HANOVERIAN
ENGLAND
1714–1837

Other Volumes in the Series

TUDOR ENGLAND
by P. J. Helm

BRITAIN AND THE STUARTS
by D. L. Farmer

ENGLAND 1815–1939
by J. Edwards

HANOVERIAN ENGLAND

1714–1837

By

LEONARD W. COWIE

NEW YORK
HUMANITIES PRESS
1967

Printed in Great Britain by
The Camelot Press Ltd., London and Southampton

PREFACE

This book seeks to provide an account of some of the important aspects of the Hanoverian period in English history. Any period of English history must still largely be a story in which political events take the leading part, but it is rightly insisted nowadays that the wider aspects of history – constitutional and religious, social and economic – must not be omitted. The opening chapters of this book, therefore, describe the general background to the period, as far as the limits of space will allow, and discuss the important constitutional, economic and other problems. The later chapters relate the narrative of the Hanoverian age mainly, though not completely, in terms of political history. To avoid repetition and to link the parts of the book together, footnotes have been used solely to indicate complementary passages wherever these occur.

This period has been described as 'the most raked-over period in English history'. Recent research has transformed the ideas of many historians about many of its aspects, but investigation is still proceeding, and there is still discussion and controversy over some important points. A book of this sort, while not claiming to make any original contribution to the study of this period, has to summarize, simplify and pass judgement on the work of these scholars. This is a dangerous and presumptuous task, but it is hoped that it has been done as carefully and honestly as possible.

The bibliography is short and selective. It indicates books which will provide the reader with further information on the most important aspects of the period, but at the same time it is confined to books which may be found in most libraries.

CONTENTS

		Page
I.	LAND AND PEOPLE	1
II.	THE SOCIAL SCENE	21
III.	GOVERNMENT AND POLITICS	39
IV.	RELIGIOUS MOVEMENTS	66
V.	SCIENCE AND CULTURE	87
VI.	THE AGRARIAN REVOLUTION	109
VII.	THE INDUSTRIAL REVOLUTION	130
VIII.	OVERSEAS COMMERCE AND COLONIZATION	154
IX.	WARFARE AND THE ARMED FORCES	185
X.	SCOTLAND, IRELAND AND HANOVER	205
XI.	THE ESTABLISHMENT OF THE DYNASTY, 1714–21	228
XII.	WALPOLE'S ADMINISTRATION, 1721–42	247
XIII.	THE WAR OF THE AUSTRIAN SUCCESSION, 1740–8	267
XIV.	THE PELHAMS IN POWER, 1748–56	282
XV.	THE ELDER PITT AND THE SEVEN YEARS' WAR, 1756–63	296
XVI.	MINISTERIAL UNCERTAINTIES, 1760–70	315
XVII.	LORD NORTH'S ADMINISTRATION, 1770–82	335
XVIII.	THE YOUNGER PITT AND NATIONAL RECONSTRUCTION, 1782–93	354
XIX.	THE REVOLUTIONARY WAR, 1793–1802	376
XX.	THE NAPOLEONIC WAR, 1803–15	389
XXI.	LORD LIVERPOOL'S ADMINISTRATION, 1812–27	403
XXII.	PARTY POLITICS, 1827–37	424
	BIBLIOGRAPHY	444
	INDEX	449

LIST OF MAPS

	Page
THE CANAL SYSTEM	151
THE COLONIZATION OF EASTERN NORTH AMERICA	167
INDIA, 1756–1818	177
THE BRITISH EMPIRE, 1815	183
SCOTLAND AND NORTHERN ENGLAND	211
IRELAND	219
EUROPE IN 1715	239
EUROPE IN 1815	399

I · LAND AND PEOPLE

A Time of Change

THE years of the Hanoverian dynasty were a remarkable period of transition in English history. It saw no less than the beginning of the change from the Old England to the New, the break-up of a way of life which had lasted for some fifteen hundred years. At the outset of the period, most of the people of England lived in remote villages and hamlets and quiet country towns and farmed the land in the old, traditional ways. Before the end of the period, the Agrarian and Industrial Revolutions were transforming both the face of the country and the position of the nation in the world. England had evolved from a small (though influential) commercial and maritime state into the foremost empire and the wealthiest, most advanced industrial power in the world. The machine age had come and already brought with it developments which made William Cobbett and others look back to the 'Golden Age' which they avowed it had destroyed.

These economic and social changes were accompanied by other important transformations and developments in the history of England and the life of her people. This was a critical period in the evolution of some of the fundamental parts of the country's constitution. The growth of the idea of constitutional monarchy and cabinet government, the emergence of the office of Prime Minister and the reform of parliament all occurred during these years. The Act of Union of 1707 between England and Scotland was tested by two rebellions in the first half of the eighteenth century, while the events culminating in the Irish rebellion of 1798 brought about the Act of Union between Britain and Ireland in 1800. Rationalism and indifference in religion was succeeded by the Methodist and Evangelical revivals, and at the end of the period the Tractarian movement was taking shape. For the greater part of the eighteenth century, war was waged against France in Europe, America and India for colonial and commercial supremacy; and the disruption of one British

Empire was followed by the beginnings of another which was to be yet greater.

All historical periods are, of course, ages of transition. The Hanoverian period, however, must have a claim to rank very high among all such periods. The years 1714 and 1837 are revealing comparative landmarks in English history. In 1714 there were still old people alive who had memories of the Puritan Commonwealth and the Restoration monarchy; in 1837 there were young children who were to live to see the outbreak of the First World War. Lord Halsbury, for instance, who was born in 1823, led the die-hard resistance to the Parliament Act of 1911, still interspersing his speeches with cries of 'Forsooth!' Yet despite these links between the Hanoverian period and our own, there is also a great chasm between them since there is no real conclusion to the Hanoverian period. It ended and the Victorian age began just as the processes of change were assuming even greater rapidity.

The Population Question

One of the ways in which the Hanoverian period differed from our own is that the English remained a small nation during these years. Conjectures about the population of eighteenth-century England are hazardous since the first official census was not taken until 1801. Many writers, including William Cobbett at the end of the century, believed that the population was declining. It is generally accepted by modern historians, however, that the population of England and Wales was about 5,500,000 when Queen Anne died, and that it slowly increased to about 6,000,000 by 1740 and then grew more rapidly until it reached about 7,500,000 in 1770 and 8,000,000 in 1790. The census figures for 1801 were 8,872,980, for 1821 were 11,978,875 and for 1841 were 15,911,757. Scotland's population in 1700 was about 1,000,000 and its census figures for 1801 and 1814 were 1,599,068 and 2,620,184. Ireland had about 2,000,000 in 1700; its first census (in 1811) gave a total of 5,937,856, which had increased to 8,175,124 in 1841. In comparison with these figures, the population of France was about 19,000,000 in 1715, probably 26,000,000 by the time of the Revolution and 33,540,910 according to the census of 1836.

The population of England, therefore, began to grow markedly in the second half of the eighteenth century and still more rapidly in the early nineteenth century. This growth, however, was uneven, being at its greatest in the late eighteenth and early nineteenth centuries. The reasons for the growth of population are, in the absence of reliable figures, still controversial. It has been generally assumed that it was mainly the consequence of a rapidly falling death-rate and especially a fall in the infantile death-rate, which was due largely to improvements in medical knowledge and provision. It is true that more hospitals were opened – 154 between 1700 and 1825, including four in London – and that advances were made in medical practice.[1] Nevertheless, the part played by the progress of medicine in lengthening human life has been increasingly questioned by medical historians. Conditions in hospitals were generally bad. Medical care was largely ineffective and cross-infection a continual danger; patients, who did not have fatal diseases on entering hospital, often acquired them after admission. It is improbable that hospitals were positively beneficial to a large proportion of their patients at this time. Florence Nightingale was later to insist, 'The very first requirement in a hospital is that it should do the sick no harm'. The increase in population did not take place around the centres of medical activity. London and other large towns remained notorious death-traps;[2] but remote Pembrokeshire had a constant surplus of population.

Several other reasons which have been put forward to explain a declining death-rate are also romantic rather than true. There is no evidence that the masses used more soap or wore cleaner underclothing. Nor was it because people drank more milk or ate more vegetables. In the towns, where the cows were kept in cellars, milk was a dangerous source of tuberculosis, while in the country almost all the milk was made into cheese, and the commonest vegetables, turnips and cabbages, were fed to cattle. The more common consumption of bread made from wheat, instead of rye or barley, may have had an effect in increasing the population, since wheat contains vitamin E, which is needed during pregnancy and is also an aphrodisiac.

[1] P. 92.   [2] P. 9.

As the eighteenth century progressed, it is true that the expectation of life became longer. An important reason for this was the halting of epidemics. There was no great outbreak of plague during the century, though many diseases were rife.[1] Small-pox was slowly brought under control first by inoculation and then by vaccination.[2] Probably the main reason for the decline of epidemics was a rising standard of living. This included such environmental improvements as better houses, which were drier and less commonly had mud floors. Another reason was the absence of famines, which weakened resistance to disease and lowered the birth-rate. Such factors produced lower death-rates, even in the unhealthy towns, in the late eighteenth and early nineteenth centuries, though it was most marked in London and the rural areas.

The national death-rate was about 33 per thousand in 1730. Its dramatic fall, when it went down to about 20 per thousand, was in the second decade of the nineteenth century, after the population upsurge had passed its peak; and there was no great decline in infant mortality until the middle of the nineteenth century, and then it did not occur in the larger towns. Indeed, recent research suggests that a decline in mortality played a smaller part in the growth of the population during this time than has commonly been supposed, and that the expansion, especially in areas affected by the Industrial Revolution, was more probably due to an increased birth-rate. A reason for this seems to have been younger and more frequent marriages. In the early eighteenth century, the average age of marriage was about 27 years for men and 25 for women, while many people remained unmarried. The nature of farm-holdings in the country and of apprenticeships in the towns restricted marriages, but the industrial developments of the century made possible earlier marriages and less celibacy. This seems to have been a factor in the expansion of the population, though it is not yet certain how important it was.

Again, in pre-industrial England the population was closely affected by the harvest which supplied the greater part of the nation's food and drink. W. G. Hoskins has calculated that most people in those days spent about 90

[1] Pp. 14–15.   [2] P. 92.

per cent of their weekly earnings on food and drink (compared with about 30 per cent by the wage-earning classes
today) and also that two-thirds of the population lived near
to conditions of poverty and want. The result of the harvest,
therefore, was vital for them and did much to determine the
growth of the population. The harvests were bad in England
during the 1720's, and there were epidemics of smallpox and
influenza which caused high rates of mortality among under-
nourished people. There followed in the 1730's and 1740's,
however, generally good harvests and low food prices, and
there was a consequent great increase in the birth-rate.
After a possible absolute check in the 1720's, the population
expanded rapidly. The children born in these years married
in the 1750's and 1760's, the period of prosperity accompanying the Seven Years' War; they also had large families, and
so again did their children who married during the prosperous years of the Revolutionary and Napoleonic Wars.
Much of the growth in population during this period seems to
have occurred in these three waves of marriage and birth.
The offspring of the last of these waves, however, were less
fortunate than their parents and grandparents. They had
young children during the years of rural overpopulation
and depression after 1815, and the need to feed them contributed to the poor law crisis of the 1830's.

The increase in population, the Agrarian Revolution and
the Industrial Revolution are all closely bound together.
There could have been no growth of population without
improvements in farming, and there could have been no
industrialization without an expanding population, since the
Industrial Revolution depended for its progress not primarily
upon exports, but upon the growing demands of the domestic
market. This was shown during the period of high food
prices during the Napoleonic War, when the ability of the
domestic market to purchase manufactured goods diminished
so sharply that for a short time the Industrial Revolution
was imperilled. The growth of population was, therefore,
both a consequence and in its turn a cause of the Agrarian
and Industrial Revolutions. As Phyllis Deane and W. A.
Cole have written, 'When the full story comes to be told, it
may well appear that at each stage in the process, the growth
of population, itself produced by economic changes in the

generation before, was one of the factors which drove the British economy upwards on the path of sustained growth'.

Towns and Countryside

The distribution of England's population, at the beginning of the Hanoverian period, was still very much as it had been in the Middle Ages. Daniel Defoe's famous *Tour through the whole Island of Great Britain*, published in 1724, shows that since agriculture was the predominant occupation most people lived where the land was richest, particularly on the corn lands of the south and east. Though there was still much woodland, especially in the southern counties, most of the land south of the Pennines and east of the Welsh moorlands had by now been brought into arable or pastural use. Considerable enclosures had already been made in the west and south-east, but in central England the land was still under the open-field system. The roads were very bad and sometimes impassable for wagons in winter, but Defoe was impressed by the few stretches of comparatively well-repaired turnpike roads over which he rode. The heaviest goods-traffic was along the rivers which were already being made more navigable. The towns were mostly some distance from each other and, except London, were small and still part of the countryside. The manufactures described by Defoe, of which the woollen industry of the Cotswolds, Wiltshire, East Anglia and the West Riding was the most important, were generally organized on the domestic system, being carried on in the homes of the workpeople themselves, particularly in the numerous small market towns to be found in every part of the country.[1] Other industries included coal-mining in the north-east, iron-smelting in Sussex and the Midlands and tin and copper mining in Cornwall; as late as 1791 a traveller spoke of 'smoky Cornwall and sunny Lancashire'.

By the end of the period, the English countryside had been subjected to developments which had already transformed it strikingly and were to continue to do so. The enclosure movement had now divided the land into a chequer-board of rectangular fields separated by hedges or stones walls in which improved breeds of cattle grazed and new crops were grown. Roads had been improved, and a network of navigable

[1] P. 140.

canals dug, though the construction of the railways was not yet far advanced. Above all, the great industrial districts of the North and Midlands had made their appearance and introduced an increasingly important way of life and system of economic production into the country.

A notable feature of these changes was the growth of the English towns, but this was not on as large a scale as is sometimes supposed. For the greater part of the eighteenth century only about a sixth of the people were town-dwellers. For centuries the towns had been spread fairly evenly over the English countryside, the siting, size, and character of nearly all of them determined by the agricultural requirements of the district. Most were small, and those that were larger owed their size and their position to commerce or local crafts. Bristol was now the largest English provincial city, but in the third quarter of the century its population was still well under 100,000. It had supplanted Norwich, which had a population of less than 50,000 and not much more than rapidly-growing Manchester. Birmingham and Liverpool each had about 35,000; Leeds had 17,000, a figure only slightly above that of Chester. On the other hand, Bradford and Brighton were both still only villages. Scotland's largest town, Glasgow, had quadrupled its population between the beginning of the century and the outbreak of the American War of Independence, but it was then still under 50,000.

Even after the further growth of population during the later eighteenth century, England was still not the most urbanized country in Europe. At the beginning of the nineteenth century, there were still several French towns larger than the leading English provincial towns. Lyons and Marseilles, each with over 100,000 inhabitants, were greater than any towns in the English provinces. The largest English provincial towns were then Manchester, Liverpool, Birmingham and Bristol, but Bordeaux and Rouen were larger than any of them. Leeds had some 50,000 inhabitants, but was the only English town of about this size, while France had Nantes, Lille and Toulouse. There were only five English towns with between 30,000 and 50,000 inhabitants – Sheffield, Plymouth, Portsmouth, Norwich and Newcastle-upon-Tyne; but there were eight

B

in France, from Amiens in the north to Nîmes in the
south. Not until well into the nineteenth century did
England become a land of big towns. The census of 1841,
however, revealed the beginning of the process. Population
was becoming concentrated in larger towns and cities in the
north and Midlands. Manchester and Liverpool each had
over 200,000 inhabitants and Birmingham, Leeds, Bristol
and Sheffield over 100,000. Industrial changes were increasingly bringing about growing populations on coal-fields, at
great ports and, at the same time, in the metropolis.

London, indeed, was unique among English cities throughout this period. Defoe dwelt again and again on its astonish-
ing size. In his time it extended from Deptford to Vauxhall
south of the Thames and from Westminster to Limehouse on
the north, while Chelsea and Kensington on the west and
Poplar, Blackwall and Greenwich on the east, together with
other prosperous suburbs on the north and south, were almost
continuous with the built-up area. During the eighteenth
century, it expanded its area particularly in the west, where
such fine squares as Grosvenor Square and Cavendish Square
were built. Before the end of the Hanoverian period, it
had begun, for the first time in its history, to grow away
from the river with the building of houses in Primrose Hill
and Bayswater. By this time also, well-to-do people were
beginning to live farther away from the City. Among them
were the parents of the Victorian statesman, Joseph Chamberlain. For generations the Chamberlains had lived in Milk
Street, off Cheapside, but when they married in 1834 they
settled in Camberwell.

London was the seat of government and culture and the
chief centre of trade and finance in the kingdom. It was the
capital city of a wealthy country and a growing empire.
Alone among the great capitals of Europe, it was also a first-
class port with a hinterland which covered a large part of
the country. This maritime trade contributed much to its
size since about a quarter of its inhabitants were in some way
connected with the port. For the greater part of the eighteenth century it was the only great English city where town
life was sharply distinguished from country life. The only
place abroad comparable with it was Paris, but London
overtook it in population before the middle of the century.

By 1740 London had about 500,000 inhabitants and by 1760 about 650,000. It constantly attracted immigrants from the country who came in search of work and wealth. Without them, the population of London might indeed have declined because of its terribly high death-rate, especially in the first part of the century. 'The waste of life', Dorothy George has said, 'was at its worst since the days of the Plague between 1727 and 1750.' There were greater contrasting social conditions in London than elsewhere its poorest inhabitants suffered grievously from destitution, disease and wretched housing.[1] Most London parishes in the first half of the eighteenth century recorded three burials for every two baptisms, and not until the end of the century was the death-rate less than the birth-rate. Then the capital's population grew much more rapidly. It was 1,000,000 by about 1810, 1,500,000 by about 1826 and 2,000,000 in the early 'forties.

Throughout the Hanoverian period, at least one person out of every ten in England and Wales lived in London, and in no other European country was this proportion approached. It was the home of Parliament, the court and the law courts. It was the arbiter of fashion and taste. Dr. Johnson was not the only writer to feel such a strong preference for London. As the National Debt rose relentlessly, successive governments became ever more dependent upon its bankers and other monied men. The London mob also played an important part in politics. The gin mania of Walpole's time was almost entirely a London vice. London had its enemies as well as admirers in the Hanoverian age. Country gentlemen and provincial merchants resented its power and wealth, while to others it represented the sway of government and administration which was so disliked and suspected in this age. In the opening years of the nineteenth century, as industrialization began to bring new importance and population to the north and Midlands, a challenge to London's national pre-eminence appeared, but this lay still in the future. Throughout the Hanoverian period, whether for good or ill, whether admired or resented, London exercised a stronger influence over the political and social, commercial and industrial life of the country than it has ever done since.

[1] P. 14.

Manners and Customs

Since the Hanoverian period was a time of transition, it is not surprising that England was during these years a country of many and striking contrasts. Conflicting forces and interests seemed to be at work in the lives of the people, often in a strong and violent manner, and these had a striking effect upon their everyday manners and customs. The consequences were most marked in the unique way of life of the teeming, excitable capital, but even in the towns and villages of the country, where the majority of the population dwelt in circumstances so different from those in London, the same national traits of the time were apparent, even if less stridently expressed.

One aspect of Hanoverian England is still displayed in its architectural survivals, which well exemplify its restrained and harmonious culture. The influence of this culture was closely connected with the leadership of the landed aristocracy whose supremacy was being challenged by the new industrial classes only at the end of the period. The aristocracy delighted in Classic architecture, nationalized into the Georgian style, which reached its final expression in the Regency period. The buildings of the Adam brothers were conspicuous for their elegance and lightness, but at the same time were reserved and formal, places for well-ordered receptions, banquets and balls. To such great houses, 'Capability' Brown gave a carefully-studied surrounding of clumps of trees, large lawns and even artificial lakes.[1] Even small houses were set amid trim walks, shrubberies and orchards. A large proportion of the country houses in England were built between Queen Anne's reign and the end of the century; and in those days before factory mass-production, skilled craftsmen could provide them with furniture, plate and ornaments, which were simple and effective in design and execution, combining fine elegance with impressive splendour.

Yet in contrast with the moderation and dignity of Hanoverian taste, all classes displayed a predilection for pugnacity and violence. 'Perhaps the most obvious but least recognized feature of English life in the eighteenth and

[1] Pp. 105–6.

LAND AND PEOPLE 11

early nineteenth centuries was its love of aggression', J. H.
Plumb has written. 'Rarely has the world known a more
aggressive society or one in which passion was more openly
or violently expressed.' This was itself paradoxical; the age
constantly deplored moral or intellectual enthusiasm, but
made no attempt to control its quarrelsome, bellicose personal
feelings. A proposal to improve the street-lighting in Cambridge aroused the objection that it would result in men
fighting instead of passing each other unrecognized. High
and low were prepared to settle their differences by individual
combat. Prominent men who fought duels included Wilkes
in 1763, Byron in 1765, Fox in 1779, Pitt in 1796, Castlereagh and Canning in 1809, and Wellington in 1829. Lower in
the social scale, men and even women were equally ready to
fight with their hands. In 1768 two women fought each
other in public in Spa Fields over a new shift, and the victor
'beat her antagonist in a terrible manner'.

Such pugnacity found equal expression in international
affairs. The great wars and vast overseas conquests of the
eighteenth century were popular with most English people.
They acclaimed such daring deeds as Clive's capture of
Arcot in 1751 or Nelson's victory at the Battle of the Nile in
1798.[1] The country was elated when the Elder Pitt called
for open aggression against France and Spain at the close of
Walpole's ministry, and it rejoiced in the next century when
Palmerston vigorously announced that France should not
make the smallest territorial gain in Belgium.[2] The abusive
articles and savage cartoons in the British press, which
Napoleon so keenly resented, both encouraged and appeased
the national urge for violence.

These passions also found their outlet in frequent and savage
rioting. Throughout the Hanoverian period outbreaks of
disorder and destruction by mobs occurred in all parts of the
country. The turnpikes were uprooted in Bristol in 1749,
the enclosures torn down in Wiltshire in 1758 and the boxes
smashed in Covent Garden theatre in 1763. In the metropolis political violence brought riots against Walpole's
Excise Bill and Pelham's Jew Bill, riots in opposition to Bute
and in favour of Wilkes, and culminated in the Gordon Riots
of 1780.[3] All over the country parliamentary elections were

[1] Pp. 165, 385.   [2] Pp. 265, 437.   [3] Pp. 257, 287, 321, 332, 351.

notoriously violent.   At the High Wycombe election of 1794, Lord Wycombe was thrown in the mud, and Squire Dashwood, another candidate, lost his hat and almost his life.   The Norwich weavers rioted over the price of mackerel in 1740 and the Shropshire colliers over the price of corn in 1756, while industrial troubles brought about the destructive Luddite Riots between 1811 and 1818.[1]   Wesley recorded some sixty riots in his *Journal*.   Even schoolboys acted similarly. There were three mutinies at Winchester between 1766 and 1793, and riots at both Eton and Harrow in 1771, while barring-out and attacking masters, destroying furniture and flagrant insubordination were as common in schools as the severe birchings and constant bullying.

The same contrast was to be found in the recreation and leisure of Hanoverian England.   This was the period of Vauxhall, Ranelagh and other pleasure-gardens on the outskirts of London which gained the approval of social reformers by offering simple amusements and cool evenings out-of-doors.   At this time also cricket emerged from the obscurity of southern villages to become a national game as a usually humane form of recreation.   Its rules were codified in 1744, and it spread under aristocratic guidance as part of the amusements of country-house life.   Aristocratic patronage similarly brought about the development of Bath and other spas, which ladies and gentlemen patronized partly to gain relief from the waters for their gout, brought upon by drinking port instead of claret owing to the French wars; but they also bathed in the pools, walked and conversed along the promenades and danced in the ball-rooms.   The seaside and sea-bathing became fashionable later in the period; George III patronized Weymouth, and George IV made Brighton famous.

At the same time, there was another side to these refined and elegant amusements.   All classes delighted in pastimes involving much brutality, cruelty and degradation.   Cock-fighting, hare-hunting, bear and bull-baiting were all popular.   So too was prize-fighting in which desperate conflicts, involving death or mutilation, took place under distinguished patronage; and the racing of women in their shifts was another popular spectacle.   Drinking was very

[1] P. 395.

prevalent. The taste for gin-drinking acquired by Marlborough's soldiers in the Netherlands started the gin mania
in London, which produced the scenes depicted in Hogarth's
cartoon, *Gin Lane*, among the poor.[1] When this was at last
suppressed, heavy drinking still continued among all classes.
Rich men drank their four bottles of port at a sitting, and
many of Wellington's officers were 'five-bottle men'.

Horace Walpole spoke of 'the outrageous spirit of gaming'
which by the middle of the century had 'spread from the
fashionable young men of quality to the ladies and the lowest
rank of the people'. Gambling became common. People
betted in all forms of sport and on every subject in everyday
life. The rich played for high stakes in games of chance.
Lord Stavordale lost £12,000 in a single throw at dice in 1770
and thanked God he was not playing for high stakes; at the
age of sixteen Charles James Fox and his elder brother lost
£32,000 after playing cards for three days and nights; and
Georgiana, Duchess of Devonshire (1757–1806), the reigning
beauty of the day, lost over £100,000 at cards with disastrous
consequences for herself and her marriage. In other circles,
tradesmen and craftsmen ruined themselves by gambling
and wives dissipated their husband's savings. The national
lotteries, until abolished in 1826, yielded a large annual
revenue to the Crown. All classes sought to share the excitement and prizes of gambling, and it was yet another sign of
their general aggressiveness.

With such vehemence and recklessness went much callous-
ness and cruelty. To see half-naked prostitutes whipped at
the Bridewell or beating hemp under the overseer's cane
ranked as a popular spectacle in London. Unwanted infants
were left in the streets to die, and homeless vagrant children –
the 'Blackguard' – roamed the towns. Sickness and suffering were met with indifference or worse; when the dying
Henry Fielding was hoisted in 1754 on to the ship at Rother-
hithe, which was to take him on his last voyage to Lisbon,
the watermen and sailors jeered at his ghastly appearance.
English merchants made profits out of the terrible trade in
negro slaves with general public approval. The poor law
was often unfeelingly applied by the parish authorities, and
industrialization brought harsh treatment for women and

[1] P. 103.

children in factories and mines. Against such an attitude philanthropists and humanitarians long struggled fruitlessly.

Together with this acceptance of cruelty and violence as an inevitable part of life went a general indifference to death. When a German pastor, Charles Moritz, visited England in 1782, the insensibility of the crowd to funerals struck him as strange – 'The people seem to pay as little attention to such a procession as if a hay-cart were driving past'. John Wesley did not question such an attitude, but rather encouraged it among his followers. He attached, as he showed in his *Journal*, great importance to the triumph of religion over bodily fear. On the voyage he made as a young man to America he was led to a fervid admiration of his Moravian fellow-passengers by their courage in the face of imminent shipwreck. He valued supremely the power of Methodist preaching to send criminals to the gallows with a conviction, almost amounting to a sense, that they were at once changing this life for a better one; he rejoiced when several prisoners in Newgate, with whom a good Methodist woman had prayed, greeted the bellman's midnight cry, 'Remember you are to die today', with shouts of, 'Welcome news – welcome news!' And nothing shocked Wesley so much in Ireland as the reluctance of condemned criminals, often mere boys, to accept their fate after they had received the Church's last consolations.

The prevailing unfeeling attitude to suffering and death, together with the ebullient love of pleasure, owed much to the cruelty and uncertainty of life itself. Amid the elegance and luxury of the age, pain, violence and death were ever present. There were no palliatives for suffering, and operations were performed without anaesthetics. Patients had to endure purges, leeches, emetics, bleeding and intentionally-induced blisters and running sores. Hysterical girls were ducked in cold water or had their hair pulled out by the roots from their head to cure them by shock. Dirt and disease abounded, particularly in the towns. The opening of the Hanoverian period saw London insanitary, unpaved and unlit and with notorious slums in St. Giles, Drury Lane, Shoreditch and Whitefriars where people were crowded together in tenements. Such conditions were repeated in the new industrial towns, and improvements in sanitation and drainage were slow to reach them. Smallpox, typhoid, typhus, dysentry and other diseases spread rapidly in these districts, tuberculosis killed young mothers, and few children survived.[1] Wealthy people might expect to live longer than the poor, but death from disease was not uncommon among them. Among women in all classes deaths in childbirth were frequent; many men married two or three times during their life.

Brutality and violence were also encouraged by the rudimentary, archaic and ineffective means of preserving law and order. Neither the unpaid constables appointed by the parishes nor the watchmen hired by some big towns were numerous or competent enough to apprehend more than a few of the thieves and pickpockets in the towns and footpads and highwaymen on the roads. For those who could not pay fees to the gaolers, prisons were horrible, overcrowded, demoralizing, insanitary places, but they were rarely used during the greater part of the period for convicted offenders, but mainly for debtors and persons awaiting trial. Rather, reliance was placed upon exemplary, humiliating and public punishments, which almost exclusively employed some form of corporal suffering and, in the absence of certainty of detection, sought to deter offenders by severity and brutality. Mutilation was no longer practised as a punishment, but branding was still common. Whipping, often at the cart's tail, was a frequent penalty for all manner of offences for both men and women. In 1737 a young woman at Grimbsy received 28 lashes about her bare shoulders at the market cross, town hall and other public places, and her punishment was not unusually severe. Women were still ducked as scolds, and the stocks and pillory were used, many people dying in them through being pelted by the mob.

Reliance upon severity led to ever-harsher penalties. Thousands of convicted criminals were transported to servitude, first in the American colonies and then in Australia. Above all, increasing reliance was placed upon hanging. During the eighteenth century, Parliament raised the number of capital crimes from about fifty to nearly two hundred. These included picking a pocket to the value of a shilling, sheepstealing, damaging Westminster Bridge, impersonating a

[1] P. 9.

Chelsea pensioner, consorting with gypsies or setting fire to hay. A boy of ten was hanged at Norwich for stealing a penknife and a girl of fourteen in London for secretly taking a hand-kerchief. In London every six weeks condemned criminals were taken in procession in open carts from Newgate to the gallows of Tyburn. This came to an end in 1783, when hangings took place outside Newgate and in public for the rest of this period. Hanging was only substituted for burning in 1790 as the penalty for women guilty of high or petty treason. All over the country, decaying corpses, their rags fouled by droppings from birds, dangled from gibbets until the practice was abolished in 1834; and in London until 1776 the heads of executed traitors rotted on Temple Bar while pedlars hired out spy-glasses for visitors to view them.

Year after year sentences at the assizes multiplied these punishments. During 1763 at the Old Bailey 433 persons were tried for murder, burglary, robbery and theft, and of the 243 persons convicted, 42 men and 5 women were sentenced to death, 122 men and 49 women transported, 10 men and 2 women branded and 5 women whipped; and by 1797 there were 97 hangings in a single year. Yet none of these punishments ensured respect for the law. Criminals were prepared to take desperate measures to avoid detection and escape apprehension. Juries sometimes failed to convict, and popular opinion often sided with those who violently and recklessly defied authority. In the south-east maritime counties smugglers flourished with the sympathy and con-nivance of the local population. The dashing highwayman was a popular hero, and his journey to Tyburn, dressed in gay clothes, was often a triumphal progress, and he died before a cheering crowd.

This was, indeed, yet another paradox of the times. English people often sympathized with those who defied the harsh penalties of the law, but they also generally accepted their necessity. Most people took it for granted that the enforcement of justice should rest upon the infliction of some form of severe, humiliating, physical suffering. They them-selves relied extensively upon corporal punishment in the training of the young. Almost everyone considered it indispensable in education. To the abbé in charge of a school in Buckinghamshire for the sons of French emigrés, who complained of his pupils' indocility, Edmund Burke said, 'You must exert your cane with more vigour, and if that does not do, you must flog – and flog soundly.' Parental discipline was equally severe. Lady Anna Lindsay said that sometimes in her childhood home 'in every closet was to be found a culprit, some were sobbing and repeating verbs, others eating bread and water, some preparing themselves to be whipped'. Nor was corporal punishment only for young children. It was common for servant-girls and apprentices to have their clothes turned up or down and be smacked or whipped openly in drawing-room or shop. They could expect little protection from magistrates, who probably corrected their own daughters in the same way. John Wilkes, as a London magistrate in his last years, spoke against the use of the birch or stick to punish apprentices, but not spanking with the hand, even of girls.

Such extensive and severe punishment in home and school was intended to make the young obedient, industrious and well-behaved, but the note of sombre, moral earnestness in their upbringing came only with the later religious revival. The public schools of these days were not great nurseries of morality.[1] Indeed, such an emphasis would not have been consistent with contemporary manners. When the painter, Joseph Farington (1747–1821) looked back on these, he found in them yet another of the contrast of the times. 'With the apparent show and polish of the former age much brutality was mingled,' he wrote, 'and great and general licentiousness prevailed in all ranks.' Coarseness of speech, grossness of manners and looseness of morals were very common.

Queen Caroline, who could speak as coarsely as any man, had to rebuke Walpole for his shocking language to her daughters; and the Earl of Pembroke, according to Horace Walpole, was 'so blasphemous at tennis that the Primate of Ireland was forced to leave off playing with him'. At the close of the century the orgies at Medmenham Abbey of the 'Hell-Fire Club' of John Wilkes and his associates were notorious, but the private morals of other politicians were not blameless. Wellington had a mistress, Melbourne was twice cited as a co-respondent, and Palmerston had four children by Lady Cowper. Gladstone said that he had known eleven

[1] P. 32.

prime ministers and that seven of them were adulterers. Illegitimate children were common in all classes. The Duke of Devonshire had three children by the Duchess and two by Elizabeth Foster, while the Duchess had one by Earl Grey of the Reform Bill. Towards the lower classes, however, the official attitude was typically harsh. In 1766 the Poor Law authorities of Gloucester, 'for the discouragement of bastardy', ordered that 'mothers of base-born children' chargeable to the parish should receive a public whipping of fifty lashes. In London the Lord Mayor and Aldermen every now and then tried to clear the streets of prostitutes, sending the worst to be whipped or put to hard labour. Nevertheless at the end of the century London was said to have some 50,000 of them, including the wives of artisans and others who lived partly by prostitution, and French visitors were shocked by English depravity.

The Beginnings of a New Age

By the end of the Hanoverian period, however, sweeping changes were taking place in the manners and customs of the English people. The Methodist and Evangelical movements were establishing new moral standards among all classes of society. There was a general increase in sensibility which found expression in many ways. In artistic and literary spheres, it produced the Gothic and Romantic movements.[1] Outdoor sports changed their character. Cock-fighting ceased to be a gentleman's amusement; bear-baiting and bull-baiting were forbidden by law in 1835; the old prize-ring disappeared soon after the Regency. The conduct of society altered, gradually accepting the influence of changes made at court by George III in the first year of his reign, when he abolished the Sunday dances at St. James's Palace and limited the gambling there and required the Archbishop of Canterbury to give up the elaborate balls held at Lambeth Palace. A new attitude towards children was also evolving. 'The domestic discipline of our ancestors', Edward Gibbon wrote, 'has been relaxed by the philosophy and softness of the age.' The public schools were undergoing reform, and a start had been made in the provision of a system of national elementary education for all children. Above all, the new outlook

[1] Pp. 98, 108.

supported social movements which had previously been
sustained with little effect by a few reformers. For the first
time such wrongs as the condition of the prisons and the evils
of the slave-trade, the sufferings of the poor and the hardships
of factory-workers aroused widespread concern. To be a
'Man of Feeling' had become praiseworthy.

This gave rise to a changed attitude towards crime and
punishment. The old humiliating penalties were gradually
abolished. The stocks were last used in 1826 and the pillory
in 1837. The public whipping of women was abolished in
1817 and their whipping in private in 1830, while the last
ducking of a woman as a scold seems to have been at Leo-
mister in 1809. Sir Robert Peel began a reform of the penal
code which drastically reduced the number of capital offences.[1]

At the same time, piecemeal efforts to strengthen the
forces of order and establish respect for the law throughout
the country were steadily effective. In 1817 a coastal blockade of Kent and Sussex was established against smuggling,
and the coastguards were established in 1831. The smugglers
were defeated in a series of pitched battles, the last being
at Pevensey Sluice in 1833. 'It was probably the first time
that any English government had gained undisputed control
of that stretch of coast and the land behind it', Dr. Kitson
Clark has commented. In the same year the London mob
were probably finally defeated in the battle of Cold Bath
Fields by the Metropolitan Police Force founded four years
previously, though similar forces were not organized in the
rest of the country until after the accession of Queen Victoria.

These changes in the English character were also assisted
by the success of the Industrial Revolution, which was now
bringing into being a wealthy, contented middle class, ready
to work hard to secure and maintain its position. The
rational aims of Utilitarianism appealed to it;[2] and it desired
administrative reform and political power. It despised
extravagance and admired thrift.[3] Its morals were un-
debauched by luxury and became increasingly severe. To
meet its outlook, Thomas Bowdler in 1818 produced his
Family Shakespeare 'in which those words and expressions are
omitted which cannot with propriety be read aloud in a
family'. Its social life presented no observable fascination.

[1] P. 416.   [2] P. 97.   [3] P. 24.

Florence Nightingale later said that all that seemed to lie before it was 'the petty grinding tyranny of a good English family'.   And this was more and more to be put before the English people as the ideal to which they should aspire.

Another change in the English character was brought by the transformation of England into the leading industrial and imperial power in the world.   Such economic advances and imperial gains combined with the religious revival and social amelioration of the times to produce a sense of moral complacency and even superiority among the English people. Their successes led them to concentrate upon their own affairs and take pride in their own achievements which seemed so much greater than those of other nations; and the 'Theorists of 1830' directed public opinion towards the overseas Empire.[1] The attitude of Britain at the Congress of Vienna and her subsequent foreign policy showed that she was already adopting that insularity which was to be so strong in the Victorian age.

[1] P. 184.

II · THE SOCIAL SCENE

The Social System

'THE feudal system survives in the steep inequality of property and privilege, in the limited franchise, in the social barriers which confine patronage and promotion to a caste, and still more in the submissive ideas pervading these people' – so wrote Ralph Waldo Emerson, who visited London in 1833, about English society. Though this American view may be somewhat exaggerated, since there was greater freedom and equality in the England of those days than in other European countries, yet society was based upon quite rigid class distinctions, and such a system was generally accepted as right and necessary.

Indeed, the rapid growth of prosperity during the eighteenth century led most people, in the countryside at any rate, to feel satisfied with the existing pattern of society. By 1730 the tension between the great landlords and the lesser gentry, freeholders and tenant-farmers had been largely resolved; the disappearance of the older Toryism of the squirearchy was a sign of this. Rising rents and prices benefited landlords and tenants together, and the great landlords were no longer envied by the lesser. Later in the century, the challenge of reforming ideas made men who possessed any position and property still more conservative. Edmund Burke's warning that Jacobinism could ruin any state 'by corrupting the common people with the spoil' of revolution seemed to them a very strong reason for upholding the country's traditional social system and the stability that went with it.

The Upper Classes

At the top of English society were the nobility, who were few in number: even at the beginning of George III's reign there were only 174 English peers. Land was the source of their wealth and power.[1] The few really great aristocratic

[1] P. 110.

21

families, whom Burke described as 'the great oaks that shade
a country', such as the Russells, Grenvilles, Cavendishes,
Talbots and Howards, owned thousands of acres and enjoyed
princely incomes. This was due partly to growing agricultural prosperity, which increased the yield of their rents, and
partly to industrial development, which led to the exploitation
of valuable minerals on many estates, or to the growth of
towns for those who were fortunate to have land situated
where they could take advantage of it. Farming prosperity
raised the annual rentals of the Earl of Egremont's estates
in Sussex from £7,950 to £14,770 and of those in Yorkshire
from £12,976 to £34,000 between 1791 and 1824; building
development increased the Duke of Bedford's income from
his Bloomsbury property from £3,700 to £8,000 between
1732 and 1771. As profitable means of investment, which
included government stock, real estate, industry and shipping,
increased, noblemen showed themselves ready to lay out their
money in these, while others, notably the third Duke of
Bridgewater, themselves became economic pioneers. In
their prosperity they lavished their wealth upon great houses
and parks, fine furniture and pictures, which nowadays their
less affluent successors display to sightseers.

Legally the peers formed one of the estates of the realm
and were privileged as members of the House of Lords. Their
importance in the state was immense. They and their
families practically monopolized political office, the foremost
ecclesiastical preferment and the higher ranks in the armed
forces. Yet the English aristocracy was not, like the French
noblesse, an exclusive caste, marked off from their neighbours
by specific and identifiable privileges, such as exemption
under the law or relief from taxation.

In many ways, the life of the nobility was similar to that
of the wealthier among the gentry or squirearchy. The
gentry were landowning families who were not connected
by birth with the aristocracy. They were often Justices of
the Peace and sometimes Members of Parliament. Their
opportunities of gaining political power were fewer than those
of the nobility and their inclination to do so usually less,
but Walpole's career showed that it was possible with determination and ability. The income of a country gentleman
might be anything between about £2,000 and £300, and the

more important among them emulated in a smaller way the building and collecting activities of the nobility.

Moreover, among both nobility and gentry primogeniture confined the inheritance of the family estates to the eldest son. This told against social exclusiveness, for the younger sons commonly took family livings in the Church, became officers in the army and navy and sometimes entered the professions or went into trade. Marriage was another way in which social mobility occurred. These younger sons often married the daughters of professional men and merchants, and their sisters might marry into the same class. Noblemen themselves were prepared to marry the heiress to a wealthy merchant family. The first Viscount Palmerston (1673–1757) married in turn two middle-class ladies, the first the daughter of the Governor of the Bank of England and the second the widow of a Lord Mayor of London; and the second Viscount (1739–1802), the father of the nineteenth-century statesman, married the daughter of a City merchant. Similarly, the three daughters of Thomas Coutts (1735–1822), the founder of the London banking-house, married the Earl of Guilford, the Marquis of Bute and Sir Francis Burdett.

The Middle Classes

After the nobility and gentry came the class designated by the contemporary term 'the middling sort' and described by Dorothy Marshall as 'comprising all those families whose income came from some non-manual occupation but who, by way of their life and attitude of mind, had no claims to be ranked with the gentry'. They formed a less cohesive group than the nobility and gentry. They differed greatly in wealth, occupation and way of life, and there was a further distinction between those in the country and those in the town.

In the countryside they were the millers and innkeepers and, above all, the farmers, both freeholders and leaseholders, who had between 100 and 500 acres of land. Under the inevitably hard and speculative conditions of farming their fortunes varied, but from the middle of the eighteenth century most of them benefited from the flourishing condition enjoyed by English agriculture.[1] The growing population brought

[1] Pp. 121–2.

an increased demand for both corn and meat, while improved transport meant reduced costs and wider markets. Production was increased by enclosures, larger farms and scientific methods of agriculture. Farmers built themselves new houses, their wives bought new clothes in the county town, and their sons and daughters more often received the same education as the children of the gentry.

In the towns, opportunities for the middle classes were increasing throughout the Hanoverian period. Growing national wealth, larger commercial and industrial organizations and almost continuous warfare were among factors which raised the numbers and status of lawyers, physicians, civil servants, clergymen, soldiers, sailors, architects and schoolmasters, whose ranks were recruited from both the gentry and the middle classes. From the beginning of the period most of the country's trade was managed by middle-class men who ranged from private bankers, shopkeepers, ironmongers, linendrapers and other fairly substantial urban figures to the great and wealthy directors who controlled companies concerned with trade, banking, insurance and every form of overseas commerce, in London, Bristol, Norwich, Hull and Liverpool. These merchants grew in numbers and wealth, but still more did the industrialists. Before the Industrial Revolution, production was in the hands of craftsmen such as spinnners, weavers, cutlers and cabinet-makers, working on a small scale and organized and financed by the merchants who marketed their goods. Factory production brought into being a new class of industrial capitalists, who came from different social origins and made varying fortunes. A calculation made at the beginning of the nineteenth century estimated that there were about 15,000 merchants in the country, but as many as 250,000 'manufacturers employing labour in all branches'. A century earlier the merchants would easily have outnumbered the industrialists.

Despite their heterogeneity, the members of the middle classes had much in common, especially those who had improved their own circumstances. They believed in hard work, discipline, frugality and order. They regarded the lavish spending of the upper classes as wrongfully self-indulgent and, indeed, often were not educated enough to enjoy expensive tastes. They resented the inefficiency and

undemocratic nature of the country's governmental institutions and became strong supporters of efforts to reform them.
They also desired moral and social reform. They encouraged
the suppression of fairs and wakes, brothels and ale-houses,
cock-fighting and bull-baiting. At the beginning of the
Hanoverian period, they supported the Societies for the
Reformation of Manners (which instituted proceedings against
such offenders as drunkards, swearers and prostitutes); and
at its end they were patronizing literary and scientific societies,
mechanics' institutes and libraries and were prominent in
the Evangelical and philanthropic causes.[1] They wanted,
as J. H. Plumb has observed, 'a more ordered, hardworking,
decent and just society based on industry, thrift and goodness'.
And by the opening years of the nineteenth century, they were
succeeding in moulding the general character of the country
more and more along these lines.

Some middle-class men scornfully shrank from efforts to
improve their social position with their newly-made wealth,
but some of the most successful merchants and industrialists
were able to enter the ranks of the aristocracy and gentry by
land purchase and marriage. A notable example was Samuel
Whitbread (1758–1815), son of the founder of the brewery,
who was educated at Eton, Oxford and Cambridge, made
the Grand Tour, married Earl Grey's sister and became a
prominent Whig politician. Indeed, with the progress of
industrialization, the aristocratic way of life had a growing
attraction for wealthy middle-class men and their wives.
Bulwer Lytton, in *England and the English* (1832), spoke of
'that eternal vying with each other, that spirit of show, that
lust of imitation which characterizes our countrymen' and
attributed it to 'the peculiar nature of our aristocratic
influences'.

As such middle-class social ambitions increased, however,
it became less easy to fulfil them. During the prosperous
years after 1750, farmers had less need to sell land to traders
and manufacturers or noble families to marry their daughters
to them. They could close their ranks and maintain their
hold on power and patronage. In Lancashire, for instance,
it became an avowed rule not to make any mill-owner a
Justice of the Peace. The middle classes became more

[1] Pp. 78–83.

numerous, wealthy and self-confident, but the aristocracy continued to safeguard their own privileged position, and this was to contribute towards the political crisis which occurred before the end of the period.

The Lower Classes

By far the greater part of the population, however, were not members of the nobility, gentry or middle classes, but were manual workers of some sort. Most of them during the whole of this period lived in the countryside and were engaged in agriculture. They were nearly all either yeomen (working farmers owning or renting from five to fifty acres of land) or cottagers (peasants owning a cottage and garden with a strip or two in the common fields and grazing rights on the waste). As with the larger farmers, their fortunes were liable to vary from year to year, and most cottagers were engaged in little more than subsistence farming. It is unlikely that the enclosures of the eighteenth century reduced the numbers of these small farmers in the way that has commonly been supposed.[1]

Wage-earners in the country were comparatively few early in the century before the advent of enclosures and agrarian improvements. A large number of farmers, particularly in the open-field districts, worked their land with the help of their family, relying for occasional labour from cottagers or rural craftsmen, many of whom were independent workers. The average wage of an agricultural labourer was about 7s. 6d. a week, but they rose quite steeply in the later years of the period.[2]

Cottage-industries, organized on the domestic system, were not immediately extinguished by the Industrial Revolution. Its immediate effect, in fact was to cause an expansion of some cottage-industries, notably weaving in Leicestershire and nail-making in Warwickshire. By the end of the century, however, such industries were in decline in several parts of the country, creating a situation which was partly responsible for the adoption of the Speenhamland System.[3] And in the last years of the Hanoverian period the urban factory-system was threatening them with universal extinction.

Industrialization also only slowly affected the life and

[1] Pp. 119–20.   [2] P. 123.   [3] Pp. 124–5.

composition of the urban working classes. By 1815, when England's total population was about ten million, between six and seven million still lived in hamlets, villages and market-towns; and the new industries had yet to become overwhelmingly large employers of labour – there were, for instance, more tailors and shoemakers than miners in Durham and Northumberland. As late as 1837, more women were employed in England in domestic service than in the cotton industry, while the building trade provided more employment than any other single occupation. Most men were still employed in rural pursuits, and perhaps about an equal proportion of the population was engaged in agriculture and industry.

Compared with those in the countryside, there were more marked differences of income and manner of life among the urban working classes, particularly in London; and before the coming of the factory-system the distinction between these classes and the social groups nearest to them was not always very definite. The best-paid skilled craftsmen, such as printers and engravers, coach-makers and cabinet-makers, jewellers and watch-makers, might enjoy an income and social status comparable with those of a small master or shopkeeper; they had served a long apprenticeship and could earn a weekly wage of anything between £1 and £4. Other skilled workers, such as glaziers, leather-makers and weavers, earned from 12s. to 15s. a week. Below them were the majority of urban workers, the 'labourers', which meant those not following a definite trade normally entered through some regular apprenticeship. They might be bricklayers, saddlers, tailors, porters, bakers, or lightermen, and their average wage was 10s. a week. Women engaged in domestic work, dressmaking and other occupations got between 3s. and 8s. a week. Wages tended to be lower in the north of England than in the south. About 1770 skilled textile workers in Lancashire and Yorkshire got between 6s. and 12s. a week and unskilled workers 3s. 6d. to 5s. Women got less and children could expect 1s. 6d. a week upwards according to their age and trade. As with rural wages, urban wages also rose sharply during the later part of the Hanoverian age.

Prices also rose during these years, particularly during the French wars, but previously – after the bad harvests of the 1720's – food was generally plentiful and reasonably cheap by the standards of the time. The poorer workers knew poverty and hunger, but few died of want. Those worst off were the thousands of women domestic workers, the aged and infirm, naval and military veterans crippled in the wars and then turned on to the streets with licences to beg, and persons unable to find work for various reasons. The numbers of such unemployed were increased by the mechanization and slumps of industrialization.

The relief of these unfortunates was still based upon the Poor Law Act of 1601, which made the Justices of the Peace responsible for appointing in every parish an overseer to collect a poor-rate and relieve the sick and aged, apprentice poor children, set the able-bodied unemployed to work and punish 'sturdy beggars' and others who would not work with whipping 'on the bare back until bloody'. This was modified by the Settlement Act of 1662 which allowed Justices to send back to their place of birth any persons likely to become chargeable upon the poor-rate, and by an act of 1723 empowering overseers to establish workhouses and deny relief to those refusing to enter them. Gilbert's Act of 1782, however, once more allowed outdoor relief, which was granted so indiscriminately under the Speenhamland System at the end of the century that the Poor Law was at last reformed in 1834.[1]

The imperfections of the Poor Law system bore hardly upon those compelled to seek relief from it. Many of them normally lived near to bare subsistence, and bad harvests or severe winters, which caused sharp increases in the cost of living, brought complete destitution and often starvation and death. Even journeymen and settled labourers suffered such deprivation at these times that they resorted to riots and strikes. Such conditions occurred in 1767–8 and 1771–3 and contributed towards the violence of these phases of the 'Wilkes and Liberty' movement.

Costume and Fashion

Changes in fashion are often closely related to the social developments of the times, and in the Hanoverian period differences in costume had a more intimate connection with

[1] P. 438.

class differences than nowadays. As might be expected the
aristocracy of eighteenth-century England were the arbiters
of fashion in costume; and their clothes, Henry Hamilton has
said, 'expressed confidence in their attainments and satisfaction with the society of which they were the ornaments'.

For the greater part of the century, a gentleman wore
knee-breeches, a large-sleeved, loose coat with a low collar
and usually profusely ornamented with buttons, deep lace
ruffles, a long flowered waistcoat, silk stockings and buckled
shoes and on the head a wig. A lady wore a richly-
embroidered silk gown, with a tight-fitting bodice reaching
from the bust to well over the hip-bone, sometimes stiffened
with whalebone stays, to hold up the bosom which was no
longer exposed, but framed in frills and laces; beneath her
dress she wore a quilted petticoat upon a whalebone hoop
and beneath it several petticoats of cambric or flannel and
thick white stockings.   Feminine toilet became very elaborate.
Hair was frizzed or closely curled, piled up high over a large
pad and whitened with thick powder; black patches were
worn on the face, which was heavily creamed and powdered.
Children were dressed much as their parents; boys had ruffles
and dressed hair, and girls were made from the age of ten or
younger to wear full-skirted, tight-bodiced gowns.

Though these fashions originated among the aristocracy
in London, they spread throughout the country during the
century.   Copying the costumes of their social superiors was
one way in which wealthy middle-class men and their wives
responded to the attraction they felt for the aristocratic way
of life.   To wear a hoop brought a merchant's wife nearer
the higher social class which she admired.   Growing agricultural prosperity led farmers' wives and daughters also to dress
more stylishly, and the mail-coaches brought the latest
fashions out to them.[1]

An artisan's wife or a dairymaid rarely wore a full-hooped
skirt, but they did try to acquire yellow and red quilted
petticoats, leather stays and pink and blue gowns.   Writers
complained that the emulation of upper-class fashions by the
lower ranks of society threatened 'the utter destruction of
order and distinction'.   Ladies who founded charity schools
for girls made sure that these future domestic servants were

[1] Pp. 122, 148.

dressed according to their station, requiring them to have
their hair cropped short and wear plain dresses, long mittens,
white aprons and mob caps; one bold charity-girl, who
powdered her hair and face with flour, was 'instantly stripped,
birched and scrubbed before the whole school'. Yet ordinary
people could not go far in adopting the elaborate fashions of
the time which were ill-suited for their workaday lives.
Their gowns and petticoats, knee-breeches and long coats
had to be plain and unadorned, while the farm-worker
continued to wear his coarse linen and woollen smock.

At the end of the eighteenth century, the Industrial Revolution and the French Revolution both greatly influenced
fashions. The textile industry made new materials readily
available – cotton and calico, chinz and muslin.[1] Ladies
began to wear an immense variety of many-patterned dresses.
Then came a general uniformity, naturalness and simplicity
in dress, the effect of the French Revolution and the Romantic
movement.[2] After the Treaty of Amiens, English visitors to
France were amazed at the new fashions there. Ladies
dressed à l'antique with a muslin gown clinging to their form
like folds of drapery on a statue, their hair plaited at the back
and falling in small ringlets round the face and greasy with
huile antique, and a large veil thrown over the head. Soon
tight bodices, hoops and even petticoats were discarded in
England. They were replaced for the lady of fashion at the
beginning of the Regency period by a single one-piece dress
with an extremely low neck, divided into skirt and bodice
by a cord or ribbon tied below the barely-veiled bosom and
made of flimsy material that was too slight to bear the weight
of a pocket, so that reticules or handbags appeared. Sug-
gestive draperies revealed more than they concealed, and
long legs were admired clearly visible through gossamer
muslin gowns. Another consequence of this 'naked fashion'
was that many ladies began to wear drawers, an undergar-
ment hitherto confined to professional dancers, and a newspaper reported that 'drawers of light pink are now the ton
among our dashing belles'. At this time also, elaborate
coiffures and powder were replaced by hair worn in its
natural colour, cut short into curls or parted in the centre and
brushed down smoothly.

[1] P. 139.   [2] Pp. 98–9.

Male costume experienced a similar trend towards plain-ness and uniformity. After 1789 Charles James Fox, who had dressed most carefully in his early days, introduced a new style of negligence to demonstrate his sympathy with the democratic doctrines of the Jacobins; and between 1794 and 1814 princely favour made a dictator of fashion of George ('Beau') Brummel (1778–1840), among whose innovations was the wearing of trousers instead of breeches in fashionable society and insistence upon subdued colours, perfect cut and exquisite linen as signs of elegance. At the same time, coats became less ornate, and wigs and powder disappeared. Only in the evening, for full-dress occasions, could princes and noblemen still dress brightly and elaborately.

Further changes took place in costume before the end of the Hanoverian age. Romanticism and simplicity in feminine dress did not last long. Small, tightly-restricted waists returned to favour and were sometimes made to look even smaller by the device of balloon sleeves which grew larger and larger until the middle 1830's; bosoms were covered, four or six starched petticoats extended long, full skirts beneath which legs disappeared. Out of doors, ample cloaks concealed the figure, and the hair was confined in a close-fitting bonnet tied with a bow under the chin, which gave an effect of extreme modesty. Young ladies might wear brightly-coloured dresses, but when older were expected to confine themselves to dark blue and purple. For gentle-men, the frock-coat and silk hat appeared, brass buttons vanished and black cravats became usual. By 1830, indeed, sombre clothes had become general for masculine attire on most occasions, the fashion being assisted by George IV, who wore a dark-blue frock-coat. Dress which was demure and modest for women and unadorned and business-like for men signalled the end of Hanoverian England and the rise of middle-class influence in society and politics.

Education

Education in Hanoverian England strongly reflected and reinforced the inequalities of the contemporary social system, besides being typically haphazard and disorganized and partly anachronistic. And these features proved to be firmly established. When the beginnings of educational reform were undertaken late in this period, they were instituted in accordance with the prevailing class divisions and along lines which typified the unsystematic and largely individualistic character of English life.

Many aristocratic and wealthy boys were still educated at home by private tutors, but increasingly during this period they were sent as boarders to the few schools – Eton, Harrow, Winchester and Westminster being the most fashionable – which had acquired a national reputation. These public schools retained the old classical curriculum, valued in the Middle Ages as a preparation for theological learning and renewed in Renaissance times to promote the study of humanistic literature, but now chiefly regarded in the words of Foster Watson as 'a definite manifestation and a great store of illustrations for grammatical rules' and studied 'not primarily as an end in itself, but as a repository of adequate and eloquent expression, a territory rich in the right thing to discourse about and the right way to say it'. This type of education was accepted by aristocratic parents as a preparation for their ablest sons to take part in the political and parliamentary life of the country. So also was the freedom accorded to the boys. The masters taught their classes and flogged those who were idle or grossly insubordinate. Otherwise discipline was in the hands of the older boys whom the younger boys served as fags. In the Long Chamber at Eton some forty scholars of all ages were locked in together for ten hours at a stretch 'and cries of joy and pain were alike unheard'. Conditions in these schools reflected the violence and brutality of the times.[1] Not only did the boys indulge in rebellions against the masters and bullying among themselves; they also raided the streams and orchards of neighbouring farmers and landlords. The Elder Pitt was so miserable as a boy at Eton that he refused to send any of his sons away to school; but in many ways such a school society with its emphasis on classical teaching, self-government and common equality was a preparation, if a rough preparation, for membership of the aristocratic ruling class of the nation.

The grammar schools, some of which were later to develop into public schools, were mostly endowed schools in small market-towns or large villages attended by the sons of the

[1] P. 12.

poorer gentry, the clergy and farmers of the locality. Able
boys might receive from them a sound preparation for a
professional career; a headmaster of Lichfield Grammar
School, which was Dr. Johnson's school, boasted that he had
flogged seven judges. They shared with the public schools a
largely classical curriculum, but some added such subjects
as mathematics, geography and French to their curriculum.
These were mainly schools in large cities where the new
industrial classes demanded such reforms. Typical of these
schools at this time was the Royal Grammar School, Newcastle-upon-Tyne, which educated Vice-Admiral Lord
Collingwood and two brothers, John and William Scott, sons
of a coal-factor's apprentice, who became Lord Eldon, Lord
Chancellor, with one brief break, from 1801 to 1827, and Lord
Stowell, a Judge of the High Court of Admiralty for an even
longer period.

Not all grammar schools, however, were capable of reform,
and during this period a large number of private schools were
opened and flourished because they concentrated upon
modern subjects and attracted parents whose boys were
destined for business or commerce. Notable among these
schools were the Dissenting academies, which originated in
the prohibition of Dissenters either to teach in grammar
schools or study at the universities. The Tories in Queen
Anne's last parliament had passed the Schism Act of 1714,
forbidding any Dissenter to keep a school, but it had little
effect and was repealed in 1719. The educational standards
of the Dissenting academies varied between those of the
grammar schools and of the universities. They trained
candidates for the Dissenting ministries, but they also taught
the new subjects desired by the trading classes. Some of the
most progressive academies, such as those at Newington
Green (where Samuel Wesley, senior, was educated and Dr.
Richard Price later taught) and Warrington (where Dr.
Joseph Priestley taught) gave instruction in scientific and
technical subjects.

Such Dissenting academies contributed a modernizing
element to English education, but there has been a tendency
to exaggerate their importance and also to overstress the
decadence of the two ancient universities. It is true that
neither university trained medical men, who either attended

Edinburgh or Leyden or went to the London hospitals.[1]   It is also true that scientific progress owed much to the Royal Society, the Royal Observatory at Greenwich and the Scottish universities during this period.   Nevertheless, it is incorrect to suppose that studies at the universities were limited to theology and classical authors.   There were scientific professorships at both universities, and a number of English pioneers of science were trained at them.   Nor is it correct to think of the fellows of the colleges at this time as growing old in their academic posts; in fact, they were pre-dominantly unmarried ,young clergymen, who took college livings as their turn came round, and only the heads of the colleges and professors were older and unmarried.   Again, as Nicholas Hans has shown, the universities were not dominated by wealthy undergraduates, who led an idle extravagant existence.   Throughout the period these students were always a small minority, but – like all small, noisy groups – they attracted undue attention, while the serious, studious majority passed unnoticed.   At the beginning of the period, about a half of the undergraduates were poor students, the sons of the clergy and lower social classes.   Local squires and incumbents were often ready to help poor boys of ability to go to the grammar school and the university and so into the professions.   After about 1760, however, there was a sudden fall in the number of poor undergraduates brought about by social and industrial developments in the country. A social cleavage grew up between the labouring classes and the new employers, many of whom had little use for education other than technical training.   This had a very harmful effect upon the universities.   Their total numbers of students fell, and movements for reform languished.   The study of the old classical subjects received a new lease of life, being valued chiefly for the social benefits they brought a privileged minority.

An educational undertaking which was a feature of aristo-cratic life during this period was the Grand Tour.   Frequently a young nobleman or gentleman, before entering the House of Commons, completed his education by driving through the principal European countries by post-chaise in the company of a tutor.   Here he was expected to obtain some knowledge

[1] P. 92.

of foreign languages (especially French) and acquire fashionable manners and elegant taste by becoming acquainted
with court and society life and seeing the famous collections
of antique sculpture and Renaissance pictures. Few came
back to England without a desire to improve their homes and
embellish them with paintings and statues, and increasing
family wealth made it possible for them to do so.[1] The
result is the magnificent schemes of interior decoration and
art collections on view today in their Georgian country
houses, which remain as evidence of the effect the Grand
Tour and their previous classical education had upon these
young men.

Their sisters had few educational opportunities. The
daughters of noble and wealthy families were usually brought
up privately at home under the care of governesses; but
towards the end of the century day- and boarding-schools for
rich girls became more common, some of them being conducted by *émigré* noblewomen from revolutionary France. In
these fashionable, expensive schools the standard of education
was usually low. The pupils learnt some arithmetic and
literature, but more time was given to music, dancing and,
above all, deportment, which were accomplishments thought
likely to secure a girl an eligible husband. There were also
schools for middle-class girls, who were prepared for marriage
in their station of life, being taught, besides reading and
writing, 'lace-making, plain work, raising paste, sauces and
cookery' (as one such school advertised). Learning for
upper and middle-class girls was thought to endanger their
matrimonial prospects; 'bluestocking' was an opprobrious
term. Dr. Johnson was not untypical in saying: 'A man in
general is better pleased when he has a good dinner upon his
table than when his wife speaks Greek.' Successful matrimonial prospects were thought also to require feminine
modesty, good manners and even submissiveness. Such
girls were not, therefore, allowed the same freedom as boys
and were birched almost as much. Dr. Johnson was again
not untypical in praising the rod when he met 'some young
ladies in Lincolnshire who were remarkably well behaved'
and was told it was because of 'their mother's strict discipline
and severe correction'.

[1] P. 110.

Educational opportunities for the children of the poor were very few.   Here and there a dame-school or a village school-master might give some children a smattering of education for a few pence a week before they were set to work at an early age.   Such schools became more numerous as industrialization increased.   A dame, charging 3*d*. or 4*d*. a week for teaching children in her own house, could earn about £17 or £19 a year.   In 1834 the Statistical Society calculated that there were about 230 dame-schools in Manchester alone, giving some sort of an elementary education to poor children.

Early in the eighteenth century the charity-school move-ment had been initiated, largely under the auspices of the Society for Promoting Christian Knowledge.[1]   These schools were established for boys and girls of the labouring poor and were supported by private subscriptions.   The children received religious instruction and an education suited to their circumstances – reading and writing, a little arithmetic for the boys and needlework for the girls.   They were clothed in distinctive uniform, and a few of the schools were boarding-schools.   By 1727 there were nearly 1,400 charity-schools in England and Wales, but thereafter the movement lost its original impetus.   Fewer new schools were founded, and there were attempts to make existing schools self-supporting by setting the children to work and selling their produce; cobbling, printing, carpentry and gardening were taught to boys, knitting, sewing, spinning and straw-plaiting to girls. Such efforts, however, were not usually profitable, since the children's work was not skilful enough to sell their products in the markets.   Most successful were those girls' schools which were converted, usually by the lady of the manor or incumbent's wife, into boarding establishments where the pupils rose early and ate plain food, were whipped and disciplined and spent long hours at housework and needle-work as a solution to the perpetual problem of finding trained and respectful domestic servants for neighbouring country houses.

About the same time some workhouse administrators made equally unprofitable attempts to establish 'schools of industry' for their pauper children, which were similar to charity-schools.   Most workhouse officials wished to get the children

[1] P. 81.

off their hands as soon as possible, and between the ages of twelve and fourteen they were 'farmed out' or 'apprenticed', the girls mostly to domestic service, the boys to farmers, chimney-sweeps, undertakers and almost anyone who would take them off the rates for a small premium; and the Industrial Revolution brought about the large-scale use of such children, commonly from a younger age, in unskilled work in factories and mines.[1] Pauper children received nothing approaching the education formerly given by craftsmen to their apprentices. Accordingly the Health and Morals of Apprentices Act of 1802 stated that factory children should receive instruction for two hours each day, but not until the appointment of state inspectors in 1833 was this really enforced and even then with little educational value. The children were often taught sitting on the floor in a warehouse or a disused part of the factory, perhaps by an elderly or disabled workman provided only with a reading-primer and a cane. Factory inspectors, whose reports described, for instance, classes of girls between the ages of nine and thirteen, stained with the blue dye from the textile-mills and too listless and heavy-eyed to learn, regarded the provision as a means of limiting the children's hours of work rather than giving them much education.

In the closing years of the eighteenth century, the Sunday school movement made a fresh contribution towards the education of the poor. This did not originate, as is often supposed, with Robert Raikes (1735–1811), a printer and newspaper owner in Gloucester. Some Sunday schools had already been founded, such as those by Hannah and Martha More in the Mendip district and Hannah Ball in High Wycombe; but from 1780 Raikes organized the already existing schools into a successful movement and gave them a publicity which led to the establishment of many others by both the Church and the Dissenting bodies. The schools usually met on a Sunday morning and taught both religion and reading and writing. In 1833 it was stated that, while six out of ten children attended some sort of school, three of these were at a Sunday school.

The growth of industrialization and the development of large towns, however, made the existing facilities for the education of the children of the poor increasingly inadequate.

[1] P. 143.

Religious people were especially concerned about their lack of Christian knowledge and inability to read the Scriptures. Two societies were founded to provide day-schools for them. These were the British and Foreign School Society, founded by Nonconformists in 1808, and the larger National Society, founded three years later by Churchmen. The National Society alone founded 3,000 schools during its first twenty years, but such efforts touched only a fraction of the children. Some Radicals wanted a national, rate-aided system of education, but religious zeal and *laissez-faire* made this impossible. The government did, however, make an annual grant of £20,000 from 1833 to be shared among the two societies. It was a small step, but state intervention in education had begun.

Later in the Hanoverian period also, the new upper classes began to show a fresh concern for education and gave their support to movements for reform. The introduction of written examinations and the award of classes in degrees at Oxford and Cambridge marked the beginning of the revival of the ancient universities; and in London, University College, founded in 1828, and requiring no religious tests was soon joined by King's College, established on an Anglican basis, and the two were linked in 1836 as the first constituent colleges of the new University of London. Modernization and moral reform in the public schools began with the head-masterships of Samuel Butler at Shrewsbury from 1798 to 1836 and of Thomas Arnold at Rugby from 1828 to 1842. This was to revive the public schools and, by extending its influence to the grammar schools, transform the whole of English secondary education.

III · GOVERNMENT AND POLITICS

The Constitution

FOR the greater part of the Hanoverian period nearly all classes and opinions united in praising the excellence of the British constitution. Horace Walpole (1717–97), the son of the great Whig minister, wrote, 'Everybody talks of the constitution, but all sides forget that the constitution is extremely well, and would do very well, if they would but let it alone', while the Tory Sir Walter Scott (1771–1832) contrasted 'our noble system of masculine freedom' with the less fortunate conditions existing in disturbed France. Edmund Burke (1729–97) thought that the English form of government was the most perfect in existence since it embodied 'those rules of Providence which are formed upon the known march of the ordinary Providence of God'. This view was shared by the Oxford jurist, Sir William Blackstone (1723–80), who held that the constitution was most in conformity with the laws of nature and so not only the most rational but also the most perfect and unalterable. 'Of a constitution, so wisely contrived, so strongly raised, and so highly finished', he wrote in his *Commentaries on the Laws of England* (1765), 'it is hard to speak with that praise which is is just and severely its due – the thorough and attentive contemplation of it will furnish its best panegyric.' Crowds sang exultantly in *Rule Britannia*,

> While thou shalt flourish great and free,
> The dread and envy of them all.

And the Birmingham mob in 1791, when local Radicals celebrated the fall of the Bastille, burnt Dissenting chapels, private houses and Priestley's laboratory with shouts of 'No Philosophers!' and 'Church and King!'[1]

Such admiration of the British constitution, which was shared by distinguished foreigners like Voltaire and Montesquieu, had been given a theoretical basis by John Locke

[1] P. 373.

(1632–1704) in his political writings. His purpose was to justify the Glorious Revolution of 1688, which had set the seal of the ruling authority of the landed classes in the state. He imagined that civil society had come into being to secure a remedy for the inconveniences of a primitive 'state of nature' and to guarantee to the individual his natural rights. James II had lost his throne in 1688 because he had violated these natural rights; the people had replaced him by another ruler, whom they had bound by the Bill of Rights.

Among these fundamental rights, Locke included not only life and liberty, but also property. Before the formation of government, he argued, there existed a right of property and particularly of landed property, which brought its owners a right to political power, since 'subduing or cultivating the earth and having dominion are joined together'. For the eighteenth century, this was a rationalization of the political and social supremacy of the landed classes.

Moreover, such respect for property was justified because it safeguarded for everyone their own natural rights. The large landowner, independent of the court and ready to defend his rights, was regarded as the strongest opponent of arbitrary government. The liberty, justice and independence this class demanded for itself were enjoyed by the rest of the nation. The meanest householder was as secure as the richest landed nobleman; both were protected by the rule of law, which embodied their rights and could not be violated by anyone, however exalted. Foreign observers were amazed that, when George II's daughter, Princess Amelia, on her appointment as Ranger of Richmond Park, tried to treat it as a private domain and exclude the public, she was sued successfully by a Petersham brewer at Kingston assizes in 1758. 'The poorest man in his cottage', said Chatham in 1777, 'may bid defiance to all the forces of the Crown.'

The eighteenth-century constitution thus accepted the idea of a ruling class in the state. Politicians justified this by further reference to Locke's ideas, holding that the people had originally escaped from the 'state of nature' by granting the power of government to such a class on condition that it protected their rights and liberties. 'We contend', wrote the staunchly Whig Bishop of Llandaff, Richard Watson (1737–1816), 'that in all just government, the people have delegated to their governors the particular degree of trust with which they are invested [and] have limited the extent of the control to which they are to be subjected.' Nevertheless, the society governed this way was avowedly aristocratic and not egalitarian. Burke upheld the constitutional rights of the Whig magnates on the grounds of propriety and justice – 'Some decent, regulated, pre-eminence, some preference given to birth is neither unnatural nor unjust nor impolitic.' All men had these rights and privileges, which were not equal, but depended upon their position in society and were safeguarded by its hierarchical nature.

Another safeguard stressed by most eighteenth-century writers was the 'mixed' nature of the constitution. Contemporary political thought held that there could be no liberty where the right of both making and enforcing laws rested with the same man or body of men. This theory of the separation of powers was regarded as an essential aspect of the British constitution. Crown, Parliament and Judicature were considered to possess their own separate powers and operate in mutually exclusive spheres, each being prevented from securing supreme power by checks and balances which regulated their relations with each other. These included the Crown's right to dissolve Parliament and veto bills, Parliament's control of finance and the judges' settled positions and salaries. The Crown and its ministers took executive decisions, Parliament made the laws, and the judges enforced them. Though this was a theory which in many ways suited the practical politics of the time, the fact remained, however, that Parliament, through its possession of legislative authority, was ultimately the supreme body in the constitution and was increasingly able to assert this during this period.

According to Locke, all power possessed by the legislature rested upon the superior power of the people as a whole. 'There remains still in the People', he wrote in *Of Civil Government*, 'a supreme power to remove or alter the Legislative, when they find the Legislative act contrary to the Trust reposed in them.' It was commonly recognized that the people were justified in rebelling against a government which violated their rights. The Whigs interpreted the Glorious Revolution in this way. Yet eighteenth-century politicians did not think that the contemporary population would exercise this right of regaining governmental power. 'It was exercised at the Revolution', said Bishop Watson; 'and we trust that there will never, in this country, be occasion to exercise it again; for we hope and are persuaded that the wisdom of the House of Hanover will keep at an awful distance from the throne men professing principles which have levelled with the dust the House of Stuart.'

In fact, the English people in the eighteenth century were well able to check a government pursuing a policy which they strongly disliked. No administration, possessing only the rudimentary means of the time to enforce its authority, dared run the risk of provoking extensive violence, and the opposition were prepared to encourage and use the threat of general disorder against the government. The agitation against Walpole's Excise Bill of 1733 was a notable instance of popular hostility being exploited for political purposes.[1] An eighteenth-century government would hardly have been able to secure the passing of the Poor Law Amendment Act of 1834 in face of the bitter feeling it aroused in the country. In the last decades of the Hanoverian period, however, during the wars against France and the consequent internal troubles, the government was compelled to acquire the means of repression to ensure its survival. Popular reaction to this situation produced the widespread agitation which accompanied the parliamentary struggle over the enactment of the Reform Bill of 1832.

The Hanoverian Monarchs

Though contemporary writers regarded the British constitution as perfect and permanent and emphasized the stability guaranteed by the careful balance of its different parts, the Hanoverian period was actually one of outstanding constitutional development. In particular, far-reaching changes took place in the role of the monarchy in the government of the country, and these were partly due to the characters of the Hanoverian kings. The social and political importance of the Crown was still sufficient to ensure that the personality of the monarch exercised an important influence upon the history of the age, and, strangely enough, this was

[1] P. 257.

particularly true in a negative way under George I and George II whose effect upon affairs of state was not strong.

George I (1714–27) was fifty-four years old when he came over to England, accompanied by many German attendants, two Turkish valets and an uncertain number of German mistresses, notable among them being Ehrengard von der Schulenburg, whom he made Duchess of Kendal. Short and fair-skinned, he possessed the bright-blue protuberant eyes and irritable expression, both of which facial features of the Guelph family were to be inherited by subsequent generations. He retained a German prince's egoism and a German officer's peremptory habits. His mother, Sophia, Electress of Hanover and granddaughter of James I of England, had died only just before Queen Anne and was thus deprived of the English throne which she had so much desired; but George I accepted it only because, like William of Orange, he thought Britain would be useful to him in the foreign politics of Hanover, where he would much rather have remained.[1] It is not true, however, that he was ignorant of English; he had a passable smattering of it and could speak French, the language of diplomacy, which most of his ministers understood. He was shy and retiring, appearing in public for his casual weekly attendance at divine service, but mainly living quietly in a few rooms in St. James's Palace. He brought no Queen with him; his German cousin, Sophia Dorothea of Celle, whom he had married at his father's wish, remained imprisoned for infidelity in the Castle at Ahlden until her death in 1726. Unlike William III and Anne, he did not care for Hampton Court or Kensington, so the court returned to London, but it would not have been the centre of social life had it not been for the Prince and Princess of Wales (afterwards George II and Queen Caroline).

George I doubted the loyalty of his English ministers. He gave much of his political confidence to foreigners – two Hanoverian ministers, Baron von Bothmer (1656–1732) and Andreas Gottlieb von Bernstorff (1649–1726), and Jean de Robethon (d. 1722), a Huguenot refugee who had been William III's private secretary.[2] These men, like the King's German mistresses, were commonly accused of selling their influence to aspiring politicians. Contemporaries seem

[1] P. 224.
[2] P. 224.

to have agreed on George I's character. Lady Mary Wortley Montagu thought him 'an honest blockhead' and 'completely free from ambition'; Lord Chesterfield found him 'an honest and dull German gentleman', who was 'lazy and inactive even in his pleasures'; and Dr. Johnson asserted that he 'knew nothing and desired to know nothing, did nothing and desired to do nothing'. Yet these verdicts probably underestimate his ability. He had a strong character and was determined not to be ruled by his ministers, but he was handicapped by his ignorance of English men and affairs. That his reign provided the Hanoverian dynasty with a successful beginning was due much to the fact that Walpole came to enjoy the King's trust and control the Crown's extensive patronage.

An unwitting contribution made by George I to British politics was the hostility between the King and his eldest son, which was to be repeated in following reigns. This owed something to the personalities of the members of the Hanoverian royal family, but was also deliberately encouraged by opponents of the government for their own ends. George II (1727–60), who was forty-four before he came to the throne, infuriated his father by championing his mother, and they quarrelled with each other for years.

The first two Hanoverian monarchs had much in common in their characters, but George II was considerably less indolent and more business-like. Like his father, he appreciated music alone among the arts, and he encouraged Handel to settle in England. His other delights were money and his guards, his attachment to whom made him envy Frederick the Great's magnificent Prussian army and detest him with an intensity that was not without effect on British foreign policy. He had as strong a preference for Hanover as his father, but, as Horace Walpole admitted, 'was not so totally careless of the affection and interests of his country as his father had been'. Though he had mistresses, his wife, the singularly intelligent and cultured Caroline of Ansbach, exercised a decisive influence over him. Of her, Lord Harvey said, 'the darling pleasure of her soul was power'; and her death in 1737 was a misfortune for both the King and Walpole, whose authority was much dependent upon her friendship with him. After her death, George II's lack of political courage ensured that his ministers did not have to fear his opposition so much.

George II, in his turn, quarrelled so violently with his eldest son, Frederick, Prince of Wales, that court and society were split into two factions. Frederick, however, died in 1751 at the age of forty-four, leaving his eldest son to come to the throne as George III (1760–1820). He was twenty-two years old when he succeeded his grandfather, but was backward mentally and emotionally. His intellectual endowment was modest, and he developed late. For the first years of his reign he remained under the influence of his strong-minded mother, the widowed Princess Augusta of Wales, and her intimate adviser, the Earl of Bute. They had taught him to hate the Whig ministers who had dominated his father, to mistrust his uncle, the Duke of Cumberland, and his 'black-hearted' followers like Fox, and to share the dislike of the insular Tory squires for 'German' measures and wars.

Bute, however, was in power only for a few months, and George III finally ceased to depend upon him in 1766. With his marriage in 1761 to Charlotte of Mecklenburg, he fast matured, and indolence was replaced by continual activity in politics. Both his virtues and shortcomings developed. He was naturally shrewd and soon acquired political experience. His sense of duty made him perform the duties of kingship with conscientious application; he rose daily at four o'clock and spent three hours on the government despatch boxes before taking his morning ride in Windsor Great Park. Nevertheless, his much discussed period of personal rule from 1763 to 1782 brought calamitous blunders for which he must share the responsibility. He carried personal hatreds into public life to the extent of objecting to a state funeral for Chatham as 'offensive to me personally'. His character was obstinate rather than strong. As Walter Bagehot wrote: 'Throughout the greater part of his life George III was a kind of "consecrated obstruction".' He undermined cabinets by encouraging disloyalty. His decisions were often wrong and unstable. His conservatism was such that Radicalism, industrial strife and American rebellion all seemed to him wicked attacks on the most perfectly constituted order of things. Finally, the strain on his unsteady mind brought him periods of mental illness as early as 1765, and after 1811, following the death of his favourite daughter, Princess Amelia, he became permanently incapacitated.

Yet he was personally more attractive than his two immediate predecessors. Horace Walpole was favourably impressed when he first met him – 'This young man don't stand in one spot, with eyes fixed royally on the ground, and dropping bits of German views; he walks about and speaks to everybody.' Though his wife was plain and unattractive, he remained faithful to her, and his family of fifteen legitimate children is a record for a British king. He had no English blood in him, but asserted in his first speech from the throne in 1760, 'Born and educated in this country, I glory in the name of Britain'; he never visited the Continent and regarded Hanover as a 'troublesome principality'. His genuine piety had its effect upon the pleasures of both his courtiers and Archbishop Cornwallis.[1] He displayed his courage during the Gordon Riots and the several attempts made on his life. His dutiful labours allowed him few pastimes, but he appreciated music, delighted in agricultural techniques and enjoyed sea-bathing, stepping into the waves from his machine at Weymouth to the tune of *Rule Britannia*. He disliked Shakespeare. His people, and especially the middle classes, discovered these qualities and approved of them. His popularity increased after the American War and the revival of prosperity under the Younger Pitt. He gained sympathy also when in his old age the reckless behaviour of his dissolute sons seemed to contribute to his loss of reason. During the years when the forces of revolution were menacing Continental monarchs, he retained the loyalty and affection of his subjects.

His eldest son, who ruled England as Prince Regent from 1812 to 1820 and then as George IV until 1830, had shared a strict and severe upbringing with his brothers, one of whom was flogged for contracting asthma. Consequently, when at the age of twenty-one in 1783, he was given a private establishment and an allowance of £50,000 a year, he abandoned himself to unrestrained self-indulgence. In 1785 he married Mrs. Fitzherbert, a young Roman Catholic widow, but did not forfeit his throne under the Act of Settlement since the Royal Marriage Act of 1772 rendered the union invalid.[2] On

[1] P. 18.   [2] P. 336.

Parliament agreeing to pay his debts of £650,000, he married in 1795 his cousin, Princess Caroline of Brunswick, but he made no pretence of being faithful to her, and after the birth of their only child, Princess Charlotte Augusta (1796–1817), she left him.   Like the previous Hanoverian Princes of Wales, he attached himself to the opposition and earned his father's hatred and contempt by becoming the close friend of Fox and other young dissipated Whigs, though neither as Regent nor King did he try to bring his Whig friends into office.   Upon his accession he tried to get Parliament to pass a bill of divorce against his wife, but feeling in her favour was so strong that the ministry had to stop the proceedings.   He earned further unpopularity through his extravagant expenditure upon his Pavilion at Brighton and his ministers' post-war legislation, particularly the hated Corn Law.   Ill-health and natural laziness combined to make him an ineffective sovereign. His character robbed the throne of the support of that moral influence contributed by his father and not to be regained until Victoria's reign.

The last Hanoverian monarch was George III's third son, the Duke of Clarence, who became William IV in 1830 at the age of sixty-four.   He did much to restore the monarchy's popularity though not its dignity.   Service in the navy had a permanent effect upon his language.   Without any of the training and few of the qualities of a king, he displayed no idea of propriety or of his position.   He was honest, stupid and obstinate, but not entirely lacking in political sense. During the Reform Bill crisis of 1832 his attitude over the creation of peers was sensible, but his action in dismissing the Whigs in 1834 was a serious error of judgement.[1]   Upon leaving the navy in 1791, he had lived at Bushey Park with Mrs. Jordan, the actress, by whom he had ten children; but when it became likely that his legitimate heirs would inherit the throne, he left her and married Adelaide of Saxe-Coburg-Meiningen in 1818.   Their two daughters died in infancy, and he was succeeded by his niece, Princess Victoria, in 1837.

The Powers of the Crown

Outwardly the position of the monarchy under the Hanoverian kings may seem to have been then very much as it

[1] P. 440.

is nowadays. The ancient forms have indeed been maintained, and there has been an unwillingness to take power expressly from the Crown, but this apparent continuity is deceptive and has deceived historians in the past. Institutions bearing the same name no longer perform similar functions, while numerous 'constitutional understandings' have in fact limited the royal prerogatives, and the events of the Hanoverian period played an important part in this process. Their general effect was to reduce the monarchy's power gradually, but the decline was not uniform, and by the end of the period it was still an important factor in the government of the country.

The Revolution Settlement of 1689 and particularly the Bill of Rights had set certain limits to the Crown's powers. The King could not be a Roman Catholic nor marry a Roman Catholic; he had to be in communion with the Church of England and to make a declaration against transubstantiation. He was to be subject to statute law since he might not suspend nor dispense with statutes, nor create any new offence by proclamations. He could neither keep a standing army in the realm in time of peace without Parliament's consent, nor revive the prerogative courts established by the Tudor monarchs and abolished by the Long Parliament.

In the years after the Revolution Settlement, the position of the Crown in relation to Parliament declined still more. Parliament began to vote money for the needs of one year only, appropriate it for specific purposes and audit accounts. Parliament also would only make possible the existence of a standing army by passing an annual Mutiny Act, the operation of which was limited to the next twelve months. Accordingly, to obtain revenue and maintain the army the King had to call Parliament every year.

At the same time, later Stuart politicians had not sought to reduce the monarch to a mere figurehead. He was left with great legal powers. It is true that Queen Anne's refusal of assent to the Scottish Militia Bill in 1707 proved to be the last time the Crown used its power to veto a parliamentary measure, but it was not legally abolished. In general, the King was expected to use all the old royal prerogatives, except those expressly annulled by statute. Law and usage, therefore, accorded the Hanoverian monarchy a considerable position in national government.

Throughout the period, the court continued to be the centre of the country's political and social life. Every decision and appointment had to be discussed and argued with the King. Potentially the King was in a powerful position to secure his wishes because a vast system of patronage was in his hands. This still included the right to appoint to every ministerial post, to commissions in the armed forces, to numerous positions in the royal household and government sinecures and to bishoprics, deaneries, canonries and crown livings in the Church. The control of thirty or more Treasury boroughs and the award of peerages were also in his hands.[1] Parliament made an annual payment to each Hanoverian king for the expenses of the Crown, and the fact that the salaries of judges, civil servants and others were charged upon this Civil List until 1831 made it a fruitful source of royal patronage. As Parliament had several times in this period to pay the King's debts, attempts were made to reform it. Burke's measures of economical reform in 1782 were a step towards this, but the Younger Pitt's administrative reforms after 1784 were more effective in checking political patronage.[2]

Consequently, when the King did make use of his power to intervene in politics, it was usually effective. Even Walpole could not have continued in office after George II's accession had not Queen Caroline persuaded the King to retain him; and the Younger Pitt would hardly have won his striking victory at the general election of 1784, when some eighty of Fox's friends lost their seats, had he not been supported by royal wishes and influence. The failure of Roman Catholic Emancipation in 1800 and the passing of the Reform Bill in 1832 were other events in which royal participation produced great political effect.

Nevertheless, the monarchy's power in fact gradually declined during the Hanoverian period. Neither George I not George II were capable of forming a policy or using their powers fully. Under them, royal patronage was generally at the disposal of ministers who possessed the King's favour. The growth of public influence in politics and of the influence of the press also undermined royal power. It became increasingly advisable for the King to have ministers belonging

[1] P. 57.   [2] Pp. 350, 366–7.

to the dominant party in the Commons and difficult for him to get rid of ministers whom he disliked. The leading Whig politicians, by uniting against George II, compelled him to retain in 1746 and accept in 1757 ministers whom he disliked because they alone possessed the support of the Commons.[1] George III's resumption of much royal patronage did not permanently strengthen the Crown's position. At first he was more independent, especially when Lord North was in office, but disasters in America brought into being a united opposition which secured the resignation of the whole ministry, except the Lord Chancellor, against the King's wishes.[2] Thereafter royal authority continued to diminish. George III's incapacitating mental breakdown and the growth of cabinet solidarity gave the Prime Minister control of more of his prerogatives. William IV's dismissal of the Whigs in 1834 was to be the last time an English sovereign exercised his prerogative of dismissing his ministers.

The Development of the Cabinet

The Restoration in 1660 restored both the King as the supreme executive authority and the Privy Council as his advisory body. The King appointed all its members, but he was expected to include a number who held only honorific posts with little or no administrative responsibility. It was too large to conduct business efficiently and secretly. Charles II and his successors consequently chose from the Privy Council a small, informal committee of advisers to take its place. By Anne's reign this had become known as the Cabinet, with definite duties and regular meetings, and the most important ministers were among its members.

Such a body had no official status, so that Blackstone in 1765 did not refer to it in describing the contemporary English constitution; but by 1714 it was in fact generally realized that it had replaced the Privy Council as the real governing body. At first the Cabinet itself seemed likely to become as overlarge as the Privy Council previously had been. From the early eighteenth century there existed a large Cabinet Council, membership of which was often honorary, and a smaller, inner Cabinet. 'The Duke [of Leeds]', Horace Walpole once wrote, 'is made Cabinet Councillor, a rank that will

[1] Pp. 275, 301.   [2] Pp. 352–3.

soon become indistinguishable from Privy Councillor by
growing as numerous.' Wartime problems, however, particularly revealed the uselessness of this larger body, which was
summoned with decreasing frequency and is believed to have
last met to consider the King's Speech in 1806. The inner
Cabinet survived to deal effectively with government business.

The smaller Cabinet necessarily included the First Lord of
the Treasury, and the Secretaries of State, and almost
invariably the Lord Chancellor and the President of the
Council as well as others according to circumstances.
Restrictions upon its membership were gradually accepted.
By about the middle of the eighteenth century, such figures
as the Archbishop of Canterbury, the Lord Steward, the
Master of the Horse and the Lord Chief Justice had ceased
to attend its meetings. And Addington's refusal in 1801 to
allow Lord Loughborough, the previous Lord Chancellor,
to remain in the Cabinet brought final recognition that it
consisted entirely of the principal ministers of the government
of the day.

At Cabinet meetings, George I had to depend on his eldest
son as an interpreter. This angered him and together with
his boredom at its proceedings led him to cease to attend it
after 1718. His successors followed his example. None of
them went to the inner Cabinet, and after 1781 their very
rare attendances at the Cabinet Council ceased. That the
King no longer attended and presided over Cabinet meetings
did not reduce his power as much as has been sometimes
supposed. He could still issue instructions to his ministers
before the meetings and review their decisions afterwards.

In the King's absence, a leading minister presided over
Cabinet meetings. Inevitably a dominating position in the
Cabinet was achieved by the minister who presided over the
Treasury and could best control royal patronage and so
exercise a power of management. Shrewsbury was the last
man to hold the office of Lord Treasurer in 1714;[1] after that
its powers were permanently entrusted to a Treasury Board,
presided over by the First Lord of the Treasury, who enjoyed
the further advantage of being able to sit in the House of
Commons himself.

Such a minister came to be described, though at first in

[1] P. 228.

derision, as the Prime Minister. Sir Robert Walpole is commonly thought to have been the first to make himself a 'prime minister' during his years as First Lord of the Treasury from 1721 to 1742.[1] Yet he was never independent of royal favour, as his insecure position upon George II's accession showed. His dominant personality and long period of office, coupled with George II's political ineptitude, gained him an ascendancy over his colleagues and the power to get dissidents to resign, but he did not choose his ministers nor did they resign when he left office. His successors, who were mostly in office for only a short time, could not exert his authority. Henry Pelham, even after getting rid of Carteret, had to share much power with his brother, the Duke of Newcastle, who in his turn had subsequently to share power with the Elder Pitt; and Lord North was much more a court favourite that a principal minister.[2] Lord North's daughter, indeed, recalled in 1839 that he would never allow his family to call him Prime Minister because there was no such thing in the British constitution. The Younger Pitt, through his controlling influence and hold over his colleagues, may be regarded as the first Prime Minister to have united support from his Cabinet; and Lord Liverpool's able control of Cabinet meetings during his long period of office from 1812 to 1827 further enhanced the Prime Minister's role.[3]

Next to the First Lord of the Treasury, the Secretaries of State were the Cabinet's most important members. Since the fifteenth century they had been two in number, and from 1688 were designated the Secretary for the Southern Department and the Secretary for the Northern Department. The former was responsible for correspondence relating to the southern states of Europe, together with home, Irish and colonial matters, and the latter for correspondence relating to Holland, Germany and the Baltic. For a short time there was also a Secretary for Scotland (1709–25 and 1742–6) and a Secretary for the Colonies (1768–82). After the establishment of the Hanoverian line in 1714, the Secretary for the North became more important and tended to specialize in foreign affairs, to accompany the King to Hanover and negotiate with foreign rulers, while the other gave more time to domestic affairs. This development was recognized in 1782 when the

[1] Pp. 251–5.   [2] Pp. 271, 301, 335.   [3] Pp. 403–4.

two original secretaries were renamed the Secretary of State for Foreign Affairs and the Secretary of State for Home Affairs. With the abolition of the Secretaryship for the Colonies, because the loss of the American colonies had reduced its functions, colonial affairs were made the responsibility of the Home Secretary until they were transferred in 1794 to the Secretary for War, created in that year to replace the Secretary at War, who had never been in the Cabinet.

Parliament and Representation

In Parliament, at the opening of the Hanoverian period, the importance of the House of Lords in the constitution seemed unimpaired, and it still rejected bills passed by the Commons. It was also the highest court of appeal and performed its part several times under the first two Georges in the exceptional and solemn judicial process of impeachment. For the greater part of the eighteenth century, it possessed strength and unity through its comparatively small numbers, which between 1714 and 1780 remained at the almost constant figure of 220, including twenty-six bishops and sixteen representative Scottish peers. George III, however, largely while the Younger Pitt was in office, created 388 new titles of which 128 were new creations.[1] The Union with Ireland added twenty-eight peers and four bishops to the House, while after 1791 Roman Catholic peers were allowed to take their seats. The Peerage Bill of 1720 was an unsuccessful attempt to limit the King's creation of new peers.[2] If it had passed it would greatly have increased the power and independence of the House of Lords, but its rejection by the Commons was an indication that, in fact, the Lords had became the less important of the two Houses of Parliament.

Indeed, during this period the main political authority of the peers was probably exerted outside rather than inside Parliament. Their landed estates brought them the domination of local government throughout the country and also an influence in county and borough elections which gave them some control over the Commons, many of whom were members or dependants of noble families. Their personal importance was shown by their preponderance, especially in the higher posts, in the ministries of the period.

[1] P. 364. [2] P. 236.

It was as a legislative and debating assembly that the Lords most markedly declined in power and reputation. 'My Lord Bath, you and I are now two as insignificant men as any in England', remarked Walpole to the outstanding orator, William Pulteney, Earl of Bath, on their promotion to the House of Lords. In the later part of the period, the Lords became more reactionary; the peerage was determined to use its privileges against middle-class ambitions;[1] and many of the new creations were closely attached to the Crown. The prophecy made by Wilkes, as peerages multiplied under the Younger Pitt, that the Lords would become the 'dead weight' of the constitution, approached fulfilment. While the Commons moved towards the abolition of established abuses, the Lords became more obstinate in defending them, and the result was the conflict between the two Houses in 1832 over the Reform Bill.

That the conflict did not come sooner was largely due to the fact that for the greater part of the period most of the members of both Houses were agreed on important matters and came from much the same social class. The House of Commons had 558 members. Twenty-four of these represented Wales and forty-five Scotland, and after 1801 there were a hundred Irish members. After 1710 county members had to have an income of £600 and borough members £300 a year from land. It was possible for merchants, financiers, manufacturers, lawyers, civil servants, officers in the fighting services and others with enough wealth or influence to secure election; the property qualification was often overridden in their favour by legal subterfuges, and they might even gain ministerial office. Nevertheless, only after 1815 were there ever more than a hundred such men in the Commons; the rest belonged to the gentry or nobility. Most of the Commons, and particularly the borough members, were either relatives of peers or dependent upon them.

The right to vote in parliamentary elections depended upon different qualifications in county and borough seats. In the counties the franchise was uniform, having been granted by an act of 1430 to all men possessing freehold property valued at forty shillings a year; but in the boroughs there was great variety, largely depending upon local medieval customs.

[1] P. 25.

In a few boroughs, like Preston, anyone could vote who stayed the night there before an election. In about twelve boroughs the voters were the 'potwallopers' (everyone who boiled a pot, i.e. all male householders or lodgers); in about forty-seven those who paid 'scot and lot' (church- and poor-rates); in about thirty-nine the burgage tenants (those possessing certain tenements); and in about sixty-two the freemen. The first two types of boroughs usually had larger – sometimes considerably larger – electorates than the others; but most of the boroughs had a small number of voters.[1] Both borough and county electors had to record their votes openly at the hustings or platform erected in some public place from which the candidates also gave their addresses.

The distribution of seats was as illogical as the franchise. Each English county, from Yorkshire (15,054 voters in 1761) to Rutland (609 voters in 1761), returned two members, and the total number of county voters was probably about 160,000 or about two-thirds of the entire English electorate. Each borough also returned two members, a borough being a town which had been granted by royal charter a corporation and special privileges, including the right to send representatives to Parliament. The last town to be made a borough had been Newark in 1677, after which jealousy of the House of Commons of this royal prerogative had compelled its disuse, so that the number of boroughs remained unaltered. Many boroughs were very small places, like Appleby in Westmorland or Bramber in Sussex. Some were 'rotten boroughs', which had been seriously depopulated – Gatton, Winchelsea and Rye were bad examples of these, while the most notorious were Dunwich in Suffolk, much of which lay under the sea, and Old Sarum in Wiltshire, which was a deserted site on a hill. The smallness of the boroughs, their restricted electorate and system of open voting also led to 'pocket boroughs', the representation of which was controlled by some landowner. Finally, the location of the boroughs was anomalous. Large towns in the north and Midlands – Birmingham, Manchester, Leeds and others produced by the Industrial Revolution – were not boroughs, but there were twenty-six boroughs in Cornwall with a total of 1,050 voters in 1783.

[1] P. 56.

E

The structure of the electoral system made possible the use of patronage and influence in politics, but not uniformly. The eighty county seats were the least amenable to control. Not only were they the most populous, but since there was only one polling town in each constituency candidates found it expensive to provide horses and carriages, beds and meals to enable their supporters to vote at the hustings. Yorkshire was the most expensive; the election of 1807 cost the three candidates in the county a total of some £250,000. It is not surprising that uncontested elections were common in the county seats.

The large preponderance of the borough constituencies and the generally small size of their electorate, even in some of the most populous, made them the most liable to influence. The pocket boroughs were, of course, the easiest to manipulate, but since only twenty-two boroughs had more than a thousand and thirty-three over five hundred voters, there were many others open to control by a local landowner who could secure by promises, bribes or threats the election of a candidate. Such influence was not, however, confined to the few great aristocratic families, and Sir Lewis Namier has shown that their electoral influence has been exaggerated. At the accession of George III, fifty-one peers and fifty-five commoners appear to have secured or effectively influenced the return of more than 190 members of the Commons, but among these even such a grandee as the Duke of Bedford had only four boroughs at his disposal, the Duke of Devonshire had three, and several dukes had none. There was no line of division in borough patronage between the great families and the rest of the peers, nor indeed between peers and commoners.

As the century passed, the cost of electioneering became ever more expensive – Lord Penrhyn, for instance, spent £30,000 in 1790 in an unsuccessful effort to control Liverpool, where 1,967 freemen had the vote. This was due to the growing importance of Parliament and increasing wealth of the country as well as to the Septennial Act of 1716 which greatly increased the incentive to obtain election to the longer-lived parliaments.[1] The cost of private patronage was also increased by the greater importance of Crown patronage after

[1] P. 234.

the Duke of Newcastle had shown how it could be used to good effect to gain the support of borough patrons who would secure the election of members favourable to the ministry.[1] To them went the numerous appointments controlled by the Crown;[2] and after the election of 1784 there were seventeen promotions to peerages. Crown patronage was also used in the ministry's interest in the constituencies. There were the small Treasury boroughs, where the voters all had government posts, and sea-ports where the granting of naval contracts and appointments to customs posts enabled similar influence to be exercised through the Admiralty.

Such exploitation of Crown patronage steadily lessened the independence of private borough patrons. The mounting expense of elections often forced them to obtain offices of profit under the Crown for themselves and their supporters, and from 1727 Newcastle made the connection closer by paying direct financial grants from the secret service account to patrons for the right to nominate candidates at elections. The usual price of a seat was £1,500 which had risen to £2,000 by 1761 and to £5,000 or £6,000 by 1801. Such an alliance of the ministry with the leading borough patrons guaranteed victory at any general election.

Several consequences followed from this growth of Crown patronage. Contested elections now became comparatively rare in small boroughs such as the Crown could dominate. In 1715 there were over sixty contests in boroughs with an electorate of less than 400, but in 1761 only fifteen. This had the further result of transferring the struggle by opposition politicians from the constituencies to attempts to win over patrons and Members of Parliament. And, finally, the effectiveness of Crown patronage aroused resentment which later in the century led to the decline of its influence over constituencies. The disfranchisement of revenue officers in 1782 contributed towards this decline.[3] So also did the rivalry of private families, who had succeeded by the end of the eighteenth century in capturing about a half of the Treasury boroughs.

It must not be thought that the system of patronage destroyed the independence of Parliament and its members. Sir Lewis Namier has shown that between 1754 and 1762

[1] P. 253.   [2] P. 49.   [3] P. 356.

the Duke of Newcastle spent in secret service money from the Treasury about £291,000, of which only 43 per cent was spent on elections and constituencies and in pensions to Members of Parliament, the rest going to the aristocracy, salaried government officials, secret agents, supporters of the ministry and Germans. Namier concludes that parliamentary corruption was 'surprisingly small' and also that 'there was more jobbery, stupidity and human charity about it than bribery'. The number of placemen – civil servants, court and household officers, government contractors and members sitting for government boroughs – in the Commons seems to have been about 200 between 1716 and 1783. They were valued, as Miss Betty Kemp has shown, as 'a vital link between a House of Commons chosen by the electorate and ministers chosen by the King'. They provided the ministry of the day with enough support to carry on the government, but were not numerous enough to reduce the Commons to subservience.

In fact, eighteenth-century patrons had probably less control over Members of Parliament than that exercised today by political parties, and ability, personality and eloquence counted for more. Similarly, voters generally had little control over those whom they sent to Parliament, though the representatives of the counties and of boroughs with large electorates, such as Bristol or Norwich, had to be more attentive to the wishes of their constituents than most borough members. The Wilkesites in 1769 introduced new ways into politics when they adopted the practice of issuing instructions to Members of Parliament whom they supported.[1]

In the House of Commons, the most independent members were the country gentlemen and their urban counterparts (mainly rich businessmen). Indeed, Namier has said that 'the distinguishing mark of the country gentleman was disinterested independence'. Such men entered the Commons with a sense of duty to the public, their ambition being primacy in their own 'country' or social circle. They were chosen as parliamentary representatives for their county or some respectable borough (or sat for a pocket borough of their own, preferably one where favours for the voters did not have to be obtained from the administration). To seek offices, honours or profits might have impaired rather than

[1] P. 333.

raised the standing of such men. They were, therefore, independent of the Crown and the ministers. They tended to be critical of financial expenditure of the court, of sinecures and of wars; suspicious of politicians and courtiers; hostile towards the presence of government contractors and pensioners in the House; and opposed to a high land tax. Since, however, their votes were determined by individual convictions and not by pursuits or party manœuvres, they were so much divided that on normal occasions their votes generally cancelled each other out.

Nevertheless, a strong movement of public opinion could produce a measure of unity among them, and then their weight would have effect. From the middle of the century, indeed, this group in the Commons, which was perhaps about a hundred strong, increasingly became an indication and expression of public opinion. They believed it their duty to support the King's government as long as they conscientiously could, but when vital issues arose, they were prepared to judge them as impartially as they could. In 1764 so many country gentlemen voted with the opposition against general warrants that Grenville's ministry barely survived; and in 1782, when the defeat at Yorktown turned public opinion completely against the American War and the government, enough country gentlemen withdrew their support from Lord North to bring him down.[1]

The rôle of the country gentlemen in politics began, however, to change towards the end of the century. The numerous peerages conferred by the Younger Pitt on leading county families seem to have lessened their traditional objection to receiving honours and consequently weakened their independent position. Yet they remained a force in Parliament beyond the Hanoverian period and well into the reign of Victoria.

Whigs and Tories

In the reigns of William III and of Anne, the Whig and Tory parties represented a real division on interest and outlook between political groups which were contesting with each other for power and disagreed over the political and religious issues of the day. The two parties originated in the

[1] Pp. 325, 353.

post-Restoration period, when each acquired the hostile nickname by which it became known – 'Tory' being a term originally used to describe Irish brigands and 'Whig' to describe Scottish covenanters. Traditionally the Tories championed the cause of the Established Church, the Crown and the landed gentry and the Whigs the Dissenters, Parliament and the merchant classes.

The accession of the house of Hanover, however, fundamentally changed the situation. The failure of the Jacobite rebellion, in which a few Tory leaders strove desperately and hopelessly for a Stuart restoration, ruined the political chances of their party and began the long period of 'Whig supremacy'. The Whig leaders were able to persuade both George I and George II that they were the only true supporters of the Hanoverian dynasty. Henceforward, no Tory held office either as a minister or even within the ranks of the government party.

The result was that those Tories who wanted a share of royal patronage abandoned their old allegiance and began to call themselves Whigs. 'By 1750', Namier has said, 'everyone at court, in office and in the central arena was a Whig, while the name of Tories, by a process of natural selection, was left to the residuum who did not enter politics in pursuit of office, honours or profits, that is, the country gentlemen, and to the forerunners of the urban radicals.' Such Tories could neither form an opposition nor provide a ministry. From 1715 there were always more Whigs than governmental places, so the active opposition as well as successive ministries were mainly Whig. It has been said that George III turned to the Tories in 1760; but Bute's origins were undeniably Whig,[1] and ministries between 1760 and 1780 continued to be drawn from the Whigs; thus the structure of politics remained the same.

Parliament did not have, therefore, a two-party system related to great national issues. In actual fact it had a multi-party system. There were many groups, each of about ten members. The Rockingham party had about eighty members, but this was exceptionable. Administrations drew their support from coalitions of such small groups, some of which were of uncertain political colouring. As late as

[1] P. 318.

1807, Edward Harbord, later Lord Suffield, said on being returned for Yarmouth, 'The old story of Whig and Tory is now forgotten; all parties are mixed together.'

Yet the party names survived in many constituencies where they still corresponded to real divisions, partly because they were identified with local factions and partly because the most lasting distinction between Whig and Tory – that of High Church against Low Church and Dissent – retained more vitality and significance in local struggles than at Westminster. Indeed, local matters were more important than national questions in most elections. There were no political issues in the elections between 1760 and 1780. Candidates in their addresses confined themselves to general remarks about the upholding of the constitution in Church and State and the preservation of liberty, while during the election of 1774 the great issue at Newcastle-upon-Tyne, for instance, was the right of the freemen to graze cattle on the Town Moor, and not the American problem.

At the very time, however, that party political differences seemed to have disappeared, Lord Rockingham and his supporters fell out of favour with George III and sought to base their opposition to the Crown upon the claim that they were inheritors of the Whigs of 1688 and were struggling to defend the constitution against the threat of destruction from the King and the party of the 'King's Friends'.[1] This claim was continued after 1792 by Charles James Fox and his followers, who supported the French revolutionaries and the cause of parliamentary reform; they styled themselves as Whigs and designated their opponents as Tories.[2]

By then the pattern of politics was changing. George III's illness and the Prince Regent's inadequacy, measures of economical reform and wartime pressures combined to push the monarch out of politics; and the social and economical problems of industrialization and later the ideological effect of the French Revolution gave rise to issues upon which real parties could be based. The election of 1784 initiated genuine political debates in some constituencies, notably about Fox's India Bill and Pitt's retention of power for three months. There followed the crystallization of great national issues – the slave trade, Roman Catholic

[1] P. 328.　　　　[2] P. 393.

emancipation and parliamentary reform – which brought national agitations into politics. When Wilberforce stood for Yorkshire in 1807 his devotion to the anti-slavery cause brought him private subscriptions which more than covered his election expenses of £58,000. Nevertheless, these issues were only gradually fought on party lines. The independent members were still important, and the struggle took the form rather of efforts, principally by societies and through petitions, to organize pressure upon them. These efforts were sometimes remarkably successful; few county members in 1831 chose to oppose the prevailing demand for parliamentary reform.

During the later years of the Hanoverian period, however, a two-party system was developing. The Whigs gained fresh substance for their claim to be upholders of popular liberty in the crisis that preceded the accomplishment of parliamentary reform. The Tories acquired cohesion through the fear of Jacobinism and were sustained through the capture of Treasury boroughs by private families; after a period of Toryism and 'Liberal Toryism' under Lord Liverpool, their party broke up, but by 1834 Peel's Tamworth Manifesto and improvements in party organization heralded its recovery and also marked a further stage towards the development of the modern party system.

Local Government

The activities of local government had a more important effect upon the lives of most people in Hanoverian England than nowadays. The abolition of the Council of the North and others prerogative courts by the Long Parliament in the seventeenth century had largely deprived the central government of its means of supervising the local authorities. Westminster and Whitehall now normally took little part in local administration, which was managed by a collection of institutions and officials, dating from different periods of the past and sometimes conflicting with each other's authority in the three main administrative units of county, parish and borough. The majority of these officials were part-time, amateur and unpaid; and as in the central government of the time, local affairs were largely controlled by the landed classes, at any rate in the countryside.

The most important official in the oldest and largest unit of local government, the county, was nominally the Lord-Lieutenant, but in the course of centuries his administrative functions had largely disappeared. Since he was usually a great nobleman of the district, his real importance lay in the local, social and political influence which he could exercise in support of the government. The Duke of Newcastle showed his appreciation of this by retaining for himself the Lord-Lieutenancies of Middlesex, Nottingham and Sussex, the three counties where his estates were largest and his need of support greatest. Indeed, a Lord-Lieutenant, by influencing local opinion, might do much to determine the result of an election and even the fate of a ministry.

The most important local administrators were the Justices of the Peace. Originally, Justices needed to have landed property in the county worth £20 a year, but in 1732 Parliament (ever-suspicious that the government appointed newly-enriched landless men) raised this to £100 a year. They were generally appointed from the local squirearchy and later in the eighteenth century sometimes from wealthy merchants who had bought estates and the clergy, whose social status was rising. Upon this medieval official sixteenth-century sovereigns had heaped so many judicial and administrative tasks that he has been called the 'Tudor maid-of-all-work'. His authority was maintained and even extended in the Hanoverian period. A single Justice, sitting perhaps in his parlour, could fine or put in the stocks drunkards, swearers or poachers, issue orders to parish officers, send unmarried mothers to a house of correction and order the whipping of vagrants. Two or three Justices, sitting together in Petty Sessions in the local tavern or their own houses, dealt with many minor offences, appointed the parish constables, over-seers of the poor and surveyors of highways, fixed the parish poor-rate and audited the local officials' accounts and ordered paupers likely to be charged on the rates to be removed from the district. In the Special Sessions after 1729, the Justices of each hundred licensed public houses and performed other local duties, such as recruiting soldiers in 1745, besides dealing judicially with non-jury cases. Finally, when all the the Justices of the county met together four times a year at Quarter Sessions, they could try all crimes except treason and also, with a jury, civil cases, besides levying county rates for the upkeep of roads and bridges, prisons and houses of correction, fix wages, license trades and deal with disorderly houses. The extent of their powers was shown by the Speenhamland System, which resulted merely from a decision of the Justices of Berkshire in 1795.[1]   Naturally such men varied in character. Contemporary literature depicts both those who were negligent or abused their authority and those who were just, conscientious and public-minded. The government continued to rely largely upon the Justices of the Peace for the maintenance of law and order in face of the disorders during and after the Revolutionary and Napoleonic Wars, but they gradually became incapable of dealing with the changed conditions of industrial England.[2]

Within the county was the ancient ecclesiastical parish, which the Tudors had made the basic unit for carrying out the detailed work of local government. There were some 9,000 of them in England, each being governed by the annual vestry meeting, usually held in the parish church under the chairmanship of the incumbent. Most were 'open vestries' to which all ratepayers could come, but in some places, particularly in London and the northern counties, these had become 'closed vestries', attended only by the largest landowners or most influential ratepayers. Since Tudor times the powers of the vestries had been increasingly abrogated by the Justices of the Peace. The parish was still legally responsible for the maintenance of order, the upkeep of its roads and the relief of its poor, but the Justices fixed the rates for these purposes each year and appointed from among the parishioners the officials who (often very unwillingly) had to carry them out. Nevertheless, an active vestry could see that parish affairs were as well managed as possible, and the churchwardens, still usually elected by the vestry, might add the supervision of the parish officials to their ecclesiastical duties. Both open and closed vestries differed in their standards of performance. Some, like St. George's, Hanover Square, Brighton or Leeds, were efficient and enterprising, taking on new duties, notably the lighting, cleaning, paving and policing of the streets, and following an enlightened policy of poor relief; but others, like Manchester which did not even check the accounts of the parish officials, were slack and corrupt.

Local government in the towns was less uniform than in the country. Some towns, especially new ones like Manchester, Birmingham or Leeds, were legally only parishes and so were administered like villages by the vestry and the Justices. Other, older established towns, some two hundred in number, were chartered boroughs with the right to govern themselves through a municipal corporation (and also to send representatives to Parliament). These ranged in size and importance from places like Haverfordwest in Pembrokeshire, which was really a fishing village, to Bristol, Norwich, Leicester, Lincoln and other ancient country towns. The size of their corporations also varied considerably; some, as at Oxford, included most of the townsmen, but others, as at Cambridge, consisted of only a few of the most influential. Some boroughs were well-governed. The corporation of Liverpool, which built docks and widened the streets, was especially progressive. Many, however, were notoriously incompetent and corrupt, dominated by co-opted oligarchs, who abused the corporate income and charities.

During the Hanoverian period the inadequacies of English local government were increasingly realized, especially in the growing towns. Some of the existing authorities, both vestries and corporations, acquired powers by statute to engage in such additional activities as maintaining the streets, providing drainage and regulating markets. More common, however, was the creation of new statutory authorities to perform specialized functions in particular districts. These grew rapidly in number from the middle of the eighteenth century and included turnpike trusts for the improvement of roads; corporations, established in London and Bristol, to administer the poor law; and, above all, improvement commissioners for paving, watching, lighting, drainage and many other additional services. The establishment of modern borough government began with the repeal of the Test and Corporation Acts in 1828 and the passing of the Municipal Corporations Act in 1835.[1]

[1] Pp. 425, 441.

IV · RELIGIOUS MOVEMENTS

The Church of England

'WHEN I mention religion, I mean the Christian religion; and not only the Christian religion, but the Protestant religion; and not only the Protestant religion, but the Church of England', said Parson Thwackum in Henry Fielding's *Tom Jones.* The Revolution Settlement had maintained and even strengthened the dominant position of the English Church. It remained the Established Church of the land. Its bishops sat in the House of Lords. The universities and the endowed schools were under its control. The Bill of Rights of 1689 required the monarch to be a member of it; and the Corporation Act of 1661 and the Test Act of 1673 laid down that all members of municipal corporations and holders of office under the Crown must communicate according to its rites. Its churches were mostly well-attended, the sermons of its divines and the pastoral charges of its bishops were widely read, and its clergy held an important place in society.

Moreover, in the early years of the Hanoverian period the Church seemed to have little fear from its rivals. It is true that a measure of religious toleration had been established. Locke had taught that toleration should be granted to all forms of religion which did not endanger the safety and well-being of the civil society and that civic rights should not depend on the acceptance of a prescribed form of belief; but the Toleration Act of 1689 had merely granted freedom of worship to Protestant Dissenters. The repeal of the Occasional Conformity Act and the Schism Act in 1719 had prevented the narrowing of that toleration;[1] and Dissenters exerted quite a considerable influence in the government of the towns; but they were still excluded from taking a leading part in national politics. Meanwhile, the old Dissenting bodies – Presbyterians, Congregationalists and Baptists – had lost much of their original fervour. Their membership was confined mainly to shopkeepers and journeymen in the older towns, and these

[1] Pp. 234–5.

were years in which they declined in numbers and influence. During the reigns of the first two Georges over fifty Dissenting ministers appear to have joined the Established Church. At the same time, Unitarian views, encouraged by the rational spirit of the age, were widely accepted by Dissenting congregations, especially among the Presbyterians, who lost about half their chapels in the eighteenth century.

The position of the Roman Catholics in England was still weaker. They had not yet obtained legal freedom of worship, though in practice this was generally tolerated. The penal legislation passed under the Tudors and Stuarts excluding them completely from public life also remained in force, and the Gordon Riots in 1780 showed the continued strength of popular 'No Popery' feeling.[1] Jacobitism hardened opinion against Roman Catholicism, and the outlook of the age was hostile to its doctrines. 'The errors of Rome', declared the Elder Pitt, 'are rank idolatry, a subversion of all civil as well as religious liberty, the utter disgrace of reason and human nature.' Roman Catholicism had now few adherents, and Irish immigration was insufficient to increase them. It continued mainly in Lancashire and Yorkshire and was kept alive in London largely by six chapels attached to foreign embassies.

Again, the Church of England had survived the events of the Glorious Revolution without serious damage to its unity. The Nonjurors, comprising eight bishops, some four hundred priests and a few laymen, had then left the Church rather than take the oath of allegiance to William and Mary, but their numbers declined, and by the end of the eighteenth century the movement was almost extinct. The Nonjurors were High Churchmen, so called not because they differed from the other clergy in ritual or ceremonial, but because they upheld a 'high' conception of the Church, the claims of the episcopate and the nature of the sacraments. Their defection left the High Church movement in the Church without its best leaders, and after a short interlude of influence in Queen Anne's reign, the exclusion of its remaining members from ecclesiastical preferment upon suspicion of Jacobitism under the Hanoverians drove it into obscurity until, from 1833, the Tractarians struggled to reassert its claims.

[1] P. 351.

The Nonjuring schism deprived the Church of England of some of the finest exponents of its piety and, despite the strength of its position, it suffered from other serious weaknesses. Historians of the Evangelical and Tractarian movements have both tended to exaggerate these, but they were real and inherent in the conditions of the time. After the fervour and controversy of the previous century, reaction and exhaustion set in and were followed by religious torpor, materialistic values and moral laxity. 'Enthusiasm' (which meant 'fanaticism') was decried and 'reason' exalted; and eighteenth-century rationalism was often hostile to traditional Christianity.

Unitarianism was one manifestation of this rationalism. Another was Deism, a system of natural religion, avowing belief in a personal God, the Creator of the universe, but regarding Him as detached from the world to which He had made no revelation. Though it exercised considerable influence on the Continent, Deism was never widely accepted in England and had little effect on English thought. It was ably refuted by English divines, particularly by Joseph Butler, Bishop of Durham, in his great *Analogy of Religion* (1736), which argued that the difficulties in the way of accepting revealed religion are no more formidable than those confronting the advocacy of the natural religion proposed by the Deists.

The form taken by rationalism in the Church of England was Latitudinarianism, which attached greater importance to ethical and moral precepts than to matters of doctrine, ecclesiastical organization and liturgical practice. The dominant influence in the eighteenth-century Church was the sermons in three folio volumes of John Tillotson, Archbishop of Canterbury from 1691 to 1694. Tillotson revolutionized English preaching by breaking away from the traditional, essentially medieval style of pulpit oratory and writing sermons in simple, practical, clear prose, but as Charles Smyth has said, 'the content of his preaching was little more than a prudential morality, based rather on reason than on revelation and appealing deliberately to sober common sense'. As proclaimed by the eighteenth-century parochial clergy, this message with its emphasis upon duty, decency and right conduct did much to prepare the way for the transformation of the English character which was to take place in the next century. Nevertheless, to quote J. H. Plumb, 'it was not a religion which had much appeal to the men and women living brutal and squalid lives in the disease-ridden slums of the new towns and mining villages. They needed revelation and salvation.' The religious revival later in the century is set against the background of the failure of Latitudinarianism to supply this.

Other weaknesses of the eighteenth-century Church were legacies from the Middle Ages. The Reformation of the sixteenth century had removed it from papal control, reformed its doctrine and worship, dissolved its monasteries and deprived it of part of its endowments, but left its medieval organization practically unaltered and failed to abolish such old abuses as pluralism and non-residence. Also inherited from the Middle Ages was the conception of the close connection of Church and State – in the words of J. N. Figgis, 'the whole atmosphere of the medieval mind was such that we cannot picture them as treating the two as really separate societies'. Power over the Church, previously exercised by Pope and Crown together, was now exercised by the Crown alone, and ecclesiastical preferments were part of the Hanoverian system of patronage. Royal ministers treated the Church as if it were a department of the government and were supported by Benjamin Hoadly, Bishop of Bangor, who insisted in a sermon in 1717 that the Gospels afford no warrant for any visible Church authority. The result of the ensuing 'Bangorian Controversy' was that the government, in order to save Hoadly from condemnation, prorogued the ancient assemblies of the English clergy, the Convocations of Canterbury and York, which did not meet again to transact business until the middle of the nineteenth century.

'No man can now be made a bishop for his learning and piety', said Dr. Johnson in 1775. 'His only chance of promotion is his being connected with somebody who has parliamentary interest.' There was a good deal of truth in this. Although the bishops no longer held high offices of state as in the Middle Ages, they were expected to be often in the House of Lords, and under the first two Georges the bench was filled with sound Whigs who voted regularly with the government. Some bishops badly neglected their sees for their London houses; Hoadly notoriously never went once

in six years to Bangor.   Most bishops, however, were not idle.
They were industrious and active and tried to do their duty
in their diocese.   The publication of the Visitation Returns
for 1743 of Thomas Herring, Archbishop of York, has done
much to correct the popular impression of the much-abused
Hanoverian bishops.   They had indeed to face enormous difficulties.   To the demands made upon their time by their
political obligations were added the burden of enormous
dioceses, which became worse with the growth of populous
industrial areas.   It was particularly difficult to perform
confirmations and visitations of the clergy during the four
or five summer months of the year in such dioceses as York
or Lincoln; but most bishops tried to perform these duties.
The Honourable Robert Drummond, a later Archbishop of
York, confirmed in his diocese during the years 1768 to 1771
no less than 41,600 candidates.

A list drawn up for George III about 1762 indicated that
the income of bishoprics varied between Canterbury, Winchester and Durham at £7,000–£5,000 a year and Oxford
and Bristol at only £300, but the poorer bishops usually
augmented their stipends by holding also deaneries, canonries,
or rich benefices.   Some cathedrals were wealthy, notably
Durham where the chapter drew coal royalties of such a
magnitude that their total was never revealed.   As the
wealth of the nation grew so did the value of many ecclesiastical preferments, with the consequence that the nobility
and gentry more frequently sought them for their younger
sons.   William Warburton, Bishop of Gloucester, commented upon this in 1752: 'Our grandees have at last found
their way back into the Church.   I only wonder they have
been so long about it.'   In 1815 eleven of the twenty-
bishops were of noble birth.   This aristocratic invasion of the
higher posts in the Church contributed towards the general
unpopularity of the bishops at the time of the Reform Bill
when the Bishop of Bristol's palace was burned and the
Archbishop of Canterbury was pelted by a furious mob.

Among the lower clergy, there were incumbents who
enjoyed stipends running into four figures a year, but there
were thousands of parishes worth less than £150 a year and
many curates with only £30–£40.   In 1704 Queen Anne
had formed Queen Anne's Bounty to augment poorer

parishes, surrendering to it the annates formerly paid to the Papacy by the clergy and transferred to the Crown at the Reformation; but its resources did not allow much being done to alleviate the position. The same abuses were to be found among the parochial clergy as among the higher clergy. In 1809, of 11,194 incumbents 7,358 were non-resident. Sometimes pluralism was practised by a wealthy absentee, who paid curates low stipends to care for his parishes, but often inadequate parochial endowments compelled a clergyman to hold more than one benefice. The agricultural prosperity of the eighteenth century improved the position of the country clergy and their social status was raised accordingly. The change is shown in the contrast between Henry Fielding's Parson Adams, who had 'a handsome income of twenty-three pounds a year', and Jane Austen's debonair Henry Tilney.

'The Hanoverian Church was justified', according to Charles Smyth, 'not by its triumph over Deism, but by the lives and labours of its parochial clergy at their best.' Tales of idle, drunken, sporting parsons do not give the whole truth. There were also many fine examples of devotion to duty in both town and country. In Leeds Parish Church, for example, the clergy attended daily for marriages from eight to eleven-thirty, for baptisms and churchings twice a day and were ready to perform burials three times a day in the winter and twice a day in the summer, while the Vicar of Stretton, a country parish in Staffordshire, had 244 communicants in a total population of 610. The diaries of three such different parish priests as James Woodforde of Ansford and Weston Longeville, William Cole of Bletchley and James Skinner of Camerton reveal a genuine belief in their calling and a concern for the welfare of their parishioners. Generally, however, the clergy had a more leisured life than nowadays, since the amount of pastoral care and the number of services required of them was not high by modern standards.

Nor was the Church without its pious, zealous laymen and laywomen. These included Dr. Samuel Johnson (1709–83), who worshipped regularly in St. Clement Danes Church in the Strand and recorded his religious life in his private notebooks, and the charitable Lady Elizabeth Hastings (1682–1739) of whom Richard Steele wrote 'to love her was a liberal education'. Indeed, one of the features of the eighteenth

F

century was what has been called the 'steady laicization of religion', brought about by the increasingly active part taken by the laity, individually and collectively, in religious organization and philanthropic work. This prepared the way for the responsible positions given to lay people in the later Methodist congregations.

Compared with recent times (and, indeed, with the previous two centuries), there was greater uniformity of worship in the Church of England, and it was predominantly Protestant. The rational emphasis of the age was antithetical to any element of mysticism and adoration. Although the Prayer Book required daily services, they steadily fell into desuetude. The Holy Communion was celebrated monthly in some churches in large towns and even weekly in certain London parishes, but only four times a year in most churches. For the greater part of the eighteenth century, new churches were of Classical design, usually in the style of the Adam brothers, and medieval churches were adapted to the prevailing mode of worship. The interior was commonly dominated by a tall 'three-decker' pulpit, perhaps placed in front of the chancel, at the lowest desk of which the clerk led the responses, while the clergyman conducted the service at the next desk and mounted to the canopied pulpit at the top to preach, changing into a black gown and probably reading his sermon, since extempore preaching was a sign of 'enthusiasm'. The nave was crowded with box-pews, and as the population was increased, side-galleries were built as well as perhaps a west gallery for the musicians and unsurpliced choir who led the singing, which was, however, confined to the metrical psalms of Tate and Brady. Worship, as Horton Davies has said, 'was performed out of a sense of decorum and duty rather than from rapture and delight'. To this worship the Evangelicals added congregational hymn-singing and fervent preaching, but otherwise it remained the same. 'I do profess *ex animo*', wrote J. H. Newman in 1862, 'that the thought of the Anglican service makes me shiver', though the worship which he found so dreary had been transformed by the movement once led by him in Oxford.

Methodism

Despite the devotion of many Churchmen, both lay and clerical, the Church of England proved incapable of meeting the conditions of the times. Especially it failed to minister to the workpeople in the ever-growing new industrial areas. To its rationalism and sobriety was added an almost complete lack of missionary spirit. The ethical piety of the philanthropic supporters of the Societies for the Reformation of Manners and the charity schools was inadequate to satisfy the needs and problems which they realized existed. More might have been done if the Church had possessed a central organization and an effective system of administration, but the Convocations had been silenced, and neither Parliament nor the bishops were capable of attempting reforms. When, therefore, a religious revival came, even though it began within the Church, it was almost inevitable that this should take an individual and independent course.

By the second quarter of the eighteenth century several religious movements had come into being, but all were to be eclipsed by the amazing success of that led by John Wesley (1703–91), a younger son of Samuel Wesley, Rector of Epworth in Lincolnshire from 1697 to 1735, and his wife, Susanna. Samuel Wesley was descended from a long line of English gentlemen and clergymen, the Duke of Wellington belonging to a collateral branch of the same family; he was a strong Tory and High Churchman, disappointed in his hopes of preferment and embittered by poverty and the hostility of the turbulent Fensmen, who were 'almost heathen' and mocked his attempts to impose High Church discipline in the parish. Through his mother, the daughter of a famous Dissenting minister, John Wesley was related to the cultured representatives of English Puritanism, and she was the formative influence upon his career. Susanna Wesley was strict, determined and intensely religious, which was demonstrated in the way she brought up her large family. She believed in 'conquering the will of children betimes' and training them in Christian habits, especially prayer and industry. To achieve this, they were made from a year old 'to fear the rod and to cry softly' and were taught to examine the state of their souls at least once a week under her direction. John Wesley inherited her unyielding will and energy, her religious zeal and disciplined ways.

John Wesley was educated at Charterhouse and Christ Church, Oxford. He was ordained, elected to a fellowship

at Lincoln College, Oxford, in 1726 and then went to act as
a curate to his father. In 1729, however, the terms of his
fellowship required him to reside in Oxford, and so began
what he later marked as the first phase of Methodism. His
younger brother, Charles Wesley (1707–88), who had followed him to Christ Church, had collected round him a few
young Oxford men, all High Churchmen, who read the
Bible and prayed together, visited the sick and prisoners in
gaol, fasted, made regular confessions and communicated
weekly, observing strictly the rules of the Prayer Book which
were generally now regarded as archaic. Already the
strictness of their life had earned them from undergraduates
the mocking nickname of 'Methodists'. When Wesley
returned to Oxford, he became the leader of the group, which
was joined by George Whitefield (1714–70), who came of
humble parentage and had entered Pembroke College,
as a servitor, an undergraduate partly supported by the
college in return for waiting at table upon the fellows
and gentlemen-commoners. The group was never large;
it numbered fourteen or fifteen by 1735, though several others
had then left the university. Their piety was sincere, but
somewhat rigid and consisting of external practices rather
than an inspired and living reality.

It was in 1735 that Wesley resolved to go to Georgia as a
missionary, accompanied by his brother, now also ordained.
He came to regard this as the second phase of Methodism.
On the voyage to the new colony, they experienced the hardships common in Atlantic sailings during the autumn gales.
In the ship as emigrants were some members of the Moravian
Brethren, a Protestant community, whose courage during the
storms made Wesley wonder whether, despite his life of high
purpose and strict discipline, he could really consider himself
a Christian until he should experience a conversion, an
assurance of personal salvation through Christ, such as they
described to him. The visit to Georgia was a failure.
Missionary work among the Red Indians was not permitted; efforts to introduce the Methodism of the university
into a colonial parish alienated the colonists; and Wesley
himself, as the *Dictionary of National Biography* expresses it,
was caught in the toils of 'unfortunate encounters with the
daughters of Eve'. In 1736 the brothers both returned to

England. They were succeeded in Georgia by Whitefield, but he also came home after an equally fruitless mission lasting only sixteen weeks.

Fortunately the outcome of the third and last phase of Methodism was very different. While in London, Wesley attended on 24th May 1738 a religious society in Aldersgate Street founded by a Moravian preacher, and during the reading of Luther's preface to the Epistle to the Romans he had the experience of conversion. His heart was 'strangely warmed', and he trusted 'in Christ, Christ alone, for salvation'. Now he knew himself called 'to promote as far as I am able vital practical religion and by the grace of God to beget, preserve and increase the life of God in the souls of men'. To this purpose he devoted the rest of his life.

At first he delivered his message in the parish churches, but his sermons expressed the spirit of enthusiasm rather than of reasonableness. His calls to repentance sometimes provoked convulsions and other hysterical scenes among his hearers. The clergy began to forbid him the use of their pulpits, and within a year, though reluctantly at first, he followed the example already set by Whitefield by preaching in the open air. Soon such 'field preaching' became his regular practice. It brought him huge audiences and took him to the un-evangelized areas and the thousands of poor who had received no religious care. Sometimes he went in danger of his life. Local authorities, apprehensive of his mission among such people, often refused to protect him against rioters and even sometimes encouraged trouble-makers to break up his meetings, but he was never daunted. He always rose at four in the morning, preached at five, as well as two or even three times later in the day. Until his seventieth year, he made all his journeys through the country on horseback, riding sixty or seventy miles day after day. During his fifty years of evangelism, he travelled 250,000 miles and preached 40,000 sermons.

The message was spread not only by gospel preaching, but also by 'spiritual song'. The greatest number of hymns were written for the movement by Charles Wesley, the most prolific and probably the most gifted of all English hymn-writers. From him came such well-known hymns as 'Christ, whose glory fills the skies', 'Jesus, Lover of my soul', 'Soldiers of Christ, arise', 'Hark! The herald-angels sing' and 'Love divine, all loves excelling'.   Hymn-singing soon became an important part of Methodist worship and spread to the Church of England through the Evangelicals, whose most notable writer was Augustus Montague Toplady (1740-78), author of 'Rock of Ages'.   Indeed, modern hymn-writing and hymn-singing were largely the creation of the Methodist and Evangelical movements.

Besides being a great evangelist, John Wesley was also a remarkable organizer.   He saw the need of permanent guidance and direction to maintain the fidelity of those converted by preaching.   Wherever Methodist congregations were gathered together, they were formed into societies. These were modelled upon the 'religious societies', which had already been formed by 'serious people', who wished to strengthen each other in religious life and practice by prayer and worship, charity and good works; there were already thirty or forty of them in London alone when Wesley started preaching.   Wesley's societies were under the control of lay preachers, whom he appointed, generally moving them from one wide round (or circuit) to another at the end of each year.   Every society was divided into classes, groups of about a dozen members living in the same locality, under class-leaders, which met during the week for prayer and instruction. The class-leader was expected to visit his members, report upon their life and character and collect financial contributions from them.   The societies sent delegates to the Annual Conference, which was not held for general discussion or debate, but to receive instruction, criticism and exhortation from Wesley, who insisted that his word must be obeyed in all matters of belief and practice.   His enemies called him 'Pope John'.

Wesley's autocracy led the Methodists to separate from Whitefield, the most striking orator of the movement.   The breach began on doctrinal grounds.   Whitefield accepted strictly Calvinist teaching about election, predestination and reprobation.   'I frankly acknowledge', he wrote, 'I believe that God intends to give His saving grace, through Jesus Christ, only to a certain number, and that the rest of mankind will at last suffer that eternal death, which is its proper wages.' Wesley, faithful to his High Church upbringing, held the

Arminian position that God ever desires men to be saved, gives them free will to choose the way of salvation and offers them grace to help them through Jesus Christ Who died for all. Whitefield secured the support of the pious Selina, Countess of Huntingdon (1709–91), and through her support his followers were organized separately from Methodism.

Wesley had not intended that his movement should separate from the Church of England. He expected Methodists to attend the services and make their communion in their parish churches in addition to their class and society activities. Nevertheless, his ways were not those of the Church and its traditional parochial system. During the formative years of his life, Wesley had been an Oxford don and not a parish priest. He wrote in his *Journal* as early as 1739, 'I look upon all the world as my parish'. His constant evangelistic journeyings, his individualistic authority and his rival organization were hardly consistent with the established means of pastoral work. The contemporary inflexibility of the Church and the hostility of many bishops to his methods soon brought difficulties. Chapels had to be built for Methodists, especially in areas where there were no churches, and when the movement spread to America, he found the refusal of bishops to ordain priests for him such a serious handicap that in 1784 he began to ordain ministers himself. Until his death in 1791 formal separation was avoided, but soon afterwards Methodists made themselves an independent Dissenting body.

When Wesley died, he left 75 circuits in England and Wales, 294 preachers and over 70,000 members, most of whom were to be found among the lower classes and particularly in the new industrial districts. Later village preaching gained adherents in the countryside as evidenced by the plain rural chapels built in the early nineteenth century (though now often closed or converted into dwelling-houses or garages). Dissent became more important and numerous, its numbers rising from one in twenty-five of the population in 1700 to one in four in 1800, Methodists forming the largest part.

Wesley thought always of Methodism as a religious movement seeking 'to reform the nation, more particularly the Church, and to spread Scriptural holiness over the land'. It developed into a popular Christianity such as had never been

known before in England, at any rate since the Middle Ages.
As a return to an ardent devotion to the person of Christ,
it was an individual, emotional faith, but it had social consequences, doing much to raise the moral standards of the
nation and to promote charity and reform.   Its organization
gave ambitious or conscientious working-men an opportunity
for power and achievement and provided many future trade
union leaders with their training.

Towards politics, however, the early Methodists shared the
conservatism of their founder, who upheld the existing social
order and condemned the colonists during the American
War.   This soon gained Methodism approval from the ruling
classes.   At first they had suspected a movement which gave
authority to artisans in its congregations – the Duchess of
Buckingham thought they were 'strongly tinctured with
impertinence and disrespect towards their superiors'; but their
attitude changed when it became clear that Methodism was
far from being a militant working-class movement, and in
1785 Wesley wrote, 'I am become, I know not how, an
honourable man'.   At the end of the century, the Methodists,
unlike the older Dissenters, showed no sympathy with the
ideas of Jacobinism and did not urge radical constitutional
changes.   It may, therefore, be true, as F. D. Maurice
thought, that Methodism saved England from a cataclysm
like the French Revolution.

Evangelicalism

Together with the Methodist movement, there was the
Evangelical revival in the Church of England.   Though this
owed some of its inspiration to Wesley, it was largely an
independent movement, and its disagreement with Methodism
contributed towards the latter's withdrawal from the Church.
The Evangelicals could not accept the Arminianism of the
Wesleys.   Their theological ideas were closest to the
Calvinism of Whitefield, but they attached most importance,
not to predestination or reprobation, but the experience of
personal conversion and salvation by faith in the atoning
work of Christ.   Evangelicism concerned itself with the inner
life of the individual soul, expressing itself in prayer and a
pastoral concern for people.   Moreover, though the Evangelicals founded societies and led movements, they organized

themselves and established their religious life upon the parochial system of the Church.

Unlike Methodism, Evangelicalism was strongest among the upper and middle classes which had not lost touch with the Church. Their numbers were not large. In 1822 there were only a dozen Evangelical clergymen in London, while in Oxford their influence was confined to the small and unimportant St. Edmund Hall. They formed strong groups in Cambridge, Clapham, Islington, Cheltenham and some places in Yorkshire and Cornwall, but elsewhere they were isolated individuals, and the first Evangelicals were not much in favour with bishops and patrons of livings. They never became a party or formed themselves into a united, powerful movement.

Nevertheless, they came to play a very important part in the Church. Professor E. W. Watson reckoned that from 1770, at the latest, they were the most forceful religious group, and their influence grew for two generations or more, partly because they had no rivals in the Church during that time. Moreover, since most people in the upper classes of society still counted themselves members of the Established Church, Evangelicalism through its influence upon them was able to exercise a profound effect upon the life of the country as a whole. This was especially so after the appointment of Evangelicals as bishops, the first being in 1815 when Lord Harrowby's brother, Henry Ryder, was made Bishop of Gloucester.

Probably, however, the movement owed most of its success to clergymen who gave themselves to preaching and pastoral work in the parishes. Among the first were John Fletcher (1729-85) of Madeley who worked for twenty-five years among the Shropshire colliers, and William Grimshaw (1708-63) of Haworth, who used to leave his congregation singing the 119th Psalm, while he emptied the taverns of his Yorkshire parish with a horsewhip, and John Newton (1725-1807), formerly the captain of a slaver, became a curate at Olney and the friend of William Cowper. Other early Evangelical leaders included Henry Venn (1725-95), who first revived religious life in Huddersfield and then went to the village of Yelling in Cambridgeshire, where he exercised a strong influence on the University. His son, John Venn

(1759–1813), was Rector of Clapham and exercised a particularly important ministry.   Also among Evangelicals of this later generation was Charles Simeon (1759–1836), Vicar of Holy Trinity, Cambridge, for more than fifty years.   Lord Macaulay, who had known him as an undergraduate, wrote, 'If you knew what his authority and influence were, and how they extended from Cambridge to the remotest corners of England, you would allow that his real sway over the Church was far greater than that of any primate.'   Simeon also helped to secure a greater Evangelical control of parishes by creating a trust fund which in time acquired the patronage of about a hundred livings.

Another strength of Evangelicalism was the number of wealthy and influential laymen who were attracted to it.   The most important of these belonged to an informal group nicknamed by Sydney Smith the 'Clapham Sect' because they lived near Clapham, a fashionable village just outside London, and worshipped at the parish church under John Venn. Outstanding among them was William Wilberforce (1759–1833), a member of a rich commercial family in Hull, a friend of Pitt and a Member of Parliament for Yorkshire; he had been converted under Newton's guidance.   There was also Henry Thornton (1760–1815), a banker and the patron of the benefice; Zachary Macaulay (1768–1838), a retired colonial governor and the father of the future historian; Lord Teignmouth (1751–1834), a retired Indian administrator; Granville Sharp (1735–1813), an experienced Radical and philanthropist; and Charles Grant (1746–1832), Chairman of the East India Company.   Towards the end of her life Hannah More (1745–1833) was closely connected with the group, since under Wilberforce's influence she turned, in 1789 with her sister, from play-writing and dinner-parties to religious writing and good works.[1]   Between about 1785 and 1830, largely through the personal position of its members, this group was able to lead public opinion and Parliament and engage in important schemes in Church and State with a success out of all proportion to its numbers.

The Evangelicals did much to revive and extend the activities of the Church.   They were prominent in the establishment of Sunday Schools and then in support of

[1] P. 37.

the National Society.[1] They co-operated with Dissenters in founding in 1799 the Religious Tract Society, for the publication and dissemination of Christian literature, and in 1804 the British and Foreign Bible Society, for the printing and distribution of the Scriptures at home and abroad. They founded the Church Pastoral Aid Society in 1836 to provide more curates and lay workers in the parishes. Above all, they launched the Church of England upon missionary work overseas. The Society for the Propagation of the Gospel had been founded in 1701, but this had largely confined itself to work among the colonists in America, while the Society for Promoting Christian Knowledge in 1698, which had done much work at home and tried, especially under its devout Secretary, Henry Newman (1670–1743) to send missionaries to India, but had to send German Lutherans instead. In 1799 a number of Evangelicals, including Wilberforce, Granville Sharp and Zachary Macaulay, established the Church Missionary Society, and the first to offer himself to it for service overseas was Simeon's curate, Henry Martyn (1781–1812). Although Martyn died of fever after a few years in India, his pioneer devotion to evangelism among the natives made a great impression in England. Through such lives as his the nineteenth century was to become a great age of missionary effort.

The Evangelicals were also responsible for a notable growth of philanthropy and efforts to raise the moral standards of the country. Of course, such aspirations were not new. Earlier the Societies for the Reformation of Manners and kindred bodies had tried to deal with the social problems of their times, as also had individual reformers like James Oglethorpe (1696–1785), who founded the colony of Georgia for debtors, Thomas Coram (?1668–1751), who established the Foundling Hospital in 1745 to care for deserted infants, and John Howard (1726–90), who campaigned against conditions in English prisons. Such efforts, however, had been limited in scope and result. The philanthropy of the Evangelicals was pursued with a new spirit and organized on a broader front. They were prominent in the humanitarian movements which sought reforms in the factories, the prisons and the criminal code.[2] Their work was to be continued by an Evangelical of a later date, Lord Shaftesbury (1801–85).

[1] Pp. 37–8.   [2] P. 25.

In some ways the most remarkable success of the Evangelicals was achieved in their struggle against negro slavery in the British Empire between 1787 and 1833. This action, William Lecky, the historian, wrote, 'may probably be regarded as among the three or four perfectly virtuous acts recorded in the history of nations'. Wilberforce led the anti-slavery movement and received particular support from Granville Sharp and Zachary Macaulay as well as from Thomas Clarkson (1760–1846), a clergyman's son who abandoned his original intention of becoming ordained in order to devote himself to the cause. Clarkson travelled 35,000 miles to collect evidence against slavery; Wilberforce used his membership of Parliament and influence with Pitt to publicize the facts. In 1788 he secured the appointment of a Committee of the Privy Council to investigate the slave-trade; it reported that 74,000 slaves were being transported each year from Africa to America, 38,000 in British ships. The next year Wilberforce introduced his first motion for its abolition and persisted until 1807 when, through the support of Charles James Fox, one of his closest sympathizers, an act was passed forbidding the participation of British subjects in the slave-trade and the importation of slaves into the British colonies. Wilberforce then continued the fight against slavery itself. Though failing health forced his retirement from Parliament, he lived long enough to see the first reformed Parliament in 1833 pass an Emancipation Act which set free all slaves throughout the British Empire, £20,000,000 being voted as compensation to the slave-owners. Other Evangelicals went on in the Anti-Slavery Society to campaign against slavery wherever it existed.

In addition to such important reforms, the Evangelicals took a leading part in bringing about the general change in the moral and religious life of the people which occurred at the end of the Georgian period. A reaction in favour of this had already set in before their influence was felt. The tone set in court circles by George III's simple piety was enduring.[1] It survived the wild extravagances of the Regency court, which did not reflect the attitude of the country as a whole and were generally condemned by public opinion. By then the upper classes were ready to support, if not the pious earnestness

[1] P. 18.

of the Evangelicals, at any rate their moral standards. The excesses of Jacobinism and Revolution in France further turned the tide against moral laxity and scepticism in England as on the Continent. Acceptance of religion became usual in influential and even fashionable circles. Bath, Brighton and other watering-places had become Evangelical centres before the end of the Hanoverian age. Attendance at public worship, Bible-reading, Sunday observance, morning and evening family prayers, grace before meals, charitable works and subscriptions to good causes, all these outward signs of Evangelical influence were practised to an extent which would have seemed impossible earlier in the period.

Another consequence of the revival of religion was the beginning of administrative reform in the Church. This was largely due to two statesmen of the time. During the years from 1812 to 1827 when he was Prime Minister, Lord Liverpool remedied one of the worst medieval abuses – the exploitation of high ecclesiastical preferment to requite the services of servants of the State. In exercising the Crown's patronage he refused to allow political considerations to influence his appointments and (in the words of a contemporary pamphlet) 'elevated unpretending merit and excellence to high places in the Church'. Of equal importance was the creation in 1835 by Sir Robert Peel of a permanent Ecclesiastical Commission to hold much of the property of the Church and make better use of it. The Commissioners proceeded to abolish sinecures, diminish the chapters of cathedrals, bring the incomes of bishops somewhat nearer to equality and increase the endowments of poor parishes. The foundation of the bishopric of Ripon in 1836, the first since the sixteenth century, was to be the first of twenty new bishoprics founded during the next hundred years. One of the most active members of the Ecclesiastical Commission was Charles James Blomfield, Bishop of London from 1828 to 1856 and described by Sydney Smith, who was a not very active Canon of St. Paul's, as inspired by an 'ungovernable passion for business'. In such ways began the administrative reformation of the Church which is still in progress.

Church-building was a further result of the religious awakening. The Tory and High Church parliamentary triumph in 1710 had led to the passing of an act to build

fifty-two new churches in London, but in consequence of the
Whig accession to power in 1714 only sixteen were completed
under the scheme. Few other churches were built during
the rest of the eighteenth century. In 1818, however,
Parliament passed the Million Act which granted a million
pounds towards the building of churches in new districts, and
nearly 300 new churches were built in industrial areas between
1819 and 1830. Blomfield took up the problem in London
with typical energy, and during his episcopate two hundred
new churches were built in the diocese. This was the
inauguration of the great period of church-building in the
nineteenth century, described by John Betjeman as 'comparable with the fifteenth century'.

In the later years of the Hanoverian period, however, the
Evangelicals, though still an important power in the Church,
had passed their greatest days. After the deaths of Charles
Simeon, John Venn and the members of the 'Clapham Sect',
the movement failed to find any more outstanding leaders.
Its enthusiasm diminished, while its lack of scholarship and
failure to influence intellectual circles proved a serious weakness. Its two most important centres, Clapham and Cambridge, were lost to it; the congregations in seaside-resorts and
other towns by no means took their place. To quote Dr.
Kitson Clark, 'After 1836 the social and political distinction
of the Evangelicals seems to fade out with Lord Shaftesbury
as a notable exception. They became people on the periphery working in the dim streets of provincial towns, while
for many people their ideas remained, what they always had
been, intellectually beyond the pale.' The younger generation tended to drift away from a movement which seemed
to lack intellectual force and find the tenets of Radicalism and
Utilitarianism more attractive.

Tractarianism

Meanwhile, there had also been a smaller revival among
the High Churchmen. Some of their most prominent
members, since they lived in another village near London,
were nicknamed the 'Hackney Phalanx' and included Joshua
Watson (1771–1855), a wine-merchant and first Treasurer
of the National Society, William Stevens (1732–1807), a
London tradesman and Treasurer of Queen Anne's Bounty,

and Henry Norris (1771–1850), Rector of Hackney.   Like
the Evangelicals, they supported religious activities and
overseas missions, but they were rigidly orthodox in doctrine, disliked Dissenters, upheld the rights of the Church
and the powers of the episcopate and priesthood and were
politically conservative.   Since the Evangelicals in the
Church Pastoral Aid Society laid down doctrinal tests for the
curates it assisted and employed lay workers, they formed
the Additional Curates Society in 1837; they also supported
the Society for the Propagation of the Gospel instead of the
Church Missionary Society.

By the second quarter of the nineteenth century, events
were combining to make Churchmen more sympathetic
towards the High Church outlook.   The repeal of the Test
and Corporation Acts and the emancipation of Roman
Catholics the next year seemed a challenge to the Establishment.   The passing of the Reform Bill in 1832 gave the vote
to a greater number of Dissenters, many of whom were bitterly
and openly hostile to the Church.   Already they were
demanding that the Church should be deprived of its powers
and privileges in the universities and elsewhere.   Some
Radicals were openly anti-religious.   'I thought these foolish
ceremonies had ceased', one of them was reported as saying
on seeing an ordination service in a cathedral.   They made
the most of the abuses of the Church, suggesting that its
endowments should be put to other and even secular uses.
Consequently many Churchmen viewed with grave suspicion
and strong dislike the proposals for financial reform which
culminated in the setting up of the Ecclesiastical Commission.

At the same time, several developments were inevitably
giving new channels to the country's religious stream.   The
events of the French Revolution and the subsequent wars
had brought Englishmen into closer contact with Roman
Catholicism.[1]   Still more, the Romantic movement in literature had developed new interests and undertakings which had
their effect upon religious thought.[2]   J. H. Newman himself
enumerated Wordsworth, Scott and Coleridge among the
influences which formed a preparation for the new emphasis
of theology.   Wordsworth's expression of his discovery of
the beauty of the natural world opened the way to a fresh

[1] P. 384.   [2] P. 100.

appreciation of the sacraments. Scott's novels developed a new interest in history, while his sober acceptance of medieval ritual and ceremony made them seem natural instead of strange and ridiculous. Of the three, however, Coleridge provided the most powerful intellectual stimulus, especially through his insistence upon the spiritual independence of the Church.

The new movement, which came out of this combination of political and intellectual circumstances at the end of the Hanoverian period, had its main beginnings in the University of Oxford. In 1827 John Keble (1792–1866), soon to be Professor of Poetry in the University, published *The Christian Year*, which has been called 'Wordsworth and water', but his poems were to rekindle an observance of fast and festival in the Church of England. Aroused by the government's plan to suppress ten Irish bishoprics, Keble preached at Oxford in 1833 an assize sermon on 'National Apostasy'. John Henry Newman (1801–90), Vicar of the University Church, always regarded this sermon as marking the beginning of the new movement. That autumn Newman and a number of his friends, among whom was Edward Bouverie Pusey (1800–82), Professor of Hebrew in the University, began to issue the long series of *Tracts for the Times*, expounding the nature of the Church of England as a divine institution, the doctrine of the apostolic succession and the Book of Common Prayer as a rule of faith. From them the Tractarian Movement derived its name, and before long its influence was spread from Oxford to the whole Church.

V · SCIENCE AND CULTURE

Scientific Discoveries

THE seventeenth century had been an age of great European scientific thinkers, and the greatest of them all was an Englishman. Sir Isaac Newton (1642–1727) lived into the eighteenth century, but his important discoveries had been made early in his life. 'Newton . . .', Dr. Einstein has said, 'determined the course of western thought, research and practice to an extent that nobody before or since his time can touch.' Though Newton discovered the spectrum and made a telescope, his greatest scientific achievement was to show that the apparent attraction of the earth on bodies at its surface could be explained by the single assumption that these bodies gravitate or are pulled towards the earth with a force which decreases as the square of the distance. As he himself claimed, he 'subjected the phenomena of nature to the laws of mathematics'. The Newtonian ideas became the basis of calculation in natural science, and the Hanoverian period was particularly notable for the practical uses to which this new knowledge was put to satisfy the demands of the time.

Newton's influence was particularly seen in astronomy, which was specially significant in this age of English naval power and ocean voyaging. Charles II had established the Royal Observatory at Greenwich in 1675 and created the post of Astronomer Royal, which was held from 1719 to 1742 by Newton's friend, Edmund Halley, who was the first to apply the idea of universal gravitation to astronomy and so was able to calculate the return of the comet named after him, while as a young man he spent a year at St. Helena and made an astronomical chart of the southern hemisphere.

A more important advance was made by James Bradley, Astronomer Royal from 1742 to 1762, who has been described as 'the founder of modern observational astronomy'. Newton's theories had stimulated efforts to secure decisive experimental evidence that the earth moved in orbit round the sun. Bradley did this by discovering, through repeated

observation, an apparent alteration in the position of a
selected star, which he explained was due to the motion of the
earth in its orbit and the non-instantaneous transmission of
light. This aberration of light meant that to catch a ray of
light from a star in a telescope an observer must turn it
slightly in the direction of the earth's annual movement.   It
was a discovery that revealed both a new method of calculating the speed of the propagation of light and a correction
which had to be applied to ensure the accuracy of measured
star positions.   Bradley's calculations also contributed
towards the success of a fellow astronomer, the second Earl
of Macclesfield, in persuading Parliament in 1752 to bring
England into conformity with the Continent by adopting
the Gregorian calendar.[1]

The greatest observational astronomer of this period, however, was William Herschel (1738-1822), who was the son
of a Hanoverian bandsman and came to England in 1757,
where he himself was a music teacher for some time; but
astronomy absorbed his interests, and from 1773 he constructed his own reflecting telescopes to make his observations.
During his lifetime he made no less than 430 telescope mirrors,
and his instruments were unrivalled until the middle of the
nineteenth century.   Among them was the great forty-foot-
long telescope erected at Slough in 1789, at which he spent
long hours, accompanied by his sister who took notes of his
observations until the ink froze on winter nights.   Unlike
Bradley, Herschel was not much of a mathematician and
remained always a descriptive astronomer, more interested in
the nature of the heavenly bodies than in their movements.
In 1781 he discovered Uranus, the first planet to be discovered
in historic times; he also established the motion of the sun in
space and the existence of variable stars and double stars,
which revolved round each other and demonstrated the
operation of the Newtonian principle of universal gravitation
in the depths of space.   George III recognized his achievements in 1786 with a pension and the specially-created post
of 'Court Astronomer'.

Herschel's construction of more powerful telescopes was
accompanied by an invention encouraged by the Board of
Longitude, set up by Parliament in 1714 to grant a reward of

[1] P. 286.

£20,000 'for the discovery of longitude at sea'. This was done by observing with a sextant the angle of the sun or a star above the horizon, but the position of a ship at sea could only be calculated from this if exact Greenwich time were known. Newton had already stressed the need for 'a watch to keep time exactly' independent of 'the motion of a ship, the variation of heat and cold, wet and dry, and the difference of gravity in different latitudes'. The reward was received in 1773 by a Yorkshire carpenter, John Harrison, whose marine chronometer was subjected to very strict tests aboard ship and provided a far more accurate aid to finding longitude at sea than had been known before. Another example of official readiness to assist the development of practical aids to navigation, based upon astronomical observations, was the purchase by the British government of the lunar and solar tables produced in 1753 by a German mathematician, Johann Tobias Mayer, as a result of Bradley's discoveries. These tables became the basis of the invaluable *Nautical Almanac*, first published in 1766.

Newton's principle of universal gravitation also prepared the way for research into magnetic and electrical attraction; and the eighteenth century saw the first rapid advances made in the study of electricity and magnetism, which had hitherto been regarded as little more than a curious phenomenon observable when certain substances were rubbed together and acquired the power of attracting light objects. The advances made in this scientific field were largely the result of co-operation between English and foreign scientists. In England Francis Hauksbee in 1709 observed the electric force of repulsion as well as of attraction, and Stephen Gray distinguished between conductors and non-conductors of electricity, while in Holland Petrus van Musschenbroek in 1745 invented the condenser or storage jar known as the Leyden jar. This produced the first electric shocks, which soon became a fad of the day, known as '*l'experience de Leyde*'.

More seriously, the knowledge of electricity gained in Europe inspired Benjamin Franklin (1706–90) to undertake his own experiments and form his theories. He first introduced the terms 'positive' and 'negative' electricity. By his famous kite experiment at Philadelphia in 1752 he also

proved the identity of thunderstorms and frictional phenomena. The immediate practical result of this experiment
was his invention of the lightning conductor, which was
fitted by George III to his newly purchased Buckingham
Palace.

The most important work in electrical studies took place,
however, later in the century, being made possible by the
invention of the Leyden jar. Investigations were made into
the chemical effects of electricity. Joseph Priestley (1733–
1804) exploded a mixture of oxygen and hydrogen by an
an electrical spark in 1776; Henry Cavendish (1731–1816)
went on in 1781 to produce water by passing an electric
spark through a mixture of oxygen and hydrogen in a closed
vessel, an experiment complemented by that of the Dutch
chemists, Rudolf Deiman and Adrian Paets van Troostwijk,
who showed that water was decomposed when discharges
from a battery of condensers were passed through it for some
time. Priestley also investigated the law of electrical attraction, which was put in precise form in 1785 by the Frenchman,
Charles Coulomb, who showed that the attraction or repulsion
between two charged bodies is inversely proportional to the
square of their distance. This was startlingly similar to
Newton's law of gravitational attraction.

In the closing years of the eighteenth century, an Italian
scientist, Alessandro Volta (1745–1827), produced his 'Voltaic
pile'. This was the greatest of all electrical discoveries. It
was the first real battery and provided by chemical action the
first continuous electric current. It prepared the way for a
new epoch in the development of electricity, the beginnings
of which came with the work of the English physicist, Michael
Faraday (1791–1867), who made the first electric motor in
1821 and in 1831 discovered electromatic induction, the basis
of electric power generation. By the end of the Hanoverian
period, however, there was as yet little sign that electricity
was to become a common form of energy.

Much more immediately successful was the utilization of
steam power which transformed industry and transport during
this period.[1] The invention of the steam-engine as a pump-
ing device took place in the later years of the seventeenth
century. The Royal Society, formed in London in 1662,

[1] P. 136.

played a prominent part in both its theoretical and practical development. The further growth from the steam-pump of Savery and Newcomen to the rotative steam-engine of Boulton and Watt was closely connected with European scientific activity. Watt, for instance, had been trained as an instrument maker for Glasgow University and heard there the lectures of Joseph Black (1728–99), who had studied steam and evolved the theory of latent heat. By showing the amount of heat absorbed when water was made into steam, this theory made Watt realize the advantage of a separate condenser in a steam-engine instead of cooling and reheating the cylinder continually.

In chemistry, both Cavendish and Priestley were also prominent. Cavendish discovered hydrogen in 1766 by the action of sulphuric action on zinc; Priestley discovered oxygen in 1774 by heating red oxide of mercury. These discoveries have been called 'the germ of the modern science of chemistry', but perhaps the most important contribution of eighteenth-century chemistry to industrial development was the invention by John Roebuck (1718–94) of an improved process for the manufacture of sulphuric acid in 1746. There were twenty-three sulphuric acid factories in England by 1823, and the price of the acid had fallen from 2s. 6d. an ounce to $2\frac{1}{4}d$. a pound. This greatly promoted its use for cleaning wool and making soap and glass, while new industrial uses for it were discovered, such as for bleaching textiles and agricultural manures. Another chemical discovery, coal-gas, was a by-product of the manufacture of coke for the iron industry.[1] William Murdock (1754–1839), when employed by Boulton and Watt in erecting mining-engines in Cornwall, installed gas-lighting in his own house at Redruth in 1792 and in 1832 caused a sensation by illuminating the Soho foundry at Birmingham with gas burning in fishtail burners to celebrate the Treaty of Amiens. In 1807 the first street in London was lighted by gas, and the Gas Light and Coke Company was founded five years later.

Another aspect of scientific work in this period was the progress made in naming and classification. In chemistry, Antoine Lavoisier (1743–94) drew up in 1789 one of the first lists in which materials were named according to the chemicals

[1] P. 133.

contained in them; and he was followed by John Dalton (1766–1844), who about 1803 introduced the atomic theory, which assumes that elements consist of atoms of definite relative weight and that compound substances consist of atoms of different elements united with one another in fixed proportions. In biology, the Swedish botanist, Carolus Linnaeus (1707–78), introduced a system of botanical binominal classification, which named all plants according to genus and species and divided them into twenty-four classes.

There were similar investigations into animal and human anatomy in medical science. Eighteenth-century medical thought, despite its shortcomings, was beginning to insist on fact and description, and progress was made in the instruction of practitioners. Previously medical knowledge had been largely gained from libraries, and doctors worked in isolation. Hospitals were now taking a greater part in medical research and instruction. At first there was little to rival foreign centres, but the medical school of Edinburgh University was opened in 1725, and the great London hospitals, including those founded in this century, afforded increasing clinical instruction. An outstanding leader in this movement was John Hunter (1728–93), who studied surgery in St. George's Hospital, London, and came to be regarded as the founder of scientific surgery and modern dentistry. His skill and knowledge were derived from far-reaching observations and experiments in the anatomy of animals and men. Conditions in hospitals, however, continued to make them dangerous to the lives of their patients throughout this period.[1]

The prevalence and deadliness of smallpox at this time produced a strong desire for measures to combat the disease. Lady Mary Wortley Montagu (1689–1762), on her return from Turkey in 1718, popularized inoculation, which was increasingly practised during the century, mainly by quacks, to inflict the disease in a mild form. In 1796 Edward Jenner (1749–1823), a country physician, first vaccinated from cowpox to confer immunity from smallpox, though this was probably not used on a large enough scale to affect decisively the death-rate from the disease for the whole country until after the end of the Hanoverian period.

Medical research seems to have been most actively pursued

[1] P. 3.

to deal with scurvy, because of its importance to the navy, which lost more men at sea from it during the wars of 1739–48 than in battle. A Scottish physician, James Lind (1736–1812), in 1754 suggested green food, fresh fruit and lime juice as preventatives. Enlightened navigators proved him right. One of the foremost was Captain James Cook, who in his voyage of 1772–5 by adopting such a diet for his company of 118 men lost only one man from the disease in over three years. Finally, in 1795 the Admiralty ordered rations of lime juice to be served at sea, and scurvy disappeared.

Literature and Journalism

The Hanoverian period inherited literary standards already established in the late seventeenth century, particularly by its greatest figure, John Dryden (1631–1700). In his prefaces and essays he had popularized a clear, simple and direct prose style, which satisfied the demands of scientific accuracy required by the Royal Society and has secured him the title of the 'father of modern English prose'. His service to verse was similar. His greatest political satire, *Absalom and Achitophel* (1681), was, without being moralizing and apostrophizing, simply a story with character-sketches depicted in epigrammatic phrases that became proverbial. In drama he created the heroic play and the comedy of society and used heroic couplets – self-contained rhymed couplets – with strength and effectiveness. Throughout, his strongest influence on literature was the example of writing depending for its appeal on reason and intellectual judgement rather than on the emotions.

Dryden had expressed and been supported by contemporary public taste. The poetry of his disciple and successor, Alexander Pope (1688–1744), was described by Leslie Stephen as 'the essence of the first half of the eighteenth century'. He was not a great thinker and had no vision or message for his times. His philsophy was the facile Deism of these years, which 'looks through nature up to nature's God'. He was most effective as a satirist, particularly in *The Rape of the Lock* (1712) in which he mocked contemporary fashionable society; but his satire was inspired by personal resentment rather than any desire to reform or amend, which typified the comfortable, complacent upper and middle classes for whom he wrote. Generally the subjects of his poetry were less important than their form. His own line, 'What oft was thought, but ne'er so well expressed', might well apply to his verse. He was usually content to use Dryden's couplet and express views current in his time or borrowed from other authors, but he sought to express himself in as perfect and regular, as polished and terse a manner as possible. He made himself the nearest approach to a Classical poet in the English language, and as such was much admired by his generation.

Nevertheless, during the first years of the Hanoverian age the most memorable writings were in prose. The growth of the coffee-houses, with their clubs and talk, had produced a public ready for facts and ideas. The development of political parties had increased the value of popular opinion for the government and its opponents. Newspapers and journals were becoming more important, and the times encouraged writers to combine literature with journalism.

Typical of these writers was Daniel Defoe (1660–1731), who had, to quote Leslie Stephen again, 'the most amazing talent on record for telling lies'. He was a pamphleteer and government spy before becoming a novelist, writing *Robinson Crusoe* (1719), *Moll Flanders* (1722) and also a *A Journal of the Plague Year* (1722), a vivid account, as by an eye-witness, of the Great Plague of 1665, written when eighteenth-century England feared that a plague, then raging across the Channel, might revisit her shores. Richard Steele (1672–1729) and Joseph Addison (1672–1719), who produced the famous literary journals, the *Tatler* (1709–11) and *Spectator* (1711–12), also participated in politics; Addison became a Secretary of State while Steele, expelled from the House of Commons for a political pamphlet, was later knighted and honoured. Jonathan Swift (1667–1745) wrote for first the Whigs and then the Tories, when he wrote his great pamphlet on *The Conduct of the Allies* (1711); but the fall of the Tories in 1714 ended his political career. He returned to Ireland to write the *Drapier's Letters* (1724), *Gulliver's Travels* (1726) and the more bitter works of his last years.[1]

By 1740 most of the literary figures of the first part of the Hanoverian period – the essayists and satirists, the writers of

[1] P. 229.

easy, polished prose or poetry – were dead or had ceased writing. The next thirty or forty years did not acquire such marked characteristics and were not dominated by any definite tendency or personality. The poetic tradition of Dryden and Pope was only really seen in two widely-differing writers: the two satires, *London* (1738) and *The Vanity of Human Wishes* (1749) by Samuel Johnson (1709–84), and *The Traveller* (1764) and *The Deserted Village* (1770), describing contemporary social and economic evils, by Oliver Goldsmith (1730–74). Among other writers, there was a tendency for the poetry of the town and society to be replaced by a poetry of nature and the countryside. This was exemplified by *The Seasons* (1726–30) of James Thomson (1700–48) and the *Ode to Evening* (1749) of William Collins (1721–59). With the discovery of nature came a love of lonely country church-yards and desolate ruins to be found in the *Night Thoughts* (1742–5) of Edward Young (1683–1765) and the *Elegy Written in a Country Churchyard* (1751) of Thomas Gray (1716–71).

The dominating literary figure of these years was Samuel Johnson, whose name is frequently linked with the period. He was a poet and essayist, but his greatest services to litera-ture were his systematic studies – his edition of Shakespeare (1765), the *Dictionary* (1747–55) and *The Lives of the Poets* (1779–81) – all of which were important pioneer works. Nevertheless, Dr. Johnson is much better known as the man than as the writer. Many who do not know his works are familiar with the *Life of Johnson* (1791) in which his admirer, James Boswell (1740–95), vividly described the personality and opinions, wit and conversation of Johnson in his later years. It is the greatest English biography; it is also very valuable to the social historian, as is Boswell's recently-discovered *London Journal 1762–63*.

The really significant feature of this period was the develop-ment of the novel, the newest form of literature. In the words of Walter Allen, 'The first great flowering of the English novel began in 1740 with Richardson's *Pamela* and ended thirty-one years later with Smollett's *Humphrey Clinker*'. Samuel Richardson (1689–1761) was a master-printer who only became a novelist in middle age. In *Pamela or Virtue Rewarded* (1740) and *Clarissa Harlowe* (1747–8), he displayed a

new interest in the deepest human experiences, depicted
with especial intimacy in the succession of emotions of his
heroines, though he was formally sensitive and studiously
moral for the sake of his female readers. Henry Fielding
(1707–54) reacted from Richardson's romantic sentimentalism
and cautious morality. His *Tom Jones* (1749) is carefully
planned and executed as a tale of adventure with a wide
range of sympathy and realistic, lively characters. The novels
of Tobias Smollett (1721–71), particularly *Roderick Random*
(1748), *Peregrine Pickle* (1751) and *Humphrey Clinker* (1771),
introduced a new note of crude realism and coarse vigour in
the picaresque style which gained him fame. Smollett did
not attain the stature of Richardson or Fielding, and neither
did Laurence Sterne (1713–68), who had meanwhile produced *Tristram Shandy* (1760–7) and *A Sentimental Journey
through France and Italy* (1768), but the sentimentality and
humour of this original and eccentric writer had a great
influence. The widely differing works of these four writers
established the English novel as a form of literary art which
was immediately popular because it attracted a public that
was less cultured and intellectual than those who read poetry
or essays, but one that was also more numerous and socially
variegated. Their experiments prepared the way for the
significant new directions taken in English fiction from the
beginning of the nineteenth century.

During the last third of the eighteenth century the effect
was felt in English literature of the two great political
upheavals of the time, the American and French Revolutions,
both of which produced violent divisions of public opinion.
Edmund Burke (1729–97) expressed himself on both issues,
opposing the government's attitude towards the American
colonists in *On American Taxation* (1774) and *On Conciliation
with America* (1775) and attacking the French Revolution in
Reflections on the French Revolution (1790).[1] Whether or not he
really understood the issues of these two political upheavals,
Burke was not, as he might seem to be, inconsistent; he feared
reliance upon pure theory in politics, condemning the British
government for governing its relations with the American
colonies by legalistic procedure and the French revolutionaries
for causing violence and extremism by attempting to put a

---

[1] Pp. 342, 371.

theoretical philosophy into practice. 'Abstract liberty', he held, 'like other mere abstractions, is not to be found.' He wanted reason to be tempered in politics by experience, custom and tradition, and continuity and expediency to be preferred to revolution and theory.

Most writers, however, were on the side of innovation. Thomas Paine (1737–1809), who served in both the American army and the French National Convention, wrote *The Rights of Man* (1791–2), the most famous reply to Burke's *Reflections*, in which he proclaimed, 'My country is the world, and my religion is to do good'.[1] Jeremy Bentham (1748–1832) also rejected compromise and experience, being the leader of the school of thought and practice known as Utilitarianism. He took as his principle, 'It is the greatest happiness of the greatest number that is the measure of right and wrong', and wished every law and institution to be tested and amended in accordance with it.[2] And William Godwin (1756–1836) displayed in his *Enquiry concerning Political Justice* (1739) a belief that, since evil is solely the result of ignorance, the application of pure reason would solve all political and ethical problems. His wife, Mary Wollstonecraft (1759–97) was a pioneer advocate of the rights of women.

Other writers applied rationalism to their chosen spheres of thought. Edward Gibbon (1737–94) was the greatest to use the rationalistic approach in the realm of history. Though his hostility to Christianity gave the centre of his vast *Decline and Fall of the Roman Empire* (1776–88) an emptiness, only hidden by the uniform excellence of his style, the work was pre-eminent in its new detachment from accepted beliefs and critical attitude towards sources of information. A similar unwillingness to abide by popular conceptions was revealed in economics by Adam Smith (1723–90), who insisted in his *Wealth of Nations* (1776) that 'it is the highest impertinence to watch over the economy of private people' and that, therefore, governments should cease to impose restrictions on industry and trade and leave individuals free to seek their own private profit, which would be the best way of ensuring public wealth.[3]

Towards the end of the eighteenth century, new influences succeeded rationalism in literature. The Methodist and

[1] P. 372.   [2] P. 407.   [3] Pp. 159–60.

Evangelical movements produced hymn-writers such as Samuel Wesley and Augustus Toplady.[1] William Cowper (1731–1800) exemplified in his poetry many of the tendencies of these years from the continuing interest in rural scenes in *The Task* (1785) to the *Olney Hymns* (1779) which include 'God moves in a mysterious way' and 'There is a fountain fill'd with blood'. Accompanying the religious revival was a generous sentiment towards humanity and a concern for the lot of the poor. Among poets expressing this were Robert Burns (1759–96), son of an Ayrshire farmer, who revolted against the religious constraints and social barriers of his country, and George Crabbe (1754–1832), who came from a poor family at Aldeburgh in Suffolk and in *The Village* (1783) described rural life with implacable realism in contrast to the romanticism of the pastoral tradition. Of the same generation was William Blake (1757–1832), engraver and poet, mystic and prophet, who expressed so mystically his passion for freedom and rebellion against the industrial developments of the age.

The new tendencies found their expression in fiction chiefly in the 'novel of terror' or 'Gothic novel', inaugurated by Horace Walpole (1717–97), son of Sir Robert Walpole, who holding sinecure offices as so many did, was enabled to indulge in antiquarianism in his Gothic villa at Strawberry Hill.[2] His *Castle of Otranto* (1764) was a mysterious tale set in medieval Italy and he is famous for his *Letters*. William Beckford (1760–1844), who also had built himself a Gothic edifice – Fonthill Abbey – wrote *Vathek* (1782), an oriental romance of magnificence, luxury and voluptuousness. The most able and popular of such writers was Anne Radcliffe (1764–1823), particularly in *The Mysteries of Udolpho* (1749) and *The Italian* (1797). The most horrific was Matthew Gregory Lewis (1775–1818) in *The Monk*. In such books, desperate villains and swooning heroines performed in tales of murder and romance, violence and supernaturalism set amid ruinous castles, rattling chains and grisly skeletons.

Blake, Beckford and Mrs. Radcliffe stood on the threshold of the literary period known as the Romantic Revival which occupied the last thirty years of the Hanoverian age. Much effort has been made to assign a constant meaning to the

[1] Pp. 75–6.   [2] P. 107.

Romanticism of this movement. The term is essentially an attempt to indicate how the new writers differed from their Classical predecessors and especially Pope. The Classical writers believed that literary perfection had been reached in the golden age of Latin poetry, the reign of the Roman Emperor Augustus; they sought to write in the manner prescribed by the critical writing of the original Augustan age as interpreted by Renaissance criticism, striving after polish and refinement, expressing accepted philosophical truths and concentrating upon man in civilized society. The Romantic writers defied the accepted rules and conventions, regarded poetry as philosophy itself, relied upon intuition and imagination to bring them to final truth and were interested in solitary man and wild nature.

It was no coincidence that the seeds of this new movement in poetry were sown in the early years of the French Revolution. Its two pioneers, William Wordsworth (1770–1850) and Samuel Taylor Coleridge (1772–1834), both belonged to the generation which believed that the fall of the Bastille in 1789 marked the beginning of a new age for mankind. Wordsworth's well-known lines express their enthusiasm at that time:

> Bliss was it in that dawn to be alive,
> But to be young was very heaven!

Soon, however, the outbreak of war and the rise of Napoleon disillusioned them, but they were rescued from moral despair by the cultivation of poetry and the study of nature, which resulted in the joint-collection of their poems, the *Lyrical Ballads* (1798). This is usually held to mark the beginning of the Romantic Revival, for it was the first deliberate and conscious attempt to protest against the predominant type of poetry. The poets purposely used simple words, unusual images and varied verse-forms and created a fresh set of poetical associations. Wordsworth set out to shed the light of imagination over simple realistic incidents and people in the countryside, while Coleridge sought to give credibility to the supernatural and miraculous, especially in *The Rime of the Ancient Mariner*. Neither had a long period of poetic inspiration. Wordsworth was long-lived, but after about 1815 he became 'thick-ankled', and poetry virtually died in

him; Coleridge fell a victim to opium; but they had a great
and lasting influence. Wordsworth's poetic vision of nature
influenced the early Tractarian movement as also did Coleridge's later philosophical prose writings.[1]

They were succeeded by a new generation of Romantic
poets: Lord Byron (1788–1824), Percy Bysshe Shelley
(1792–1822) and John Keats (1795–1821). All shared an
early death, but they lived intensely and wrote brilliantly.
Keats wrote no political poetry, but Byron and Shelley, who
belonged to the aristocratic class traditionally engaged in
politics, regarded the later conservatism of Wordsworth and
Coleridge as a betrayal of their ideals. Shelley wrote much
political satire, indignantly lashing in *The Mask of Anarchy*
(1819) the 'arch-anarch' Castlereagh for his reactionary
policies; and Byron gave his life for the cause of Greek
independence. They devoted themselves both to the new
ideas in poetry and to the new ideals of nineteenth-century
liberalism and progress.

In the realm of fiction, the novels of Jane Austen (1775–1815),
achieved artistic perfection within their own limits. They
stand apart from the Romantic Revival and fall rather within
the tradition of Fielding; but Sir Walter Scott (1771–1832)
made an important contribution to the movement. Scott
shared the interest in the medieval past of Beckford and Mrs.
Radcliffe, but had a truer historical sense. Though his
finest novels are those set in seventeenth- and eighteenth-
century Scotland, whose life and traditions he knew so well,
Ivanhoe (1820), *The Talisman* (1825) and other medieval
novels were extremely popular and perhaps exercised most
contemporary influence, particularly, again, upon the
Tractarians.[2] Scott also influenced historians in an important manner. He realized that human thoughts and morals
vary with time and place and class (in contrast to the essentially eighteenth-century character of even Gibbon's emperors,
magistrates, priests and plebeians); he also concerned himself
with details of past costume and habits and environment as no
previous historical writer had ever done. As a young man,
Macaulay realized this and indicated the kind of history he
was himself to write twenty years later when he said in 1828,
'Sir Walter Scott has used those fragments of truth which

[1] P. 85.   [2] P. 86.

historians have scornfully thrown behind them. But a truly great historian would reclaim those materials which the novelist has appropriated.'

Behind the literary developments and great writers of these later years of the Hanoverian period was a growing educated reading public, particularly among the cultured middle classes, which appreciated and enjoyed them. They also joined with the educated clerks and artisans to form a large newspaper-reading public, especially when improved communications took the London news to the provinces. They read Wilkes's *North Briton*;[1] and they stimulated the starting of a number of daily newspapers – the *Morning Chronicle* in 1769, *The Times* in 1785 (though not with that title until 1788) and the *Observer* in 1791. Also started were the *Edinburgh Review* (1802) and the *Quarterly Review* (1809), containing political articles and literary reviews, and *Blackwood's Magazine* (1817) and *The London Magazine* (1820), specializing in essays, poetry and correspondence. Though their appeal was less wide than that of the daily newspapers, these magazines did much to create and stimulate nineteenth-century public opinion.

Music and Painting

The Hanoverian period was not a very distinguished one for English music. After the death of Henry Purcell (1659–95), a decline set in. During the first half of the eighteenth century, the dominant figure was George Frederick Handel (1685–1759), a Saxon who settled in England in 1712 and became naturalized in 1726. Both George I and George II patronized him, so many of his compositions are connected with royal events – the *Water Music* for a river-fête in 1717, the anthem *Zadok the Priest* for George II's coronation in 1727, the *Dettingen Te Deum* of 1743, *Judas Maccabeus* to honour the defeat of the 'Forty-Five, and the *Firework Music* to celebrate the Treaty of Aix-la-Chapelle. When *The Messiah*, first performed in Dublin in 1741, was heard in London two years later, the King set the example of standing at the 'Hallelujah Chorus'; and from 1749 Handel performed this oratorio each year at the Foundling Hospital Chapel, raising £7,000 for this charity. He was buried with high honours in

[1] P. 323.

Westminster Abbey, where in 1784–5–6 and 1791 were held magnificent Handel Commemorations, warmly supported by George III

The leading English composer of this period was Thomas Arne (1710–78), who chiefly wrote songs for the theatre; he also composed 'Rule Britannia' and arranged 'God Save the King'. As might be expected, music depended considerably upon fashionable patronage. Some noblemen, such as the Duke of Chandos had private orchestras. Others patronized the Academy of Ancient Music, which lasted from 1710 to 1792, and in 1761 founded the Noblemen and Gentlemen's Catch Club to sing glees, which were very popular during the century. Two friends, Maurice Greene (1695–1755) and William Boyce (1710–79), composed some fine church anthems, and the Three Choirs Festival (of Gloucester, Worcester and Hereford) was initiated in 1724, but the Cathedrals were not yet centres of English church music.

Later in the period, music gave no indication of achieving revival through experiments like those being made in the other arts. Charles Dibdin (1745–1814) wrote sea-songs which accorded with popular enthusiasm for the navy, and Tom Moore (1779–1852) achieved social success by writing and singing poems set to Irish folk tunes. Generally, however, the status of performers was low. There was a marked decline in the amateur cultivation of music, which tended to be relegated to the ladies of the 'comfortable classes' and regarded as a mere 'accomplishment'. A high standard was maintained in London by the Antient Concerts (1776–1828), which were limited to compositions at least twenty years old, and the London Philharmonic Society (1813) which often commissioned for its concerts music written by distinguished foreign composers, including Beethoven's *Ninth Symphony*. In 1823 the Royal Academy of Music was founded to improve the position and training of English musicians, but its effect was only gradually felt. The influence of music remained much less than that of poetry and even painting in the national culture.

English painting in the eighteenth century was mainly confined to portraiture and conversation pieces. The tradition was established by Sir Godfrey Kneller (1646–1723), who painted innumerable, not very interesting, portraits of his distinguished contemporaries and was court painter to every monarch from James II to George I.   At this time the portrait-painter was commonly called the 'face-painter', his function being almost limited to producing a likeness for an important patron which should be orthodox, recognizable and flattering.   These were the portraits which the landed gentry, wealthy merchants and Indian 'nabobs' commissioned to hang in their mansions.

Nor was there any important change until the advent of William Hogarth (1697-1764), who disliked the grand manner and painted, without flattery, vigorous portraits of contemporary life.   As he said of himself, he 'grew so profane as to admire *nature* beyond the finest productions of art'. Instead of taking well-dressed noble lords and ladies as his subjects, he chose the tradesmen and apprentices, draymen and beggars and even the criminals, drunkards and harlots of contemporary London.   He was also a moralist, insisting that there was better morality in his *Gin Lane* than any allegorical gods and goddesses, but he was none the worse artist for that.

The demand for fashionable portraiture continued throughout the century, and fortunately two great artists raised it to a new and splendid level, though they still painted in the Classical style.   Both Sir Joshua Reynolds (1723-92) and his friend and rival, Thomas Gainsborough (1727-88), were successful and prosperous as portrait-painters and produced a magnificent collection of stately portraits of men and women of this graceful age.   Yet if they had not been led by the demands of the day to paint portraits, they might perhaps have chosen other subjects.   Reynolds would have chosen historical and Gainsborough devoted more time to landscape subjects.

During the last years of the Hanoverian period, the revolt against old traditions and the desire to experiment became apparent in painting as in poetry.   This was seen in the work of Sir Thomas Lawrence (1769-1832), the most fashionable portrait-painter of Regency society, who abandoned Reynolds' care that pose and drapery should conform to the grand Classical style; he sought rather to use dress and setting, as well as the face or poise, to indicate a mood.   He was an elegant painter, but introduced into his pictures a liveliness,

H

a dash and sometimes a carelessness unusual in official portraiture.

A similar desertion of the Classical framework appeared also in landscape-painting, in which artists began to adopt a more intimate and so more romantic attitude to nature. This again was part of the spirit of the age which was expressed in poetry. The leaders of the movement were two artists of genius, John Constable (1776–1837) and J. M. W. Turner (1775–1851). Constable contented himself more often with the landscapes of his native Suffolk, but tried to depict the exact appearance of the weather, the green meadows, the foliage of the trees and the clouds with an effect that Henry Fuseli, the contemporary painter and art-critic, said made him call for his umbrella. Constable, in the words of Eric Newton, 'evolved for this purpose a nervous, shimmering brush-stroke with broken tones flicked with pure white', an experiment which aroused many protests. Turner was more successful in gaining public approval because people liked the way he stressed the romantic and picturesque in landscape but he also was experimenting in his efforts to render nature intensely, concentrating on new and impressive ways of painting sunlight. Later Turner became less popular when he went on to experiment in painting light in an impressionistic manner, but some of his most famous pictures, such as *The Fighting Temeraire* (1838) and *Rain, Steam and Speed* (1843), belong to these years.

Architecture, Decoration and Furniture

In architecture, the first half of the eighteenth century saw the development of the Early Georgian style from the Anglicized Classic manner of building evolved by Sir Christopher Wren (1632–1723). Like all Classic architecture, this style was much concerned with form, symmetry and proportion. The magnificent country mansions, built for the aristocracy, were Classically correct and monumental in architecture rather than convenient and comfortable. The favourite plan, to be seen in Holkham Hall, Norfolk (1734–60), by William Kent (1684–1748) and Blenheim Palace, Oxfordshire (1706–24), by Sir John Vanburgh (1664–1726), was a large central block, approached by steps and monumental portico, flanked on either side by symmetrical low wings to give greater

scale to the centre.   The strict concern for ordered formalism
even extended to the designing of gardens, which were laid
out with wide terraces and stately flights of steps.   Smaller
houses, such as those in Cheyne Row, Chelsea, and Church
Row, Hampstead, were of simple rectangular shapes, depending for adornment upon mouldings round the windows and
elegant door surrounds.

The Late Georgian style of the middle and closing years of
the century became continuously more refined and simple.
On the whole, great houses were less massive and heavy,
relying for effect more upon touches of individual grace, a
cupola or a few pillars perhaps, than upon mere ponderous-
ness.   The shift in taste reflected the effect of the discovery of
the ruins of Pompeii and Athens as well as the domestic
simplicity of the young George III's court.   The greatest
influence was that of the Adam brothers – James Adam
(d. 1794) and Robert Adam (1728–92) – who introduced a
refinement and lightness typical of the social elegance of the
time; and as designers of everything pertaining to the interior
embellishment of their buildings – fireplaces, ceilings, furniture, joinery and even china – they also became known as
decorative artists.[1]   Famous Adam houses include Osterley
Park, Middlesex (1761), Syon House, Middlesex (1762),
Lansdowne House, London (1765), Ken Wood, Highgate
(1776), and Stowe, Buckinghamshire (1777).

The surroundings of country houses changed from the
earlier formal, symmetrical arrangements to naturalistic,
informal, yet carefully contrived designs.   Consequently, the
houses built from the Restoration to the time of Vanburgh
(including those of the age of Wren) now stand, not in the
surroundings designed for them, but in alien landscapes
substituted at this time.   The former formal gardens had
owed their origin to French and Italian influence, but this
new style was an English development, known on the Continent as 'le jardin anglais'.   The greatest English landscape
gardener of the eighteenth century was Lancelot ('Capability')
Brown (1715–83), who laid out Kew Gardens, replanned St.
James's Park and swept away the hedges, walks and enclosed
gardens of Blenheim Palace to create the magnificent parkland
scenery which remains today.   Brown's remarkable faculty

[1] P. 107.

for pre-judging landscape effects made him the natural leader of the new style of landscape architecture. In his appraisal of the 'capability' of an estate, he tried to bring out the undulating lines of the natural landscape. Usually he ran the contoured parkland right up to the mansion, keeping deer or cattle away by a ha-ha or boundary ditch. The sweeping turf he accentuated with groups of oak or chestnut trees, while wooded slopes were arranged to give glimpses of a widening river or lake, behind which arose encircling woodlands following the periphery of the park. His designs were sometimes criticized as being bare or hard in outline, but this is not so now that many of the trees he planted are in their prime and producing an effect which he could never have hoped to see.

The end of the century saw the expansion of London and other towns. Much of this was accomplished in an orderly and properly planned manner through the civic sense of landlord and architect, particularly in Bath and the Bloomsbury squares in London. From 1776 the Bedford and Foundling Hospital estates in Bloomsbury were planned as a quiet respectable suburb with wide streets, spacious squares and dignified and sometimes monumental architecture. Specific and stringent clauses were inserted in the building leases to preserve the houses as gentlemen's private residences, so that even today there is an extraordinary shortage of public houses in the area.

At the same time as rows of future slums were being built for the industrial workers around the factories in the new manufacturing towns, Georgian architecture reached its final expression in the Regency period, when an exceptional purity of design was obtained by the use of flat painted stucco walls, sash windows with thin wood members, projecting eaves and elegant balconies. Its dominant architect was John Nash (1752–1835), though he concerned himself with broad architectural effects rather than with the perfection of detail. By securing the Prince Regent's patronage, he gained the opportunity to plan a magnificent, aristocratic residential district in London, extending from Regent's Park to Carlton House, and in this he combined whole groups of buildings and crescents and terraces with colonnades and open spaces, trees and grass in a most satisfying manner.

The effect of Romanticism in architecture was seen in the Gothic revival, which began about 1750, when Horace Walpole built his villa at Strawberry Hill, and became more important with the advent of James Wyatt (1746–1813), who between 1800 and 1807 built for William Beckford the extraordinary Fonthill Abbey, which superficially resembled a huge cathedral.[1] As yet, however, the Gothic revival was confined largely to the introduction of Gothic mannerisms into buildings which were still essentially Classical in form and was practised only by a few eccentrics and villa-builders. It was firmly resisted by the representatives of early nineteenth-century radical enlightenment, whose buildings – Dissenting chapels and seminaries and, above all, University College, London – were strictly Classical. The great popularity of the Gothic movement lay ahead in the Victorian period.

Throughout the Hanoverian period, interior decoration was closely connected with architectural development and also the influence of the Grand Tour upon young noblemen.[2] The large, high state rooms of Georgian mansions were lavishly decorated with painting, stucco and marble. Walls were sometimes panelled (deal or pine generally replacing cedar, walnut and mahogany early in George III's reign), sometimes of painted plaster, sometimes hung with damask, velvet or tapestry, while printed or hand-coloured wallpaper was popular as a cheaper substitute. About 1740 the extreme French rococo style came into fashion with its scrolls, curves and lavish use of gilt and mirrors.

From about 1760 the brothers Adam introduced a new style of decoration, based on a study of ancient Greek and Roman architecture and the details of antique works of art brought by noble collectors from the Continent. Its main features were painted panels in low-relief, thin cobweb-like lines of decoration and flat fan-shaped ribs, all executed in hard plaster in ceilings, fireplaces and relief on the walls, the motifs commonly being medallions, festoons, vases and other Classical elements. Moreover, a complete harmony was obtained; the carpet was woven to repeat the pattern on the ceiling, and the furniture and fittings made in a single style through collaboration with artists and craftsmen.[3]

The effect of Romanticism in decoration was seen in a

[1] P. 98.   [2] Pp. 34–5.   [3] P. 108.

Gothic taste which followed Horace Walpole's pseudo-
medieval decoration of Strawberry Hill (which included
'stone-coloured Gothic wallpaper'). Furniture of all kinds,
often of a very meretricious type, was made in this semi-
ecclesiastical style. There followed, stimulated by the import
of lacquer, porcelain and textiles from the Far East, a taste in
decoration and furniture for Chinese or Indian motifs such
as pagodas, exotic birds and dragons and lattice work. The
main monument to this taste is the Prince Regent's Royal
Pavilion at Brighton; but these fancies remained exceptional
throughout the period.

Furniture, in its turn, was designed in relation to interior
decoration. By 1720 the simple and dignified Queen Anne
style was showing signs of less restrained French and Italian
influences, while the growing prosperity of the country made
possible the replacement of walnut as the fashionable material
by mahogany imported from the West Indies and Cuba.
Elaborately carved and gilt mirrors and side-tables were
popular, the chief exponent of the new style being William
Kent, who had studied in Italy and was the first architect
to include movable furniture within his architectural schemes.

The new ideals of the Adam brothers were assimilated by
Thomas Chippendale (1718?–79), who collaborated with
them in making furniture in the style of their Classical
revival. Continental exuberance was replaced by a marked
austerity and greater sense of proportion. There was also a
revival in the art of marquetry; new woods, stained and
shaded, were used for decoration, particularly satinwood.
George Hepplewhite (d. 1786) skilfully modified the style,
his aim being 'to unite elegance and utility and blend the
useful with the agreeable'. Thomas Sheraton (1751–1806)
designed yet more slender and fragile furniture, increasing its
elegance with costly veneers and metal inlays.

Furniture became more intensely Classical with the
influence of the Regency version of the French *directoire* style.
Classical precedents were studied, while Napoleon's Egyptian
campaign brought an interest in Egyptian remains. The forms
of antiquity were copied or adapted for tables, settees and arm-
chairs. Designs were sought from the 'best antique examples'
of ancient Greece, Rome and Egypt, though in the last years of
the period 'Grecian severity' was the predominant ideal.

VI · THE AGRARIAN REVOLUTION

The Development of Large Estates

DURING the sixteenth and seventeenth centuries, moderate-sized estates had predominated in the English countryside through the accumulation of land by the gentry who were rising in economic status; but from the early eighteenth century large estates were being established at the expense of the smaller ones. By 1785, for instance, the amount of land held in properties of less than a hundred acres had fallen by two-thirds in twenty-four Oxfordshire parishes and by four-fifths in ten Gloucestershire parishes. Before the end of the eighteenth century, nearly half the cultivated land in England was owned by five thousand families.

This process was accomplished mainly by purchase. Small owners were encouraged to put their land into the market by being offered good prices – prices, in fact, which might be in excess of the capital value of their properties as sources of income. They were usually only too ready to have the money to pay off their debts or to put into trade, or even make use of it to stock larger farms as tenants. The purchasers, who continued to buy land in this way to increase still further the size of their great estates, were partly noblemen, wishing to increase their holdings in the country, and partly those made wealthy by trade – the most successful middle-class men who had prospered considerably from the vast expansion of English overseas trade and industry.[1] These men used their profits to build up landed estates for themselves. Sometimes they belonged to the younger line of a noble family, such as the Elder Pitt's grandfather, Thomas Pitt, who purchased estates in Berkshire and Cornwall with the wealth he gained in India.[2]

The motives of such purchasers of estates were social rather than economic. They desired to secure land not so much for profitable investment as for the prestige and political power that went with its possession. The ownership of land made it

[1] P. 25.　　　　　　　　　　　　　[2] P. 296.

possible to enter county society and often gain a title.   It
was also a qualification for participation in local government,
since the landed nobility and gentry by acting as Lords-
Lieutenant, Deputy Lieutenants, Sheriffs and Justices of the
Peace, managed all civil and military administration in the
provinces.[1]   Equally power in the central government rested
upon the possession of land.   The power of the Whig ministries under the first two Georges depended upon the control
of votes in Parliament.   Extensive landed property gave its
owners a powerful local influence over elections, especially
where pocket and rotten boroughs existed, and those able to
control elections could demand a share of ministerial patronage, which was likely to be needed to place younger sons in
the Church, the armed forces and the public services.   Hence
the growth of large estates in the eighteenth century, a process
which, whether accomplished by prudent marriages by
noblemen or lavish purchases by merchants, was actuated by
motives stimulated by the contemporary character of polite
society and of local and national government.

Having built up large estates, such landlords were anxious
to maintain them and they adopted a number of devices to
ensure this.   The 'strict settlement', devised in 1660, enabled
landlords, who could afford to provide against certain con-
tingencies, to protect their inheritance against individual
extravagance; and their near monopoly of the profits of
political office and development of non-agricultural revenues
guaranteed them against agricultural misfortune.[2]   Thereafter, the pressure of a growing population added to their
prosperity.[3]   By between about 1720 and 1790 rents had
doubled, and in the next twenty years they doubled again.   The
landlords could afford to be lax with their tenants and had
political reasons for being so.   For the sake of a popularity which
they needed at the county elections, many kept rents low and
released leases without question.

This laxity might not hasten agricultural progress.   The
large landowners might possess the means of improvement,
such as considerable resources, home farms and professional
stewards, but they often lacked the necessary incentive.
Agronomists like Arthur Young vainly urged landlords 'to
sacrifice popularity for the sake of 5s. per acre per annum'

[1] P. 63.   [2] P. 22.   [3] P. 2.

and argued that 'the extravagant son of White's', whose 'rents fly with the dice' and had, therefore, to press his tenants to raise their yield, was worth 'ten times more to his country than the gentlemen of regularity and moderation', but the political landlords knew better than Arthur Young where their ultimate interests lay.   Political power, not agricultural efficiency, assured their position in England.

New Methods in Agriculture

Such an attitude meant that often large landowners were not inclined to encourage the development of new agricultural methods or to take an interest in the new scientific farming.   Increasing knowledge of the details of contemporary estate management, indeed, reveals that this part of the Agrarian Revolution was much less rapid and dramatic than has been commonly supposed.   Nor were English farmers pioneers here.   Since quite early in the seventeenth century, farming standards in the divided Netherlands had been generally recognized as the highest in Europe.   Expensive land and high wages combined there with urban requirements to produce a very efficient agricultural system. Attention to breeding and stall-feeding with fodder-crops secured larger cattle than elsewhere; and the fertility of the land was improved by constantly ploughing in clover and other crops.   As late as 1802 a careful German observer considered that agricultural productivity in the Austrian Netherlands was still a third greater than in England.

The 'Norfolk system of husbandry', which became famous in the late eighteenth century, was defined by Arthur Young as having seven main points – enclosure by agreement, the use of marl and clay, a proper rotation of crops, the culture of hand-hoed turnips, the growing of clover and rye grass, long leases and large farms.   The advantages of this new system are well known.   The rotation of crops, in which corn and roots were sown in alternate years, meant that the same field could be kept in continuous production and did not need a fallow year, since the crops used different depths of soil – the corn family, being fibrous-rooted, draw their nourishment from the top spit of the soil, while the root crops draw theirs from the lower spit by long tap roots.   Again, in the past most of the stock on a farm were killed off about November

and salted down, leaving only the haulage animals and breeding couples to be maintained throughout the winter; but now
the cattle could be kept alive by being fed with turnips for
winter keep.

It is now known that this system was of Dutch origin and
was first practised in north-west Norfok in the closing years
of the seventeenth century. Its introduction is commonly
associated with the name of Viscount Charles Townshend
(1674-1738), whose estates were at Raynham Hall, Norfolk,
but it was well established on the Walpole estates at Houghton
Hall some years before 1700 and continued to be practised
throughout Sir Robert Walpole's time. Indeed, J. H. Plumb
has suggested that had Walpole lost his struggle in 1730 with
Townshend and retired to his Norfolk estates, he would
doubtless be known to posterity as 'Turnip Walpole'. The
new system was adopted, not as the result of the revolutionary
ideas of a few men, but rather through the work of many –
landowners, farmers and country clergymen.

Other changes came about in much the same way. The
seed-drill of Jethro Tull (1674-1741), which sowed seed in
rows by a horse-drawn machine instead of broadcast by
hand, was based upon experiments made by other men before
him. Robert Bakewell (1725-95) of Dishley Grange, near
Loughborough, experimented from about 1745 in the
improved breeding of sheep and cattle, but so also did others,
including the brothers, Charles Colling (1751-1836) and
Robert Colling (1749-1820), developers of the shorthorn cow,
John Ellman (1753-1832), breeder of Southdown sheep, and
George III, who introduced a stock of Merino sheep on his
model farm at Windsor. Thomas William Coke, later Earl
of Leicester, of Holkham (1752-1842), the best-known of the
English improving landlords of the period, was certainly an
efficient and successful landowner, but the gross rental of his
estates in Norfolk was about doubled between 1776 and 1816
and not increased four, nine or ten times, as is often stated.
'The monetary gains made by Coke', Steven Watson has
written, 'have been grossly and almost universally exaggerated.' He was not a worker of miracles, who brought
fertility to a sandy waste and converted north-west Norfolk
from a rye-growing into a wheat-growing district, for agricultural progress was a feature of the Holkham estates during

the whole of the eighteenth century, and wheat had been grown in Norfolk as early as the sixteenth century. Coke was certainly interested in the new techniques, and probably his greatest contribution to their dissemination were the famous sheep-shearings which he began in 1778. These were a combined farm-walk and agricultural show at which landlords and farmers saw his innovations and the new Southdown sheep he patronized.

Perhaps a main reason why many later eighteenth-century agriculturists are well known, while their predecessors have gone unrecorded, is because their work coincided with the rise of agricultural journalism and official publications which chronicled their names and activities. Prominent among the writers on agriculture were William Marshall (1745–1818), Sir John Sinclair (1754–1835) and, above all, Arthur Young (1741–1820), who himself twice failed as a practical farmer, but exerted an important influence in favour of new agricultural ideas in the descriptions of his tours and other writings. These men were prominent in the Board of Agriculture, a body set up and provided with funds by the government in 1793 to spread among farmers knowledge of the improved ways of cultivation and stock-breeding. It collected information, published reports and encouraged the organization of farmers' clubs and agricultural societies, ploughing matches and county shows. Its campaigns in favour of the commutation of tithe, more rapid enclosures and increased corn laws brought hostility from many quarters and resulted in its abolition in 1818, but during its existence it hastened the adoption of new agricultural methods.

Agricultural change, therefore, was not only less sudden in its beginning than has often been supposed, but also less rapid in progress during the eighteenth century. Such tardiness was largely due to the agricultural conservatism (for political reasons) of the great landlords and the caution, and lack of capital, of many farmers. So, as late as 1760, the only counties in which marked agricultural development had occurred were Essex, Hertfordshire, Leicestershire, Norfolk and Suffolk. Further progress came about through the efforts of the 'great farmers', especially those near the growing London market. Arthur Young went so far as to ascribe 'every great and beneficial practice' to them and not to the landowners.

Moreover, it was not until late in the period that mechanization on the farm began. The invention of the first useful threshing-machine in 1788 (to which steam-power was later applied) was followed in 1794 by a chaff-cutting machine which produced cattle-fodder, but the first effective reaping-machine was an American invention and was not patented until 1834.

Thus, the Agrarian Movement in England cannot be regarded as a cataclysmic movement. It was a slow process, evolutionary rather than revolutionary, and the changes covered by such a phrase came more gradually than the name implies and over a longer period than some historians have believed. On the one hand, important changes in estate management, usually attributed to the last quarter of the century, had been introduced into estates earlier and sometimes much earlier. On the other hand, the general adoption of such changes throughout the country was only gradual. Though the new methods had been devised before the last part of the century, it was only in these years that rising prices, the efforts to spread knowledge, and the influence of educated landowners and farmers combined to produce a marked agricultural expansion.

The Enclosure Movement

During the first half of the eighteenth century, there was no great demand for English farming to increase the national food-supply. The population increased only slowly.[1] The prices of agricultural products remained low. Except for the years 1739–42, harvests were good between 1730 and 1750, and cereal supplies appear to have outpaced demand, even though since 1688 a bounty of 5s. a quarter had been paid on all corn exported whenever the home-price of corn fell below 48s. a quarter. In fact, the average price for the whole period between 1713 and 1764 was only 34s. 11d. a quarter. Only in the three years of dearth did it rise much above this, and in some years it even fell below 25s. a quarter.

There followed, however, a combination of circumstances in the second half of the century which changed the situation. These were a marked increase in the population, the need for corn exports to pay for expanding trade with the colonies and

the Continent, the growth in the non-food-producing proportion of the population caused by the Industrial Revolution,
the demand for a higher standard of living, and the food-
shortage, rise in prices and drain on manpower brought about
first by the Seven Years' War and then by the Revolutionary
and Napoleonic Wars. The effect of these factors was felt
within a period of forty to fifty years, and together they
created a greater demand for home-produced food.

The inevitable consequence was a sharp and continuing rise
in the prices of agricultural products. The average price of
corn in the period from 1764 to 1794 was 44s. 7d. a quarter.
From about 1765 English exports of corn declined and imports
grew, until from 1790 there was an excess of imports over
exports, and in 1773 the system of bounties on exported corn
was abolished. Restrictions on the importation of foreign
corn, which had existed since the Middle Ages, were also
relaxed in 1773 by an Act declaring that when the home-
price of corn rose to 48s., foreign corn might be imported free
of duty. This figure was raised to 54s. in 1791 and to 66s. in
1804. In fact, however, rising prices rendered these provisions
largely inoperative. Since imports were restricted by wartime
conditions, the home-price of corn continued to depend on the
English weather, and there were bad harvests at the beginning
of the Revolutionary War and again later in the Napoleonic
War.[1] In the decade after 1804 the average price at which the
importation of foreign corn began to be duty free was nearly
100s. and in 1812 was nearly double that.

A desire to increase the productivity of the land, stimulated
largely by these rising prices, was the chief motive for the
great expansion of the enclosure movement. The parts of
the country where this was most extensive were those areas in
which the medieval open-field system of farming survived.
In this the arable land was usually held in strips scattered
among three great open fields, each of which followed in the
course of three years a rotation of two corn crops and a fallow
period. In addition, the owners of strips held rights of
pasturage over all the arable lands of the village as well as
over the stretches of uncultivated common or wasteland, and
of gathering fuel in the woodland; and they shared the
meadowland, which was divided into lots for hay. Enclosure

[1] Pp. 380, 395.

meant the replacement of these large areas of open land by smaller, individually-owned fields in which the proprietor could raise crops or livestock as he chose.

At the beginning of the Hanoverian period, however, the open-field system was not practised everywhere in England. There were many parts of the country where it had never been established. These included much of the land in the counties along the border with Wales, in Shropshire, Hereford-shire and perhaps Staffordshire, while large areas in Westmor-land, Cumberland and Northumberland and in Cornwall and Devon were probably brought into separate cultivation through the reclamation of rough, wild country. Again, there had been earlier enclosures, particularly in the sixteenth century for the creation of sheep-pastures. These enclosures, however, were largely confined to the Midlands, East Anglia and parts of the Home Counties and did not affect more than 30 per cent of the arable land in these districts. In all, about 744,000 acres were enclosed during this period, which repre-sented just over 2 per cent of the total area of England or 4 per cent of the cultivated area. Consequently, while slightly more than half of the total area of England was under cultivation, perhaps three-fifths or about 10,500,000 acres were still farmed under the open-field system. Only 10 per cent of the total area of Nottinghamshire and less than 50 per cent of that of Northamptonshire had been enclosed by 1700.

While the main reason for the sixteenth-century enclosures was to produce wool for the prosperous cloth industry, those of the eighteenth century were to grow more food. Enclosures were not always accompanied by the introduction of the new methods of farming, though clearly the conditions of the old system did not encourage the efficient growing of crops or breeding of sheep and cattle. Landowners were often under pressure to promote enclosures from farmers and the tithe-owners who wished to increase their profits from the land. Public opinion grew more favourable towards enclosure and overcame the fear of social consequences which had existed since Tudor times.

The particular purpose of eighteenth-century enclosures differed, naturally, according to the circumstances of time and place. Generally speaking, however, the low price of grain in the first half of the century and the general prevalence of the old inefficient and expensive ways of arable farming produced enclosure for pasture and cattle breeding, while later in the century the rising price of grain and the spread of new agricultural ideas led to enclosure for crops. During the first period, the wide belt of grazing land in the Midlands was enclosed and in that following the corn-growing areas of East Anglia, the East Midlands and the North-East. It has been estimated that the area of wheat land was increased by at least 365,000 acres between 1771 and 1808.

The simplest and cheapest method of enclosure was in a parish where a dominant landowner could do so by buying out freeholders and copyholders, not renewing leases and terminating tenancies, or where it could be done by agreement among the parishioners. It was a usual method in the first half of the century, when enclosure was on a small scale and had to be done cheaply; but later, when enclosures were larger and the incentives greater, landowners were increasingly prepared to override opposition by resort to an enclosure Act. A majority of proprietors in a parish or group of parishes petitioned Parliament for leave to bring in a Bill, which was then passed in the normal way, though at the committee stage objections to the Bill were heard, and it could not succeed unless supported by proprietors who owned the larger part of the land. The enclosure itself was carried out by commissioners appointed by the Act. Such Acts became markedly more numerous during the century. Only five were passed between 1714 and 1720, but 67 between 1721 and 1740, 205 between 1741 and 1760, 4,039 between 1761 and 1780 and 900 between 1781 and 1800.

Generally the first lands to be enclosed in most parts of the country were the open fields of villages, the larger before the smaller. Considerable areas of waste remained unenclosed much longer, especially in the northern counties of England. Arthur Young said in 1773, 'You may draw a line from the north point of Derbyshire to the extremity of Northumberland, of 150 miles as the crow flies, which shall be entirely across waste lands'; but by 1800 over 200,000 acres of waste had been enclosed in the two counties of Northumberland and Durham. In that year also only half a dozen counties remained in the whole of England with more than 3 per cent of their land unenclosed. The appearance of the countryside had been transformed.[1]

The enclosures of the sixteenth century had inspired contemporaries with alarm and indignation; they painted a picture of villages destroyed and villages dispossessed by landlords to make way for large, profitable sheep-runs, a picture still largely accepted today, though its inaccuracy has been revealed. Similarly, the first enthusiasm for enclosures in the eighteenth century was followed by fears that it had borne unjustly on the rural poor, particularly by depriving them of commonage and pasturage rights. The words which Arthur Young said he heard in a Berkshire ale-house – 'Parliament may be tender of property; all I know is that I had a cow, and an Act of Parliament has taken it from me' – still enjoy an unexampled promotion from tap-room gossip to frequent textbook quotation.

Recent investigation, however, suggests that there has been exaggeration here, as with the effects of the sixteenth-century enclosures. It is true that the two or three men who usually formed an enclosure commission were normally chosen by the lord of the manor, tithe owner and large proprietors, and no doubt they were liable to pressure from these wealthier men, but they were likely to be surveyors and other skilled professional men who worked on one enclosure after another and seem to have done their work conscientiously. Of fifty-three enclosures studied by Professor Beresford, half took over four years to complete and eight of these over eight years. Moreover, investigation into a number of enclosure Bills has shown that the commissioners seem carefully to have considered all claims and shown reasonable consideration for rights and interests. Irregularity and unfairness were probably not nearly as usual as has been commonly supposed. An examination by W. E. Tate of 171 Nottinghamshire enclosure Bills, passed between 1743 and 1845, suggests that the number of improper awards made 'cannot be more than 16 per cent of the total. By any fair computation it must necessarily have been very much less.'

It has also been alleged that the results of enclosures inevitably fell hardly upon the smallholders, who were therefor forced either to sell the land they had received and become

[1] P. 6.

landless labourers or go to the towns. It is said that the cost of legal charges and of hedging and ditching their new land was more than they could afford. Sometimes the initial expenses were doubtless heavy for them, but they could in these later years of the century get such good prices for their produce that they could probably afford to pay them, and the cost of enclosing their land has been exaggerated by towns-men who have never planted a thorn-hedge. It is also said that the smallholders did not have the experience and capital needed to adopt the new agricultural methods on their holdings. These methods, however, did not need expensive machinery or artificial fertilizers or much additional labour; the average smallholder could manage successfully with the labour of his family and sensible experimenting with crop-rotation, winter-feed and improved breeding standards.

It is, in fact, not true, as a fairly recent writer has stated, that 'the new methods of farming on a large scale tended to extinguish the independent yeoman class, mostly freeholders with 100 acres or less'. Such smallholders had already, since the early eighteenth century, been selling their farms to wealthy landowners who wished to build up large estates and were willing to pay good prices for land. Smallholders continued to do this after enclosures, and others now sold their land because they were attracted into the factory-towns by the wages and opportunities of industry. From their families came such industrial leaders as Jedediah Strutt, John Wilkinson, Abraham Darby and Sir Robert Peel senior.[1] That the yeoman class declined rapidly after enclosures can-not, however, be substantiated. Numbers are difficult to check because many such men, with rising prosperity and social status, began to describe themselves in official docu-ments as 'farmers' and not 'yeomen'. In some parts of the country, such as Derbyshire, Leicestershire, Lincolnshire, Nottinghamshire and Warwickshire, land tax returns seem to show that there was actually an increase in their numbers between 1780 and 1802 after parliamentary enclosures.

There is less evidence about tenant farmers. It is certain that after enclosure landlords raised rents, and it may be that they wished to consolidate small farms into larger holdings. It is likely, however, that the small tenant farmers survived

[1] Pp. 130 f.

I

in larger numbers than has been supposed. Landlords could not always get as many wealthy, large tenant farmers as they wanted, and increased production enabled small tenants to pay good rents, especially during the prosperous war years.

Much the same is probably true of the very small freeholders, cottagers or peasants, possessing three acres or less. Those with valid legal rights to the use of common were compensated with land in enclosure awards, though they might suffer the loss of fuel through the enclosure of wastes and woodlands.[1] At any rate, an investigation of some areas in Suffolk has brought the conclusion that 'the enclosures did not lead immediately to any substantial changes in the proportion of land owned by peasant proprietors'. The poor most seriously affected by the enclosures were the comparatively small class of illegal squatters on common and waste land, who were evicted without compensation through enclosures; they must have had to work as labourers, though at the worst they only exchanged one form of poverty for another.

There is certainly no evidence for the belief that the eviction of numerous small freeholders and tenant farmers as a result of enclosures created a vast new body of landless labourers; but farm labourers, as an important class in the countryside, were a result of the enclosures and the new agricultural methods. Full-time, wage-earning workers were few before the advent of large farms and more intensive agriculture.[2] The new developments did create a growing demand for regular agricultural labourers, but this varied in different parts of the country and was probably not on a large scale until towards the end of the period. Northumberland, for instance, was an area of quite large farms, but at the end of the Napoleonic Wars its average agricultural unit was one employer with $2\frac{3}{4}$ hands to help him. The need for farm labour was doubtless partly supplied by evicted squatters, but much more by the increasing population of these years.

It is, indeed, improbable that enclosures brought about rural depopulation. On the contrary, the population of agricultural villages generally increased. Investigations in Bedfordshire have indicated that 'there is no evidence that eighteenth-century enclosure was accompanied by loss of

[1] P. 123.   [2] P. 26.

population. Indeed, some of it would point to the fact that it was actually increasing a little more quickly in the enclosed than in the open villages.' Nor is this surprising. Enclosures and improved farming and contemporary prosperity enabled such villages to support a larger population and offer it employment. Far from the new industrial towns drawing their population from country-dwellers driven off the land by enclosures, they were rather supplied by the surplus resulting from the increase in population which could not be employed in agriculture even with the greater opportunities brought by the Agrarian Revolution.

It was this rural overpopulation which came to dominate the situation of many villagers by the end of the century. From it and the decline of rural industries – and not enclosures – came underemployment and unemployment and the great increase in the poor-rates. And it was made worse by the depression which followed the ending of the Napoleonic War.[1]

Prosperity and Poverty

The agricultural prosperity of the later eighteenth century brought striking increases in the rent-rolls of landowners.[2] A French traveller in England in 1810 found that some rents had trebled in fifty years and yet farming was prosperous enough to pay them without difficulty. Despite severe wartime taxation on land and growing expenses through the rising cost of living, the nobility strengthened their position in the country during these years. The squirearchy also benefited, having now more money to spend on their manor houses and gardens, and were able to send their sons to the expanding public schools. So too did the clergy. The rise in the value of tithe and glebe enabled them to build new rectories or vicarages with nurseries and wine-cellars, stables and large gardens, which were to present their modern successors with unwelcome problems.

Equally prosperous were the tenant-farmers, especially those who rented a considerable acreage on a long lease, put labour and capital into their farms and adopted the new methods and grew the new crops. The consequence was a new class of farmers, some of whom, at any rate, imitated the

[1] P. 406. [2] P. 22.

way of life of their social superiors. They added rooms to their farm-house – a better bedroom, a dining-room where the farmer and his family took their meals instead of eating with their men in the kitchen, and a parlour with a carpet on the floor and fashionable mahogany furniture in place of the old oak settles. Their wives, instead of themselves making butter, curing bacon and brewing beer, began to content themselves with supervising the performance of such menial tasks by hired servants.

Moreover, the children of such farmers often received a similar education to those of old-established landed families. Their sons were sent away to school and university. Their daughters were fashionably dressed, made to read such books as *Rules of Civility* and *The Ladies' Cabinet* and introduced by governesses or school-mistresses to the same ladylike accomplishments and discipline as the girls in the manor-house. A correspondent in a womens' journal wrote feelingly of a farmer's daughter of sixteen who 'had as many strokes of the rod merely for curtseying too stiffly'; but the upbringing of these girls seems generally to have aroused more expressions of wrath than sympathy. Arthur Young was angered to find 'a pianoforte in a farmer's parlour', 'a post-chaise to carry their daughters to assemblies' and money sometimes paid to educate them 'at expensive boarding schools', while a writer in a magazine found it deplorable that 'instead of dishing butter, feeding poultry or curing bacon, the avocations of these young *ladies* at home are studying dress, attitudes, novels, French and musick'. Apparently the fact that 'the *exhibitions* of girls in the country vie with those in the capital' was an unwelcome indication to some people that the profits of agriculture were giving successful farmers a new outlook and new social inclinations.

The extent to which smallholders and labourers shared in the rural prosperity of these years is more difficult to determine. They were certainly better off in some parts of the country than in others. In the North and the Midlands, where the needs of industry for factory-hands tempted agricultural workers into the towns, farmers had to pay higher wages than were usual in the purely agricultural districts of the South. In other parts of the country, the 'canal mania' of the 1790's also drew men from the land, as did the requirements of the

armed forces during the wars against France.   The removal
of young and able-bodied men from agriculture, at a time
when many farmers needed labourers to increase production,
tended to raise wages wherever it occurred.

In fact, agricultural wages kept closer to rising costs than
those in industry, but since they were often near to subsistence
level many labouring families would have starved if they
had not risen.   Usually agricultural wages improved in
sympathy with the cost of living and by the end of the
Napoleonic Wars had overtaken it.   By 1795, for instance,
the cost of living had risen to 130 per cent of the level of 1790
while agricultural wages were up by 125 per cent, and in 1815
the figures were 150 per cent for living costs and 187 per cent
for agricultural wages, though between 1793 and 1814 there
were seven very poor harvests when living costs exceeded
agricultural wages.

The fact that agricultural wages on an average kept pace
with prices does not, however, tell the whole story.   As
prices rose, farmers abandoned the practice, customary in
some parts of the country, of supplementing wages by payments in kind.   In addition, the enclosure of waste and
woodland brought punishment upon those who tried to
maintain their previous rights to free fuel.   As early as 1764,
for instance, a woman, described as 'an old offender', was
taken from the Clerkenwell Bridewell to Enfield, where she
was publicly whipped at the cart's tail by the common
hangman for cutting wood in Enfield Chase.   Resentment
at this was strong enough in some places to bring about riots
and the pulling down of fences on dark nights.

Resentment was caused also in some parts of the country
by the spread of game-preservation.   This had not seriously
affected the rural poor earlier in the century, in days of
unorganized shooting with primitive guns over largely
unenclosed lands.   With the growth of wealth among the
landed classes, however, shooting habits changed, guns
improved, the massive battue developed, more keepers were
employed, and pheasants were introduced for the first time
on many estates.   Since this occurred at the same time as
farmers were bringing more and more land under the plough,
some country people were deprived disastrously of a traditional means of supplementing their food with wild-fowl or fish.

The result was the encouragement of poaching and the passing of ever more severe Game Laws. The first important Act in 1771 allowed a single Justice of the Peace to punish the killing of game at night by from three to six months imprisonment and a subsequent offence by from six to twelve months and a public whipping, and another Act in 1800 permitted two or more persons convicted of possessing any implement for taking game to be imprisoned for up to two years with whipping. Such penalties encouraged resistance to arrest, and subsequent Acts provided for the transportation of armed poachers, and landowners were allowed to place man-traps and spring-guns in their woods. These measures did not suppress poaching; poachers organized themselves into gangs and fought desperate battles with gamekeepers when surprised. Between 1827 and 1830 there were over 8,500 convictions under the Game Laws, yet many assize juries refused to convict even on the clearest evidence, and informers, 'too well aware of the coldness of pump and pond', hardly existed. Not until, 1831, however, was it recognized that the laws were so harsh as to defeat their own ends, and the more severe penalties were abolished.

By the later years of the eighteenth century, labour was ceasing to be scarce in the countryside, and some parts were beginning to feel the effects of overpopulation. At the same time, the northern textile mills were now increasingly depriving rural families of the chance to supplement the produce of a smallholding or the wage of a labourer by domestic spinning and handloom weaving. Among the rural districts which were most rapidly becoming impoverished were those where a cottage-industry was in decline.

Such an area was Berkshire, affected by both over-population and a decaying textile industry. In 1795 the Justices of the Peace of this county met in the Pelican Inn at Speenhamland, a hamlet now part of Newbury, to consider exercising their powers to fix the wages of labourers under the terms of the Statute of Artificers of 1563, but instead they decided 'to alleviate the distresses of the poor with as little burthen on the occupiers of the land as possible' by supplementing wages from the poor-rates according to a scale which depended upon the price of corn and the size of a labourer's family. Some parishes had already begun as

early as 1783 to make up wages in such a way, but the Speenhamland magistrates drew up a table which could con-
veniently be adopted elsewhere. The Speenhamland System,
as it became known, spread throughout the country until by
1834 it operated in every county except Durham and Northumberland.

In some counties wages were subsidized to a considerable
extent. Arthur Young found in Suffolk in 1801 that a typical
labourer received 9s. in wages and 6s. in poor-relief a week.
The poor-rate had started to rise throughout the country in the
later years of the eighteenth century. Its product increased
from an annual average of £689,000 in 1748–50 to £1,521,000
in 1776 and to £1,912,000 in 1783–5. The general adoption
of the Speeenhamland System made it rise more rapidly. It
reached £4,077,000 in 1803, £6,656,000 in 1812, £5,724,000
in 1815 and £8,000,000 in 1818.

In the summer of 1795 there had been serious riots in
several places, when mobs attacked bakers' shops and seized
foodstuffs, and George Canning held that the Speenhamland
System saved England from the outbreak of widespread
disorder in the middle of the war against France. This may
well have been so, but its long-term consequences were
serious. The smallholder, perhaps working his land with
the help of members of his family, paid his share of the
increased poor-rate together with the larger farmer, who
employed a number of labourers. Farmers could pay low
wages, and their labourers had little inducement to agitate
for an increase or move to districts where there were better
opportunities of employment, since wages would always be
made up to a subsistence level by the parish. It was, in fact,
often more profitable for lazy labourers to be completely
workless and dependent upon the overseers; and the parish
authorities paid the rents of these pauper tenants, whose
landlords also gained since they did not have to pay poor-
rates on such property. These were the consequences of
adopting, practically all over the country, a measure of poor-
relief originally designed to relieve serious need in a county
especially affected by local agrarian and industrial developments.

The burden imposed upon the countryside by the high poor-
rates resulting from the Speenhamland System was borne at

first by a prosperous agriculture. The Revolutionary and Napoleonic Wars, the Continental System and the bad harvests which occurred during these years kept the price of corn high. In 1814, however, circumstances changed. The downfall of Napoleon, the cessation of the blockade and an excellent harvest in 1813 brought about a quick and dramatic decline in the price of corn. By 1815 it had fallen to 63s. 8d. a quarter. The landed classes became alarmed. There had been a great increase in arable farming during the wars, and traces can still be seen in the countryside today of marginal land which was ploughed up in those years. Farmers were now unable to get an economic return for their grain, and landowners feared that their tenants would not be able to pay their rents, even though these were believed to have been reduced by as much as £9,000,000 in 1816. They secured the appointment of a committee of the House of Commons to consider the question.

Following the committee's recommendations, Parliament in 1815 passed an Act forbidding the importation of foreign corn into Britain until the domestic price reached 80s. a quarter. It was believed that this Corn Law would bring to farmers a reasonable and steady profit for their crops, but it did not do so. Too many farmers were attracted by the return promised in the measure, and the result was over-production of corn. At first bad harvests made it appear as if the legislation had succeeded. The price of corn rose to 76s. 2d. in 1816 and 94s. 0d. in 1817, but then began to fall again until it was only 43s. 3d. in 1822. Many farmers, who had borrowed heavily to buy land at inflated war prices, were ruined.

After declining for five years, corn prices began to recover somewhat, becoming as high as 66s. 6d. in 1825, but this still did not approach the figure expected from the Corn Law. There was a further fall in rents, and the landed classes again agitated for parliamentary action. So in 1828 the Corn Law was modified; prohibition was replaced by a sliding scale of duty. When the price of corn was less than 62s. a quarter, imported corn was to pay a duty of 25s. 8d. a quarter. Every rise of a shilling in the price was to be accompanied by a reduction of a shilling in the duty, but when corn reached the price of 73s., it could be imported at a nominal duty of only a shilling. It was hoped that this change would check the price-fluctuations which had taken place ever since the Corn Law had been passed, but since these fluctuations depended upon the chances of the harvest, the new system of protection had no remarkable effect. During the next five years the price varied between 58s. 6d. and 66s. 4d., and then a series of good harvests from 1832 to 1835 kept it low. Corn production increased by $5\frac{1}{2}$ million quarters, and up to 1840 imported foreign corn only amounted to a fifteenth of the total amount consumed in Britain. The agitation for the repeal of the Corn Law did not seriously revive until the successive years of bad harvests and industrial depression which occurred from 1836 onwards.

The condition of British agriculture remained an important national problem because as late as 1830 about half the population still depended for its livelihood upon rural occupations, between a quarter and a third of the families being returned as engaged in agriculture. About five-sevenths of these were the families of labourers, and rather less than half of the remainder were those of occupiers who hired no labour. The increase in the number of agricultural labourers, which had occurred by now, produced in the countryside, as Elie Halévy observed, 'two separate classes whose interests were totally distinct and discordant – on the one side the landowners and farmers who wanted their produce to be dear and wages cheap; on the other the labourers who wanted high wages and cheap bread'.

A rise in the price of corn, therefore, meant distress and discontent among the agricultural labourers. Moreover, the situation was made worse by post-war economic difficulties and unemployment.[1] And in the years of peace, agricultural output was increased to keep pace with the demands of the substantially growing population by better farming methods which low prices led farmers to adopt in preference to employing more labour. Employment did not increase sufficiently to absorb the growth in rural population. There was a serious, though often mainly seasonal, surplus of labour. This was most serious in the south-eastern counties, where there were no possibilities of alternative employment in industrial towns, and where there was considerable use

[1] P. 406.

made of threshing machines, which meant that farmers could stand off men longer during the winter when their need for food, fuel and clothing was greatest. The diet of most labouring families in this area was bread and cheese for six out of seven days of the week, though some labourers kept a pig, and many had smallholdings; the widespread cultivation of potatoes did not begin until the 1820's.

Consequently this area suffered recurrent spells of winter unemployment which produced agrarian disturbances. The high prices of 1816 led to rural rioting here, which spread to parts of East Anglia. The rioters burnt ricks and houses and damaged threshing machines and demanded higher wages and laws fixing the price of bread and flour. Around Ely they armed themselves with sticks and iron spikes and threatened to march on London with a flag inscribed 'Bread or Blood!' After much property had been destroyed, the disturbances were suppressed by the yeomanry with some loss of life. Five rioters were hanged, nine transported and ten imprisoned.

Food prices did begin to fall and round about 1822 reached the level of about 1790. Dr. Clapham has estimated that over the country as a whole the farm-labourer was slightly better off by the 1820's than he had been before the Revolutionary and Napoleonic Wars. At the beginning of hostilities in 1793, a common agricultural wage was 9s. a week in the south and 8s. in the north. By now after various fluctuations during the wars and after, it stood at 11s. or 12s. in most parts of the country, while the cost of living was less than 10 per cent higher than in the pre-war period

Yet there were areas in the eastern and southern counties where agricultural wages had fallen to the pre-war level of 8s. or 9s. and changed little until after 1834. It was in these counties that the poor-rate was most freely used to supplement wages under the continued operation of the Speenhamland System, and in the later 1820's many justices and parish officials made efforts to keep down the rates. The families of labourers were given doles of potatoes and oatmeal instead of money to spend on wheaten flour; the girls were set to work to gain a few shillings by making lace. Farmers refused to raise wages, and some even tried to reduce them, while others changed from corn-growing to pastural farming, which required fewer labourers and might bring better returns.

The failure of the harvest of 1830 finally brought about in the agricultural districts of southern England during the winter months the disturbances which J. L. and Barbara Hammond have described as the 'last labourers' revolt'. It was a spontaneous, unorganized movement which spread rapidly from Kent to Dorset. The labourers demanded higher wages or assured Poor Law allowances. Again stacks were fired and agricultural machinery smashed, but personal violence rarely went beyond the ducking of harsh overseers of the poor in village ponds. The new Whig government acted with severity. Nine rioters were hanged (six of them for arson), 457 were transported (nearly 200 for life) and almost as many imprisoned for varying terms, though the only death had been that of a man killed by the yeomanry. The ministry, though now actively pursuing its measures of parliamentary reform, refused to consider any positive measures to relieve distress.

The situation of English agriculture was still difficult at the end of the Hanoverian period. The early prosperity accompanying the Agrarian Revolution had disappeared with the end of hostilities against France, but improvement was at hand. Before the end of the period, the Poor Law Amendment Act of 1834 made things easier for farmers.[1] And so did the Tithe Commutation Act of 1836. Soon more potent factors were to take effect. The new railways were to link the growing towns with the countryside. An increasing population and rising standard of living were to bring an expanding home market not yet open to rival foreign or colonial producers. To the demand for wheat was added a growing demand for meat and dairy produce. The result was a prosperity which was unaffected by the repeal of the Corn Law in 1846 and which made the middle years of the century the 'golden age of English farming'.

[1] P. 439.

VII · THE INDUSTRIAL REVOLUTION

The Economic and Social Background

THE same period of the eighteenth century which brought in
the Agrarian Revolution saw also the beginnings in England
of the Industrial Revolution, a term coined in 1837 by the
French economist, Auguste Blanqui, to denote the fundamental economic changes occurring in the economic life of
the country during these years. As with the Agrarian
Revolution, the speed with which these changes took place
has perhaps been exaggerated. Professor Nef has argued that
it should be regarded as effectively beginning not in 1760,
the traditional date, but rather in 1780. It is true that there
were few large towns in England until well into the nineteenth century and that the composition of the population
changed only slowly.[1] It is true also that it was not until the
second quarter of the nineteenth century that industrial
change began markedly on the north-east coast of England
and made it into one of the chief centres of economic power
in the country. Nevertheless, the term probably describes
more accurately industrial development in England than the
Agrarian Revolution does agricultural development. Once
industrialization had begun, development was more rapid
here than in agriculture, and inventions and improvements
had a more revolutionary effect.

Moreover, while English farmers were not pioneers of
agricultural change, English inventors and manufacturers
were so in the matter of industrial innovations, and industrial
development enjoyed a great initial advantage in England.
By 1830, it has been calculated, Britain was producing three-
quarters of Europe's mined coal, half of Europe's cotton goods
and iron and most of Europe's steam engines.

That the Industrial Revolution started earlier in England
than in the rest of Europe was due partly to a number of
economic circumstances. The country possessed abundant
coalfields associated with easily-mined deposits of iron ore.

---

[1] Pp. 7–8.

It also possessed a long and deeply-indented coastline, affording numerous excellent harbours which permitted the growth of great ports, especially as many of the inlets penetrated into rich and fertile parts of the country, and there were no mountain barriers to hinder communication with the interior. Such navigable inlets and good harbours made the country's rivers commercially important, and further they were not subject to serious floods and were rarely frozen. Moreover, the fact that most of the longest English rivers flowed eastwards was a fortunate economic factor since their mouths faced the great river outlets of the Continent.

England's early industrial pre-eminence was also due to political and social circumstances. Since the Glorious Revolution of 1688, the country had enjoyed political stability and religious toleration. It took advantage of the security of its island position to establish the naval power which protected it from invasion and obtained overseas colonies. It had not inherited crippling internal customs barriers and medieval economic restrictions, and its people were ready to invest in new commercial and industrial undertakings. Its society was open. Merchants could enter the ranks of the nobility.[1] Such social mobility encouraged money-making. Effort was possible and rewarded. Capital could be concentrated in the right places through the development of a sound banking-system by the middle of the century. Its wars stimulated the making of munitions, and expanding overseas trade demanded an increasing variety and number of manufactured goods, as also did the growing population and rising standard of living. The scientific movement of the seventeenth and eighteenth centuries in England produced results which were of important practical application in industry.

In other European countries at this time some of these economic and social circumstances were present, but in England alone did they combine to such effect. For instance, it seems that until well after the Treaty of Paris of 1763 the output of some of the large French industries, especially iron and cotton, was greater than that of their English rivals. This might be expected, indeed, when the population of France was three or four times the size of that of England; but these French industries could not expand in a country where

[1] P. 23.

most manufacturers were still organized in a system of guilds, which were hostile to initiative and technical improvements, and where the *bourgeoisie* invested their capital in hereditary legal and administrative posts rather than in trade and industry.   Consequently England was able to overtake France and establish an absolute supremacy in industrialization which she maintained well into the nineteenth century until overtaken herself by Germany and the United States of America.

An early aspect of the Industrial Revolution in England was the invention of new techniques to meet contemporary requirements, such as, for instance, the smelting of iron with coke.   Other early improvements took the form of mechanical inventions which were mainly labour-saving devices demanded by the limited skilled or semi-skilled labour force then available to manufacturers.   These devices were evolved notably in the textile industry.   Later inventions still further increased manufacturing production by utilizing new forms of power.   In the same year, 1769, Arkwright gave the water-frame to the cotton industry and Watt patented his steam-engine.   Finally, the development of machinery and new forms of power led to the growth of the factory-system with its serious social problems.   And all this was accomplished and made possible by a corresponding development of transport.   'The Industrial Revolution', Professor Meredith has said, 'was the work of a mere handful of men.   Some ten or twelve individuals revolutionized or created each of a number of great industries.'

Iron, Coal and Steam

In writing about the Industrial Revolution in England, Jacquetta Hawkes took as its starting-point 'the time about two hundred years ago, when men began to smelt iron with coke'.   At the beginning of the eighteenth century, the iron industry was dispersed in a number of areas, East Sussex being an important one and the Forest of Dean another.   The location of these areas was determined by the presence not only of iron ore but also of trees and running-water.   The industry had to be situated near to woodland since it used charcoal for smelting – about an acre of timber being needed to make sufficient charcoal to produce two tons of pig iron. It also needed to be situated on running-water to provide the power to work both the bellows of the blast-furnaces and the trip-hammers of the forges. Hence many ironworks were to be found along the Rother, Cuckmere, Severn and other rivers.

At this time the iron industry was largely stagnant. This was due not so much to the exhaustion of the forests as to the high costs of operating small, scattered ironworks which might have to bring their ore from a long distance. The War of Jenkins's Ear, however, increased the demand for iron and so stimulated efforts to find a means of using coal for smelting without its sulphurous fumes making the iron impure and brittle. As early as 1709 Abraham Darby (1677-1717) at Coalbrookdale used coke instead of charcoal in his blast-furnace, and his method was improved by his son, Abraham Darby II (1711-63), but it was not widely adopted outside Shropshire in the first half of the century.

During the 1760's, however, smelting with coke became usual, and the industry began an expansion which again was stimulated by the renewal of hostilities in the Seven Years' War. With the restoration of peace in 1763, fresh demands enabled the industry to continue its growth by producing cylinders and engine-parts for manufacturers, fire-grates and pots and pans for domestic needs and wagon-way rails for transport. The capabilities of the industry were further increased by the provision of an improved blast for the furnace such as was achieved at Coalbrookdale by the installation of a Newcomen engine.[1] The number of blast-furnaces steadily increased in England – from under 20 in 1760 to over 80 by 1790, and from 177 in 1805 to 372 in 1830, In 1797 England became, for the first time, an exporter of iron; by 1812 exports exceeded imports, and from 1800 to 1850 about 20 per cent of the pig-iron produced in England was exported.

The improvements in smelting no longer made it necessary for the iron industry to be dispersed among woods and beside rivers. Now it gradually concentrated itself among the coal-fields. The last Sussex furnace closed at Ashburnham in 1825; and by then the industry was largely established in the Midlands, Yorkshire, Derbyshire, South Wales and the Scottish Lowlands. Among the great ironmasters of this period was

[1] P. 136.

John Wilkinson (1728–1808), who established the first furnace
to produce coke-smelted iron in the Black Country at Bradley
in 1757 and invented a more accurate way of boring cannon
in 1774; he executed large government orders for cannon
and shot, supplied miles of cast-iron pipes for the water-
supplies of Paris and New York and insisted that when he
died he should be buried in an iron coffin beneath an iron
obelisk.   Another was John Roebuck, who had received a
medical education and previously discovered an improved
way of making sulphuric acid.[1]   In 1759 he set up the Carron
Ironworks in Stirlingshire, which used the local coal and iron
ore and before the end of the century had become the greatest
munition works in Europe; its carronades – short cannon of
large bore – being particularly celebrated.   An early sign
of the success of the new industry was the erection of the first
permanent cast-iron bridge over the Severn at Ironbridge
near Coalbrookdale in 1779 by Abraham Darby III (1750–91)
and Wilkinson.

The mounting expansion of the iron industry in the later
eighteenth century was made possible by another invention.
The coke-operated blast-furnaces still made pig-iron or cast-
iron, which contained carbon and was brittle.   The new
machine age increasingly required wrought or malleable
iron, capable of taking greater stresses and strains, but to
make this the iron had to be heated with charcoal and
hammered in the forges to remove impurities, which was a
long and costly process.   The problem was solved by Henry
Cort (1740–1800), a naval contractor and an ironmaster of
Fontley in Hampshire, who in 1794 patented his puddling
process which by using coke in a reverberatory furnace
produced wrought iron fifteen times as quickly as before; he
also invented grooved rollers to change ingots of wrought iron
quickly and cheaply into usable bars and sheets.

The iron industry could now achieve further concentration
and large-scale production.   In the middle of the century,
the annual output of pig-iron was only about 18,000 tons; it
increased to about 68,000 tons in 1788, to 125,400 tons in 1796,
to 250,000 tons in 1806 and to 678,000 tons in 1830.   By the
end of the century coke had completely superseded charcoal
in making wrought iron, the export of which from Britain

[1] P. 91.

quadrupled between 1806 and 1832. Elsewhere in Europe
and in America small charcoal furnaces continued to operate
until the middle of the nineteenth century. Britain had thus
inaugurated the new age of iron production at least half a
century earlier than the rest of the world.

An important result of this was that, at the end of the century, England also had a pre-eminence in skilled work in
metal which produced a new group of engineers who designed
machine-tools. Two of the most ingenious pioneers were
Joseph Bramah (1748–1814), the 'universal inventor' of
patent locks, the beer-engine, the water-closet and, for
industry, the hydraulic press, and Henry Maudslay (1771–
1831), who invented the screw-cutting lathe and the slide-
rest. Among Maudslay's pupils were Joseph Whitworth
(1803–87), who was to construct a measuring-machine by
which was elaborated his system of measures and gauges, and
James Nasmyth, inventor of the steam-hammer in 1839. The
importance of such machine-tools was their precision and
delicacy, mechanical operation and ability to ensure the rapid,
and therefore cheap, production of machines.

The new iron age was also the coal age, for the demands of
the iron industry did much to expand coal-mining. At the
beginning of the eighteenth century, the coal industry was
already important, and pit-shafts of over 200 feet in depth
and large underground galleries were already known.
Ability to send coal by sea to London made the Northumberland and Durham coalfields the largest and most productive.
Coal was used for domestic purposes, brewing and distilling,
smelting and casting brass, making bricks and tiles and
manufacturing glass, nails, hardware and cutlery. Wartime
and industrial needs led to a great growth of coal-mining,
and coalfields in Yorkshire, the Midlands, South Wales and
Scotland became more important. Coal production rose
from about 2,500,000 tons in 1700 and 4,750,000 tons in 1750
to over 10,000,000 tons in 1800 and 16,00,0000 tons in 1829.

Such an increase came about not only through greater
demand, but also through the solving of technical problems in
the mines, which had prevented deeper shafts and more
extensive workings. One was the danger from the explosive
gas, fire-damp; this was overcome by the safety lamp of Sir
Humphry Davy in 1815. Another was the need for

K

improved means of conveying the coal to the surface, which
was achieved in the later part of this period by the introduction
of pit-ponies, iron-rails and winding-machines. The further
difficulty of transporting the coal from the mines to its
markets was solved by the construction of wagon-ways and
canals.[1]

Perhaps the most intractable problem facing the mines,
however, was the danger of flooding. Thomas Savery (1650?–
1715), a military engineer, patented in 1698 a machine for
raising water by the use of steam; the water was sucked up by
creating a vacuum through condensing steam in an enclosed
vessel. Savery entered into partnership with Thomas
Newcomen (1663–1729), who in 1708 replaced his machine –
which was never very successful – by an atmospheric steam-
engine in which steam, injected into a cylinder, was con-
densed to make a vacuum so that atmospheric pressure forced
the piston down, and then a fresh injection of steam forced
it up again. The upright piston was attached to a pivoted
beam, the other end of which was attached to a pump. It
could raise fifty gallons of water a minute from a depth of 156
feet, making it possible to work seams in and below the
watery layers and so considerably increase coal output.
By 1765 there were a hundred Newcomen engines draining
mines in the north-east of England alone. Later it was also
used to feed reservoirs and to blow the hot air into blast-
furnaces, while at Boulton's works in Birmingham and
Wedgwood's pottery in North Staffordshire it was employed
to pump back water that turned the water-wheel operating
the machinery.

The Newcomen engine, however, had three serious defects.
It wasted fuel lavishly (though this did not matter much in a
coalmine) because the cylinder was alternately heated by the
injection of steam and cooled with cold water to create a
vacuum; it was limited to an up-and-down motion; and it used
steam pressure to drive the piston only in one direction.
These defects were all remedied by James Watt (1736–1819).
He realized the advantage of adding a separate condenser to
the engine in 1765.[2] Watt first worked with Roebuck at the
Carron Ironworks and after 1774 more successfully with
Matthew Boulton (1728–1809) at his Soho Ironworks, near

[1] Pp. 149, 152.   [2] P. 91.

Birmingham, where craftsmen, trained to make ornamental hardware, could make the delicate valves he needed, and Wilkinson's method of boring cannon at nearby Bradley gave him accurate cylinders. The new engine was four times more powerful than that of Newcomen, but it was still practically limited to operating pumps. Watt went on to make his engine a universal source of power in 1781 by fitting a crank-shaft and cogwheel to the piston which gave it a rotary movement, capable of turning machinery; and the next year he made it into a double-acting steam-engine in which steam was admitted alternately on each side of the piston with further economy of fuel and greater speed of rotary action. A Boulton and Watt engine, installed at the Whitbread brewery in London in 1785, to pump water from the brewery well and drive the barley mills, replaced for £1,000 and a bushel of coal an hour 24 horses costing £916 a year to keep. By 1800 some five hundred of these engines were operating in mines, ironworks and cotton-mills.

'I shall never forget Mr. Boulton's expression to me, "I sell here, sir, what all the world desires to have – *power*"', so wrote James Boswell on his visit to the Soho factory. The steam-engine, indeed, brought two advantages essential to industrial development: it provided sufficient power to work every type of manufacturing machinery, and it freed factories from the restriction of location dictated by reliance upon water-power. The coming of the steam-engine was stimulated by the demands of the coal industry, but at the same time it would not itself have been achieved without the resources of the coal and iron industries with which its evolution was so closely connected. Not only did its general manufacture and adoption depend upon the increasing output of coal-mines and ironworks; the initial exploitation of Watt's inventions was only made possible by the accurate iron-casting at Soho and Bradley and by the business acumen and organizing ability of Boulton. 'It would not be worth my while', said Boulton, 'to make for three counties only; but I find it worth my while to make for the world.'

The Textile Industries

At the beginning of the eighteenth century, the greatest English industry, next to agriculture, was still the woollen trade. Cloth had been England's major export since the sixteenth century, and from 1720 to 1760 this grew by about a third in amount. The greater demand for wool, coinciding with improvements in inland transport, assisted the competitive advantages of districts where production could be made most efficient. The Cotswolds, Wiltshire and East Anglia were overtaken by the West Riding, which could benefit from the proximity of water for fulling, dyeing, and, later, power, and added a larger worsted manufacture to its range of cloth. During these years the English woollen industry became increasingly concentrated and specialized in the Pennine villages of this part of Yorkshire, which by 1760 produced almost half England's exports of woollen cloth of every type.

By then, however, the industry was facing growing encroachments upon its products from neighbouring Lancashire where the small cotton industry developed spectacularly during the eighteenth century into Britain's greatest exporting business. This industry had been established in England by Flemish refugees during Elizabeth I's reign, importing raw cotton first from the Levant and then from the West Indies. At first the English industry produced a coarse cloth called fustian, a mixture of cotton and linen. When feminine demand required pure cottons, calicoes and muslins, these were brought from India, but the woollen manufacturers induced Parliament to prohibit these imports in 1701 and 1721. This had the unintended result of affording the English cotton-spinners, weavers and calico-printers a protection which enabled them to become increasingly serious rivals to the older textile industry. Pure cotton goods began to come from the looms for the home market, while the growth of the slave trade provided a further stimulus since cloth went to pay for African slaves and was sold to clothe them on the plantations.[1] Imports of raw cotton, which had averaged just over 1,000,000 lb. a year between 1698 and 1710, rose to over 1,540,000 lb. in 1730, to over 3,870,000 lb. in 1764 and to over 56,000,000 lb. in 1801. The value of cotton goods exported rose from £23,000 in 1701 to £46,000 in 1751 and to £7,050,000 in 1801.

The rapid progress of the cotton industry was largely

[1] P. 155.

accomplished by a series of inventions which accelerated production. The slowness of the old ways of spinning and weaving was overcome by new devices and machines made possible by the development of the iron industry. The first important invention of the century applied to weaving. In 1733 John Kay (d. 1764) devised the fly-shuttle by which the weaver could jerk the shuttle across the loom and back again using one hand only. The speed of weaving was doubled; and a single weaver could make cloths of any width whereas previously two men had sat together at a loom to make broad cloths.

Kay's invention, however, caused a growing shortage of cotton thread since four spinners were now needed to supply one weaver with sufficient thread. A similar mechanical aid to spinning came in 1764 when James Hargreaves (c. 1745–78), a Lancashire spinner, invented the spinning-jenny. This was a spinning-frame containing a number of revolving spindles worked by one spinner, who might only be a child. The first spinning-jenny had eight spindles, but this was soon extended to sixteen and finally to 120. By 1788 there were some 20,000 spinning-jennies in operation in England.

The devices of Kay and Hargreaves were both hand-operated, but in 1769 the water-frame, a spinning-frame worked by water-power, was invented by Richard Arkwright (1732–92) who entered into partnership with another inventor, Jedediah Strutt (1726–97). Though the water-frame spun a stronger thread than had ever been possible before, it could not produce fine thread, which still had to be hand-spun. In 1779, however, Samuel Crompton (1753–1827) combined the principles of the spinning-jenny and the water-frame in his spinning-mule. This was at first worked by a water-wheel, but later by a steam-engine. It could produce fine threads and made possible the popularity of costumes of new materials among fashionable ladies.[1]

By now the balance between spinning and weaving had been reversed. Thread could now be produced more rapidly than it could be used. A period of prosperity began for the hand-loom weavers. The processes of weaving being more complicated than those of spinning, the first power-loom was not devised until 1785. Its inventor was a Leicestershire

[1] P. 30.

clergyman, Edmund Cartwright (1743–1823). It remained, however, a clumsy machine until improved early in the nineteenth century by William Radcliffe and John Horrocks. The improved power-loom had ten times the capacity of a hand-loom, but by then there were enough weavers to deal with the supply of thread, so it was not at first extensively employed. Even in 1813 it was estimated that there were not more than 2,400 power-looms in Britain as against nearly a hundred times as many hand-looms. After the Napoleonic War, however, power-looms were introduced more rapidly. There were about 14,000 by 1820 and about 100,000 by 1833. At the end of the Hanoverian period the hand-loom weavers were facing acute unemployment and distress.

The adoption of machinery was much less rapid in the woollen industry. The spinning-jenny was not generally used until about 1785, and in 1837 the power-loom was still exceptional. This was partly because wool was too breakable for the machines. Also, while the invention of the cotton gin by Eli Whitney in 1793 made possible a large supply of fibre from the southern plantations of the United States of America for the Lancashire mills, not until after 1815 did the Australian sheep-farms provide similar quantities of wool. Again, the ancient industry was restricted by past government controls and strong traditions, the woollen workers were better able to resist change, and past prosperity tended to make employers conservative. Finally, the demand for woollen cloths, at home and abroad, was less elastic than for calicoes and muslins, and wealthy people were discarding woollen underclothing for the lighter cotton.

Consequently, the woollen industry continued throughout the Hanoverian period to be conducted according to the old domestic system, in which a capitalist middleman, the clothier, purchased the raw wool, distributed it to the spinners and weavers, who worked in their own homes, and marketed the finished cloth. The slow introduction of machinery and power into the industry resulted in the survival of this semi-independent organization in many villages until well into the nineteenth century. As late as 1856, only about a half of those employed in the Yorkshire woollen industry worked in factories.

The decline of a similar domestic organization in the cotton industry was more rapid, particularly in spinning. The spinning-jenny devised by Hargreaves was used in the spinner's home, but the machines of Arkwright and Compton required power which could not easily be supplied under domestic conditions. Accordingly, there came into being factories, which were more profitable and made the fortunes of a new class of factory-owners. This process was assisted by previous developments in the silk-industry. In 1721 John Lombe had built on the River Derwent near Derby a five-storied, stone-built silk-mill in which the silk-throwing machinery was driven by water-power and tended by women and children. The silk-industry was comparatively small, and by 1765 there were only seven such mills in England, but they served as a model for enterprising cotton-spinners.

One of the first of these was Arkwright himself, who established a spinning-mill, modelled on Lombe's mill, in 1771 at Cromford, also on the River Derwent, and owned eight other mills when he died in 1792. Others were ready to follow his example. 'We all looked up to him', said the first Sir Robert Peel, the wealthiest of these early cotton-spinners. By 1788 there were forty-one spinning-mills in South Lancashire. Most of these first mills relied upon water-power and were, therefore, built by the side of swift-flowing Pennine streams; but from 1785 steam-power drove the mules, and factories could be built in towns. While there were only two cotton-mills in the Manchester district in 1782, ten years later there were fifty-two, each employing about 300 workers. By 1811 four-fifths of the cotton goods manufactured in Lancashire were made of mule-yarn, mostly spun in urban mills. Weaving remained a domestic industry longer, but from about 1820 it became common for cotton-spinners to add weaving-sheds, containing power-looms, to their mills.

The Factory System

Although the textile industries, as originally organized, had been the classic and largest example of the domestic system, other industries were also managed along these lines. For instance, in the Midland nail industry the capitalist allocated pig-iron to families who turned it into nails for him in their small domestic workshops, and a similar arrangement prevailed in pottery. At the same time, there were industries which, through their very nature or the cost of operative equipment, could not be conducted according to the domestic system, such as ship-building, coal-mining, paper-making, sugar-refining, iron-making or cloth-finishing. Many of these establishments were small and rural rather than urban, but they represented an embryonic factory system since they required their workers to perform the different processes of an industry in one place.

The effect of the new processes, machines and forms of power in the eighteenth century was to hasten this progress in a number of industries, whether they had originally dispersed or concentrated their production. The new inventions required capital equipment beyond the resources of small-scale or domestic operation. The capital of the Carron Ironworks rose from £12,000 in 1760 to £150,000 in 1771. Such investment required an equally rapid increase in the unit of production. Early in the century the largest Shropshire iron-furnace produced 500 tons a year and the smallest 200 tons, but in 1788 the average output was 1,100 tons which rose to about 1,500 tons in 1796 and 1,900 tons in 1806. The concentration of production became more rapid with the use of a water-wheel or steam-engine moving an axle to operate by means of gear wheels or belts all the machines engaged in the various processes of manufacture. A pioneer of this development was Josiah Wedgwood (1730–95), who founded in 1769 his great Etruria pottery works in Staffordshire, which used a steam-engine to run the lathes and employed no less than ten thousand workers in a well-planned division of labour, when Arthur Young visited it some years later. In adopting the factory system and developing large units of production, however, the cotton industry was easily pre-eminent. By the end of the Hanoverian period, it was still true to say, in H. Heaton's words, 'cotton was a lonely hare in a world of tortoises'.

The cotton-mills also displayed most markedly the contrasts in working conditions between the old and the new organization of industry. Under the domestic system, the spinners and weavers, working in their own cottages, had been able to determine for themselves their hours and conditions of work, but the mill-owners quickly developed a rigid system of industrial discipline. Hours were long and holidays few.

There were fines for lateness, talking at work or even opening a window. The machines were noisy, and the atmosphere of the mills was kept hot and moist to prevent the cotton threads snapping when stretched. It was the need to submit to this new discipline and working conditions that the first generation of factory-workers found especially hard.

Another feature of the cotton-mills was their employment of large numbers of women and children because they were more docile, their wages were lower, and their nimble fingers and shorter stature enabled them to undertake delicate threading tasks among the machinery. In 1816 the mills of Manchester employed twice as many women as men and almost as many children as adults. Earlier than that the proportion of children was even higher for the first cotton-mills, depending on water-power, were built by streams in the Lancashire moors where little local labour was available. The mill-owners, therefore, made use of pauper apprentices, whom they could have from the parish authorities.[1] To these first mills thousands of pauper children were sent by wagon or barge from London and other large towns to be fed, clothed and lodged in apprentice-houses by their employers. The later cotton-mills, which used steam-power and were established in towns, employed the labour of 'free' women and children which was cheaper since they could be discharged when trade was bad.

The conditions under which women and children were employed in the mills provided factory reformers with their first cause. Their hours of work were rarely shorter than those of the men; children of seven years or younger commonly worked from twelve to eighteen hours a day. Discipline was imposed upon them by physical punishment; overseers frequently kept both young women and children at their tasks with a strap, cane, or thin, wooden billy-roller from a spinning-machine. Yet the first factory reformers were slow in getting support for their campaign. It had long been generally accepted that poor children should be set to work as soon as possible. Young children were 'inured to labour' in charity schools and workhouses and apprenticed under the domestic system or employed by their parents – and, said a contemporary, 'their parents were the hardest of task-masters'. Child labour was common in old-established

[1] P. 37.

industries and farming.   In Midland brickyards little girls each caught and threw fifteen tons of bricks between six in the morning and eight at night; and in the eastern counties boys and girls between five and sixteen years old were hired by their parents in pot-houses to 'undertakers', who employed them in agricultural gangs on such tasks as weeding or cutting thistles in the corn under the stick or whip of a foreman.   The cotton industry inherited this tradition, and, moreover, the overseers in the mills were themselves operatives, whose brutality was a reflection of that commonly suffered by wives and children in lower-class homes.   'Much cruelty is daily practised in many a cottage,' stated the Factory Commission of 1833, 'which is not unfit to rank even with the strap and billy-roller.'

There were instances in which mill-children (and mill-hands generally) were better treated by many individual employers.   As early as 1780 the mill built by Samuel Oldknow at Mellor had a pleasant and well-designed apprentice-house where the children were kindly treated, well fed and taught.   David Dale (1739–1806), who built a mill at New Lanark in conjunction with Arkwright, erected cottages for his work-people, employed children only from the age of ten and limited their working-day to ten hours.   The mill was taken over by Robert Owen (1771–1858), who married Dale's daughter and continued his policy, making a show-place of both factory and village, which included the first infant school in the kingdom.   From 1817 Owen became interested in social experiments, which included model villages (nicknamed 'Owen's Parallelograms'), communist colonies in America, co-operative societies and labour exchanges.   These were mostly failures and consumed much of his fortune.   His last great experiment and failure was the Grand National Consolidated Trades Union of 1834.[1]

The first attempt at factory legislation was due to the first Sir Robert Peel (1750–1830), himself a large employer of child-labour, who secured the passing of the Health and Morals of Apprentices Act of 1802, which limited the working-day of pauper-apprentices in cotton-mills to twelve hours, forbade night work and required them to receive daily instruction.[2]   By then, however, with the growth of steam-

[1] Pp. 441–2.   [2] P. 37.

powered mills in towns, the employment of pauper children was declining, and Owen persuaded Peel to promote the Cotton Factory Act of 1819, which applied to all children working in mills, forbidding their employment below the age of nine and limiting the working day of those between nine and sixteen to ten-and-a-half hours. The enforcement of both these acts, however, was assigned to the Justices of the Peace, and this did much to make them ineffective, for in many of the manufacturing areas the magistrates and their parish subordinates were incapable of regulating the vast new mills.

Some years later, the Factory Act of 1833, passed largely through Lord Shaftesbury's efforts, limited the labour of children in textile mills between nine and thirteen years old to 48 hours a week or not more than 9 a day and of those under eighteen to 68 a week or not more than 12 a day. The appointment of four factory-inspectors under the measure ensured that it was at least partially effective, and after the registration of births, marriages and deaths was introduced in 1836, enforcement was made easier.

Improvements in Transport

Neither the development of the factory system nor the growth of large towns which went with it would have been possible in England without very considerable improvements in transport. Until 1750 most English trade was sea-borne since good roads were few and navigable rivers mostly short. The best way of transporting goods on land was by pack-horses, which travelled, sometimes more than a hundred in a line, on stone causeways laid alongside or down the middle of highways, and the best way for travellers making long journeys was to use relays of post-horses.

An Act of Parliament of 1555 (which was not repealed until 1835) ordered each parish to maintain its own roads, and in 1654 magistrates were empowered to make local assessments and hire labour; but this obligation was perfunctorily observed. Although coaches and wagons were growing in number, wheeled traffic remained difficult and dangerous during much of the eighteenth century. Vehicles commonly had to go along open fields beside the roads to avoid stretches of mud and ruts and pot-holes. At the beginning of the century it usually took three weeks to do the four hundred miles by post-chaise from London to Edinburgh.   When the future Emperor Charles VI came to England to visit the Duke of Somerset in 1703, his coach capsized a dozen times before he reached Petworth; and in 1739 George II and Queen Caroline once spent a whole night going from Kew to St. James's during which they were overturned in their coach near where Chelsea Football Ground now is.

Efforts had begun in the later seventeenth century to introduce improvements in road administration by turnpike trusts.   The first Turnpike Act of 1663 empowered the justices of several counties to set up turnpikes and charge tolls on roads for traffic improvements.   Local companies secured as turnpike trusts similar control over short stretches of road through private acts of Parliament from the early eighteenth century.   Such trusts increased rapidly from 1750 to 1770, when some eleven hundred trusts levied tolls over 21,000 miles of roads, and a General Turnpike Act in 1773 made their establishment easier.   Though only covering a minority of the highways with greatly varying efficiency and mostly in debt, they had by the later years of the eighteenth century linked the larger towns with usable roads.   The many pleasant toll-houses, with their large windows looking each way along the highway, survive as reminders of those days.

The turnpike trusts made possible improvements in road-building by employing great highway engineers who replaced the old horse-tracks by something like modern roads.   Among the pioneers was John Metcalf (1717–1810), commonly known as 'Blind Jack of Knaresborough', who despite his infirmity constructed about 180 miles of turnpike road in Yorkshire and Lancashire.   Later came John Macadam (1756–1836), Surveyor-General to the London turnpikes and inventor of the road surface, composed of a tight mixture of broken stones, sand and water, which still bears his name, and Thomas Telford (1757–1834), who built many miles of roads and numerous bridges.   Bridge-building, indeed, was another feature of this period.   To the historic London Bridge was added, in 1750, Westminster Bridge, so often depicted under construction by Canaletto, and by the end of the Hanoverian age London had four more bridges.   Two of them (and the rebuilt London Bridge) were by John

Rennie (1760–1821), who built many masonry bridges, while Telford's favourite undertakings were his iron bridges, the best-known being the suspension bridge carrying his London to Holyhead road over the Menai Straits.

The most striking effect of these improvements was to make passenger transport by road much faster and more pleasant. Dr. Johnson told Boswell that if he had no duties he would spend his life 'in driving briskly in a post-chaise with an amiable woman'. In the middle years of the century, stage-coaches, which ran regularly between fixed stages (usually inns) appeared on the roads. Such coaches took two days from London to Bristol and between ten and twelve days from London to Edinburgh. In 1782, John Palmer, who managed the theatres at Bristol and Bath, suggested to Pitt that the Post Office should use specially-designed coaches to carry the mail faster than the post-boys on horseback who had done it since Charles I's proclamation of 1635 inaugurating the General Post Office. In August 1784 the first of these new coaches, carrying mail and passengers, left Bristol at 4 o'clock in the afternoon and fulfilled its schedule for the 119 miles journey by reaching London at 8 o'clock the next morning. Next summer mail-coaches were running from London to Leeds, Liverpool, Manchester and Nottingham and by the autumn to Birmingham, Carlisle, Dover, Gloucester, Holyhead, Milford Haven, Shrewsbury and Worcester. Mail-coaches usually charged passengers tenpence a mile inside and fivepence a mile outside, which was about twice the charge on ordinary stage-coaches, but they were also twice as fast, for by eliminating stops and changing their four horses about every ten miles, they soon averaged between 100 and 120 miles a day. They paid no tolls and turnpike gates had to be opened to them. The last twenty years of the Hanoverian period brought even greater speeds, the best coaches doing between ten and twelve miles an hour. The first mail-coach from London to Edinburgh in 1786 took 60 hours, which was reduced by 1834 to two days; and in 1837 the coach leaving London at 8 o'clock at night for Bristol arrived there at 7.45 the next morning. By then the great system was at its best, but its days were approaching their end.

The mail-coach system had important social and economic effects. Crimes of violence on the roads diminished as the multiplication of accelerated vehicles scared away footpads and defeated the highwaymen. The blunderbuss carried by the first coach-guards gave way to a long horn for alerting toll-gate keepers and ostlers with fresh horses. Travel became possible for more people than before. A writer complained that it had become too easy for the wives of country squires and clergymen to go to London where 'they must presently be in the mode, get fine clothes, go to plays and treats, and by these means, get into such habits of idleness and love of pleasure as makes them uneasy ever after'. The old 'rider-out' was replaced by the new commercial traveller, who supplied the families of the wealthier professional classes and farmers with fresh luxuries and needs. Some brought in their bags charming miniature samples of furniture, pottery or silver (now prized as antiques). Others had dresses and sashes, silks and satins, which young ladies in the little market-towns excitedly recognized were 'fashions of the newest pattern' described in such periodicals as *The Ladies' Monthly Museum* or illustrated in the fashion plates invented at the end of the century. And others came with copy-books, globes and even 'little jemmies and tartars' – canes and birches – for parents and governesses.

The mail-coaches also assisted the journalistic developments of the time;[1] and similarly brought about a great improvement in the postal service. Among those who benefited from the more efficient conveyance of news and correspondence were the early trade unions, now beginning as local clubs of skilled craftsmen in the manufacturing towns, particularly in the cotton industry among the jenny-operators, mule-spinners and even handloom-weavers. A better postal service assisted their efforts to extend their organization beyond a merely local basis, despite attempts to deprive them of this new advantage by Home Secretaries who sometimes ordered local postmasters to stop letters or news-packets addressed to suspected members of these bodies. Businessmen also gained from the improved service, particularly in placing orders and remitting payments.

Although the improvements in road-transport brought important advantages to internal trade, they had no significant consequences for industry as they did not make the

[1] P. 101.

transport of heavy goods much swifter or cheaper. Where roads were good enough for wheeled traffic, pack-horses were replaced by stage-wagons, and the load that could be moved was increased from a few hundredweights per horse to a ton or more; but these wagons were large, lumbering vehicles, carrying passengers as well as merchandize and drawn by six or eight cart-horses at a walking pace. In 1760 it still costs 40s. a ton to carry loads the thirty-eight miles between Liverpool and Manchester. Nor did roads always exist where industry needed them. Before 1767 the coal of Merthyr Tydfil was carried by ponies and donkeys along mountain tracks to Hereford and Cardiff.

Coal had, indeed, to be carried almost entirely by sea, and its transport from the inland coalfields was a serious problem for the rising industries which needed it. This stimulated the construction of the first canals at the same time as the roads were being improved. The great period of inland waterway construction in England was inaugurated by the Duke of Bridgewater's Canal in 1761. Engineered by James Brindley (1716–72), an unlettered millwright, this canal linked the Duke's coal-mines at Worsley with the growing town of Manchester seven miles away, crossing the Irwell by an aqueduct at Barton. Coal could now be taken to Manchester for 5s. instead of 10s. a ton by road. By 1767 the canal had been extended to the mouth of the Mersey at Runcorn, so joining the textile area of south-eastern Lancashire to the port of Liverpool.

Before then another extension (opened in 1777) was planned from the Bridgewater Canal through the salt-mining district of Cheshire to the Potteries, then past Burton to connect the Mersey with the Trent and so with the Humber; later it was connected to Birmingham and Coventry and so to Oxford and London. This Grand Trunk Canal received capital support from Wedgwood for it brought him Cornish clay and access to large towns and ports for his products. In 1777, also, the Leeds and Liverpool Canal was opened, crossing the Pennines where roads were few and difficult and connecting Liverpool with Hull (thereby eliminating a long sea-voyage), Lancashire cotton with Yorkshire wool and the Atlantic with the Baltic. All these canals were planned by Brindley and so were others, including the Forth and Clyde Canal and the Stafford and Worcester Canal linking

Wolverhampton and the metal-working Midlands with the Severn; these were opened in 1790 and 1791, nearly twenty years after Brindley had died, exhausted by his labours.

Brindley simplified the construction of his canals by keeping as far as possible to a single level, which was partly why most of the routes he planned traversed the Midlands. Further canals, closely connected with the spread of industrial development, were built by Telford, Rennie and others. These included the Thames and Severn Canal (1789) linking London with Bristol, the Shropshire Union Canal (1793) linking Birmingham with the Severn, the Kennett and Avon Canal (1794) connecting the Thames and Severn, and the Grand Junction Canal (1805) linking London with Liverpool.

The canals were dug by a new class of mobile 'navvies', largely Irish labourers, who later worked on the new roads and railways. The years from 1790 to 1794 were a period of 'canal mania' when Parliament authorized the construction of 81 canals. By 1837 £11,000,000 had been invested in the four thousand miles of canals which linked the important industrial areas with each other and the four great ports of London, Liverpool, Bristol and Hull.

The canals provided industry with transport which was cheap and capable of carrying bulky goods. Often a canal was cheaper to make than a road. Always it saved time, labour and cost in operation: a writer in 1792 asserted that canals were 'roads of a certain kind on which one horse will draw as much as thirty horses on ordinary turnpike roads'; and Professor Jackson has carefully estimated that 'the cost of canal carriage normally did not exceed one-half and in most cases was from one-fourth to one-third of the cost of land carriage'. A single horse could move a load of fifty tons or more on water. For goods in large bulk, the canals were especially economic and convenient, as the canal barge, with an average capacity of thirty tons, was a bigger unit than anything on the roads. Over half the canals were designed chiefly for the carriage of coal. Industrial raw materials were also commonly carried by canals. Manufacturers could send their products to markets all over the country and directly to the nearest sea-port. Grain could be sent easily to the large towns, reducing the price of bread and preventing a famine in times of dearth; and, similarly, farmers

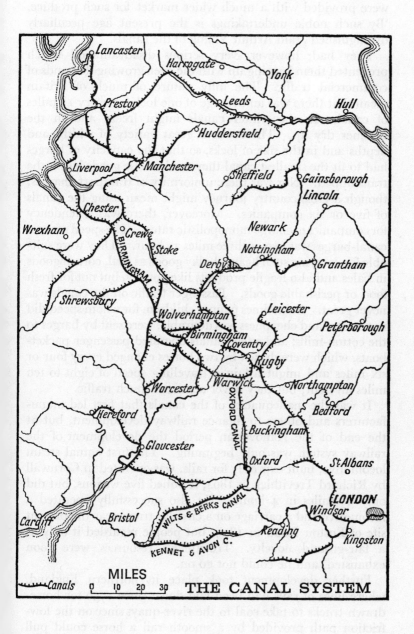

THE CANAL SYSTEM

were provided with a much wider market for such produce. 'By such noble undertakings is the present age peculiarly distinguished', said Arthur Young of the canals.

They had, however, very serious disadvantages, which prevented them keeping up with the ever-growing demands of commercial traffic. The hilly nature of much of Britain mean that there was an average of one lock for every $1\frac{3}{4}$ miles of canal. In the winter canals might freeze and in the summer dry up. There was a great variety of widths and depths and in the size of locks, so that the capacity of barges had to fit the smallest canal they used or else goods had to be transhipped. Nor was there uniformity of transport charges, though a cross-country journey might mean using the canals of five or six companies. Moreover, there was a tendency for companies to charge monopolistic rates. The speed of most canal-barges was two or three miles an hour. They were suitable for carrying such heavy, bulky goods as coal, corn or goods in bales and also fragile products like pottery, but not for fresh food or perishable goods. Passenger traffic on the canals was never great. Sometimes pauper children, for whom speed did not matter and cheapness was desirable, were sent by barges to the cotton-mills; and a few canals operated passenger packet-boats, which were drawn by two horses changed every four or six miles and might attain a travelling speed of eight to ten miles an hour, but they never attracted much traffic.

It was the inadequacies of the canals that first led manu-facturers and others to finance railway development, but at the end of the Hanoverian period the development of the railway system was only beginning. The first actual steam locomotive, built expressly for rails, was operated in Cornwall by Richard Trevithick in 1804; it pulled five wagons, but did only $9\frac{1}{2}$ miles in 4 hours. He also successfully operated a locomotive and a carriage on a circular track near the present site of Euston Road in 1809, but people regarded it only as a fair-ground novelty. Trevithick's resources were soon exhausted, and he could not go on.

Further development took place in northern England, where lines of rails had been laid down since 1750 for horse-drawn trucks to take coal to the river-quays since on the low-friction path provided by a smooth rail a horse could pull three, five or even ten tons. In 1815 George Stephenson

(1781–1848), a fireman in charge of a pumping-engine at Killingworth Colliery built a steam locomotive which effectively hauled trucks of coal along the railway from the mine to the River Tyne. It did four to eight miles an hour with a load of ninety tons, and in such an area its possibilities were recognized. When the Stockton and Darlington Railway was built in 1825, Stephenson persuaded the company to use his locomotives; and in 1830 his *Rocket* at the Rainhill trials of the Liverpool and Manchester Railway drew a train with a load of thirteen tons at more than fifteen miles an hour for sixty-three miles, the cost of its fuel being approximately $1\frac{1}{2}d.$ a mile. Within two years only one stage-coach was plying between the two towns. The nature of the challenge to both roads and canals was apparent.

There were by 1837, however, no more than 400 miles of railway working in Britain, mostly in the North, and all the lines were short, still chiefly built to carry coal to the ports. London's first railway came in 1836 when the first section of the London and Greenwich Railway was opened by the Lord Mayor amid the noise of barrel-organs, sizzling flares, blaring bands and a general fanfare. The first trunk line, the London and Birmingham Railway, though opened as far as Boxmoor in 1837, was not completed until the next year.

The use of steam-power for ships was also beginning. It had, in fact, begun earlier than on land because it was possible to use the early, heavy steam-engines to propel boats. In 1803 William Symington (1763–1831) ran the *Charlotte Dundas* on the Forth and Clyde Canal. Nine years later Henry Bell (1767–1830) plied the *Comet* on the Clyde between Glasgow and Dumbarton so successfully that steam-ship services were operating between Holyhead and Dublin, Greenock and Belfast by 1816 and Dover and Calais by 1818; and in 1833 the *Royal William* crossed the Atlantic under steam from Nova Scotia to London in twenty days. By 1837 a number of paddle-steamers were sailing to America and India, but they carried sails as well and used their engines only on calm days. An eminent scientist said to the British Association in 1838, 'Men might as well project a voyage to the moon as attempt to employ steam navigation across the stormy North Atlantic Ocean'; and nearly thirty years were to pass before British shipyards built more steamships than sailing-ships.

VIII · OVERSEAS COMMERCE AND COLONIZATION

The Development of Seaborne Trade

WHILE English industrial expansion was only beginning under the first two Georges, commercial expansion was already considerable. The customs officials began to keep statistics of English trade in 1697, and while Sir George Clark has shown that these must be treated with care, they do at any rate give some idea of the general trends of this expansion. They place the value of English exports in 1700 at £6,500,000, which was about a sixth of the value of domestic trade, but by 1760 exports are shown to have more than doubled in value, and the home market cannot have increased at such a rate. This was a great and hitherto unparalleled growth.

The customs statistics give also some indication of the pattern of British trade. In the first year of the statistics, the most important sources of English imports were the American and West Indian plantations, seven-eighths of the total being tobacco and sugar. Next came Holland, then Germany and then Turkey. The East India Company's imports were only fifth and Ireland sixth. The only other substantial sources were Spain, the Canaries and the Baltic. For exports from England, the first country was Holland, and the American colonies were second. Germany was third, Ireland fourth, and the Spanish Netherlands fifth, but this was occasioned by the needs of the English wartime army in Flanders. Portugal was eighth, but no other country bought any considerable quantity of English goods.

Some sixty years later, in the last year of peace before the Seven Years' War, most English imports came from the West Indian Islands, followed by the East Indies and the American mainland colonies. Then came Germany, Italy, and Russia. There followed the Baltic with Ireland eighth and then Spain, Holland and Portugal, three countries which re-exported various colonial goods. The plantations now received more English exports than any other country, while Portugal was fourth, Ireland fifth and Spain sixth.

Behind these figures lie the important trade developments of the period. They show, for instance, the decline in trade of the Dutch (who had no manufactures of their own and steadily lost their pre-eminence in exporting Eastern products) and the opening up of Russian commerce. Above all, these figures are related to two factors which did much to assist the increase of British trade – the colonies and the slave trade. The ever-growing population of the colonies provided England with an excellent market for her manufactures, especially those in wool, iron and leather, while the steady flow of tropical products, particularly raw cotton, sugar and tobacco from the West Indies, sent to England to be processed and re-exported, gave her the basis for a lucrative distributing trade in Europe. If imports and exports were added together, the colonies as a whole had by far the largest share of English trade. The slave trade was dominated by British slavers from 1750, which was just at the time when the expanding cotton industry was able to take advantage of the profitable triangular basis on which it was organized.[1] Cotton cloth (together with firearms, hardware and trinkets) provided the means of purchasing slaves in West Africa (and also clothing for them when purchased); and the shipping of the slaves to the American and West Indian plantations helped to pay in turn for the tropical exports to England.

The extent to which the rapid increase of exports was due to the growth of a large re-export trade was intimately connected with the system controlling colonial trade. The earliest English colonies had been founded in the first part of the seventeenth century by merchants, religious groups and individual proprietors with little government intervention. The advantages of the colonies were thought to be social; they provided an outlet for surplus or troublesome population. From the middle of the seventeenth century, however, their economic value was realized, and there was a growing desire to divert the gainful trade of the Dutch with the English colonies to England herself. Soon after the execution of Charles I in 1649, the new Commonwealth set up a Commission for Plantations to consider 'how the

[1] P. 138.

Plantations may best be managed and made useful for this Commonwealth; how the commodities thereof may be so multiplied and improved, as those Plantations alone may supply the Commonwealth with what it necessarily wants'. The result was the passing of the Navigation Acts of 1650 and 1651; the first prohibited all ships of foreign nations from trading with any English colony without a licence from the Council, and the second forbade the importation of goods into England or any of her colonies in any other than English ships or in the ships of that European state in which the merchandise was grown or manufactured. At the Restoration these Acts were re-imposed by the Navigation Act of 1660 with the addition of a provision that certain colonial products might be sent only to England or to another English colony and not direct to a foreign country. These 'enumerated articles', as they were called, included sugar, tobacco, cotton, ginger and dyestuffs, and their range was increased as new colonial products, such as naval stores, rice and iron, became important. The system was completed by the Staple Act of 1663, which required that all European goods going to the colonies must first go to England and pay duties before being shipped overseas.

These later Stuart acts (together with various protective customs duties and import prohibitions) formed the basis of the navigation system designed to give English merchants and manufacturers a monopoly of the colonial market and to make sure that England obtained from her colonies raw materials essential for her defence or economic prosperity. It was a system which remained substantially in force for the greater part of the Hanoverian period; and during that time it accorded with the ideas of the commercial policy followed in varying forms by the leading European countries and commonly known as mercantilism. This assumed that national wealth could be increased if the State encouraged its means of production and protected them from foreign competition. And the chief prize sought by a mercantilist government was a favourable balance of trade which brought the country wealth, supported its population and created a shipping fleet which would be valuable in time of war.

The effect of the English navigation system upon her most important colonies – those on the American mainland –

varied.   The southern colonies, whose plantations produced
the most important of the 'enumerated articles', traded
naturally under the system, sending their crops to England
and receiving large quantities of manufactured goods in
return.   The northern colonies, however, produced crops
and could manufacture articles which competed directly
with those of England and were, therefore, subject to the
restrictions of these Acts, but the practical damage done to
such colonies was slight.   They had but few industries, and
England gave them a ready and protected market for their
raw materials and crops.   Moreover, Walpole's settled policy
of *quieta non movere* had an ameliorating influence.[1]   Walpole,
it is true, agreed to the Molasses Act of 1733 which the West
Indian planters demanded to prevent the export of cheaper
French and Dutch sugar to America in competition with
theirs, but it was seldom enforced.   Northern merchants did
not hesitate to break laws which hampered their trade and
they were able to do so with impunity.

Some American manufacturers, notably those of woollen
cloth or wrought iron, suffered parliamentary prohibition
because they threatened to compete seriously with British
industries; but such prohibitions affected only a few people in
America, who made some complaints, but were not as
vociferous as the young men of England when the manufacture
of beaver-hats was prohibited at a time when these American
productions were at the height of fashion.   American hostility
to the system, in fact, was largely psychological.   Colonists
felt that they might be able to do better without economic
restrictions and resented regulations which they had no share
in enacting.   'America deplored the prohibition of industry
which she was in no position to undertake', Steven Watson
has said; and the greater part of colonial trade was conducted
along legal channels, being influenced at least as much by the
good prices paid by England for colonial products and the
cheapness of English manufacturers as by legislative requirements.   Resolutions of the First Continental Congress of
1774 approved the navigation system, and Franklin offered to
have the Acts re-enacted by every American colonial legislature and to guarantee them for a century if taxation of
America were abandoned.

[1] P. 258.

That the navigation system did not enforce an artificial pattern of trade may be seen by the fact that after the American War of Independence, trade between Britain and her former colonies, despite prejudice against it on both sides, continued to expand. As Peter Marshall has said, 'For Britain the loss of the thirteen colonies was greater in terms of prestige than of material interests; the economic independence of the United States lagged far behind the winning and use of political sovereignty'. British exports to America rose from £2,000,000 in 1763 to nearly £3,000,000 in 1793 and to £7,000,000 in 1800. On the other side, the adoption of Witney's gin enormously increased exports of raw cotton from the southern slave-plantations of America, and by 1830 the United States was supplying three-quarters of all the cotton used in British mills. She was Britain's largest customer, and cotton goods formed much of what she bought.

The manufacturing pre-eminence secured for Britain by her Industrial Revolution gave her in the later part of the Hanoverian period an even greater expansion of foreign trade. Her cotton and metal industries no longer required the advantages of the easier, privileged colonial markets. As their products became cheaper, they were able to invade not only the European but all other markets with their irresistible goods. By 1800 British exports and imports, which had been valued at just over £16,325,000 and £14,800,000 respectively in 1775, had risen to £38,120,000 and over £30,500,000. During that same time British shipping had almost trebled in tonnage, because, firstly, of the withdrawal from American shipyards of the protection of the navigation system, and then the wartime decimation of French and Dutch shipping. Britain had gained a final superiority in the carrying trade and a source of invisible exports which made her balance of trade even more favourable.

Between 1806 and 1812 the Continental System severely strained Britain's economy, particularly during the later difficult years.[1] Exports dropped to less than £35,200,000 in 1808, but recovered to £50,000,000 by 1812, and this was despite the outbreak of war with America in that year which temporarily reduced British exports to the United States from £7,147,000 to £1,432,000. Thus the general effect of war

[1] P. 395.

upon the expansion of British trade was not significant, and it continued to grow after 1815 despite fresh peacetime difficulties.[1] Exports rose from nearly £52,000,000 in 1820 to nearly £67,000,000 in 1830 and to over £97,000,000 in 1840 and imports from £36,500,000 in 1820 to over £46,000,000 in 1830 and to £62,000,000 in 1840.

The effects of the Industrial Revolution in Britain, which ensured this great development of British overseas trade, are seen also in the changes in composition of her exports and imports during the Hanoverian period. At first manufactured woollen goods were her most important export.[2] In the earlier part of the period, they provided more than two-thirds of the value of British domestic exports, but by 1830 this proportion had fallen to nearly an eighth, while cotton goods now accounted for nearly a half. Next in importance in 1830 were iron and steel products, including hardware and cutlery, which amounted to just over a tenth of the total. Of imports, at the beginning of the period rather more than a third in value were textile raw materials and just under a third were food, drink and tobacco. These proportions were about the same in 1830, though those of food, drink and tobacco had slightly increased. On the other hand, while at first just under a third of the value of imports were manufactured goods, again largely textiles, these were of negligible importance in 1830; and while at first about a third of all imports were re-exported, this had fallen to less than a third by 1830.

The large increase in seaborne commerce, which accompanied British industrialism, went with growing criticism of mercantilism and the navigation system. In 1776, the year of the American Declaration of Independence, Adam Smith (1723-90), a Scottish professor and noted economist, wrote his *Wealth of Nations*, which was an attack on economic protectionism and monopoly. He argued that the exchange of goods was governed by mutual needs and brought mutual benefits and that, therefore, artificial restrictions on the free and natural course of trade were harmful to the interests of all participating nations. If trade were left free, nations would supply each other's requirements, so that 'the different states into which a great continent was divided would so far resemble the different provinces of a great empire'. It is true that he defended the Navigation Act as encouraging the country's sea power, and (he pronounced) 'defence is of much more importance than opulence'; but this, and other exceptions which he made to uncontrolled free enterprise, were largely disregarded in an age ready to link his outlook with the *laissez-faire* ideas of the French Physiocrats and extend it beyond economics to other spheres of life.

The American War of Independence weakened faith in the navigation system, but British industrialization sustained opposition to it. Previously England had not possessed productive supremacy over other nations and could not obtain all the raw materials she needed without regulating their supply, while the close connection between merchant shipping and naval power convinced the warlike statesmanship of the times that the mercantile marine must be protected. By the later eighteenth century, circumstances had changed. British pre-eminence at sea seemed assured, and industrialization made British manufacturers advocates of free trade. They needed to dispose of their goods without impediment and feared no foreign competition. Even if the removal of British restrictions did not encourage other European nations to do the same, vast and unprotected markets lay elsewhere in the tropics and sub-tropics. Manchester, Sir John Clapham has said, 'lived on shirts for black men and brown men and yellow men and for the Moslem world'.

The Younger Pitt was influenced by the *Wealth of Nations* to take the first step towards freer trade. He reduced some customs duties.[1] Moreover, Adam Smith had argued that the nearness and large population of France should make her a good market for British goods. Pitt secured a commercial treaty with France in 1786 which promised benefits to English manufacturers and French vineyards. The Revolutionary and Napoleonic Wars checked the liberation of trade, and Parliament's refusal in 1816 to continue the wartime income tax necessitated import duties for revenue purposes; but commercial circles continued to oppose control. A petition by London merchants in 1820 declared 'that the maxim of buying in the cheapest market and selling in the dearest, which regulates every merchant in his individual dealings, is

---

[1] P. 367.

strictly applicable as the best rule for the trade of the whole nation'.

The first substantial abrogation of the navigation system was achieved by William Huskisson, who was at the Board of Trade from 1823 to 1827; he procured in 1826 the repeal of those parts of it restricting colonial trade and revised the tariff system by abolishing prohibitions (notably on silk goods) and substituting moderate for prohibitive duties mainly on a range of manufactures.[1]   Since the Whig government elected in 1830 was more interested in administrative than financial reform, the remaining control of trade was not removed until after the Hanoverian period.

The First British Empire

Though starting later than other European nations in the establishment of overseas colonies, the foundations of the British Empire were laid under the Early Stuarts, and by the early eighteenth century it consisted of coastal settlements in North America, several West Indian islands and trading posts in India. Of these possessions, the most prized were the West Indies – the Bermudas, Bahamas, Jamaica, the Virgin Islands, Barbuda, St. Kitts, Antigua, Montserrat and Barbados. They became increasingly important in British trade.[2] They supplied Britain with sugar, which was worth more than the total exports of the American mainland colonies and gave employment to many British ships; they took British cotton goods and other manufactures, while they lacked industries competing with those of Britain. They also needed negro slaves for their plantations, supplied from Africa by British merchants, and from them slaves could be sent to the British and Spanish mainland colonies. British opinion in the eighteenth century long regarded these islands as more valuable than either the American colonies or the Indian trading posts.

In North America the English had a series of colonies along a narrow coastal belt on the eastern seaboard stretching from the river mouths of Maine in the north to the borders of Spanish Florida in the south, though the southernmost colony of these original thirteen – Georgia – was not founded until 1733. The Treaty of Utrecht assigned Britain the French

[1] P. 418.   [2] P. 155.

colony of Acadie, which became Nova Scotia, the name given
to it by James I, and recognized her possession of Newfoundland and the Hudson Bay Territory, where the Hudson's Bay
Company had, despite French opposition, maintained forts
to engage in the fur trade and was now endeavouring to
extend its operations to the Great Lakes and the West.   The
Treaty also recognized British protection of the Red Indian
tribe of the Iroquois, which was understood to take the
boundary of the colony of New York to Lake Ontario.   In
North America, as elsewhere, France remained an important
colonial and commercial power, and rivalry between her and
Britain continued, despite the twenty-five years of peace in
Europe after the Treaty.[1]   Though Spain, Portugal and
Holland still possessed considerable overseas possessions, their
age of colonial expansion was over.   Britain and France were
now isolated as the main contestants for overseas power, and
the issue between them was far from being decided at the
beginning of this period.

In North America, English settlement was still practically
confined to oceanic coastlines and penetration into the
interior was opposed by France.   So far the two nations had
clashed mainly over fishing in the Gulf of St. Lawrence and
the Canadian fur trade.   A wider conflict was initiated in
1718 when the French founded New Orleans, a hundred
miles above the mouth of the Mississippi, as a strategic trading
post in their new colony of Louisiana; and they rapidly linked
this with their older settlements around Montreal and Quebec
by establishing along the Mississippi, the Ohio, the Great
Lakes and the St. Lawrence a chain of defensive trading posts
which culminated in strongly-fortified Louisbourg on Cape
Breton Island designed to dominate the river-entrance.   The
French had only to hold these positions to check English
advance westwards from the seaboard colonies, while they
might penetrate past Lake Champlain and the Hudson Valley
to the Atlantic, dividing the English colonies and facilitating
their conquest.

The American colonists had, therefore, to advance against
the French if they were not to be confined to the relatively
small area east of the Appalachian Mountains.   They greatly
outnumbered the French, being in 1700 about 200,000, more

[1] P. 261.

than ten times as many as their rivals. Nevertheless, the French had considerable advantages. France was a stronger nation militarily than Britain and could send over more troops; and the highly centralized government of New France could conduct war better than the loose association of independent-minded colonial governments. In addition, as explorers and traders, the French knew the countryside and were friendly with the Indians, while the American farmers and settlers often knew little of the border territory and aroused the Indians' hatred by taking their lands. So nearly all the Indian tribes supported the French, who hired them to raid American territory, burn settlements and kill the inhabitants or drag them off westwards. As the rival outposts along the ill-defined boundaries moved closer to each other, desperate fights between English and French frontiersmen and traders and their Indian allies continued and were unaffected by the absence of official hostilities.

Nor did this situation produce the immediate events which involved Britain in renewed warfare with European powers. These occurred in the waters of Spanish America, an old area of English maritime endeavour. The Treaty of Utrecht had granted Britain the *Asiento,* a monopoly for thirty-three years of selling negro slaves to the Spanish colonies, and the right to send one ship each year to Porto Bello. These concessions were assigned to the South Sea Company, contributing towards the South Sea Bubble.[1] The trade caused constant local friction. Both sides practised fraud and violence. The British abused the 'annual ship' by refilling it from so-called supply vessels, and West Indian colonists ran illegal cargoes into Caribbean ports; the Spanish *guarda costas* retaliated by exercising the right of search to hinder British shipping and seizing the cargoes of many honest traders. War with Spain came in 1739 through the incident of Captain Jenkins's Ear.[2] Walpole was forced into hostilities by a general clamour which was supported by trading interests, the opposition and his own colleagues.

The War of Jenkins's Ear was essentially a maritime contest.[3] Since Spain and Britain supported sides in the War of the Austrian Succession, it soon became part of this wider contest, and in 1744 fresh colonial and naval war

[1] P. 242.   [2] P. 264.   [3] P. 265.

broke out between Britain and France. In America this was
known as King George's War. It did little to settle the rivalry
between the two nations. Apart from the daring and
decisive capture of Louisbourg by a British naval squadron
with the help of colonial troops from Massachusetts in 1745,[1]
fighting was an intensification of brutal incidents along the
borders of New England and New York by both sides, only
resulting in a temporary check on frontier settlement.

A similarly indecisive outcome characterized Franco-
British conflict in India, the other great area of rivalry which
achieved fresh prominence in this war. At the beginning of
the eighteenth century the English East India Company
had three principal factories through which it sent silk and
calicoes, tea and coffee to Britain. These were, on the west
coast, Bombay, part of the dowry of Charles II's Queen
Catherine of Braganza, and other subordinate posts on that
side of India; on the east coast, Madras, founded in 1639,
and its dependent factories on the Coromandel Coast and in
the Bay of Bengal; and in Bengal, Calcutta, founded in 1690.
Its rival was the French *Compagnie des Indes Orientales*, formed
in 1664, whose chief factories were Pondicherry, south of
Madras, and Chandernagore, north of Calcutta. The first
years of the century were a time of steady and quiet prosperity
for the British in India, which made the fortunes of the first
'nabobs' such as Governor Pitt of Madras;[2] and peace was
maintained with the French company. This situation was
changed, however, with the appointment of Joseph François
Dupleix (1697–1763), an able, restless organizer, as Governor-
General of the French Indies in 1741. He resolved to take
advantage of the decline of the Mogul Empire and make
himself master of southern India by putting his candidates on
two native princely thrones, those of the Nizam of the Deccan
and of his nominal vassal, the Nawab of the Carnatic. When
the War of the Austrian Succession broke out, the French
secured local naval supremacy and stormed Madras in 1746,
but the two British naval victories off Cape Finisterre prevented the exploitation of this success.[3] When the Treaty of
Aix-la-Chapelle ended hostilities in 1748, the French relinquished Madras in return for the British restoration of
Louisbourg.

[1] P. 279.   [2] P. 296.   [3] Pp. 196–7, 279.

Peace in Europe, however, did not restrain Dupleix's ambitions in India. By 1750 both his candidates were on their thrones. The English claimant to the Carnatic, Mohammad Ali, was besieged in Trichinopoly by his rival and seemed likely to have to surrender, which would leave the English company without an ally in India and helpless before Dupleix.

The situation was saved by Robert Clive (1725–75), who had reached India as a writer in the Company's service in 1744, tried twice to shoot himself, but then found satisfaction by transferring himself from the boredom of writing out trading-bills to a captaincy in the small force of English and sepoys kept by the Company to protect its factories. He persuaded the Council at Madras to allow him to attack Arcot, the capital of the Carnatic. A daring dash with a force of 200 English and 200 sepoys in the summer of 1751 secured Arcot without difficulty. This attracted (as Clive had intended) part of the force investing Trichinopoly, and he was closely besieged by an army of 10,000 for fifty days behind crumbling walls and dry moats. His men repulsed repeated attacks by drug-excited natives and battle-elephants and, when the enemy withdrew, he had lost over a third of his force, but it was the turning-point of the struggle. Trichinopoly was saved, and Mohammad Ali became Nawab of the Carnatic. Clive returned to England in 1753 to be greeted as a victor, but Dupleix was recalled to France the next year, discredited in the sight of the directors of his company who were interested only in peaceful trade.

The struggle for India was, however, not over. The Seven Years' War brought open fighting between the two companies. The Nawab of Bengal, the young Surajah Dowlah, who was inclined to support the French, seized the opportunity in June 1756 to capture the wealthy city of Calcutta; many of its English inhabitants perished in the 'Black Hole of Calcutta'. Clive had returned to India the previous year. After being engaged in suppressing the pirates infesting the Malabar Coast, he had just taken up his new appointment as Governor of Madras. He was ordered to sail with ships and troops to Bengal and early in 1757 recaptured Calcutta. With three thousand men, a third of them British, he then met the Bengal army of 50,000 and a few French auxiliaries at Plassey and gained an overwhelming victory. Mir Jaffier, one of the Nawab's generals, had been bribed by Clive and kept out of the fighting, but the British owed the day more to Surajah Dowlah himself who fled in panic with his men before the battle was properly joined. Mir Jaffier was made Nawab of Bengal, and his son murdered the captured Surajah Dowlah a few days later. The East India Company now ceased merely to be a trading corporation, for all Bengal, with a population twice that of England, came under its control. Clive did not return to Madras; he remained in Bengal until it was subdued and sailed for England in 1760 with a fortune of £300,000, much of it a gift from Mir Jaffier.

While Clive was in Bengal he was able to send help to Madras when it was threatened by the French expedition which had at last arrived under the Comte de Lally, the son of an Irish Jacobite refugee; and in 1760 a force led by Sir Eyre Coote defeated Lally at Wandewash. Lally retired to Pondicherry, where he had to surrender the next year. The English company was now also supreme in the Carnatic. By the Treaty of Paris in 1763 the French regained their factories, but these were to be trading depots only and not garrisoned or fortified. The Company now not only practically monopolized India's commerce, but had entered upon an irreversible process of conquest and rule, soon to bring fresh problems in which Clive himself was involved.[1]

Meanwhile, the British had secured an equally complete triumph in North America. Here, indeed, actual warfare preceded the outbreak of European hostilities. While Pennsylvanians were pioneering over the Alleghenies and Virginians staking out holdings in the West, the French began in 1749 to build new forts along the Ohio valley, invading territory claimed by the English colonies. When George Washington was sent in 1754 with Virginian militia men to assert the English claim, he was repulsed – an action which began the French and Indian War between Britain and France in North America. The next year British troops under General Braddock were surprised and badly defeated by the French whom he had expected to oust from Fort Duquesne at the Forks of the Ohio; and in August 1756 the Marquis de Montcalm, the new French commander in

[1] Pp. 176–8.

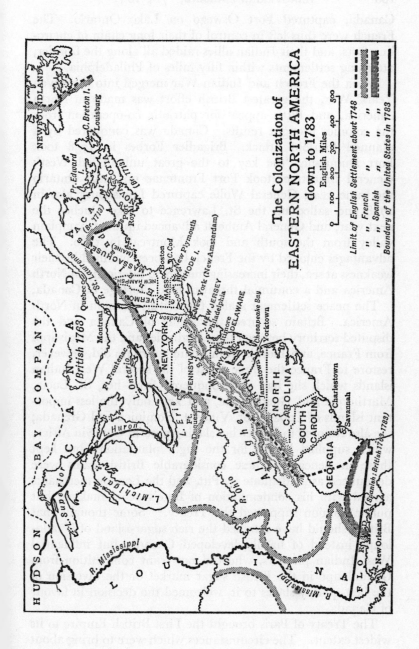

The Colonization of
EASTERN NORTH AMERICA
down to 1783

English Miles

0   100   200   300   400   500

Limit of English Settlement about 1748 ——
   "   "   "   "   " French - - -
   "   "   "   "   " Dutch
   "   "   "   "   " Spanish
Boundary of the United States in 1783

HUDSON   BAY   COMPANY

NEWFOUNDLAND

C. Breton I.
Louisburg

Pr. Edward I.

NOVA SCOTIA
(Br. 1713)

ACADIA

(Br. 1713)

St. Lawrence R.

Quebec
(British 1763)

Montreal

NEW FRANCE
(British 1763)

C A N A D A

L. Superior

L. Huron

L. Michigan

Ft. Frontenac

L. Ontario

L. Erie

Ft. Duquesne

R. Ohio

Alleghany Mts.

VERMONT

NEW HAMP.

MASS. (MAINE)

MASSACHUSETTS

Boston
C. Cod
RHODE I.
CONN.

NEW YORK
New York (New Amsterdam)
Hudson R.

NEW JERSEY
Philadelphia
PENNSYLVANIA
Baltimore
MARYLAND
DELAWARE
Chesapeake Bay
Yorktown
Jamestown
VIRGINIA

NORTH CAROLINA

SOUTH CAROLINA
Charleston

GEORGIA
Savannah

LOUISIANA

R. Mississippi

R. Mississippi

FLORIDA
(Spanish; British 1763–1783)

New Orleans

Canada, captured Fort Oswego on Lake Ontario. The French were thus left in control of their long chain of encircling forts, and their Indian allies raided all along the frontier, attacking settlements within fifty miles of Philadelphia.

When the French and Indian War merged into the Seven Years' War, the greatest British effort was made in North America, and Pitt's appeal for patriotic co-operation from the colonies brought results. Canada was conquered by a planned fourfold attack. Brigadier Forbes in 1758 took Fort Duquesne, 'the key to the great unbounded West'; General Bradstreet took Fort Frontenac on Lake Ontario the same year; General Wolfe captured Louisbourg also in 1758 and sailed up the St. Lawrence to take Quebec the next year; and General Amherst advanced up the Champlain valley from the south and took Montreal in 1760. The advantages enjoyed by the French had been nullified by their weakness at sea, their increasing numerical inferiority in North America and a continual threat of food shortage in Canada.

The peace settlement sealed the British triumph in North America. Britain secured the whole of Canada and the disputed territory between the Alleghenies and the Mississippi from France, and Florida from Spain. Britain did, however, restore to France the three finest of the several West Indian islands which she had also conquered from her, St. Lucia, Martinique and Guadaloupe, and kept only the less important islands of Tobago, St. Vincent, Dominica and Grenada; she also restored to France her slaving posts at Gorée in Africa, which supplied labour for the sugar plantations, but kept those in Senegal. These considerable British gains were denounced as inadequate by Pitt, and the London merchants agreed with his condemnation of Bute's peace-making, but public opinion supported the Treaty.[1] Some thought that Britain should have retained the rich sugar-island of Guadaloupe instead of hardly-developed Canada; but influential West Indian planters, who did not want competition from Guadaloupe in the British sugar market or the diversion of the best-quality slaves to it, welcomed the decision in favour of Canada.

The Treaty of Paris brought the First British Empire to its widest extent. The circumstances which were to bring about

[1] P. 313.

its downfall were also inevitably inherent in the settlement.[1]
Nevertheless, it placed Britain in such a commanding commercial and maritime position of supremacy in the world
that she was able to survive the disruption of her eighteenth-
century empire and go on to renewed colonial efforts which
were to bring her greater and more widely dispersed colonial
possessions.

The American War of Independence (1775–83)

The ultimate origins of the American War of Independence
are to be found primarily in conditions that had developed in
the colonies through a long period of years.   They had been
founded, not by government-controlled expeditions, but by
private individuals, trading companies or religious refugees;
and they were separated from England by three thousand
miles of the Atlantic Ocean across which it commonly took a
sailing-ship seven weeks to sail either way.   Therefore, the
colonies were thrown largely upon their own initiative and
were able to conduct their own affairs to a great extent,
which gave them an increasing spirit of self-reliance and
self-determination.   By 1775 most of the colonies had a
governor appointed by the Crown, but his powers, except over
trade and defence, were not great, and there were frequent
quarrels between the governors and the assemblies, elected by
the settlers in each colony and responsible for making laws
and imposing taxation.   Though the British government
made efforts in the eighteenth century to increase its power
over the colonies, it could not exercise a strict control over their
affairs.   Moreover, the colonies had developed their own way
of life and institutions, their own economic interests and social
and political ideas, which still further weakened their ties with
England and accentuated their feeling of self-sufficiency.

This feeling seems to have reached something like a climax
with the end of the Seven Years' War, which gave Britain
possession both of Canada in the north, so long a source of
French threats to the colonies, and of the vast western region,
which the colonists had eagerly coveted in the face of French
efforts at settlement.   A new sense of freedom and opportunity grew up in the colonies.   Above all, there was a growing expression of the feeling that the colonies should be free to

[1] P. 313.

manage their own affairs. This was to be found mainly among a group of educated men, writers and thinkers, such as Samuel Adams, Benjamin Franklin, James Otis and Thomas Jefferson; they were supported by a set of radicals of poor education or none, mainly mechanics and back-woodsmen, who were to give the revolutionary movement, once it started, much of its violent energy. These two groups remained a small minority among the colonists, even when the fighting actually began, but they were the most politically active and conscious, and so determined to use American grievances (caused by Parliament's measures from 1765 onwards) to resist the British government that no concessions it might have made would have placated them for long.

On the other hand, Britain after the Seven Years' War faced new problems of imperial organization. The unity of her greatly-extended possessions had to be preserved, and they had to be strengthened and defended. The merchants and landlords in Parliament particularly wanted taxation to be reduced by placing a larger share of the cost of imperial administration and defence upon the colonies. The British national debt had doubled since 1756, and the cost of main-taining civil and military establishments in America had risen fourfold since 1748. There were complaints that few colonies had imposed adequate taxes to meet the government's needs during the war. And in 1763 Pontiac's Conspiracy, a formidable uprising by the Indians of the Ohio Valley (who feared for their hunting-grounds after the French defeat) convinced the British government that a military force would have to be maintained in the colonies.

George Grenville hoped to use the trade laws to raise the colonial contribution towards imperial defence. His first step was the Sugar Act of 1764, a revision of the earlier Molasses Act.[1] It reduced the duty on foreign molasses imported into the American colonies, but the new duty was to be more effectively enforced, which was a blow for the mainland colonies, for hitherto they had largely avoided paying any duty. There followed the Stamp Act of 1765 requiring revenue stamps on newspapers, pamphlets, licences and commercial and legal documents, which affected every man of property in every colony and also the lawyers and

[1] P. 157.

journalists who were well-skilled in the arts of politics and public persuasion. They sought a reason for their opposition to the measure and found it in the principle of 'no taxation without representation'. The British government maintained the undoubted legal right of the King in Parliament to exercise supreme authority over every British subject whether he were in England or the colonies, but the Americans now took their stand on constitutional right. The Bill of Rights of 1689 had condemned 'levying money for or to the use of the Crown by pretence or prerogative without the consent of Parliament'. Since the Americans did not elect representatives to the Parliament at Westminster, they urged that they should enjoy this same right. 'Taxation without representation is tyranny', said James Otis, the Massachusetts lawyer, in 1765.

This agitation was followed by well-planned acts of resistance. The radicals, organized as the Sons of Liberty, held public demonstrations, attacked the houses of revenue officers and destroyed the stamps. New England merchants, whose profitable West Indian trade was menaced by the Sugar Act, began to boycott British imports. And Samuel Adams, another Massachusetts politician, induced the representatives of nine colonies to send delegates to the Stamp Act Congress of 1765 in New York, and these protested to the King against parliamentary taxation. In 1765 the Marquis of Rockingham had succeeded Grenville,[1] and the next year, largely because of pressure from British merchants whose trade had suffered from the American 'non-importation' movement, he withdrew the Stamp Act, only to replace it by the Declaratory Act asserting Parliament's right to legislate for the colonies. The agitation ceased, but not for long.

Rockingham was replaced by the Elder Pitt in 1766.[2] His Chancellor of the Exchequer, Charles Townshend, boasted that he knew of a way of raising revenue from America without causing offence. It was external taxation such as the colonies had accepted for the regulation of trade. His American Import Duties Act of 1767 imposed taxes on certain articles imported from Britain.[3] The American expounders of the English constitution straightway moved on from 'no taxation without representation' to 'no legislation without

---

[1] P. 326. [2] P. 328. [3] P. 331.

representation'. 'If Parliament could bind the colonies, they were all slaves', said the Speaker of the Massachusetts Assembly. The previous means of protest and resistance were renewed, including the powerful one of 'non-importation'. Samuel Adams also repeated his efforts to bring the colonies into closer co-operation; his Massachusetts Circular Letter, which called for united resistance, received considerable support, and the assemblies of Massachusetts and Virginia were dissolved for favouring it. The result was another withdrawal by the British government, now that of Lord North who came into office in 1770. He immediately repealed the duties on colonial imports with the exception of the tax on tea, which was retained to assert the right of taxation – 'a peppercorn in acknowledgement of right is of more value than millions without'.

Once again agitation subsided in the colonies, but by now antagonism had been stimulated to the point of violence. This was clearly revealed in 1770 by the Boston Massacre, a brawl between Boston rowdies and British troops, and in 1772 by the affair of the *Gaspée*, a revenue cutter which smugglers burnt off Rhode Island. The lull came to a sudden end with the passing of the Tea Act of 1773, which had little or nothing to do with the colonial problem, but was designed primarily to help the East India Company out of financial difficulties and to dispose of its surplus stocks of tea by allowing it to take its tea directly to the colonies so avoiding the middlemen and the British (though not the American) duties. This measure halved the cost of tea in America, but it threatened the profits of smugglers and revived the never-dormant issue of taxation. The Boston Tea Party of 1773, in which the local Sons of Liberty, disguised as Red Indians, dumped the tea from the Company's vessels into Boston harbour, was one among several other less well-known 'tea parties'.

Lord North and his colleagues believed that the time had now come to act firmly in America. There followed the 'Intolerable Acts' of 1774. These were the Boston Port Act, closing the port of Boston until the colony should pay for the destroyed tea; the Massachusetts Government Act, remodelling the colony's charter of 1691 to permit greater British control; the Transportation Act, providing for the removal of British officials, charged with murder in suppressing riots, to

England for trial; and the Quartering Act, compelling Boston to provide lodging and food for British soldiers. The Quebec Act, passed in the same year, was not a punitive measure; it was intended to pacify the French Canadians. They were to be administered by a governor and a consulattive council, but the Act tolerated Roman Catholicism and perpetuated French civil law in the new British province, besides adding to it the territory west of the Alleghenies as far south as the Ohio. American propagandists effectively suggested that Britain intended to use its 'Popish slaves' to subdue the colonies and limit their expansion.

Reaction in America to these measures was swift. Committees of Correspondence, first promoted by Samuel Adams in Massachusetts, were formed in other colonies to facilitate the spread of propaganda and co-ordinate the organization of the radicals. Their insistence that all the colonies must support Massachusetts to avoid a similar fate met with wide response. The outcome was the assembling in Philadelphia in 1774 of the First Continental Congress, a gathering of representatives of the Committees of Correspondence and similar bodies from most of the colonies. It issued a Declaration of Rights, demanding the repeal by the British government of all legislation passed since 1763, declared its support for Massachusetts and adopted an Association, an agreement boycotting British goods.

This was very near to open rebellion, and the actual clash of arms came in April 1775 when troops, sent by General Gage, the Governor of Massachusetts, to seize arms stored by the radicals at Concord, were fired on at Lexington. When the Second Continental Congress met the next month, the moderates prevailed upon it to send the Olive Branch Petition to George III, asking him to redress American grievances, but he rejected it as coming from a rebel assembly; and the radicals secured the passing of motions for the raising of an army and the appointment to command it of George Washington, who was to inspire his countrymen with his conviction of the justice of their cause and with confidence in its ultimate victory. The first major engagement of the war was the Battle of Bunker Hill in June in which the colonists, trying to drive the British from Boston, were defeated by Gage, though with heavy casualties.

The military course of the war need not be followed in detail. Between 1775 and 1777 the British commanders were slow to exploit their military and naval strength on orders from the British government, which hoped to open peace negotiations after a display of force. Boston was evacuated in 1776 by General Howe, Gage's successor, who, however, captured New York that autumn, but did not exploit his victory. Meanwhile, American ideas of independence had been stimulated by the appearance in January 1776 of Tom Paine's pamphlet, *Common Sense*, a vigorous statement of the case for complete independence – 'Now, now – now – at this very moment must these uncorrupt and democratic Colonies throw off the trammels of an effete and vicious monarchy', he wrote; and in the summer the Continental Congress issued the Declaration of Independence. The American resolve to fight was further strengthened when the British government hired 17,000 Hessian troops to supplement their forces in the colonies. In 1777 General Burgoyne led an expedition from Canada to isolate the New England Colonies from the rest, but failed to join up with Howe, who had captured Philadelphia that September after landing in Chesapeake Bay, and had to surrender at Saratoga in September. This brought France into the war early in 1778 on the side of the colonists, to be followed by Spain in June 1779 and Holland in 1781. Britain's naval weakness lost her command of the sea;[1] and Howe's successor, General Clinton, was forced by a threat from the sea to withdraw to New York and Rhode Island.   Failure in the north led the British to concentrate in the south in 1779 and 1780; they first gained successes in Georgia and South Carolina, but reverses followed in 1781, and in October their chief army under General Cornwallis was forced by a combination of French ships at sea and American and French troops on land to surrender at Yorktown. The war was practically over in America (though not elsewhere).[2] The Treaty of Versailles in 1783 recognized the independence of the United States of America and its claims to the vast Central Plains which the Quebec Act had joined to Canada, besides returning to France some of the West Indian islands she had lost in 1763 and her slaving-posts in Senegal; and Spain recovered Minorca and Florida.

[1] P. 190.   [2] P. 352.

'In plain truth', J. T. Adams has said, 'we see that the American Revolution was only saved from being an abortive rebellion by two factors, neither of which could be counted upon in 1776 – one the character of Washington, the other the marshalling against England of European powers.' Even without these factors, however, and even if there had been greater competence on the British side, the difficulties of subduing the colonies were immense – their huge area and vast spaces, their remoteness and wildness, their sparse population and self-sufficiency in food, the obstacles against moving a regular army within them and the advantages enjoyed by the self-supporting colonists in holding them. Any chance of success by the British depended upon the isolation of New England and continual command of the sea. Without these, it became impossible.

The New British Empire

The American War of Independence bore very much the aspect of a civil war. As the movement for complete self-government grew, a substantial number of colonists remained loyal to the British Crown. Many served in the royal forces, while others suffered harsh treatment and confiscation of property. In 1783 and 1784 between fifty and sixty thousand of them, known as the United Empire Loyalists, went to Canada, and most of them settled around the Great Lakes. Canada was still governed by the Quebec Act of 1774.[1] The new settlers wanted representative institutions, but feared oppression by the French Canadians, who were twice as numerous as themselves. In 1791, therefore, Pitt's Canada Constitutional Act divided the country into two provinces – Upper Canada (Ontario) and Lower Canada (Quebec). Each was given an elected assembly, but the British government retained ultimate power through an appointed governor and executive council. During the war of 1812–14 between Britain and the United States, both provinces united in repulsing American invasions of Canada.

After the war, however, discontent and dissension grew in Canada. In Lower Canada, French nationalism became very sensitive, and the elected Assembly clashed with the Governor and the British officials in his Council, who were

[1] P. 173.

also suspected of favouring British traders and immigrants in the province. In Upper Canada, on the other hand, the newer British immigrants complained that all the best lands and official posts and the Governor's favour went to the older pioneers, an arrangement which they termed the 'Family Compact'. Also, the Act of 1791 had designated areas as the Clergy Lands to endow the Anglican and Presbyterian clergy, which irritated Methodists and other denominations not thus favoured. During the winter of 1837 extremists staged rebellions in both provinces. Both were fiascos but their effect upon the British government was to be important for the future of Canada and the whole Empire.[1]

Problems of government had also risen in the other important overseas territory still held by Britain. Events in India soon showed that the Company, formed for trade, was unfit for political power. After Clive's departure in 1760, the attempt to govern Bengal by British officials acting through the agency of dependent native sovereigns failed disastrously. The Company's officials were inexperienced or unscrupulous, anxious to make rapid fortunes and return to England as 'nabobs'. Their methods were exactions from native rulers and officials, private trading free from tolls and dues and plunder from native traders and cultivators. Mir Jaffier was deposed and replaced by his son, Mir Cossim, who paid for his throne with rewards and presents, but then resolved to assert his authority against the Company by force of arms. Though gaining the support of the Mogul Emperor and the Nawab of Oudh, he was defeated by the Company's troops at the Battle of Buxar in 1764 and deposed in favour of Mir Jaffier. Oudh submitted the next year.

This victory preserved and extended British power in India, but the effects of ill-government remained, and the Company turned again to Clive, who returned to Bengal as Governor from 1765 to 1767. During this second period of administration, he first made a treaty with the Mogul Emperor which added to the Company's military occupation of Bengal the right to control its revenue and justice, though the actual collection of revenue and administration of justice was performed by native officials. This was his dual system, which meant that the Company took the surplus profits of the

[1] P. 184.

administration of Bengal while leaving government largely in
the hands of the Nawab and his servants.   Next Clive tried

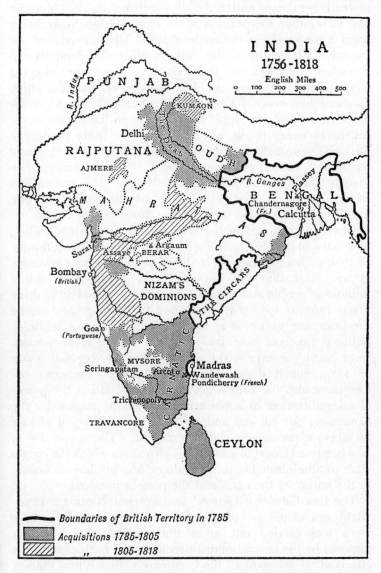

to reform the abuses which had been responsible for his
appointment.   After dismissing the whole Council at Calcutta, he forbade officials to accept gifts or avoid duties on

private trading, but he could not persuade the Directors of
the Company to remove the grounds of corruption by
increasing salaries and forbidding private trading, and he
had to improve the position of the chief officials by granting
them a monopoly in the trade of salt.   He also reduced the
excessive allowances of the military officers and suppressed
a mutiny which followed this action.   These reforms effected
a temporary improvement, but he aroused hatreds which
followed him when he returned to England.   In 1772 his
enemies secured the appointment of a parliamentary committee to examine his whole conduct in India, including
financial transactions – about which Clive said, 'I stand
astonished at my own moderation!'.   The committee acknowledged that he had 'rendered great and meritorious
services to his country', but would not fully exonerate him,
and in 1774 depression and sickness drove him to suicide.

Clive was followed in India by officials of no great ability,
and many of the old abuses reappeared, while the great famine
of 1770 in Bengal seriously reduced the Company's revenue.
It was clear that the Company was incapable of ruling
millions of people and was also in serious financial difficulties.
From 1767 to 1771 corruption and famine together caused
the Company's revenue to fall by £400,000 a year, while its
military expenses rose by £160,000 in the same period.
Lord North's answer to the situation was the Regulating Act
of 1773, which divided authority in India between the
Company and the British government by vesting the power
of administration in a Governor-General appointed by the
Company, but advised and controlled by a Council of four
members appointed by the government.   There was also to
be a Supreme Court of Justice at Calcutta, in which the judges
were to administer English, Hindu or Moslem law according
to the nature of the cases and the persons involved.

The first Governor-General was Warren Hastings (1732–
1818), one of the greatest Englishmen to go to India, whose
work was carried out amid the considerable difficulties
imposed by the new administrative system.   Suspicious of the
effects of power upon all the Company's officials and sharing
the popular jealousy of the wealth of many 'nabobs', the
government appointed to the Council members likely to
keep a critical watch upon the Governor-General.   The

result was continual friction between Hastings and the Council, led by Sir Philip Francis.[1] Only after the Bengal climate had killed two of the councillors and Francis had retired to England in 1780, after being shot by Hastings in a duel, did he secure a Council which supported him. He was also hampered by interference and demands for high dividends by the Directors in London and by the incompetence of subordinate officials. An attempt by Charles James Fox in his India Bill of 1783 to remedy these problems by placing the whole administration of India in the hands of seven government-appointed commissioners foundered in a storm of political controversy, and the situation remained unchanged.[2]

Nevertheless, Hastings did much to transform the sovereignty established by Clive in India into an administrative system. The Company had already realized that Clive's dual system was bound to mean the oppression of the people by unscrupulous native officials. Hastings energetically swept it away. The Nawab of Bengal became a pensioned figurehead. British collectors controlled local revenue and justice under a revenue board and courts of appeal at Calcutta. Efforts were made to enforce the rules against the acceptance of presents and to separate the functions of government from the management of trade.

Moreover, Hastings had to defend the territory of the Company from France, who followed her declaration of war on Britain during the American War of Independence by preparing to send an expedition to India and employing agents to incite some of the strongest Indian princes against the British. These were the chiefs of the Marathas in Central India and Hyder Ali, the Rajah of Mysore, a large state in the south. In 1780 Hyder Ali invaded the Carnatic in force, ravaging the country as far as Madras, at the same time as the Marathas menaced the borders of south-western Bengal, and a French force landed in the Carnatic. As Hastings said, 'the crisis demanded the most instant, powerful and even hazardous exertion of the government'. He negotiated peace with the warlike but disunited Marathas and sent a hastily-raised force against Hyder Ali, which defeated him and so saved Madras. His coolness and promptitude averted the junction

[1] P. 334.   P. 359.

of the French with the two native armies, which might have overthrown the British in southern India. France gained nothing at the Treaty of Versailles from her intervention.

When Hastings returned to England in 1785, it was to face impeachment. Francis, who had accumulated a large fortune in India, convinced Burke that Hastings was responsible for the corruption of British rule in India.[1] Important charges against him concerned the forceful measures he had adopted to raise revenue from the native rulers in the Ganges valley – the Rajah of Benares and the Begums of Oudh – to pay for the Company's dividends. Others concerned the hanging of a native, Nuncomar, for forgery, and a punitive expedition against the Rohillas, a tribe of mountain marauders. The proceedings dragged on from 1788 to 1795. The Lords acquitted Hastings on every charge. He was ruined by the expense of the trial, but received a generous pension from the Company for the rest of his life. 'I gave you all', he said, 'and you have rewarded me with confiscation, disgrace and a life of impeachment.' Pitt told the Commons that Hastings had served his country well, but justified the impeachment, which he had supported, on the grounds that 'though the constitution of our Eastern possessions is arbitrary and despotic, still it is the duty of every administration in that country to conduct itself by the rules of justice and of liberty as far as it is possible to reconcile them to the establishment'. In fact, only as efficient an administrator as Hastings could have made the system of government in India function at all.

Pitt had, indeed, already remedied the worst defects of the Regulating Act by his India Act of 1784, which remained in force until 1858. It set up a Board of Control in India (consisting of a Secretary of State, the Chancellor of the Exchequer and four Privy Councillors) to take charge of all the country's civil, military and revenue affairs. The Governor-General was to be appointed by the Cabinet and assisted by a Council of three members. A subsequent act of 1786 gave the Governor-General power to override the Council and act as Commander-in-Chief. The Company retained control of its commercial interests and Indian patronage. This system made the government the effective ruler of British India and enabled Hasting's successors to

[1] P. 368.

perform their duties without the opposition which had hampered him.

Nine-tenths of India was still under native rule. Neither the British government nor the Company wanted further conquests, but the warlike activities of neighbouring native states and French intrigues during the struggle against Britain made inevitable the growth of both directly-controlled territory and the number of dependent princely states, especially under Lord Wellesley, who was Governor-General from 1798 to 1805, when the danger was still serious, though diminished by the British capture of the Cape of Good Hope, Ceylon and the East Indies from the Dutch in 1795. An elder brother of the Duke of Wellington, Wellesley acted vigorously and effectively. He defeated Napoleon's allies, Tipu, Sultan of Mysore and the Nizam of the Deccan, and placed their states under British supervision. He did the same to Oudh in the north and annexed the Carnatic in the south. Finally he defeated the Maratha chiefs, compelling them to surrender territory and accept a British alliance. This policy of subsidiary alliance and annexation doubled the Company's territory and extended its influence over the whole of the sub-continent. To quote J. A. Williamson, 'In seven years he had transformed the British from one of the Indian powers into the supreme power'. This was, however, too costly for the Directors and too aggressive for the government, which wished to concentrate on the war in Europe and tried to halt the expansion of British rule.

Indeed, the East India Company's financial position grew worse with each addition to its territory. Its trading activities declined through concentration on collecting taxes and maintaining soldiers. Profits from Indian commerce were now made by individual traders who benefited from its monopoly. Accordingly, the Company surrendered this monopoly in 1813 and twenty years later relinquished all trading, confining itself to administration and patronage.

Expansion of British power continued. In 1815 the Marquis of Hastings established supremacy over Nepal, and in 1824 Lord Amherst annexed parts of Burma. During the closing years of the Hanoverian period, Lord William Bentinck, Governor General from 1828 to 1835, took advantage of an interlude of peace in India to try to reform its conditions of life. He prohibited the burning of widows, the killing of unwanted baby girls and the murders of the Thugs. He also developed native education, which was to be in English, a common language among India's many tongues. The story of exploitation and conquest was unfolding into administration and humanitarianism.

The growth of British power in India, though reluctantly accepted by the government, was in accordance with the contemporary tendency of imperial expansion, which was towards the tropical trade so essential for Britain's industrial development. The additions brought to the British Empire by the Revolutionary and Napoleonic Wars were tropical islands or plantations – St. Lucia, Tobago, Trinidad, Guiana, Mauritius and Ceylon – and naval bases on the trade routes – Malta, the Ionian Isles and the Cape of Good Hope. After the American War of Independence, the establishment of fresh colonies in lands with a temperate climate suitable for permanent white settlement did not seem desirable. It was thought that such undertakings would be expensive and useless since when the colonies became strong enough to be self-supporting they would inevitably want to break away and become independent.

The reluctance to form settlement colonies was seen clearly in Australasia. Before the end of the American dispute, Captain James Cook (1728–79) had made his eventful second voyage during which he claimed both Australia and New Zealand for Britain.[1] The pioneer British settlers, however, did not reach Australia until 1788, and then they were transported convicts and their guards. When their sentences expired, most of the convicts remained in the country as free men, but the government did not wish free emigrants from Britain to be encouraged to settle there. By 1837, however, a growing number of such emigrants were arriving in Australia, being particularly attracted by the development of sheep-farming from 1797 in New South Wales, but the official attitude was still discouraging. New Zealand at this time had over two thousand white settlers, among whom were both escaped convicts and missionaries, but was not to be annexed by Britain until 1840.

Political indifference towards the Empire was, however,

[1] P. 93.

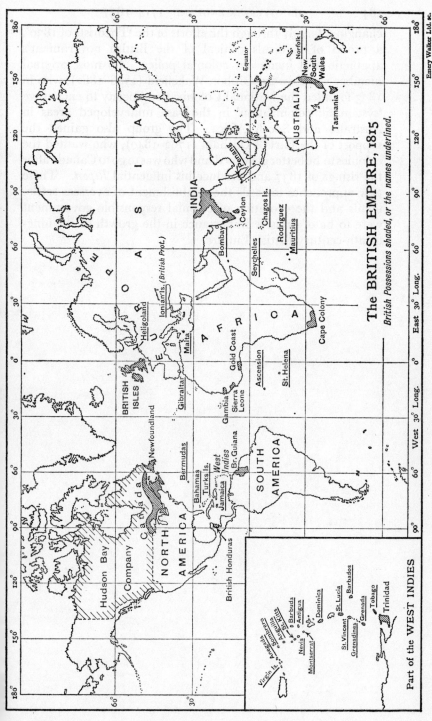

The BRITISH EMPIRE, 1815

British Possessions shaded, or the names underlined.

Emery Walker Ltd. sc.

Part of the WEST INDIES

N

changing, largely through the efforts of the 'Theorists of 1830', a group of Radicals critical of the British government's apathetic and inefficient colonial policy. Its most original member was Edward Gibbon Wakefield (1796–1862), who in 1833 founded the National Colonization Society to encourage 'systematic colonization' in the vast, undeveloped areas in Australia and South Africa. The group also gained the support of the Earl of Durham (1792–1840), who wanted the colonies to be better governed and who was to go to Canada after the risings of 1837 and produce his influential *Report*. These new approaches towards the establishment of overseas settlements and the evolution of colonial responsible government were to be of decisive importance in the growth of the nineteenth-century British Empire.

IX · WARFARE AND THE ARMED FORCES

A Century's Wars (1715–1815)

THE Hanoverian period began very soon after the end of the struggle against the France of Louis XIV. The two wars in which Britain fought, the War of the League of Augsburg (1689–97) and the War of the Spanish Succession (1702–13), were major European contests, and her part in them was large and decisive. Without her the Grand Alliance against France could not have endured to its successful conclusion. The Duke of Marlborough (1650–1722) was given the command of the allied forces in the Netherlands in 1702, and his great victories brought France down to defeat. There were no decisive battles at sea to match his military successes, but the British navy effectively supported land operations in Spain and Sicily, and Gibraltar and Minorca were captured. The Treaty of Utrecht, which ended the hostilities against Louis XIV (who died in 1715) was mainly Britain's work and brought her valuable commercial and colonial gains.

After the conclusion of peace, Britain had still to take a leading part in European affairs, and the danger of internal rebellion, to which George I's accession exposed her, made it more important than ever that her position in Europe should be secured. The six-and-a-half years' work of Stanhope in foreign affairs established an alliance with France and Holland strong enough to uphold the Utrecht settlement, particularly against Spanish ambitions, and prepared the way for Walpole's great ministry of financial reconstruction and peace.[1] For eighteen years Walpole was able to maintain for Britain that peace which he considered essential for the security of the dynasty and the well-being of her commerce. It ended in 1749 when popular opinion drove him unwillingly into war against Spain. This proved to be only the prelude to a long struggle for dominion between Britain and the Bourbon powers. The attempts of Stanhope and Walpole to pacify Europe gave way to a

[1] Pp. 237–41.

reversion of the pattern of the Grand Alliance. The pacific era of Walpole and Fleury was merely a short interlude in the eighteenth century. From the War of Jenkins's Ear and the War of the Austrian Succession to the Revolutionary and Napoleonic Wars, the Anglo-French overseas struggle was merged into the European conflict as it had been in the War of the Spanish Succession. This rivalry became the most enduring feature of the century, and has led some historians to call the wars in which it found expression the 'Second Hundred Years' War'.

The Elder Pitt's conduct of the Seven Years' War (1756–63) brought a new strategic conception to British methods of waging war. The greater attention given to naval and colonial warfare, which had marked the last years of the War of the Austrian Succession, was deliberately adopted by him as the best way to make use of Britain's naval power and economic resources and also to attain the gains she valued most. The navy participated directly in the destruction of French power in North America and India.[1] It also blockaded France, eliminating French overseas commerce and preventing the despatch of assistance to her colonies. Raids were made on the French coast, and some troops were sent to Germany, but the main reliance was upon allies – particularly Prussia – who were subsidised to contain French power in Europe.[2]

This new strategy was hardly, as it has often been described, Pitt's invention. From the early years of the eighteenth century, there had been a school of thought, largely Tory, which had put it forward as the best course to be adopted in wartime by Britain with her small population, weak and inefficient army and, at the same time, huge shipping reserves available for naval purposes. It had been argued that such a policy would not only be most likely to bring victory for Britain, but would also make war profitable for her by the capture of the enemy's overseas trade. These were the ideas Pitt so successfully put into effect in his conduct of the Seven Years' War.

During the American War of Independence (1775–83), however, the same policy could not preserve the possession of the thirteen colonies for Britain because she did not possess the means for carrying it out. A period of desuetude had

[1] Pp. 302 f.   [2] P. 304.

left her navy weaker than its rivals and incapable of fulfilling the functions required of it. At the same time, while the American colonies were joined by France, Spain and Holland in opposition to Britain, she was not only without allies, but had also to face an unfriendly Europe. The League of Armed Neutrality of 1780, formed by the Baltic powers, did not, in fact, achieve much in practice, but Britain's diplomatic isolation was complete. The absence of those two pre-requisites for success – naval supremacy and Continental allies – coupled with the geographical difficulties of warfare in North America and the muddled, inefficient and patronage-ridden administration at home, lost Britain the war.

Nor did this policy repeat its original success when Britain went to war with Revolutionary France in 1793, though by then she had again acquired command of the sea. The Younger Pitt thought that the war would be short and that Britain should fight it with limited objectives. He believed that it could be fought by his father's methods of naval supremacy and colonial conquests, British military raids and subsidized allies on the Continent. Unfortunately, Pitt was ignorant of war and lacked his father's genius for waging it. The ruthless, nationalist France of the Revolution was a much more formidable adversary than the old Bourbon kingdom which it had destroyed. And there were this time no Continental allies for Britain the equal of Frederick of Prussia and Ferdinand of Brunswick who had served his father. The French coasts were effectively blockaded by the navy, but Pitt misused British sea-power and her limited military resources by sending her best troops in 1793 on an expedition to the French West Indies where they captured some islands of no consequence and suffered terribly from disease. In the same year expeditionary forces sent to Holland and Toulon were defeated.

Before long Britain had to recognize that her efforts must be concentrated in Europe where the struggle would be won or lost. Pitt's policy of forming European coalitions, sub-sidized by Britain, against France was continued until the fourth and last victory was gained, but this was not achieved without considerable British military intervention on the Continent. A British expeditionary force was sent to Spain, where it gained success and renown under the Duke of

Wellington (1769–1852). Nevertheless, it was still British sea-power which made this possible, and the final hostilities ended symbolically with Napoleon's surrender to a British warship and his conveyance to St. Helena in another.

The war ended with British naval and military prestige both very high. Her command of the seas was unquestioned and her trade the most extensive in the world. The continued maintenance of naval supremacy after 1815 relieved her of the threat of foreign attack, except perhaps for a short time in 1831.[1] Government policy was to maintain the peace of Europe, prevent the rise of a fresh military domination of the Continent and support the cause of peoples seeking the right to self-government. Both the post-war foreign secretaries, Castlereagh and Canning, accepted these ideas, and, though their methods were different, both men depended upon the influence of sea-power to achieve their ends. This was equally true of Castlereagh's resistance to the attempts of the rulers of the Congress system to establish a new imperialism in Europe and of Canning's preservation of the independence of the former Spanish colonies in South America and support for the cause of Greek independence.[2] And shortly before the end of the period, Palmerston was similarly able to prevent Belgium from falling under French control.[3]

The Navy

It is clear, therefore, that in war and peace the maintenance of naval supremacy was an essential requisite for British foreign policy during these years. The House of Lords in an address to Queen Anne in 1707 stated, 'We do, in the most earnest manner, beseech your Majesty that the sea affairs may always be your first and most peculiar care'. The nation was then already sea-conscious and proud of the navy as the safeguard of its inviolability and the protector of its trade and colonies, but it was the war against Spain and France from 1739 to 1748 which aroused enthusiasm for the navy to popular heights. Events showed plainly the importance of sea-power. Admiral Vernon captured Porto Bello by naval attack and with a force of only six ships; Warren captured Louisbourg, while the two naval victories off Cape Finisterre frustrated French efforts to regain it; and, on the other hand, Madras was lost to the French because Britain had lost command of Indian waters.[1] This war made the navy definitely the first of the armed services in the estimate of public opinion, and its exploits were commemorated in James Thomson's *Rule Britannia*, David Garrick's *Heart of Oak* and many other more ephemeral ballads which were sung with gusto up and down the land.

Yet at the beginning of the Hanoverian period the navy as a permanent, specialized sea-force, organized and maintained by the government, was little more than half a century old. This navy in the modern sense was the creation of the Commonwealth. Before then there had been a small nucleus of warships, but the fleets which fought naval battles were composed mostly of armed merchantmen, taken into service upon the outbreak of war. The change was necessitated by the demands of hostilities with the Dutch, which continued beyond the Commonwealth intermittently for about thirty years.

The large-scale, bloody engagements of these Anglo-Dutch Wars led to far-reaching developments in naval warfare. To make it easier to control in battle, Admiral Robert Blake (1599–1657) divided the fleet into three separate squadrons, the ships of which were distinguished by red, white and blue flags. He went on to make an important change in tactics at the Battle of Portland in 1653 when he ordered his ships in each squadron, instead of fighting in a bunch, to form a line. This was the beginning of the line-ahead formation, the basic formation at both Trafalgar and Jutland. With it came also the broadside, which was beyond the firepower of even the largest converted merchantment. The Commonwealth government had to build the *Naseby* (later renamed the *Royal Charles*) and other line-of-battle ships. These were regular men-of-war, and henceforward they replaced hastily-secured merchantment as the backbone of a fighting fleet. The navy had become a regular, organized force.

At the same time, throughout the Hanoverian period British sea-power depended closely upon trade and overseas expansion. While the politically powerful commercial community demanded a strong navy to protect its trade and the colonies which played such a large part in sustaining that

1 P. 164.

trade, the navy in its turn drew men from the mercantile marine for service in time of war and found in the overseas possessions the bases from which to initiate land operations. It is true that eighteenth-century France also possessed these factors necessary for sea-power, but her trade was never as large as that of Britain, and she had to sacrifice naval to military needs by maintaining out of her limited financial resources the greatest army in Europe to uphold her position on the Continent.

Though Britain and France remained contestants for the possession of a maritime empire and commercial and naval supremacy until the end of the Napoleonic War, since Britain was relieved by her island position of the need to have a strong army she was able to maintain the largest fleet in the world in war and peace. By the end of the seventeenth century, she had become the greatest naval power, and France never dislodged her from this position. In 1721 she possessed 124 ships of the line and 105 smaller vessels, about a quarter of which had been built since 1714. These numbers were about the same on the outbreak of war with Spain in 1739, though lack of maintenance under Walpole meant that only 35 ships of the line were fit for immediate action. By 1762, however, she had 141 ships of the line and 224 smaller vessels, though again there were reductions in maintenance under Grenville which had disastrous consequences during the American War of Independence. The numbers had increased, however, by 1783 to 174 and 294, forming easily the most powerful navy yet seen. When she went to war with Revolutionary France, her ships of the line had fallen again to 141 in number, but 115 of them were ready for service, and so were most of her 157 frigates.

France made repeated efforts to build up her naval strength, but she never attained Britain's figures. The effect of Louis XIV's wars left her with only 49 ships of all sizes. Twenty years later she had 50 ships of the line. Despite quite heavy losses in the war of 1740–8 against Britain, she had 57 ships of the line and 24 frigates by 1754; but her losses in the Seven Years' War were much more serious, and by its conclusion she had only 35 ships of the line and 10 frigates, few of which were in good condition. Further efforts gave her 64 ships of the line and 54 frigates by 1770, and ten years later the figures were 86 and 78. She had been able to challenge British naval power in the American War of Independence, but the financial strain was severe, and the Revolutionary War found her able to put less than a third of her ships to sea immediately.

France did, however, possess the advantage of commonly fighting with Spain as an ally. After practically ceasing to exist after the War of the Spanish Succession, the Spanish navy rapidly revived in the next two decades. By 1735 it had 34 ships of the line. The losses in the great wars of the middle of the century were not heavy, and her ships of the line grew to 58 in number by 1774 and 72 by 1789. Spain never ranked as a formidable naval power in this period, but there were occasions, notably in 1740 and 1779, when the combined French and Spanish fleets outnumbered the British in capital ships sufficiently to become dangerous.

Another advantage enjoyed by France was that throughout the eighteenth century her ships (and those of Spain too) were better designed than were the British. During all this time France had a school of naval architecture; one was not opened in Britain until 1810, and it soon came to an end. Though Britain built more warships than her rivals, they were not as heavily armed. When the Revolutionary War began, the largest British ships, those of the *Victory* class, nominally mounted 100 guns, but France had eight sail of the line with from 110 to 120 guns, while the magnificent *Vengeur* (later *L'Impérial*) had 130 guns and was justly claimed to be '*le plus fort et le plus beau vaisseau qui eut jamais été construit dans aucun pays du monde*'. Again, British ships were not as effective in fire power, since one of 70 guns could not engage a French or Spanish ship of its own class, while a French ship of 50 guns could well take on a British ship of 70 guns. Finally, British ships were neither as seaworthy nor as stiff in a breeze. In a light squall a British ship might heel enough to prevent the opening of the ports of the lower deck, where the heaviest guns were mounted, so that only 12- and 18-pounders could be opposed to an enemy's 32- and 40-pounders.

British officers recognized the superiority of enemy ships. Such men as Collingwood spoke often of the 'Spanish beauties' they fought. The Admiralty also recognized their superiority. It paid handsomely captains who captured a warship, and the heavier ones were invariably recommissioned as flagships in the British fleet. Captured ships also served as models for British ship-builders. Thus, when the French frigate, *La Pomone*, believed to be the fastest warship afloat, was captured at the end of the eighteenth century, they used her lines in constructing new vessels, while the *Sanspareil*, taken from the French in 1794, inspired the lines of a British ship of the same name laid down as late as 1845.

The British navy, however, pioneered the two inventions which did most to increase the efficiency of eighteenth-century warships. From 1761 it began to copper its ships' bottoms, which reduced fouling by weeds and consequent loss of speed. This gave the navy a temporary advantage until its enemies did the same. A more lasting advantage came about the same time through the introduction of the carronade, a short-barrelled, large-calibre gun, mounted on the upper-deck, with a low muzzle-velocity and easily handled. It made an important contribution to the victories of Nelson's time, and French gunners succeeded in acquiring sufficient experience to use it with equal skill.

The great advantage enjoyed by the British navy over its enemies lay in the ability of its officers. Unlike the army, naval commissions could not be bought. The officers came mostly from the landed gentry and professional classes. They usually entered the navy at the age of thirteen as officers' servants, and their appointment to the rank of midshipman depended entirely upon the captain of the ship. Promotion to commissioned rank, however, was regulated by a system initiated by the efficiency-loving Samuel Pepys, who was Secretary of the Admiralty in Charles II's reign. No one could become a lieutenant until he had served at least six months as a midshipman and passed a technical examination. A seaman who had served as a mate for six months could also take this examination, so that promotion from the lower deck was possible, but it was rare in this period, one of the few remarkable exceptions being Captain Cook. Political and family influence affected appointments to higher posts, but this had its advantages as senior officers might have to act as ambassadors, governors and representatives of the Crown in far places under testing circumstances. On the whole, the system of promotion produced officers with experience, training and self-reliance, who compared favourably with their aristocratic French counterparts.

Britain also benefited from their long years of active service in the wars of the eighteenth century. During the period of peace from 1713 to 1739, few ships were in commission, few officers gained knowledge of conditions at sea, and few new ones joined the service; but the outbreak of war encouraged a band of younger men who were to make the century outstanding in naval successes. Prominent among them was George Anson (1697–1762), who sailed round the world between 1740 and 1744 and won the first Battle of Finisterre in 1747 which foreshadowed a change in the pattern of maritime warfare. During that war he also introduced the policy of blockading France and destroying her commerce to which the French in reply, in this and subsequent wars, had to have recourse to privateering, the *guerre de course*, which inflicted losses upon British merchants, but could never destroy the British navy. During the Seven Years' War, as First Lord of the Admiralty, he proved himself also a fine administrator. Especially important was the system of classifying warships which he introduced. As the size of warships had increased, vessels of very different armaments, from over 100 to less than 50 guns, were allowed to sail in the line of battle, which was dangerous as the enemy naturally concentrated its fire on the smaller ships to try to break the line by overwhelming them. Anson applied the system of rating to ships of the line – First (three-deckers of 100 or more guns), Second (three-deckers of 90 guns) and Third Rates (two-deckers of 74 or 64 guns) – and these alone were to sail in the line.

Other sailors of this generation whose names became household words as admirals included Edward Hawke (1705–81), George Rodney (1719–92) and Edward Boscawen (1711–61). By the end of the Seven Years' War, indeed, the British navy was unrivalled in its officers, who ably carried out the Elder Pitt's perfection of maritime strategy which used naval power to conquer colonial territories by combined operations from overseas bases.

The navy was never short of officers; many families had a seafaring tradition, but the demands for seamen during the wars of the period were insatiable. Its wartime establishment rose steadily from 35,000 in 1740 to 70,000 in 1760, 85,000 in

1780, 129,000 in 1802 and 140,000 in 1811. The fundamental difficulty of manning the fleet when war began was that no one below commissioned rank was a regular serviceman. With a warship's paying off at the end of a commission, its company was discharged from the service as well as from the ship. In peacetime, no ships of the line were kept fully manned and most were laid up, while the number of seamen and marines was drastically reduced. In 1750 Pelham even brought it down to 8,000, but this aroused protests from other ministers, and he had to raise it to 10,000.[1] In the late eighteenth century the peacetime establishment was fixed at 16,000. This system existed owing to the general economy of the country and because it was reckoned that the navy could obtain the men it needed in war from merchant sailors and fishermen, but the actual recruitment of seamen was made difficult because there were never enough volunteers, and the impressment of men from these classes was regularly practised, even in peacetime. When during the Revolutionary War, sufficient men could not be obtained from the seafaring population, Pitt's Quota Acts of 1795 arranged for the recruitment of other men by quotas levied on the counties and large towns according to their populations, but the local authorities tended to send their undesirable characters – thieves, vagabonds, idlers and agitators – to serve in the fleet.

These methods had to be used because men disliked the conditions of service in the navy. Their main objection was not to naval discipline or to the flogging that maintained it. Far from complaining about flogging, most seamen seem to have approved of it. By this time, a captain could not award more than two dozen lashes of the cat-o'-nine-tails on the bare back without a court martial. There were hated captains who abused their position and resorted to severe and frequent flogging on their ships, but these were exceptions. William Bligh, for instance, often regarded as a brutal captain, only ordered seven floggings during his voyage in the *Bounty* to the Pacific between 1787 and 1789. In an age when corporal punishment was common, the cat was generally accepted, and, moreover, seamen realized that they might be hanged ashore for many of the offences for which they were flogged afloat.

[1] P. 282.

Men did not want to serve in the navy mainly because the standards of pay and living were well below those in merchant ships. Seamen's wages were the same as during the Commonwealth, although by the beginning of the eighteenth century the cost of living had risen 30 per cent, and they were often not paid to them until six months after arrival in a home port, while they were frequently cheated by the pursers. Since warships had to fight as well as sail, they were overcrowded; the men lived and slept among the guns, sometimes as many as 1,300 in a ship. Voyages of weeks and months were common, often in sultry climates. The food might be bad and was always monotonous; salt beef and salt pork were issued on alternate days, green vegetables were rare and fresh water was limited. It is not surprising that the *Annual Register* for 1763 recorded that in the Seven Years' War 1,512 seamen were killed in battle and 133,708 died of disease or were missing.

Such conditions produced constant desertions, unchecked by wholesale restriction of shore-leave and drastic punishments. Over 42,000 seamen deserted between 1776 and 1780, and these figures are not untypical for the whole period. Public opinion was complacent about conditions in the navy, and the social gulf between officers and men did much to perpetuate abuses in the ships. The mutinies at Spithead and the Nore in 1797 took everyone by surprise.[1] Richard Parker, the leader of the Nore mutiny, was a 'quota-man' impressed by Pitt's acts of 1795 and probably others were prominent among the mutineers. Their lists of grievances said little about the cat, but much about pay, food and leave. After the mutinies, pay was increased and other reforms conceded, while the care taken of their men by such commanders as Howe and Nelson became more common. In their concern for their crews, they represented a new conception of duty among naval officers.

This had been paralleled by the gradual evolution of a fresh approach to naval tactics. The introduction of the large capital ship and the line-ahead formation had been followed by the adoption of a tactical system designed to regulate naval battles. Previously fleets had rarely manœuvred during an engagement, which had usually been

[1] P. 379.

a series of isolated combats between ships. Under the line-ahead formation, each ship should follow closely the one ahead, so that the fleet formed a single long line; and it was vitally important to 'keep the line' so that the approaching enemy was exposed to the combined broadsides of the whole fleet, for if an enemy ship 'broke the line', by sailing between the bows of one ship and the stern or the next ahead, it could use its broadsides while remaining itself invulnerable. At the Battle of Beachy Head in 1690 the French broke the allied line with disastrous results, and consequently the next year Admiral Edward Russell issued *Fighting Instructions* which came, in the eighteenth century, to be binding upon all admirals. Their main purpose was to 'keep the line' and prevent the enemy breaking it.

Unfortunately this had the practical effect of stultifying the initiative of admirals in battle thus leading to indecisive engagements. Battles became gun-duels between two rival fleets, drawn up in parallel lines, which produced no important result. Between Barfleur in 1692 and The Saints in 1782 British fleets fought fifteen actions in which they preserved the fighting line throughout, and in none of these did they defeat the enemy or even capture or sink a single one of his ships. Among the occasions in which British fleets were robbed of victory through conformity to the *Instructions* were the Battle of Toulon in 1744 when Admiral Mathews abstained from vigorous pursuit of the Franco-Spanish fleet; the action off Minorca in 1756 where Admiral Byng, though personally brave, believed that he must preserve the close-hauled line of battle under all circumstances; and the Battle of Chesapeake Bay in 1781 in which Admiral Graves caught the French fleet in confusion, but maintained his line so completely that Admiral de Grass was able to manœuvre away.

Only six victories were won by a British fleet during this period of ninety years, and these all occurred when an admiral was prepared to take advantage of an article in the *Instructions* which allowed him to break formation and chase the enemy with all his ships if he judged the battle to be already decisively in his favour. Anson did this on an important occasion in 1747. While waiting for a month in the Bay of Biscay for the French fleet, he constantly exercised his fleet in battle formations and manœuvres. On the appearance of a French squadron, escorting two convoys, one for America and the other for India, he changed the correctly formal line into a general pursuit which effected the capture of all nine escorting warships by nightfall. A few months later Hawke intercepted another French attempt to send reinforcements overseas and in the same way took six of the eight enemy warships.

The more adventurous spirit produced in British officers by the century's wars led to a gradual ignoring of the *Instructions*, and the culmination came when Rodney won the Battle of The Saints in 1782 by deliberately setting out to break the enemy's line. As the two opposing fleets passed on opposite course, he ordered the captain of his flagship, the *Formidable*, to put over his helm and led his squadron through the French line, throwing it into confusion. He captured five ships, including the flagship, the *Ville de Paris*, of 112 guns, then the largest and strongest warship afloat, with De Grasse aboard. One of his junior admirals here was Samuel Hood (1724–1816), who later passed on to Nelson his knowledge of naval warfare.

Nelson could take advantage of the freedom henceforward allowed to British admirals to exploit their tactical genius, and he became the most brilliant naval strategist among them. He displayed the 'Nelson touch' audaciously at the Battle of Trafalgar, his last and greatest victory. Just before rejoining the *Victory*, he made a diagram on a small table, with his finger dipped in wine, to show Lord Sidmouth how he proposed to attack the combined Franco-Spanish fleet. 'Rodney', he said, 'broke the line in one point. I shall break it in two.' The thirty-three enemy ships were extended in a half-moon five miles long, and Nelson with his twenty-seven ships struck at their centre in two columns. While no British ship was lost, the enemy were deprived of twenty-two of their heaviest vessels, and none of the others ever fought again. Superior seamanship, gunnery and initiative in command won the battle, and these were the qualities which gave Britain the command of the seas for the rest of the war and beyond.

For the rest of the Hanoverian period, the navy adapted itself to the new tasks of peace. All over the world ships charted the oceans for the Hydrographic Department (founded in 1797). An expedition in 1816 attacked Algiers

and released fifteen thousand men and women enslaved by
the Barbary Corsairs from European ships in the Mediterranean, while the West Africa Squadron (a quarter of whom
died of fever in 1829) continually hunted down slave-ships.
The destruction of the Egyptian fleet at Navarino in 1827
secured Greek independence, and was a dramatic example of
the influence of British sea-power, usually exerted more
quietly.[1]

Improvements were made during these years in the sailing
warships, such as better hull designs and flush upper decks,
and 130 guns became the regular armament of first-rate ships
of the line.   Although before the end of the period, there were
already steam-driven merchant ships, the navy was slow to
adopt the invention, since the early steamers were moved by
paddle-wheels, likely to be vulnerable in battle and to interfere with the accommodation of guns upon the broadside.
Moreover, Britain's sea-power was based upon her 'wooden
walls', and the new invention seemed likely to destroy her
existing superiority over other nations.   'Their Lordships
felt it their bounden duty to discourage to the utmost of their
ability the use of steam vessels, as they considered that the
introduction of steam was calculated to strike a fatal blow at
the naval superiority of the Empire' – so wrote the First Lord
to the Colonial Secretary in 1828.   A paddle-steamer was
built for the navy on Brunel's advice in 1822.   At Queen
Victoria's accession, the only steamers in naval service were
small tugs to tow sailing warships out of harbour.   Turner's
The Fighting Temeraire shows the situation at this time.   There
was little to suggest that the last days of the sailing warship
were approaching.

The Army

Throughout this period the army did not enjoy the same
national popularity as the navy.   The pride inspired by
Marlborough's earlier victories had not lasted as long as the
war, while fears aroused by Cromwell's major-generals and
James II's Irish-officered army were still strong.   When
peace came, no one wanted 'a burthensom and useless army
at home'; and since 1689 a standing army in peacetime was
only legalized from year to year by the passing of the annual

[1] P. 422.

Mutiny Act authorizing the enforcement of military discipline.

The strength of the British army had attained a maximum figure of 200,000 in war under Marlborough, but this had fallen to 30,000 by 1714. Jacobite threats led to the raising of its strength to 36,000 in 1716, but it fell steadily to 16,300 in 1718 and 12,400 in 1721. From 1722 to 1738, during Walpole's ministry, it was usually between 16,000 and 18,000. In the period of war from 1739 to 1748 it rapidly increased to about 36,000 and attained its maximum of 74,000 in 1745. During the years of peace it was maintained at about 19,000. The Seven Years' War again led to its rapid growth, immediately to nearly 68,000, and finally to 150,000, but this was reduced to some 30,000 in 1764. The later wars of the century compelled Parliament to increase the army's numbers continually; they were 110,000 in 1780 and 168,000 in 1800. Politicians, however, were often tempted to bid for popularity by taking advantage of opportunities to cut them down. Addington in 1802 reduced the army's establishment to 95,000. Soon afterwards, under the threat of invasion, Pitt increased its numbers to 175,000, and between 1810 and 1815 they remained at about 300,000, but peace brought rapid reductions until by 1821 they were down to less than 100,000, of whom under half were at home.

Though at the end of each war in the eighteenth century, the establishment of the army was reluctantly fixed at a larger number than before the outbreak of hostilities, it was still too small to meet a threat of foreign invasion or other emergency. Troops had then to be taken from the Irish establishment, usually kept at 12,000, or hired from Holland, Hanover or Hesse-Cassel; and when war came, foreign troops were also hired to bring the forces abroad up to effective strength. The army was even too small to perform its normal peacetime duties properly. These were twofold. First, it had to assist, in the absence of police forces, to maintain law and order at home. Dragoons were employed to suppress smuggling, and cavalry patrols operated against footpads on the road between Kensington and London. Troops were called out to suppress riots and disorder or even strikes of workmen or gangs of poachers. Secondly, the army had to garrison the colonies, and its numbers did not allow an organized system of reliefs. 'In what other army',

o

Wellington asked, 'was it ever heard of that parts of it were to serve for twenty years in the East Indies, then come home to stay for five and then be sent to some other tropical or insalubrious climate?' The rates of mortality in these overseas garrisons were terribly high. Few British soldiers survived ten years' service in India. When a regiment was ordered abroad its ranks might be halved by desertion.

Indeed, the peacetime discipline and morale of the army were low. Deductions from their pay for food, billets and clothing might leave privates with only a few pence a week. In Scotland and Ireland the troops were housed in barracks, but in England steady opposition to the building of barracks prevented their systematic development until 1793. Until then most regiments were divided into six or eight detachments and billeted on unwilling innkeepers in as many small towns, a system which made training and discipline very difficult to enforce. In such circumstances, flogging seems to have been often more frequent and severe than in the navy. Courts Martial not infrequently awarded punishments of 800 or 1,000 lashes of the cat in the eighteenth century; a limit of 300 lashes was imposed in 1812, which was reduced to 100 lashes in 1832. In the eighteenth century also camp-followers were sometimes flogged, and there are records of disorderly women receiving up to 200 lashes of the cat, but the usual punishment for them was a whirligig, a pivoted wooden cage in which the woman was spun round for an hour to make her 'giddy and landsick'.

Under the circumstances, few but social outcasts joined the ranks of the army – 'the mere scum of the earth' was Wellington's well-known description of them. Enlistment in peacetime was for life until the act introduced by William Windham in 1806 substituted terms of years with higher rates of pay for re-enlistment. Normally, however, the army did not use press-gangs, but obtained its recruits mainly from volunteers enlisted by regimental officers and debtors and criminals freed from prison on condition they joined the army. When war came, extra numbers were sought in various ways. Acts allowed bounties to be paid to parish authorities for the impressment of their paupers. Bounties were paid to men enlisting for short periods. Individuals were encouraged by the offer of rank to raise independent companies of fencibles, who were regular troops for home service for the duration of hostilities; and during the threat of Napoleonic invasion companies of part-time volunteers were formed for coastal protection. There was also the militia, descended from the fyrd, the Anglo-Saxon national force composed of all free men. An Act of 1663 had placed the obligation to provide a quota of men from each county upon property owners, but men called on to serve could provide substitutes. The militia was liable to service anywhere in the kingdom, but was never effectively trained. The Elder Pitt's Militia Act of 1757 transferred the responsibility for supplying men to the counties, each being required to furnish a quota of men, apportioned among its parishes and chosen by lot; substitutes were still allowed. The militia was embodied during the Seven Years' War and the subsequent French Wars, supplying drafts for both home defence and overseas service.

The officers of the army usually came from much the same social classes as naval officers, but during peacetime many neglected their duties and even absented themselves from their regiments. Indeed, so little was required of them that the temptation to take their profession lightly was strong, and when they took the field, it was often with a great deal of carriages and baggage. Another weakness suffered by the army was the system of buying and selling commissions. This meant that moneyed officers could obtain promotion over the heads of their more experienced but poorer comrades, whose only chance of rising from the lower ranks might come through wartime's casualties and opportunities to distinguish themselves in action. It also meant that officers regained the cost of their commissions by making what profits they could from administering and equipping the regiment. A colonel, indeed, was practically the proprietor of his regiment, and through his hands passed bounties for recruiting and contracts with victuallers and suppliers. Not until 1751 were regiments known by official numbers and titles instead of the names of their colonels.

This was a small point in itself, but it was also part of a movement towards military reform in the first half of the century. George I displayed much interest and some capacity in military affairs; he took a 'great aversion' to the purchase system of promotion and, though unable to get it abolished, encouraged the fixing of prices for commissions and the possession of some military ability by those who bought them. The Royal Regiment of Artillery was founded in 1727; its commissions were not for sale, and in 1741 Woolwich Academy was established to provide it with well-trained officers. The Duke of Cumberland, who gained such unpopularity during the Forty-Five, reformed several abuses when he was Commander-in-Chief, among them restrictions on the number of officers' private carriages brought on campaigns and on their leave. He also encouraged the promotion of keen, young officers, such as Howe, Wolfe and Lawrence, who were given their chance by the Elder Pitt and proved their worth at Dettingen, Fontenoy, Minden and Quebec.

There followed, however, the army's disasters in the American War of Independence and then in the West Indies and Holland and Toulon. Fortunately the most thorough reform of the army in the century was now undertaken by another royal duke with an unfortunate reputation, the Duke of York, who was Commander-in-Chief from 1798 and has been described by a recent historian as 'the ablest and most powerful administrative chief the army had had since James II'. The way for him had been prepared by Burke's Act of 1783 which transferred recruitment and finance from the regimental commanders to the government. The Duke of York insisted that he must control numbers, efficiency and discipline. He placed a new emphasis on 'merit' and 'scientific' attainments and on drill and manœuvre and to achieve this established in 1799 the Royal Military College at High Wycombe (which was removed to Sandhurst in 1812). He also ordered the formation in 1800 of the 95th Regiment (later called the Rifle Brigade), which was armed with an improved rifle, given inconspicuous dark-green uniforms instead of red coats and led by picked officers who were encouraged to establish discipline by efficiency rather than flogging. This new formation gradually instilled a new spirit in the army as a whole. A further important reform came in 1806 when Parliament abolished enlistment for life, substituting for it the possibility of enlistment for a short period and higher rates of pay for men who re-enlisted.

The Duke of Wellington disliked many of these reforms. He thought the 'democratizing' of promotion had gone too far and scorned the new officers as 'coxcombs and pedants'. Nevertheless, he used the improved army with supreme success. His opportunity came in 1808 when the British government decided to send an army to the Iberian Peninsula to encourage Portuguese and Spanish resistance to Napoleon. This was a theatre of war well-suited to British military intervention; sea-power enabled an expeditionary force of 40,000 men to be landed and maintained at Lisbon, which Wellington in 1810 protected with the lines of Torres Vedras, an elaborate series of defensive earthworks and well-placed artillery.[1] Though the French usually had more than 300,000 men in the Peninsula, these had to remain scattered in order to garrison hostile territory and live off the country-side. Here also Wellington's 'direct and narrow realism', as a biographer has called it, could exploit these advantages. His forces were limited – 'If I lost five hundred men without the clearest necessity', he said, 'I should be brought to my knees' – but for two years he fought as few battles as possible, being content to remain behind his fortifications, supporting the operations of the Spanish guerrillas and emerging in the summer to attack detached enemy forces. He inflicted heavy losses on the French and strained their resources until in 1812 he was at last able to take the offensive and offer them battle.

Moreover, when he fought, Wellington succeeded in finding the tactical answer to the methods of warfare which had made Napoleon's armies supreme on the Continent. The French won their victories through bombardments by heavy cannon, commonly twelve-pounders firing iron round-shot, and charges by massed columns of infantry using the bayonet and squadrons of cavalry equipped with long, heavy lances. Wellington countered this by choosing his fighting-ground so as to afford cover for his deployed ranks or squares of infantry from artillery fire as long as possible, by screening his battle-front with skirmishers and by training his soldiers to hold out steadily on the defensive. His infantry were assisted in doing this by their possession of 'Brown Bess', a firelock much superior to any then carried by Continental armies, with which a

[1] P. 397.

well-drilled British regiment could fire three volleys or more in a minute.

These tactics won Wellington the Battle of Waterloo, the only one he fought against Napoleon himself. Although he could not choose his theatre of operations to suit his strategy, he was able to select his own position for fighting and follow his tactical methods. He kept his troops under cover on the reverse slope of Mont-St. Jean, where they would suffer little from the enemy artillery, and when Napoleon delivered a heavy bombardment from a great battery of 78 guns and sent his columns again and again against the British line, it resisted with the discipline it had acquired in the Peninsula. From ten in the morning to the evening, Wellington's army withstood the cannonade and cavalry and infantry attacks, shattering them with salvoes of musket and grapeshot and sending in cavalry to complete the rout, until the sound of Blücher's guns announced that aid was on the way. Wellington then advanced his complete line of infantry with artillery and cavalry support and drove the French in confusion from the field. The British army had defeated Napoleon. It was now to face nearly forty years of general peace and neglect.

X · SCOTLAND, IRELAND AND HANOVER

The King's Dominions

'His Majesty's dominions, on which the sun never sets' – the phrase was first used in 1829 by the Scottish author, John Wilson, who wrote as 'Christopher North'. He was writing, of course, about the overseas British Empire, but at the beginning of the Hanoverian period, although Britain possessed the American colonies and other overseas possessions, most people still meant by the 'King's dominions' the territories of the British Isles which the Crown had acquired in the course of history – Ireland and Scotland. In addition, the Crown still maintained some sort of a claim to the French throne and ruled the Electorate of Hanover in Germany.

The Royal Style asserted this position. George I was proclaimed as 'King of Great Britain, France and Ireland', and he was already Elector of Hanover and Duke of Brunswick-Lüneburg. The position was more strikingly revealed in the royal coat of arms. James I and his successors had combined the lions passant of England and the fleur-de-lys of France in the first and fourth quarter, the lion rampant of Scotland in the second and the harp of Ireland in the third. George I superimposed on all this the elaborate heraldic badge of Hanover, consisting of two lions for Brunswick, hearts and a lion for Lüneburg and a white horse for Westphalia.

This crowded shield was the result of royal ambition or dynastic succession which had brought these territories into the ambit of England. By the Hanoverian period, however, the connection with France had long been entirely fictitious. Edward III and Henry V had claimed the Kingdom of France in the Middle Ages, and their descendants continued to be proclaimed as its rulers long after the last English armies had been driven from its soil. The coronations of the first three Georges were still attended by 'two persons representing the Dukes of Normandy and Aquitaine', who each wore 'a mantle of crimson velvet furred with ermine and a cap of cloth of gold lined with ermine'. At George I's coronation, the dukes were represented by a couple of professional actors; and the only part of the spectacle that amused Jacobites in the Abbey was the jaunty way in which the sham dukes clapped on their caps when the peers assumed their coronets at the crowning of the King. The representatives of the two French dukes last appeared at George III's coronation. They and the fleur-de-lys in the royal arms vanished when the formal claim to the Kingdom of France was abandoned on behalf of the Kings of England at the change of the Royal Style in 1801.

English attempts to conquer Scotland in the Middle Ages had met with the same final failure as in France, but when James VI of Scotland became also James I of England in 1603, the two kingdoms were brought under one sovereign. Parliamentary and economic union, however, was not achieved until the passing of the Act of Union in 1707. This abolished the Scottish Parliament, but preserved the separate judicial system and the establishment of the Presbyterian Church and secured free trade between the two countries. Scotland was to send 16 peers and 45 commoners to the Parliament of Great Britain at Westminster. So by the time of the Hanoverian accession, England and Scotland had at last joined to form a United Kingdom, but juncture was recent and its time of testing was very soon to come.

Ireland at this time was still a separate kingdom under the British Crown. The English connection with the island had begun in 1171, when Henry II proclaimed himself Lord of Ireland and received homage from the Irish chiefs, but effective English authority was confined to the Pale, an area around Dublin which continued to shrink in size for centuries. The Tudors attempted to assert their authority in Ireland. By Poynings' Act of 1494 no legislation was to be introduced in the Irish Parliament without approval by the King in Council. From 1537 Henry VIII and his successors undertook a virtual reconquest of Ireland and introduced the religious changes of the Reformation, which most Irish people rejected. The sixteenth and seventeenth centuries brought successive rebellions and repression in Ireland and also the confiscation of land for settlement by Protestants from England and Scotland. James II made his last stand in

Ireland, but William III's victory at the Battle of the Boyne in 1690 and the Treaty of Limerick the next year established the ascendancy of the English government and Protestantism.

Finally, there was Hanover. After the death of Princess Anne's son, the young Duke of Gloucester, Parliament had passed the Act of Settlement of 1701 to maintain the Protestant succession to the throne. The claims of the decendants of Charles I were set aside, and it was enacted that if William III and Anne left no heirs the succession should pass to Sophia, Dowager Electress of Hanover (who was a grand-daughter of James I) or her Protestant descendants. Sophia died shortly before Queen Anne in 1714, and so her son succeeded to the British throne as George I. Hanover never formed part of the British Empire, but its monarchy was united with that of Great Britain throughout the period of the dynasty to which it gave its name.

Scotland

'Now there's ane end of ane auld sang', said the flippant and cynical Earl of Seafield as he signed the Act of Union of 1707. To some extent the act did, indeed, conclude the separate existence of Scotland as a nation. The sixteen Scottish peers elected to the Parliament of 1715 by their fellows were said to be, to a man, those whom the government wanted to have returned, and no distinctively Scottish party appeared in the Commons. Scottish members, in fact, invariably supported the existing government until 1832

The smallness of the electorate and the nature of the electoral system facilitated political manipulation. The thirty county members were elected by landowners whose estates were held directly from the Crown and were worth not less than £400 Scots (£33 6s. 8d. sterling) a year. Only about a half of the county voters, however, were genuine landowners; the rest were 'parchment barons', tenants whose landlords had made them nominal estate-owners to secure them a vote. Yet, even though their numbers were multiplied in this way, there were fewer than three thousand Scottish county voters at the end of the eighteenth century. The sixty-six royal burghs were represented by fifteen members, but only Edinburgh had a member of its own. The remaining burghs, irrespective of size, had been divided in 1707 into groups of four or five, each returning a member who was chosen by an electoral college composed of delegates, one being appointed from each burgh by its self-perpetuating town council. Such a system made it cheap and easy for the government to get its supporters elected.

At the beginning of the Hanoverian period, the economic benefits which many Scots had expected from the Union had yet to materialize. Freedom of trade had brought little advantage to Scotland because she had few industries and little to export. Indeed, the immediate result of the Union had been to ruin the woollen industry of the Lowlands by depriving it of protection against imported superior English cloth. Many Scotsmen also resented the stricter enforcement of customs duties resulting from the Union, and this grievance was responsible for the famous Porteous Riots of 1737 in Edinburgh when the commander of the city guard, which had fired upon a crowd demonstrating at the execution of a smuggler, was lynched by an armed mob.[1]

Yet feeling against the Union in the Lowlands, where the great majority of Scotland's population lived, was neither deep-seated nor lasting. From about 1720 the area's economic life revived. The western coast developed a trade with the colonies, and this especially benefited Glasgow which, on the eve of the American War of Independence, had deprived Liverpool and Bristol of most of the tobacco trade. Efforts were made to reform agriculture by the Society of Improvers, founded in 1723, while the linen industry expanded rapidly with encouragement from the Board of Trustees, set up in 1727. By the middle of the century, indeed, the Lowlands enjoyed a prosperity which well reconciled it to the Union.

It was otherwise with the Highlands. Times were more peaceful, but since the population grew more rapidly than the resources of a country with such a sterile soil and wretched climate, the restlessness of the Highlanders remained. Conditions, indeed, had hardly changed since Montrose had led the royalist cause there during the civil strife of the seventeenth century. The mountainous countryside and scarceness of roads still isolated the glens from the rest of Scotland. In religion, the people were mostly Episcopalian

[1] P. 264.

and Roman Catholic, and their clergy had suffered Presbyterian persecution after the Revolution settlement of 1689.
They continued their age-long raids on Lowland farms to
supplement the poor herds which never fetched enough to
buy the grain they needed. Parliament still allowed the
chiefs to exercise their hereditable jurisdictions and feudal
rights which empowered them to settle disputes and
administer justice among their clans, who were also their
tenants and military retainers. The disobedient were
punished by the seizure of cattle and burning of cottages. If
a chief called out his tenants for military service by the fiery
cross, the clansmen followed willingly or were 'forced out',
and they formed an effective militia, fearless, trained to arms
and rapid on the march.

The Lowlands displayed little enthusiasm for the Roman
Catholic son and grandson of James II who in their turn
sought the throne, but from the first Jacobites believed they
would get the support they needed from the Highlands. In
1708 a French squadron, with the Old Pretender, Prince
James Edward, on board, reached the Firth of Forth, only to
have to retire before a stronger British fleet and take him back
to France. Jacobite hopes were dampened, only to be
stimulated into action again after George I's accession.

The new Whig ministry's first actions aroused deep Tory
resentment in England.[1] The Jacobites around the Pretender
could not agree where a landing should be made. Eventually
the argument was settled by the Earl of Mar, known as
'Bobbing John', who had been deprived of the Secretaryship
of State for Scotland by the government. In September
1715 he raised the standard of revolt at Perth and was joined
by about five thousand clansmen, but he failed to move southwards until November, when his way was barred near Dun-
blane by an army under the Duke of Argyll, leader of the
powerful Campbells, who supported the Revolution settlement. The resulting Battle of Sheriffmuir was indecisive,
but Mar retreated and abandoned his forces, which were
finally dispersed by the Earl of Cadogan in February 1716.
Meanwhile, a rising of the Jacobites of the border and
northern England had ended in a general surrender at
Preston.[2] The cause was already lost when James Edward

[1] P. 232.   [2] P. 233.

landed in Scotland in January 1716, and he returned to France within a month. The risings had failed largely through the ineptitude of their leaders, lack of French support, divisions among the clans and apathy in England.[1]

After the 'Fifteen the government on the whole acted with moderation.[2] In Scotland continued tolerance of the increasingly uneasy anachronism of the clan system made possible another serious rebellion. The Jacobites hoped this might occur in 1719 when Spain was ready to support their cause, but though a small Spanish squadron landed three hundred troops in the western Highlands, they and the Highlanders who joined them were routed by government troops at Glenshiel. After this, the government made some effort to subdue the Highlands. The Disarming Act of 1725, requiring clansmen to give up their weapons, was largely circumvented, but more effective were the measures taken between 1726 and 1737 by General Wade. He built some 250 miles of roads linking Perth, Inverness and the Great Glen (which was held by Fort George, Fort Augustus and Fort William); he also raised kilted companies of loyal clansmen, and these were formed in 1739 into a regiment, the Black Watch, which fought at Fontenoy.

The government trusted that these measures would discipline the Highlands, but they provoked a last desperate armed resistance to change when the outbreak of war between Britain and France in 1744 encouraged the Jacobites to make their most dangerous attempt on the throne. The French had projected an expedition of 15,000 troops under Marshal de Saxe in 1744, but its troop-ships had been wrecked at Dunkirk and its escorting fleet driven out of the Channel by a storm. By the next year they had other plans. When the Young Pretender, Prince Charles Edward, landed in the western Highlands in July 1745 with only seven companions, the British navy had turned back his supply ship.[3] Still worse, he landed against French wishes, but a number of the clans rallied to him. As most of the British army was engaged on the Continent in the War of the Austrian Succession, there were hardly more than 3,000 recruits garrisoning Scotland, and their commander, Sir John Cope, left the route to the Lowlands open. Charles captured Edinburgh and

[1] P. 233.   [2] Pp. 233-4.   [3] P. 278.

routed Cope's force at the Battle of Prestonpans in September. Five weeks later, Charles led an army of 5,500 men southwards through Carlisle and Manchester to Derby, which he

SCOTLAND
AND
NORTHERN
ENGLAND

– – – Route of Young Pretender 1745-6
———— Wade's Roads constructed 1725-40
· · · · · · Other military roads
up to c.1780

English Miles

20 10 0   20   40   60

reached in December, hoping that success in England would bring him French help. The news caused alarm in London; but the clansmen were beginning to desert Charles, while few Jacobites joined him, and little French help came. He reluctantly began a retreat which ended in crushing defeat for his Highlanders on Culloden Moor in April 1746 by the seasoned army brought from Flanders by the Duke of Cumberland.   After five months of wanderings and narrow escapes, Charles escaped to France.

For three months after his victory, Cumberland set out to terrorize the Highlands and gained his name of 'Butcher' by his ruthless shooting of suspects, burning of cottages and destruction of crops.   And this time the government acted with greater severity.   Some eighty prisoners were tried and executed, while over eleven hundred were transported or banished.   The government also made a determined effort to pacify the Highlands after this last desperate resistance. In 1746 Parliament passed a new Disarming Act, which was rigorously enforced, and prohibited the wearing of tartans; and in 1748 it abolished hereditable jurisdictions.   This broke up the clan system and brought quiet to the Highlands, but did not solve the other problems of this over-peopled barren region. Its population increased too fast even for its own wretched standard of living, and an exodus from the crofts began about 1830 and was to continue until the end of the century.

After the 'Forty-Five, Scotland had no political history. The Secretaryship of State for Scotland, which had frequently been left vacant, was abolished in 1746, not to be revived until late in the nineteenth century.   The French Revolution inspired demands for parliamentary reform, but these were silenced by the political trials of 1794 at which Radical agitators were sentenced to be transported for fourteen years. As in England, repression continued beyond the French Wars, and in 1820 occurred the 'Radical War' in Glasgow when cavalry encountered a number of demonstrating weavers, three of whom were subsequently executed.   In 1832, however, a month after the English Reform Bill was enacted, Parliament passed the Scottish Reform Bill, similarly reforming the franchise and raising the number of Scottish members in the Commons to fifty-three.

A similar merging of Scottish writing and thought into that of Britain took place.   The later Hanoverian period was the 'Athenian Age' of Scotland, years of great achievement in scholarship, learning and literature.   Yet the leading writers of the movement continued a development which had begun in the sixteenth century when John Knox wrote in English instead of the old Scots tongue he had learnt as a child. Philosophers and historians such as David Hume, William

Robertson and Adam Smith carefully avoided scotisms in their work as far as possible. Even Robert Burns, who wrote his best poetry in the speech of the contemporary Scottish countryside, derived much of his technique from a study of the greater English writers. And Sir Walter Scott's novels, including those set in Scotland, aroused a lively interest and exerted a powerful influence in England.[1] Parallel with this development was the increasing tendency, already apparent before the 'Forty-Five, for wealthier Scottish families to send their sons to be educated at the English public schools and universities.

Finally, this period also brought to Scotland the beginnings of the series of social and economic changes, similar to those in England, which made up the Agrarian and Industrial Revolutions. In the countryside of the Lowlands agriculture was transformed by 'improving' landlords with a consequent marked increase in productivity. Small family farms were replaced by 'factory farms', and there was a new social grouping of landowners, substantial tenant-farmers and landless, semi-migratory farm-labourers. Even more striking was Scotland's industrial growth. Numerous new coal-mines were sunk in the middle counties from Ayrshire to Fife, and iron-making similarly developed, most spectacularly at the Carron Ironworks.[2] The steamship was first evolved on the Clyde.[3] Glasgow grew as a port and the centre of an industrial area. The linen industry was overtaken in output by the cotton mills. Roads were built by turnpike trusts and bridges by Rennie and Telford, while the opening of the Forth and Clyde Canal in 1790 made it possible to transport heavy goods across central Scotland. There was a steadily increasing shift of population from the North and South to the already long-settled and populous central region, where alone coal and iron were found. This was the most remarkable period in Scottish history, and it was essentially made possible and moulded by the country's association with England in the United Kingdom.

Ireland

Very different was the history of Ireland during this period. The island remained conquered, but not absorbed.

[1] P. 100.   [2] P. 134.   [3] P. 153.

The Williamite settlement of 1691, which was followed by further confiscations, completed the transfer of landownership to the new Protestant settler aristocracy, so that by 1714 only a seventh of the land still belonged to the native Roman Catholics who comprised five-sixths of the population; and even this was further reduced in subsequent years by legislation favouring Protestant against Roman Catholic heirs. The ascendancy seemed firmly in control. Its families, whose names now appear on the tombstones and war memorials in the Protestant churches, lived in their country houses, and the monuments to their estate-agents stood in the villages with inscriptions yet undefaced.

To preserve the position of the ascendancy and safeguard against insurrection, a series of penal laws was enacted between 1695 and 1727 against the Roman Catholics. Roman Catholicism itself, the religion of two million Irishmen, could not effectively be proscribed; its worship was in practice tolerated, and its teachers conducted their 'hedge schools', mostly giving instruction in the English language which was rapidly replacing Gaelic as the tongue of the people. Nevertheless, a whole code was passed which excluded Roman Catholics from the towns, the legal profession, public office, the armed forces and several branches of trade and manufacture, deprived them of the vote and gradually made them incapable of holding any considerable estate. A consequence of these disabling laws was that for nearly a century Irishmen went abroad to enlist in the Irish Brigades of France, Spain and Austria. Between 1690 and 1730 some 120,000 of these 'Wild Geese' are said to have served in these foreign armies.

The established Church of Ireland was similar to the Church of England, and political power was restricted to its members. Protestant Dissenters, though not subject to the same disabilities as Roman Catholics, were excluded by tests from local government and parliament. The government in Dublin was like that of England. The Irish Parliament represented only the wealthier members of the established Church. The House of Lords consisted of 28 bishops and about the same number of lay peers, who attended irregularly. The importance of individual peers depended largely on their influence in the House of Commons, of whose 300 members

234 were returned by boroughs, many owned or controlled by noblemen.

The position of the Protestant ascendancy in Ireland was not, however, to remain as secure as it appeared at the opening of the Hanoverian period. Very early it suffered the consequences of resentment by the Presbyterians of the north-eastern counties against the Anglican landowning class. In 1718 many leases, formerly granted on easy terms, expired in these counties, and upon renewing them, the landlords doubled or trebled the rents. Such rack-renting drove thousands of Presbyterian farmers, already embittered by their lack of political and religious equality, to emigrate each year to New England. As they went, the landlords accepted Roman Catholic tenants, and so in Donegal, Fermanagh, Derry and other parts of Ulster, numbers of 'plantation villages', founded by Scottish settlers in the seventeenth century, ceased to be Protestant communities.

A more serious weakness was the absence of constitutional or responsible government in Ireland. British domination in Ireland was completed by the Declaratory Act of 1719, which declared the British Parliament's right to pass acts binding on Ireland. Control from Westminster was exercised with the object of upholding English political power rather than strengthening the ascendancy. The Lord-Lieutenant, usually a prominent English nobleman, was generally expected only to reside in Dublin when the Irish Parliament sat, which was for about six months every two years. Then he returned to London, delegating his functions to two or three Lords Justices, one of whom was usually the Speaker of the House of Commons. They were assisted by the Privy Council, which was required by the current interpretation of Poynings' Act to approve the Irish Parliament's legislative intentions before sending them for the English Privy Council's consideration. The main purpose of this government in Dublin was to maintain the existing administrative system in Ireland and secure Parliament's approval of the measures and supplies required by the British ministry, which was done through the 'undertakers', the chief borough-mongers such as the Duke of Leinster, who agreed to support the government through their dependants in the Irish Parliament in return for pensions and offices.

P

What really made such English political control detrimental to the ascendancy was the determination of certain economic interests in England to use it to prevent Irish competition. Manufactures likely to threaten an English industry were suppressed, the export of farm produce to England or the colonies was forbidden, and the woollen trade was restricted. Such a policy impoverished Irish agriculture. The absentee landlords, finding wool-growing brought little profit, let their estates to middlemen, and these let out small holdings at rack-rents to Irish cottiers, who held their land under an old system by which their rents were fixed annually by public auction, so that they lacked both security of tenure and compensation for improvements they made on their holdings. Frequent agrarian outrages by the Whiteboys, Defenders and other secret societies, both Roman Catholic and Protestant, expressed the resentment of the peasants at their plight.

Still more, the condition of the country aroused a growing sense of frustration and nationalism among the ascendancy itself. Jonathan Swift, Dean of St. Patrick's Cathedral, Dublin, from 1713 to 1745, gave early expression to this, especially in his *Drapier's Letters* (1724) which successfully rallied Irish opinion against 'Wood's Halfpence' – an Englishman's monopoly of minting copper money. Protestant fears of Roman Catholicism diminished, particularly as Ireland was quiescent during both the 'Fifteen and the 'Forty-Five, and the spirit of the times favoured toleration. A Roman Catholic middle class, engaged largely in the provision trade, was developing, and it received support in its dislike of the English economic restrictions from the section of the ascendancy most actively concerned with commerce and industry. From about 1760 a Patriot Party, led by Henry Flood (1732–91), appeared in the Irish House of Commons. George III, in order to weaken the 'undertakers'' power and re-assert direct British influence, ordered the Lord-Lieutenant in 1767 to reside continuously in Ireland.

The American War of Independence gave the Irish patriots their chance. Troops were sent from the Irish establishments to America and elsewhere, leaving the country exposed to foreign threats, and the government accepted the Patriot Party's offer to raise a defensive force, the Irish Volunteers. Before long this had some 80,000 men, all Protestants, all over the country. Among its officers were prominent patriots, anxious to exact concessions from Britain. Moreover, the Patriot Party now had a new leader of great ability and character in the Irish Parliament – Henry Grattan (1746–1820), who agitated in the name of the 'Protestant Nation' for a 'free constitution and freedom of trade'. Between 1774 and 1782 the Irish Parliament removed many of the disabilities suffered by the Roman Catholic middle classes as well as the few surviving Roman Catholic landowners, while in 1780 Protestant Dissenters were made eligible for public office. Meanwhile, the Irish Parliament, with the Volunteers' support, in October 1779 voted supplies for six months only to uphold its demand for free trade and the British parliamentary opposition supported Irish grievances. Lord North had to carry through the British Parliament measures relaxing the restrictions on Irish trade and industry. After this victory, the Volunteers next agitated for legislative independence, expressing their demands at a convention held early in 1782. The Rockingham ministry wished to conciliate Ireland, and so the British Parliament now repealed both Poynings' Act of 1494 and the Declaratory Act of 1719.

These measures of 1782 were greeted with high hopes in Ireland. The free Irish Parliament became known as 'Grattan's Parliament' and voted him in gratitude £50,000. Parliament, however, did not control the administration in Dublin, which was still appointed and directed from London. Moreover, Parliament remained exclusive and corruptible. Most of the ascendancy would not agree to parliamentary reform. The franchise remained the same as in England, restricted to the forty-shilling freeholder in the counties and varying in the boroughs from place to place; the 'pocket' and 'rotten' boroughs continued; and Roman Catholics were not granted the vote, despite the efforts of Grattan who declared 'the Irish Protestant can never be free while the Catholic is a slave'.

Economically these years were more successful. The Younger Pitt's attempt to secure freedom of trade for Ireland with Britain and the colonies failed;[1] but Irish trade, assisted by considerable parliamentary subsidies, grew, and textile

[1] P. 367.

manufactures and other industries developed rapidly. Corn-growing and cattle-raising expanded, each sending a surplus to Britain's industrial towns. Large corn mills were built and also warehouses and inns for the needs of the consequent carrying trade. The prosperity of the time was seen in the building of country mansions and town houses and especially in the new streets and squares of Dublin which became the centre of a distinguished social life and by 1800 had a population of nearly 200,000. Peasant poverty remained, and agrarian terrorist societies continued their activities, but the middle class grew increasingly wealthy and important and more insistent, therefore, in its wish for a share of political power.

The French Revolution encouraged the demand of this class for parliamentary reform. In 1791 Wolfe Tone (1763–98), a Protestant lawyer, took the lead in forming in Dublin and Belfast the Society of United Irishmen to unite Roman Catholics and Protestants in securing a free and representative parliament. The organization became popular in Ireland and was particularly strong among the Ulster Presbyterians. Pitt believed that concessions must be made and joined with Grattan to induce the Irish Parliament in 1793 to make several concessions to the Roman Catholics, including the right to vote, though not to sit in Parliament. The Irish government went on, however, to arouse resentment by abolishing the Irish Volunteers in the same year; and early in 1795 occurred the 'Fitzwilliam episode'. Pitt gave the office of Lord-Lieutenant of Ireland to Lord Fitzwilliam, an Irish landowner and a Whig, who planned to secure full Roman Catholic emancipation and through a misunderstanding thought that Pitt's instructions allowed him to do this. When he aroused conservative opposition in the ascendancy, Pitt had to recall him after only three months' tenure of office. He left Dublin amid a popular ovation.

The episode seriously increased Pitt's difficulties in introducing further reforms, and the disappointment it aroused helped to make the United Irishmen a revolutionary body. In 1795 Tone went to France for aid and late in 1796 accompanied a French fleet from Brest with fifteen thousand troops under General Hoche, which reached Bantry Bay, only to be dispersed by gales. The following year another large

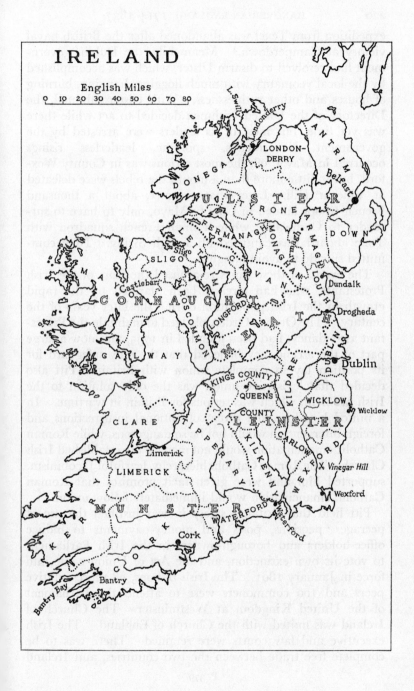

IRELAND

English Miles
0 10 20 30 40 50 60 70 80

L. Swilly

Londonderry

LONDON-
DERRY

ANTRIM

DONEGAL

Belfast

U L S T E R

TYRONE

DOWN

FERMANAGH

ARMAGH

MONAGHAN

LEITRIM

CAVAN

Blackwater

LOUTH

Sligo

SLIGO

Dundalk

M A Y O

Castlebar

C O N N A U G H T

ROSCOMMON

LONGFORD

M E A T H

Drogheda

DUBLIN

GALWAY

Dublin

KINGS COUNTY

KILDARE

QUEENS
COUNTY

WICKLOW

Wicklow

CLARE

TIPPERARY

L E I N S T E R

KILKENNY

CARLOW

WEXFORD

Limerick

Vinegar Hill

LIMERICK

Wexford

K E R R Y

M U N S T E R

WATERFORD

Waterford

C O R K

Cork

Bantry Bay

Bantry

expedition from Texel was abandoned after the British naval victory at Camperdown.[1]   Meanwhile, the Dublin government had resolved to disarm Ulster, which was accomplished by the local yeomanry with much flogging, hanging, burning of houses and other ruthlessness.   With Ulster subdued, the Directory of the United Irishmen decided to act while there was yet time, but most of its leaders were arrested by the government.   Nevertheless, sporadic, leaderless risings occurred in May 1798; the most serious was in County Wexford, but in little more than a month the rebels were defeated at Vinegar Hill.   Later that summer, about a thousand French troops landed in County Mayo, only to have to surrender to Cornwallis, while a small French squadron with Tone aboard was captured off Lough Swilly.   Tone committed suicide to avoid hanging.

The events of these times re-aroused the fears of the Irish Protestants, who had already been alarmed by the rapid growth in the Irish population during the later years of the century.   The Orange Order, pledged to maintain the Protestant ascendancy, had been founded in 1795, and now a large part of the ascendancy believed that the only safeguard for its position lay in complete union with Britain.   Pitt also decided that legislative union was the only solution to the Irish problem, which was serious for Britain in wartime.   In a united kingdom, the threat of national insurrections and foreign intervention would not be so dangerous, while Roman Catholic emancipation would not menace the established Irish Church.   The Roman Catholic hierarchy, fearful of Jacobinism, supported him and were given tacit promises that Roman Catholic emancipation would immediately follow union.

Pitt held that Britain's safety in war justified the use of peerages, pensions, posts and money-payments to induce office-holders and borough-owners in the Irish Parliament to vote its own extinction, and the Act of Union came into force in January 1801.   The Irish bishops, 28 representative peers and 100 commoners were to attend the Parliament of the United Kingdom at Westminster.   The Church of Ireland was united with the Church of England.   The Irish executive and law courts were retained.   There was to be complete free trade between the two countries, and Ireland

[1] P. 379.

was to be allowed to trade fully with the Empire. Roman Catholic emancipation, however, came to nothing. Pitt was thwarted by dissension in his cabinet and George III's refusal to agree to any such measure.[1] He resigned office in 1801.

After the Union, Ireland's economic situation became steadily more serious. Her population was increasing twice as fast as Britain's, despite the emigration of Irish labourers seeking work in England and Scotland. By 1821 it was nearly seven million and the densest in Europe; and it was over eight million in 1841. Moreover, this occurred in a country hardly affected by the Industrial Revolution. Only the Ulster linen industry flourished; elsewhere once-considerable rural domestic industries declined. Hitherto the produce of the land had generally been able to feed Ireland's population, but now, although the output of corn and meat was increasing, it was insufficient to prevent a falling standard of living. Most Irish people lived near to starvation and depended upon a single staple crop, the potato, while five-sixths were housed in mud huts or one-roomed cottages.

The agrarian situation was still dominated by high rents, insecurity of tenure, the confiscation of tenants' improvements and uneconomic and repeatedly subdivided holdings. Farming methods were primitive as ignorant peasants knew nothing of contemporary agricultural innovations, and there were few improving landlords ready to invest capital in the land; extensive areas of bog or moorland remained uncultivated through lack of drainage. Parliament, however, failed to deal with the problem. British public opinion, accepting the ideas of *laissez-faire*, was hostile to interference with the rights of property, while the House of Lords, which contained many absentee Irish landlords, strongly opposed reform. The government's answer was to pass a succession of coercion acts and to establish in 1836 a semi-military police force, the Royal Irish Constabulary.

Even in an age which was growingly opposed to religious discrimination, Protestant suspicions were still strong enough to maintain an unwillingness to consider Roman Catholic emancipation among British politicians. The issue was precipitated into a crisis, however, by Daniel O'Connell (1775–1847), the son of a small Roman Catholic landlord in

[1] P. 386.

Kerry and, in his early days, a successful criminal lawyer. He opposed the Union from its beginning and began an active campaign against it with a movement for religious equality. Since he could not obtain support from the Irish aristocracy, he used his outstanding powers of oratory to unite the Irish people in the cause. In 1823 he formed the Catholic Association with the assistance of the parish priests. Since it had branches in almost every parish, by 1825 its subscription of a penny a month, the 'Catholic rent', was yielding £1,000 a week. Numerous meetings were organized, as many as two hundred being held on a single day in 1828. The Irish forty-shilling freeholders were persuaded to defy the landowners and vote for Protestants in favour of emancipation in several constituencies.

Then O'Connell decided to take advantage of the situation created by the granting of equality to Protestant Dissenters in 1828.[1] He himself stood for County Clare at a by-election that year and was returned. As a Roman Catholic he could not sit in Parliament, but he announced his intention of standing for every Irish constituency which fell vacant. Wellington and Peel were convinced that there was a grave danger of civil war in Ireland, and the Catholic Emancipation Act was passed in 1829. It admitted Roman Catholics to Parliament and to all offices except those of Lord Chancellor and Lord-Lieutenant of Ireland. Though an accompanying act limited the Irish county franchise by depriving forty-shilling freeholders of the vote and raising the qualification to £10, the way was opened for the appearance at Westminster of a middle-class, nationalist Irish party, which was strengthened when the Irish Reform Act of 1832 opened some borough seats to Roman Catholic influence.

In Parliament, O'Connell considered that the time had not yet come for a widespread campaign for the repeal of the Union, and he was not to attempt this until 1823. Meanwhile, he supported the Whigs as the best way of getting redress for Irish grievances, but the gains from this policy were few, even when the Whigs depended upon the Irish vote in the Commons from 1835. The Irish people could not understand his tactics; he lost influence, and demands for extremism and violence were ominous for the future and

[1] P. 425.

alarmed public opinion. Less regarded was the suffering caused by occasional partial failures of the potato crop in different parts of the country, but these foreshadowed the terrible consequences which were to be inflicted upon the country by the Famine of 1846.

Hanover

The Electorate of Hanover originated in the hereditary lands in northern Germany of the ancient Guelph family. During the thirteenth century, this territory was repeatedly partitioned among several branches of the family (as was common in Germany) but by 1634, owing to the gradual failure of heirs among these branches, their lands had been merged into the two duchies of Brunswick and Lüneburg. In 1680 a law of primogeniture was accepted for the duchies which in 1705 united them under the rule of George Louis, who had been created an Elector by the Holy Roman Emperor in 1692. In this way the Electorate of Brunswick-Lüneburg (commonly known as Hanover) was established, less than ten years before its first Elector also became the ruler of Great Britain and Ireland. It had in 1714 a total area of some 500 square miles and a population of almost three-quarters of a million.

The Elector of Hanover ruled his small state despotically yet at the same time benevolently and paternally, and his subjects accepted his government uncritically. The various districts comprising the Electorate each had its own small *Landtag* of knights, bishops and burgesses, but these exerted hardly any influence on public affairs. Even after George ascended the British throne in 1714, he continued to administer Hanover in fundamentally the same way. Before leaving for England, he issued a special decree which in every aspect of government allowed his ministers merely to make decisions on routine matters and required the Elector's decision to be sought on every important question. The first two Georges rigidly enforced this decree, continuing to supervise the whole range of Hanoverian administration while they were in London and enjoying their unquestioned authority over the Electorate in contrast to the checks and delays imposed on them by the complicated British system of parliamentary government.

Hanover and Britain were thus ruled as two completely independent states. In fact, Hanover was officially regarded as a foreign country in Britain. Nevertheless, the Hanoverian connection inevitably affected Britain's foreign policy and domestic administration, though it is not easy to ascertain to what extent this was so. Both George I and George II openly expressed their preference for Hanover as compared with Britain, which diminished their popularity and authority among their British subjects and embarrassed their ministers. Moreover, during the forty-six years of their reigns, these kings went to Hanover nineteen times, usually for about six months on end, when they were replaced by a Council of Regency with limited powers, and these frequent absences handicapped the government of the country. The summoning of Parliament had to be delayed until George I was recalled from Hanover during the South Sea Bubble crisis of 1720. George II was in Hanover when the Young Pretender landed in Scotland in 1745 and did not return to London until a fortnight after the news had reached the unprepared government. George II also had to be urged to leave Hanover almost at the outset of the Seven Years' War, when he replied, 'There are kings enough in England. I am nothing there; I am old and want rest and should only go to be plagued and teased there about that damned House of Commons.'

During this period, the opposition regularly asserted that successive ministries were subordinating British interests to those of Hanover. There seemed, indeed, to be some evidence in the early years of George I's reign that Hanover strongly influenced British politics. The language difficulty alone made it inevitable that the new King should rely most upon his advisers' opinions and the Hanoverian trio who came over with him – Bothmer, Bernstorff and Roberthon – were generally unpopular and undoubtedly influential.[1] They had communicated with the Whig opposition in Queen Anne's reign and in 1714 recommended that it should assume office under Townshend and Stanhope. For the next few years, they were able to have an effect upon both policy and appointments, but in 1719 Stanhope's determination not to allow Bernstorff, who was bitterly hostile to Prussia, to interfere in British foreign policy led to a general decline in their

[1] P. 43.

power, and it disappeared when Walpole assumed office in
1721. George I himself was ready to turn more and more
away from his familiar Hanoverian advisers and rely on
Walpole. It remained true, however, under the first two
Georges that ministers who expressed a concern for Hanover,
such as Carteret (who also knew German) and Newcastle,
earned royal favour – and also gained much parliamentary
and popular opprobrium.

It was naturally in foreign policy that Hanoverian influence
was generally regarded as being exerted, and George I
ascended the British throne with the very object of achieving
this. Hanoverian foreign policy had for some time been
based on an alliance with the Holy Roman Emperor, from
whom the Guelphs had obtained the electoral dignity which
gave them importance in Germany. The alliance seemed the
best way of protecting Hanover against possible threats from
the two rising powers, Prussia and Russia, and also of fulfilling the hope that the Electorate might gain the remnant
of Sweden's territory in Germany. The Emperors, on their
part, valued the alliance as providing a means of upholding
Imperial authority in northern Germany against these two
same rising powers, and they still regarded Sweden, though
in decline, as a danger to their power.

Britain's constant friendship with the Empire in the early
years of the Hanoverian period was most frequently put
forward by the opposition as evidence of the subservience of
her foreign policy to Hanoverian interests. Yet this Austrian
connection had been part of Whig policy since William III's
reign and now seemed essential to sustain Britain's resolve
to maintain the Utrecht settlement and oppose Spanish
policy. Walpole, who considered George I's Hanoverian
advisers obnoxious, persistently supported the Imperial
alliance, and the breach with the Empire in 1726 indicated
that it could only operate if it served British interests. Similarly, British policy towards Sweden was fundamentally
governed, not by Hanoverian ambitions, but rather by her
reliance on timber, tar, hemp and other naval stores from the
Baltic. Undoubtedly Hanoverian pressure was brought to
bear on British foreign policy at different times, but events
suggest that this never resulted in the sacrifice of important
British interests, particularly during the three major wars of

the period in which Britain participated – the Great Northern War, the War of the Austrian Succession and the Seven Years' War.

The Great Northern War, the culmination of the struggle between Sweden and Russia in the Baltic, had begun in 1700. George Louis had, in fact, intervened in the war before he became King of Britain, with the object of obtaining from Sweden the ports of Bremen and Verden. Britain was also concerned because the Swedish fleet was attempting to stop British merchant ships from trading with the Baltic provinces occupied by Russia, and because it was known that hostility to Hanover had led Charles XII of Sweden to negotiate with the Jacobites. In 1715 and 1716, therefore, Stanhope sent a British fleet to the Baltic to make a show of power and protect British shipping. Though the Treaty of Nystad gave Hanover Bremen and Verden in 1721, when the war ended with a Russian victory, Britain had intervened primarily to protect her interests against Sweden. These interests had previously required the maintenance of good relations with Sweden, and after this episode brought about by Swedish aggressiveness, Britain resumed a friendly policy towards her.[1]

For Britain the prelude to the War of the Austrian Succession was the War of Jenkins's Ear, caused by British commercial differences with Spain, and its merging into the wider struggle was due rather to British fears of French aggrandizement than to a desire to defend Austria against Prussia. Hanoverian influence did not bring Britain into the war. George II, indeed, though sharing his family's traditional policy of friendship with Austria and hostility towards Prussia, was so alarmed in 1741 at the prospect of an invasion of Hanover by both French and Prussian troops that he declared the Electorate neutral until Carteret got him to change his mind.[2] Hanover's troops were taken into British pay and fought on her side. British interests had clearly not been overriden by Hanoverian policy.

The same occurred in the Seven Years' War. It is true that George II's concern for Hanover precipitated the Diplomatic Revolution which ushered in the War.[3] Austria's refusal to send troops to defend Hanover led to the conclusion

[1] P. 238.   [2] Pp. 268–9.   [3] Pp. 290–1.

of a treaty with Russia by which the Czarina Elizabeth undertook to protect Hanover in return for a British subsidy, and alarm at the prospect of Russian troops in Germany induced Frederick the Great to sign the Convention of Westminster in 1756 by which Prussia agreed to protect Hanover. At the same time, British interests had not been sacrificed to Hanover. The alliance with Austria was already at breaking-point, and Britain acquired a powerful new Continental ally which played a vital part in her war policy. Moreover, Hanover fought throughout the War and suffered for it. When the defeated Duke of Cumberland signed the Convention of Klosterseven in 1757 which accepted French occupation of Hanover, Pitt persuaded George II to repudiate it, and the French were driven from the Electorate. The verdict of Lord Hardwicke, who was Lord Chancellor from 1737 to 1756, was that Hanover was more 'hazarded by her union with Great Britain'.

After 1760 Hanover ceased to play any part in British politics. George III in no way shared the attitude of his predecessors towards the Electorate.[1] A consequence of this was that he enjoyed greater freedom in his choice of ministers. George II's ministers had earned unpopularity because they were expected to consider Hanoverian interests, but George III gave no occasion for this form of attack, and thus he could make more frequent ministerial changes and choose from more politicians. Hanover itself was now brought more closely into line with British policy and suffered disastrously in the Napoleonic War through being connected with a country unable to protect her from military attack. The Electorate, after a brief Prussian occupation, was overwhelmed by France and made part of the Kingdom of Westphalia. In 1815 Hanover became a kingdom and was granted additional territory by the Congress of Vienna; and in 1837 the connection with Britain ended, since by the Salic law women were excluded from ruling the country, and Victoria's uncle, the Duke of Cumberland, succeeded to the throne.

[1] P. 46.

XI · THE ESTABLISHMENT OF THE
DYNASTY, 1714–21

The Hanoverian Succession (1714)

EARLY in the morning of Sunday, 1st August 1714, Queen Anne, worn out with anxiety, child-bearing and a complication of diseases, died at Kensington Palace in the fiftieth year of her age and the thirteenth of her reign. During the last year of her life, while her strength was visibly failing, the succession question had become an increasingly dominant political issue, and it split the Tories. The Act of Settlement of 1701 had been passed under a Tory ministry headed by Robert Harley, Earl of Oxford (1661–1724), who was still in power. The Pretender's Roman Catholicism and French associations made most Tories prepared to let the Act take its course, but there were dissidents. The Whig opposition, on the other hand, firmly favoured the Hanoverian succession, knowing that the new King would put them in office.

Oxford procrastinated, but a growing apprehension of the danger of exclusion from power facing the Tories drove the ambitious Henry St. John, Viscount Bolingbroke (1678–1751), to action. For some time he had been jealous of Oxford, whose deteriorating powers had by now reduced him to irresolution and far too frequent drunkenness. In July 1714 Anne was persuaded to dismiss Oxford from the Lord Treasurership. Bolingbroke, although still only a Secretary of State, was left as the most influential minister, but now that the event had transpired for which he had schemed for so long, he had no definite plan, and Anne died five days later, after giving the Lord Treasurership to Charles Talbot, Duke of Shrewsbury (1660–1718), who had been prominent in bringing about the Revolution of 1688.

On the day the Queen died, several Tory leaders met in London for discussion. Only Francis Atterbury, Bishop of Rochester, was for action. He wanted them to ride down to the Royal Exchange, where he was ready himself to proclaim James III as King. Bolingbroke, however, sensed that the situation was lost. Even surprise action would not win them the country.   He told the Bishop, 'All our throats would be cut'.   The Bishop stormed out of the meeting.

As in 1688, it was the Whigs, not their opponents, who were ready for action.   The Whig lords of the Privy Council had meanwhile met at St. James's Palace and ordered George I's proclamation.   By the Regency Act of 1707 power now was to pass to a Council of Regency composed of 25 Lord Justices.   They were the seven great officers of State and 18 others nominated by the Elector.   When Bothmer, then the Hanoverian resident in London, gave the Privy Council from his black box the Elector's list of names, four were those of moderate Tories and fourteen were Whigs, chosen because they had supported the Hanoverian succession and were likely to carry out George I's policies.   They were firmly in control.   Their drastic steps were confined to the dismissal of Bolingbroke from his Secretaryship of State and of the Duke of Ormonde (1665–1745), who had been involved in negotiations with James Edward early in 1714, from his office of Captain-General.   The news reached Jonathan Swift, who was staying in the vicarage of an old friend at the small Berkshire village of Letcombe Bassett, and he realized that he could only retire to his empty deanery in Dublin.[1]

The Tory collapse in 1714 was partly due to a failure of leadership.   The landed gentry, the traditional backbone of the party, could not give it competent leaders.   Nor were any forthcoming from outside their own class.   The bishops gave them no able statesmen.   The old royalist aristocracy was too weakened by poverty and the extinction of ancient families to be an effective political force.   Oxford was an ailing and broken man, and Bolingbroke had plotted and failed.   On top of this, the Tories faced the succession crisis as a divided and uncertain party, unlikely to encourage or follow any active, aspiring politicians within its ranks. The Whigs were better served by the influential landed families, whose origins and power came mostly from the political developments of the previous century, and the wealthy commercial classes, who supported them to form the party.   Their leaders were able to act, even though a Tory ministry was in power and the throne was vacant.

Moreover, the Tories despite their Indian summer of

[1] P. 94.

power in Anne's reign, seemed increasingly discredited by the contemporary climate of opinion. The Whigs had on their side the new ideas which seemed likely to prevail in the future – limited monarchy, parliamentary supremacy, religious toleration, imperial power and economic expansion. To most people, the Jacobite cause embodied the very political and religious forces opposed to these developments. There was no popular enthusiasm for the Elector of Hanover, but the Old Pretender's religion alone deprived him of most people's support. 'England would as soon have a Turk as a Roman Catholic for King', said Bolingbroke. Most of the landed classes and the clergy had to recognize, though often grudgingly, that their interests would be less endangered under Hanoverian rule, while the great merchants and most of the middle class feared that political strife would harm trade and end the period of prosperity initiated by the Treaty of Utrecht. The proclamation of George I aroused no violent demonstrations, and stocks in the London money-market remained high as the danger of civil war receded.

George I landed at Greenwich on 18th September 1714 and the next morning took up residence at St. James's Palace. A few days later the list of the new ministry, drawn up on Bothmer's advice, showed that the Whigs were to reap the fruits of their victory. George mistrusted the Whigs only less than the Tories. He feared they were 'king-killers', who would try to use him for their own ends, but he realized that they were more likely to agree to a foreign policy favourable to Hanover than the Tories.[1] Although the ministry was not drawn entirely from the Whigs, all the important posts were given to them and not to the Tories, who still had a majority in both Houses of Parliament. Many of the new ministers were old Whig politicians, prominent in opposition during the last years of the previous reign and hostile to the Utrecht settlement.[2] They were likely to secure support from Whig lords and moderate Tories, wealthy merchants and men of property, but their return to office was not to last long. Within a few years most of them were dead. More important for the future were the two Secretaries of State – Charles, Viscount Townshend (1674–1738), and James, Earl of Stanhope (1673–1721).

[1] P. 60.   [2] P. 237.

Townshend, the Northern Secretary, came of an old Norfolk family and as Lord-Lieutenant of that county could exercise considerable parliamentary influence.   So far he had not had a distinguished public career, but had been in Holland on diplomatic business, where he had met and impressed Robethon, and marriage with a sister of Robert Walpole brought him prominence in the Whig party.   Lady Mary Montagu, a friend of his wife, described him as 'reasonable and honest'; he was industrious, persevering and ambitious, a poor speaker but an assiduous debater in Parliament.   The other Secretary, Stanhope, was also new to high office, being better known as a soldier and diplomat than as a politician. In the War of the Spanish Succession, he had served first under Marlborough in the Netherlands, then as Commander-in-Chief of the British forces in Spain (when he captured Minorca) and finally spending two years as a prisoner of the French.   His keen interest in foreign affairs was fortified by a knowledge of French and Spanish, and by the experience of diplomatic circles gained while his father was ambassador successively at The Hague and Madrid.   In the Tory Parliament he had been a successful debater for the Whigs and during the Queen's last year of life actively organized support for the Hanoverian cause.   The two Secretaries soon made themselves the leading members of the new ministry.

The general election, obligatory after a monarch's death, was held in January 1715.   The government tried hard to make it a Whig victory.   Patronage was freely used, and a royal proclamation asked the electors to return 'such as showed a firmness to the Protestant succession when it was in danger'.   The result was that the Tory majority, obtained from a war-weary country in 1710, was replaced by a majority of about 150 for the followers of those favoured by the new régime.   It was also, however, probably an expression of the mood of the electorate which still preferred the Hanoverian succession to the danger of civil strife.

The 'Fifteen

With their majority now assured in the Commons, the administration set out to control the country and cripple their opponents.   The impeachment was begun of ministers who had negotiated the Treaty of Utrecht, on the grounds that they had betrayed national interests. Bolingbroke and later Ormonde fled the country and entered the Pretender's service. Both were attainted for treason, and the Whigs could represent all Tories as traitors. Oxford remained and was sent to the Tower for two years. At the same time, Whigs replaced Tories as Lord-Lieutenants and Justices of the Peace and in every administrative department from the royal household to the excise office.

Fear now sharpened the Tory bitterness at defeat. Tory propagandists exploited with considerable success the deep-seated dislike of authority among the lower classes and their sufferings during the exceptionally severe winter of 1714–15. In London and elsewhere there were continual riots, attacks on Dissenting chapels and demonstrations in favour of Ormonde against the unpopular Duke of Marlborough (1650–1722), who had replaced him as Captain-General. The Riot Act of 1715 made it a felony for an assembly of twelve or more persons to refuse to disperse. Marlborough and Shrewsbury took the precaution of resuming the courtly messages they had sent to the Pretender during Anne's reign.

This situation was bound to make it seem to the opponents of the régime that the time might be opportune for an attempt to overthrow it. When Bolingbroke reached Paris in March 1715, he found that the Jacobites there were openly preparing for such an adventure. Louis XIV had not hindered their plans, and they had high hopes of assistance from him. After some hesitation, Bolingbroke decided that they had a chance of success, but insisted that a rising must be made in southern England which he believed could not be conquered by a Scottish movement. The Pretender, though eager to lead an expedition, could not make up his mind. 'He talked like a man who expected every moment to set out for England or Scotland', Bolingbroke wrote, 'but who did not very well know for which.'

Events overtook the indecisive Jacobites. In September 1715 Louis XIV died. 'My hopes', Bolingbroke wrote, 'sank as he declined and died when he expired.' The French Regent, the Duke of Orleans, wanted the British government's friendship.[1] He ordered the ammunition, collected at Havre for the Pretender's use, to be unloaded. And five days after

[1] P. 240.

Louis XVI's death, the Earl of Mar called out the Highland clans at Perth, vainly precipitating a Scottish rising which was already disintegrating when James Edward made his brief visit to the country in January 1716.[1]

Meanwhile, Jacobite hopes of an effective English rising had faded. The confusion and lack of secrecy, which characterized their plans, enabled the Earl of Stair, the British ambassador in Paris, and the government's agents in England to report closely on their plans; and Stanhope and Townshend took vigorous precautions. During the summer of 1715 a squadron watched the French ports along the Channel; new regiments were added to the army; Bath, Oxford and the western ports were garrisoned; suspected members of the Commons and the Lords were arrested; and arms and horses of Roman Catholics, particularly in London, were seized.

These precautions had their effect. In October Ormonde sailed into Torbay and fired three guns from his ship to signal the Jacobites on shore, but received no reply. In Northumberland the Earl of Derwentwater raised a small force of tenants, which was joined by a few hundred Lowlanders under Lord Kenmure, but their attempt to rouse the Roman Catholics of the north-western counties was frustrated by their defeat at Preston in November.

At the same time, the 'Fifteen revealed the absence of widespread, active support for the Pretender in England. Jacobite incidents were few. Ladies in Manchester sang old Cavalier songs; Oxford undergraduates beat up royal recruiting sergeants; and charity boys were whipped at school for lighting bonfires in London streets. The squires and parsons, who drank to the king over the water, remained quietly in their manor houses and rectories when the time for action came. Tory exasperation with the government did not extend to readiness to risk an uncertain rebellion against it. As Lord Stair succinctly wrote, 'There are very few among them whose love for the Pretender goes so far as to make them lie three nights under a hedge in November'. Both dynasty and government emerged from the rebellion strengthened by its revelation of the weakness of the opposition.

The government could afford, therefore, to be clement by the standards of the times when the rebellion was over.

[1] Pp. 209–10.

Derwentwater, Kenmure and some thirty other Jacobites were executed, while several hundred were transported to work in the West Indian plantations. On the other hand, for the Tory party the rebellion meant permanent exclusion from political power. Stanhope took advantage of it to remove the remaining Tories from the government; and, since all Tories might have Jacobite sympathies, the possibility of any future joint Whig and Tory ministry did not now seem practical politics. The King and his Hanoverian advisers could not hope to play off one party against another, but must work only through the Whigs.

The Foundation of the Whig Supremacy (1716–19)

After the 'Fifteen the ministry, now for the first time consisting only of Whigs, set about strengthening and prolonging its power. It successfully consolidated the Whig victory and began the process which was to maintain their supremacy in politics for the greater part of the century. The first step was to extend the duration of the existing House of Commons with its Whig majority. Under the Triennial Act of 1694 a general election was due in 1718. The government promoted the Septennial Act of 1716 which extended the life of this and subsequent parliaments to seven years. The argument put forward in its favour was that the country's unsettled condition made an election dangerous, but there were other considerations as well. A parliament of three years was too short for stable government, particularly in those days before the evolution of party discipline and organization. Arthur Onslow, Speaker of the Commons from 1728 to 1761, said that it began their emancipation from the control of both the Crown and the Lords. It certainly increased the power of the borough-mongers to the advantage of the Whigs. Without the act, they would hardly have managed to prolong their dominance for so long.

The government's next action, which Stanhope keenly desired, was to remove the measures enacted by the Tories in the last years of Queen Anne's reign to weaken the political and social influence of the Whigs' Dissenting allies. These were the Occasional Conformity Act of 1711, designed to prevent Dissenters from evading the seventeenth-century Corporation and Test Acts by receiving the Sacrament in a church in order to qualify for civil, municipal or military posts, and yet continuing to worship in their chapel; and the Schism Act of 1714 forbidding Dissenters to teach or keep a school. Both were repealed in 1719, but Stanhope got no support for his plans to modify the Test and Corporation Acts and grant relief to Roman Catholics.

In Anne's reign, the Church of England had appeared to exercise considerable influence. It was a brief period of triumph for the High Church party.[1] The ill-advised impeachment of one of its divines, Dr. Henry Sacheverell, had largely brought about the fall of the Whigs in 1710. Though the High Church clergy were now hardly more able than the Tory squires to challenge effectively the Whig government's authority, the ministry was determined to assert its control over the Church. An unusual number of bishop-rics fell vacant soon after 1714, which were filled with Whigs, From 1717 the Convocations were not allowed to transact business in order to save Bishop Hoadly from a condemnation which would have emphasized the lower clergy's opposition to the government.[2] The Church was thus brought under Whig domination, and the government's clerical critics were silenced, but at the cost of damaging the Church's life and inhibiting efforts at reform within it.

The government's action after the 'Fifteen fortified it against immediate threats from its enemies, but it also brought about a split in the Whig party. The Whigs had previously been out of political office for some years and now lacked generally-recognized leaders who could assert an authority over them and preserve unity. Moreover, since the Tories had no chance of forming a government, an effective opposition formed itself from dissident Whigs, who were critical of the ministers and anxious for power themselves, a situation which was to last as long as the Whig supremacy.[3]

The first Whig cleavage occurred among the leading members of the ministry. Townshend disagreed with Stanhope's foreign policy, and so did his brother-in-law, Walpole, the First Lord of the Treasury, who disliked the possible expense of an aggressive policy.[4] In addition, Stanhope had influence with the King's German mistresses, while the Lord

Privy Seal, the Earl of Sunderland (1674–1722), enjoyed the King's favour, which was increased when he joined the royal visit to Hanover in 1716.   The frustration of Townshend and Walpole made them critical of their colleagues, and they found support among other discontented Whigs.   George, encouraged by Stanhope and Sunderland, interpreted this as disloyalty; in 1717 he dismissed Townshend, and Walpole resigned with him.   Hitherto, indeed, parliamentary opposition had been designated as treasonable, but Townshend and his supporters were now able to combine opposition to the government with loyalty to the dynasty by taking the side of the Prince of Wales, who had already quarrelled furiously with his father.   Early in 1718 the Prince bought a house in Leicester Square, 'where', said Walpole, 'the most promising of the young gentlemen of the next party and the prettiest and liveliest of the young ladies formed the new court'.   It rapidly became the chief meeting-place for members of the opposition.

The ministry was reconstituted under Stanhope and Sunderland, who became First Lord of the Treasury.   It sustained a small majority for itself by the use of Crown patronage on a novel scale; but Stanhope feared that if George I died his son might destroy the ministry's majority in the House of Lords by the addition of new peers, in the same way that Queen Anne had created twelve Tory peers in 1712 to secure the passing of the Treaty of Utrecht. George I himself was ready even to limit his own right of making peers if he could thwart his son's actions.   Accordingly in 1719 the government introduced the Peerage Bill, which proposed that when six more peers had been created the House's maximum membership should be reached.   This measure would have given the ministry a permanent majority in the Lords, safe from any future destruction by the Prince of Wales and his friends, but the Whig opposition roused opinion in the Commons against it.   Walpole made a persuasive speech in which he urged members not to deprive themselves or their families of the prospect of promotion to the peerage.   The argument carried the country gentlemen with him.   The Commons rejected the Peerage Bill by a large majority.

This defeat compelled Stanhope to bring back Townshend and Walpole into the ministry.   They were ready to return since they wanted political power and had now made themselves too dangerous to be excluded from it. In 1720 they accepted office, Townshend as Lord President of the Council and Walpole as Paymaster-General of the Forces.

Stanhope's Foreign Policy (1714–21)

Meanwhile, despite domestic problems and dissensions in his party, Stanhope had been pursuing a skilful and successful foreign policy. In 1714 Britain's position in Europe was by no means an easy one. The long war against France had raised the National Debt to more than £54,000,000 on which the annual interest paid was £3,500,000, and contemporary opinion regarded this as a burden threatening to bankrupt the country. Her old allies, Austria and Holland, were both dissatisfied with the Treaty of Utrecht, and France's attitude, as long as Louis XIV lived, was uncertain. Spain, though she had far declined from her dominant position in Europe a century ago, was going through a period of considerable regeneration, and her rulers were ready to attempt to restore her power in Italy and the Mediterranean and to assert her claim to the French throne. There was the danger that the Pretender might get foreign aid against the new régime in Britain. Sweden had already made contact with the Jacobites, and she was also fighting Russia for control of the Baltic, an area of concern to both Britain and Hanover.[1]

The Whigs had inherited the Utrecht settlement from the Tories. Despite Britain's great gains from it, the Whigs had thought it a disgraceful surrender because the Bourbon monarchy was left in possession of Spain, and they had fought hard in Parliament against its acceptance. The Elector of Hanover also resented the Treaty, feeling that he had been deserted during the negotiations with his ambitions unsatisfied, and in choosing his ministers from among the Whigs in 1714 he was influenced by their attitude towards the peace settlement. Nevertheless, both King and ministry after 1714 had to follow a foreign policy which aimed at upholding the settlement since, besides providing a safeguard for the Electorate's interests, it contained the European recognition of the Hanoverian succession and provided for Britain's commercial development.

[1] P. 226.

The Prussian minister in London once described Stanhope as 'the only Englishman I knew possessed of a universal spirit'.   At a time when many politicians hardly saw beyond parliamentary affairs and the struggle for political power, he realized that Britain's prosperity and safety depended much upon the foreign situation.   His policy was to revive the tradition of the Grand Alliance (though this time it was not directed against France) and rescue Britain from her European isolation, to restore her friendship with Austria and Holland and ensure the stability and peace which she required.   A soldier rather than a negotiator, he was by nature impetuous and spoke of himself as 'ever inclined to bold strokes'.   His approach to foreign problems was inclined to be active and aggressive, and he was ready to risk war to gain an objective. Yet, while preferring decision and action, he was not without success in discussion – he himself used to say that he always imposed on foreign ministers by telling them the naked truth. Above all, his determination and confidence carried him far, gaining for him the confidence of allies and allaying the hostility of opponents.   Bolingbroke described him as 'not apt to despair, especially in the execution of his own projects'.

The Great Northern War between Sweden and Russia presented Stanhope with an immediate problem.[1]   His policy had to be to combine support for the political objectives of Hanover with protection for the economic interests of Britain, and here his diplomacy, with the assistance of a British fleet, was largely successful.   The cession of Bremen and Verden to Hanover at the end of the War satisfied George I, while their occupation by a friendly ruler assisted British commerce in the Baltic and Germany.   Stanhope was less successful in his attempt to form 'so strong a league of North German and Scandinavian powers that Russia would be forced to abandon the dangerous hegemony she had acquired in the Baltic' through her final defeat of Sweden.   Charles XII died in 1718, and the Czar Peter the Great was not easily intimidated. Carteret was sent to Stockholm to conduct protracted negotiations, and a British fleet was again despatched to the Baltic in 1720, this time to protect Sweden, but Russia took all her Baltic provinces except Finland.   This, however, was not as harmful to British trade as Stanhope had feared.   Russia

[1] P. 226.

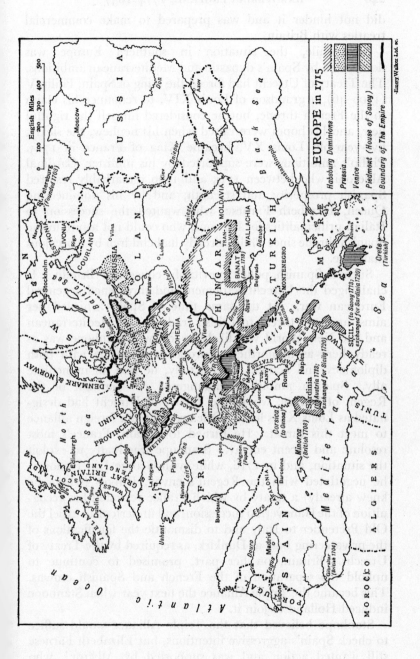

did not hinder it and was prepared to make commercial treaties with Britain.

Meanwhile, the situation in southern Europe was dominated by Spain's dynastic and Mediterranean ambitions. The Treaty of Utrecht had forced the King of Spain, Philip V (1700–46), a grandson of Louis XIV, to renounce his claim to the French throne, but he considered himself the rightful heir, and his hopes were raised when his nephew, the sickly, five-year-old Louis XV, became King of France in 1715. Philip's ambitions were supported by his minister, Cardinal Alberoni, who between 1715 and 1720 remarkably restored Spanish prosperity and strength, and by his domineering Queen, Elizabeth Farnese, who wanted the succession to Italian principalities for her sons, who could not aspire to the Spanish throne since Philip already had children by a previous marriage.

Such a Spanish policy inevitably concerned Britain. It challenged the Utrecht settlement and threatened a general European war. At the same time, if Spain achieved her aims, an early threat to British trade in the Mediterranean and the New World was likely to follow. Stanhope was as ready here as in northern Europe to intervene with both diplomacy and action. Fortunately, he had an immediate ally. Spanish ambitions endangered the position of the Regent of France, whom the Treaty of Utrecht had designated as Louis XV's heir. Orleans wanted a foreign alliance to meet this threat. He turned to Britain, France's most resolute and recent enemy. Stanhope was ready to exploit the situation, and in 1716, while with George I in Hanover, he negotiated with the Regent's envoy, Dubois (whom he knew already) a treaty by which France repeated her recognition of the Hanoverian succession, and undertook to expel the Old Pretender to Italy and to dismantle the fortifications of the privateering base at Dunkirk, as required by the Treaty of Utrecht. Britain, on her part, promised to continue to uphold the separation of the French and Spanish crowns. This became the Triple Alliance the next year when Stanhope induced Holland to join it.

Stanhope believed that the Triple Alliance would suffice to check Spain's aggressive intentions, but Elizabeth Farnese still wanted action and was supported by Alberoni, who

himself favoured renewed Spanish influence in Italy.   In
1717 a Spanish force occupied Sardinia, granted to Austria at
Utrecht.   At the same time, the Pretender was invited to
Spain, and an abortive attempt to land an expedition under
Ormonde was made in 1719;[1] while a plot to overthrow
Orleans in France occurred in 1718 with Spanish support.
Stanhope's reply to this was to set out on a special mission
to Paris and Madrid.   In Paris he negotiated the Quadruple
Alliance of Britain, France, Austria and Holland in 1718 for
the maintenance of the Utrecht settlement; but he could not
persuade Alberoni, who had now landed 35,000 Spanish
troops in Sicily, to abandon his plans.   Stanhope had already
despatched Byng with a fleet to the Mediterranean, and it
now captured fifteen of the twenty-nine Spanish ships off
Cape Passaro.

Philip sought peace.   He dismissed Alberoni, acceded to
the Quadruple Alliance and renounced his claim to the
French throne.   The Treaty of London in 1720 accepted the
Emperor Charles VI's wish to exchange Sardinia for Sicily,
which he received from Piedmont, and Elizabeth Farnese's
elder son, Don Carlos, was recognized as heir to the Duchies
of Tuscany and Parma.   It was a triumph for Stanhope.
Not only had he succeeded in uniting the four powers to form
the Quadruple Alliance, but had preserved it and made it
effective by persuading Orleans, whose policy was unpopular
in France, to support the British stand over Italy.   This
alliance was Stanhope's greatest achievement.   Besides serving its immediate purpose of checking Spanish aggression, it
was also to be the basis of British foreign policy for some years
to come.

The South Sea Bubble (1720)

In the hour of triumph for his foreign policy, Stanhope and
his ministry were overwhelmed by a serious domestic crisis,
the South Sea Bubble.   Its origins went back to 1711 when
the South Sea Company was formed on the proposal of
Harley, then Chancellor of the Exchequer, to convert a
substantial part of the government's short-term debt, created
by the war against France, into a permanent debt at fixed
interest.   The holders of £9,000,000 of this debt had to

[1] P. 210.

exchange their securities for shares in the new joint-stock company.   In return the government guaranteed an interest of 6 per cent on the debt taken over by the company, which was granted a monopoly of the trading rights in South America to be obtained from Spain when the war ended. The project was intended to strengthen the Tory party against the support the Bank of England and East India Company always gave the Whigs and to persuade the City merchants to support the peace by the prospects of fresh profits from Spanish commerce.

Accordingly, the Company was granted the management of the *Asiento* and the annual ship concession secured at Utrecht.[1]   These did not, however, produce for the Company such large-scale trade with the Spanish colonies as had been hoped.   Both were limited in scope and proved valuable chiefly to smugglers who infringed the Company's rights by engaging in the more valuable contraband trade which they made possible.

Disappointment with its commercial activities and the outbreak of war with Spain in 1718 made the Company's directors ready to extend its scope as a financial corporation holding government securities.   On its part, the government had inherited a large and expensive post-war National Debt.[2] In 1717 Walpole, with Stanhope's support, reduced the various loans at differing rates of interest to a single debt with a common rate of interest and established a Sinking Fund into which the proceeds of certain taxes were paid each year for the gradual reduction of the debt.   The success of Walpole's measures doubtless made Sunderland, as First Lord of the Treasury, ready to consider favourably a scheme put forward in 1720 by the South Sea Company that it should take over the greater part of the National Debt.   The offer, as finally accepted by Parliament, resulted in the Company incorporating £31,000,000 of the National Debt in its own capital, paying off £7,000,000 of this at once and receiving from the government a rate of interest which would be reduced from 5 to 4 per cent in 1727.

For the government, the scheme would transfer the National Debt to a single creditor, unable to demand repayment at will, and reduce considerably the enormous sum still being paid in

[1] P. 163.   [2] P. 237.

interest. The Company's gain would come from increased prestige and the profit it expected to make in offering its shares for the surrender of government securities since the terms on which the exchange was to be made were left intentionally vague, and it also intended to issue additional capital of its own, out of which it proposed to make large sums. To get governmental and parliamentary support for the scheme, the directors distributed shares in the Company at nominal prices to ministers, Members of Parliament and the King's favourites during the passage of the act legalizing the arrangements.

The directors could only make a profit and cover these large bribes if the Company's shares fetched a high price, and circumstances in 1720 made this likely. Growing confidence in the Hanoverian dynasty had assisted an expansion of trade, but pre-industrial England lacked sufficient opportunities to invest its wealth profitably. A similar situation in France was at this time boosting the shares of the Mississippi Company of John Law, which rose from 300 to 18,000 livres in a few weeks and were to crash that year as disastrously as did those of the South Sea Company. England was about to succumb to a fever of speculation in which the national passion for gambling found frenzied expression. This was made possible by the facilities for the selling and buying of stocks and shares which had been developing in London from about 1690. The brokers in these days transacted business in the street and coffee-houses (including Jonathan's in which the Stock Exchange was to be founded in 1762) of Change Alley, a narrow thoroughfare between Cornhill and Lombard Street in the City, still to be seen, though now enclosed between the white-tiled walls of Martins Bank.

The Company's shares began to rise even during negotiations with the government. Between March and April 1720 its £100 shares rose from 183 to 320. The South Sea Act received the royal assent in April. By June they had reached 890 and in August touched 1,000. The peak price was partly maintained by the Company purchasing stock illegally in the open market and sanctioning loans on the security of South Sea stock. Large fortunes were gained. A director was said to have made £3,000,000 in three months.

As events turned out, the wisest were those who sold out before the end of the summer, among them Thomas Guy, who made a profit of £180,428 with which he established his hospital.

Nor was the South Sea Company alone in attracting speculators. Early in 1720 speculation had begun in several new or revived joint-stock companies. This grew astonishingly after Parliament approved the South Sea scheme. All sorts of other industrial, commercial and financial companies were formed. Many were respectable, but others, despite their dedication to such high-sounding objects as importing diamonds, fixing quicksilver or draining bogs in Ireland, were unrealistic or dishonest. Yet many were over-subscribed at once. All sorts of people participated in these schemes. The Prince of Wales became a governor of the Welsh Copper Company, despite Walpole's protests, and made £40,000 before a remonstrance by the judges secured his resignation. In June Parliament, alarmed at so many rivals to the South Sea Company, passed the Bubble Act, which made companies without a royal charter illegal.

The directors of the South Sea Company took advantage of this Act in August by applying for writs against four companies, only to alarm the market and precipitate the inevitable decline in the over-valued shares of their own and other companies. By mid-September the South Sea shares had fallen to 410 and at the end to 175. The news that the Company's chairman and several directors had sold out hastened the decline. A panic of selling followed. Hundreds of families suffered severe losses. The Duke of Portland was brought near to bankruptcy, and Sir Isaac Newton and Walpole, who had both made a profit by selling out in the spring only to be tempted to buy again in the summer, lost money. Many companies failed, and banks closed their doors. Unemployment and food riots followed.

The economic damage sustained by the nation as a whole, however, was neither widespread nor permanent. The two other leading financial corporations, the Bank of England and East India Company, remained unshaken. No general depression occurred. The episode's most lasting effects were the difficulties imposed on the raising of joint-stock capital throughout the period by the Bubble Act.[1]

[1] P. 142.

Walpole had been no more far-seeing than other people, but he had not suffered heavily and was free from suspicion of corruption. He also happened to be out of London when the crash came in September. This gave him an initial prestige, and he had the ability to exploit the situation rapidly to his advantage. He put forward a scheme, devised for him by his banker, when Parliament at last met in December. This restored confidence by transferring £18,000,000 of South Sea stock to the Bank of England and East India Company. The estates of the directors, valued at just over £2,000,000, were sold and most of the proceeds went to meet the Company's liabilities. The Company now disappeared from history. It remained a trading company, suffering fairly constant losses, until it surrendered its commercial privileges in 1750.[1] It then continued largely as a financial house until finally dissolved by Gladstone in 1853. Before then Charles Lamb had served as a clerk in South Sea House and idled among its 'great bare rooms and courts' and become familiar with the 'long worm-eaten tables', 'pictures of deceased governors and sub-governors' and 'dusty maps of Mexico' which were the relics of past greatness.

The South Sea Bubble's political result was the fall of the government, which had participated in the original scheme. Many members of both Houses of Parliament had speculated in the Company's shares, and some had made considerable profits. Several ministers were suspected of having taken bribes. Stanhope was the subject of strong criticism, though he had a reputation for disinterestedness and had not held any shares. Walpole alone emerged with enhanced reputation, and his skill and tact in defending his colleagues gained him royal favour and the nickname of 'The Screen'. Even he, however, could not entirely prevent Parliament from proceeding with its intention to 'punish the authors of our present misfortunes'. John Aislabie, the Chancellor of the Exchequer, was sent to the Tower for 'infamous corruption'. Two other ministers were probably saved from a similar fate by death, one by suicide and the other from smallpox. Stanhope died of a stroke after vehemently defending the ministry during a bitter debate in the House of Lords. Sunderland, though cleared of corruption by a vote of the

[1] P. 280.

Commons, had to resign and died not long afterwards. In April 1721 the King had no choice but to make Walpole First Lord of the Treasury and Chancellor of the Exchequer, a position which he was to retain, with a single short interval. until 1742.

Walpole's great period of office has overshadowed that of his predecessor. Nevertheless, Stanhope's services to Britain and the Hanoverian dynasty were considerable. He laid the foundations of the Whig supremacy, despite the dissensions which had arisen in the party; he had defeated a Jacobite attempt to seize power and made the country realize that their best interests lay with the continuance of the Hanoverian régime. This had given the kingdom an economic stability which enabled it to come through the South Sea Bubble so well. Above all, his foreign policy had rescued Britain from her post-war isolation and put her actively at the head of an alliance which was to give Europe a lengthy respite from hostilities. Walpole's successes would hardly have been possible had they not been based upon the earlier efforts of Stanhope at home and abroad.

XII · WALPOLE'S ADMINISTRATION, 1721-42

The Rise to Power (1701-22)

ROBERT WALPOLE was born in 1676 in the old manor house at Houghton in Norfolk, the third son in a family of nineteen. The Walpoles had been a prosperous family in this south-western corner of Norfolk since the late thirteenth century. They were typical of the landed county families of this time, who did not usually participate in national politics, but exercised local power as Justices of the Peace or Deputy Lieutenants and occasionally entered Parliament.[1] As a younger son, Robert Walpole seemed destined for holy orders and was sent to Eton and King's College, Cambridge, but on the death of his two elder brothers his father required him in 1698 to come home to learn the management of the estate to which he was now the heir. Two years later he married the daughter of a wealthy Baltic timber merchant and granddaughter of a former Lord Mayor of London, and before the end of the year his father died. With the Walpole estate went a couple of pocket boroughs, Castle Rising and King's Lynn. Walpole was immediately returned to Parliament for Castle Rising in succession to his father and held it until William III's death. In Queen Anne's first Parliament he represented King's Lynn, which he retained uninterruptedly until his fall from power forty years later.

Walpole entered Parliament just before the passing of the Act of Settlement, made necessary by the death of Anne's only surviving son, the Duke of Gloucester, the year before. From the first Walpole, with the aid of Townshend (who had been the ward of Walpole's father and later was to marry Walpole's favourite sister), attached himself to a group of Whig noblemen known as the Junto, none of whom secured office upon Anne's succession. The Queen's religious and political sentiments made her prefer Tory ministers, but growing Tory opposition to the prolonging of the War of the Spanish Succession led to the increasing continuance of

[1] P. 63.

Whigs in the administration until in 1708 Anne was forced to
accept a wholly Whig ministry, an event which brought
Walpole the post of Secretary at War in succession to Bolingbroke.

With Britain at war and Marlborough abroad in command
of the allied forces in the Netherlands, Walpole had an
important office, and he also became Treasurer of the Navy
in 1710.   By spending more than his income, by his convivial
gifts and his industry and administrative ability, he became
prominent among the younger Whigs.   He also acquired
a good training in financial administration.   His capabilities
were such that he was not dismissed by Harley until 1711.
He immediately became active in opposition and wrote two
such skilful pamphlets attacking the Tories that in 1712 he
was expelled from the Commons and imprisoned for a short
time in the Tower on a baseless charge of corruption.   He
came back to Parliament in 1713, but the experience left
him with a detestation of the Tories and a readiness to be
ruthless with political opponents.   His ambition and love of
power remained undiminished.

The Hanoverian succession brought him back to power.
Since the most important offices went to the older members
of the Junto, he had to be content with the Paymaster-
Generalship of the Forces, but in 1715 he bcame Chancellor
of Exchequer and took an important step towards setting the
national finances in order.[1]   In 1717, however, he followed
Townshend into opposition, driven partly by differences over
foreign policy, but also by the realization that the only
alternative to standing by his friend was to find himself
isolated and powerless in the ministry.   Ambition and
financial need, however, made him determined to get back
into power on his own terms as soon as possible, and he and
Townshend organized an opposition against Stanhope and
Sunderland which set a pattern for the future and brought
them both back into office in 1720.[2]

Walpole was restored to his old post of Paymaster-General
of the Forces shortly before the South Sea Bubble burst.   He
deftly seized the opportunity it gave him.[3]   Contemptuously
ignoring the popular anger and public insults he received, he
tenaciously and courageously exerted all his parliamentary

[1] P. 242.   [2] Pp. 235–7.   [3] P. 245.

skill to save the court and the ministry from the disaster threatened by its implication in the scandal and thwart the Tory opposition. He did not, however, as Dr. Plumb has shown, save the country's finances from ruin. These had not, in fact, been very seriously damaged.[1] Walpole's financial arrangements were of no great consequence.

Walpole's triumph was not economic, but political, and it was to be the turning-point in his career. In the reconstitution of the ministry, brought about by death and disgrace, Walpole became First Lord of the Treasury and Chancellor of the Exchequer, and Townshend was Secretary of State for the Northern Department, while the members of the two Whig factions shared the other posts. Walpole had now greatly increased his political influence, but Sunderland, though forced to resign, still retained the favour of George I and was busy with plans and intrigues. Sunderland's sudden death in 1722, however, brought Walpole political dominance, though there remained Townshend as a rival who was only to be ousted after a struggle of nine years.

The Man and his Policy

When he obtained the power he had pursued, Walpole was in his forty-ninth year. He had gone a long way since his father had recalled him from Cambridge to learn a squire's duties. At the same time, he retained all his life much of the outlook and characteristics of that class. He always, it was said, opened his game-keepers letters before any official correspondence; he drank well of port wine; and, according to Dr. Johnson, 'said he always talked bawdy at his table, because in that all could join'. Pride of family made him determined to turn Houghton into a magnificent country seat. Between 1722 and 1735 he replaced the old manor house by Houghton Hall, one of the most extensive mansions in England, and filled its saloons with superb furniture designed by Kent and hung its walls with a great collection of paintings which his grandson sold in 1769 to Catherine the Great of Russia. No sooner was his house finished than he rebuilt the parish church which was crowded with his family monuments; and by the time of his death he had planted over 300 acres of woodland where there had previously been only heathland.

[1] P. 244.

With little interest, he gained power in an aristocratic society by outstanding abilities. His early days in politics showed him the importance of patronage, and he is said to have defined the gratitude of place-expectants as 'a lively sense of *future* favours'. During his first years of power, therefore, Walpole lost no opportunity to ensure that he and he alone had the favour of the Crown which gave him control of its patronage. In the past, several office-holders, such as the Lord Chancellor, the Commander-in-Chief, the Master-General of Ordnance and the Customs and Excise Commissioners, had been able to act as dispensers of patronage; but Walpole concentrated patronage in his hands and used it to build up a solid body of supporters among his relatives and friends and to offer favours to those whose services or votes he needed. 'All those men have their price', he said. Such management was one of the ways by which he kept himself in power for so long.

Nine-tenths of the jottings which Walpole made in note-form for his consultations with George II were about patronage; and the success of management depended on his retention of the Crown's support. He was not at first a favourite with either George I or George II. but he gained the confidence of each because he followed a policy which they realized was in the true interests of their dynasty. He also took care to make himself an outstandingly proficient minister of the Crown; and George I came to say of him, 'He never had his equal in business'. He mastered the details of finance, government and trade, and though never appearing to be in a hurry, he worked hard, filling many a day with correspondence, interviews and meetings, taking time off for drinking, hunting and his mistresses only to return to his tasks again, and during parliamentary sessions assiduously attending the Commons where he was, according to Lord Chesterfield, 'an artful rather than an eloquent speaker'. He was able to prove his value as a royal servant and also, fortified by powerful gifts of argument in debate, to hold his own against the attacks of opponents upon his position and his policies.

Excelling as a competent, efficient administrator and a master of political tactics, Walpole was well suited to carry out the main object of his policy – the consolidation of the Hanoverian dynasty and the Whig supremacy. This he

believed could best be done by conciliating the landed
gentry, encouraging trade, avoiding religious controversy
and keeping the country out of war.   He sought to reduce
taxation and especially the land tax, which pressed heavily
on the gentry's estates; he preserved the freedom of the
magistrates from central control; he maintained the privileges
of the Church and refused to modify the Test and Corporation
Acts; he refrained from enforcing strictly the navigation
system in America; and he persisted in friendly relations with
France as long as possible.   'Quieta non movere' – 'Let sleeping
dogs lie' – was his motto which, though not creative or
inspiring, was full of sound sense in the circumstances.   While
his political adroitness increased the power of the Whig
magnates at St. James's and Westminster, the landed gentry
retained all that they valued in Church and countryside, so
that their attachment to the dynasty slowly grew and was to
contribute later in the century to the revival of the Tory
party in active politics.

The Struggle for Supremacy (1722–30)

Walpole has often been described as 'the first Prime
Minister'.   He was never a Prime Minister in the modern
sense.   His power rested ultimately upon the Crown, as
was shown on the death of George II's wife, Queen Caroline,
and the entry of the Prince of Wales into politics.   Nor was
Walpole ever called upon to form a whole ministry of his own;
some of his ministers were always the King's own choice.
Moreover, the idea of the equality of all royal ministers
remained.   Walpole was only called a 'prime minister' as a
term of abuse by his opponents, who accused him of seeking
pre-eminence among his colleagues and comparing him
with contemporary France where the post of a 'premier
ministre', possessing authority over other ministers, had been
created.

Nevertheless, Walpole did gain a position of superiority
that was novel in English politics.   His control and use of
patronage put him in fact above his colleagues, and so did his
mastery of the business of government.   His power was also
increased by his realization of the importance of the House
of Commons in the contemporary situation.   Hitherto the
principal ministers had always sat in the House of Lords,

leaving the government's policy to be defended in the Commons by less important and influential members of the ministry. Walpole was not ennobled on his appointment as First Lord of the Treasury in 1721. He remained in the Commons to manage it in the royal interest and did not become Earl of Orford until the end of his career in 1742. Walpole's pre-eminence, however, was not secured without effort. He had to fight for it by gaining public support for himself and, above all, by eliminating all ministers likely to rival his power in a struggle lasting nine years before it was finally resolved in an outcome which left Walpole in a still stronger position and had an important effect on the development of the cabinet system.

Early in 1722, before Walpole had been a year in office, George I insisted upon a general election in the hope of gaining a parliament more favourable to himself and prevent Walpole building up his influence at the Treasury. The election on the whole produced a parliament ready to support whatever ministers the King might choose, but Walpole was saved from a cabinet reshuffle by Sunderland's death, and then in April came the discovery of a fresh Jacobite conspiracy. Walpole straightway made the most of it. The new Parliament suspended the Habeas Corpus Act for a year and imposed a tax of five shillings in the pound on Roman Catholics and Nonjurors to pay for the troops hurriedly encamped in Hyde Park. An unimportant lawyer, Christopher Layer, was hanged, and two other Jacobite agents were imprisoned. Walpole also seized the opportunity to strike at the Pretender's most formidable supporter in England, Atterbury, who on doubtful evidence was exiled by Parliament for life. Walpole certainly believed that the Jacobite threat to the régime was genuine and serious. The measures he took in 1722, though moderate, were sufficient to ruin Jacobite finances and turn popular opinion still more against them. They also served to remove any Tory threat to his personal position. There were some 170 Tories in the Parliament of 1722. There had been many fights for seats between them and Jacobites, but Walpole was able to brand all Tories as Jacobites and discredit them in the public regard. Above all, Walpole had taken action impressive enough to suggest that opposition to him was disloyal. His own political prestige was highly enhanced. 'It contributed', wrote Onslow soon afterwards, 'very much to fixing Mr. Walpole's interest and power with the King and manifesting fresh proof of his abilities and usefulness as a minister.'

Even in his hour of triumph, however, Walpole's ascendancy in the ministry was not assured. The other Secretary of State, besides Townshend, was the brilliant, arrogant Lord Carteret (1690–1763), who was Stanhope's pupil in diplomacy. Walpole rapidly came to regard him as dangerous both to the country and to himself. He shared Townshend's fear of Carteret's desire for a spectacular foreign policy.[1] He also feared the growing influence Carteret was gaining over George I by supporting Hanoverian interests. And especially he feared Carteret's leadership of the Sunderland faction within the ministry, the members of which were now alarmed at Walpole's influence and wanted to get rid of him. Walpole, however, was able to move first by taking advantage of the affair of 'Wood's Halfpence'.[2] Though the contract was, in fact, regular and fair, Swift aroused a storm of resentment in Ireland against it, largely because the right had originally been granted to the Duchess of Kendal, who had sold it at a handsome profit. Carteret was known to have opposed the scheme; George was angry that his prerogative of providing for the striking of coin should be questioned. Carteret was dismissed from his Secretaryship of State in 1724 and sent to Ireland as Lord-Lieutenant with the ironic task of settling the disturbance he had helped to create. Wood's patent was withdrawn in return for a pension from the Irish funds.

That was the end of the Sunderland group. Walpole was now in high favour with George I, who knighted him in 1725. He got the King to appoint as the new Secretary of State the Duke of Newcastle (1693–1768), who with his brother, Henry Pelham (1695?–1754), had supported Sunderland and now transferred their allegiance to him. Newcastle was a capable debater and had high political judgement, but he already exercised great political influence, as a landowner with estates in five counties, and came to excel as an assiduous and careful organizer of patronage for the government.[3] He

[1] P. 259.   [2] P. 216.   [3] Pp. 57–8.

strengthened Walpole's position immensely in both Houses of Parliament.

It had been commonly supposed that Carteret would be succeeded by William Pulteney (1684–1764), who had gone into opposition with Townshend and Walpole and was still without an important post. He was an accomplished orator and had considerable financial ability, but was both avaricious and ambitious and likely to rival Walpole. In 1724 he got only promises of future promotion from Walpole, and after waiting a year, he began to attack him in the Commons. Walpole now felt strong enough to abandon without recompense a subordinate colleague who tried to intimidate him, and Pulteney at once lost his lucrative sinecure as Cofferer of the Royal Household.

The strength of Walpole's position was shown in 1727 when George I died. Many expected that George II would dismiss his father's favourite minister, but he soon found that no other minister could get parliamentary approval for a new civil list, and Queen Caroline was determined to keep him in power. Within several months George II had come to depend upon Walpole in the business of government, and this dependence grew stronger each year.

It was all the more necessary that Walpole should have the new King on his side because the incipient rivalry between himself and Townshend was now culminating in a prolonged crisis. Carteret's disappearance had eliminated their last serious common rival, and once Walpole had secured the support of George and Caroline he depended less on Townshend than in the previous reign. The friendship between the two men had been weakened by the death of Walpole's sister, Lady Townshend, in 1726, and Townshend resented Walpole's challenge to his family's leading position in Norfolk. At the same time, Walpole increasingly mistrusted and opposed Townshend's foreign policy.[1] Walpole's conclusion of the Treaty of Seville with Spain in 1729 marked the defeat of Townshend's policy. Townshend waited hopelessly for a year and then resigned to retire to his long-neglected Norfolk estates and acquire an unmerited reputation as an agricultural pioneer.[2]

In manipulating Townshend out of office, Walpole acted

[1] P. 260.   [2] P. 112.

with patient dexterity.   He had never liked the large Cabinet Council, fearing that it might split into two hostile factions which would destroy the government, and used it only for formal business, but now he resorted to the smaller, inner Cabinet to undo Townshend.   He gathered a group of a few ministers, who were particularly active when Townshend was with the King in Hanover.   He made sure that these were ministers who shared his views so that opposition to Townshend's plans came from them all and not from him alone.   The ministers were also few enough for him to manage; he could discuss business separately with them before they met and be likely to secure a unanimous decision from them.   So Townshend was isolated and finally ousted from his post.

Walpole's expedient played an important part in the evolution of the cabinet system and of the idea of the corporate responsibility of its members on matters of policy.[1] Townshend's resignation, because of serious differences about policy with the other ministers, came to be regarded as a precedent for the future.   It also further strengthened Walpole's position as the minister presiding over this 'efficient' cabinet, and he, therefore, kept it in being.   While Townshend's previous resignation in 1717 had seriously weakened the Whig ministry, in 1730 no one accompanied him.

Financial and Economic Policy (1721-33)

During Walpole's first period of office as First Lord of the Treasury, he had instituted a Sinking Fund in 1717 to pay off the National Debt.[2]   By 1727 about £8,500,000 had been paid off from the Sinking Fund, and had Walpole used the Sinking Fund as he originally proposed, the National Debt might have been extinguished in quite a short time, but he did not hesitate to divert it to meet deficits in the revenue caused by extraordinary expenditure or a reduction in taxation. Consequently the actual reduction in the National Debt effected by the Sinking Fund was very small, but he had shown that it was a useful financial reserve for a government for other purposes, and subsequent politicians were to follow his example.

Moreover, the very existence of the Sinking Fund created

[1] P. 52.   [2] P. 242.

confidence in the National Debt. Investors at home and abroad became more ready to place their money in it. This enabled Walpole to reduce the interest to a uniform 4 per cent by 1727 and to raise a new loan at 3 per cent. Indeed, while the National Debt's size and high rate of interest had previously presented the government with a troublesome problem, which it had vainly tried to transfer to the South Sea Company, it was now an actual source of strength for the Hanoverian régime since investors, who valued the security and profit it afforded them, realized that they would suffer if there were a change of dynasty.

The same connection between finance and politics appeared in Walpole's attitude towards taxation. The chief direct taxes were the window tax and the land tax. The first Walpole retained, but the second he wished to reduce and even abolish. He called it 'a burden, so long and so grievously borne by a small proportion of the whole collective body of the nation'; these were the Tory squires whom he wished to conciliate. The defeat of his Excise Bill in 1733 prevented its abolition, but he kept it as low as possible. He at once reduced it from 3s. to 2s. in the pound, and until war came in 1739 it only exceeded this during the foreign troubles between 1727 and 1729, while it was as low as 1s. in 1732 and 1733.

The government also relied considerably on indirect taxation, which took the form of excise duties, imposed upon such home-produced articles as candles, leather, soap and salt, and customs duties, levied at the ports on a whole range of foreign imports. Customs duties were largely evaded by the widespread smuggling of the time.[1] In accordance with contemporary ideas, Walpole tried to suppress smuggling by enacting laws providing for severe penalties, including the death penalty, on smugglers, but evasion was so easy and the profits so great that these measures gained little success compared with the resentment they aroused. Walpole came to believe that the best way to remedy the government's loss of revenue would be an extension of the excise system, which was more effective (and, therefore, no less unpopular) and would also, he noted, increase governmental patronage.

Walpole proposed to do this by developing the system of

[1] P. 16.

bonded warehouses in which imported goods were stored and were liable for excise duty if they were taken out for domestic sale, but not if they were re-exported. This not only checked smuggling, since a receipt for the tax could be demanded from those selling dutiable goods, but also helped importers who did not have to pay an immediate duty on each foreign cargo they received. In 1723 he transferred tea, coffee, cocoa and chocolate to this system, achieving a rise in revenue although he reduced the duties on them; and in 1733 he proposed to extend it to tobacco and wine.

His Excise Bill, however, was seized upon by the opposition in the Commons, which had been growing in numbers and eminence.[1] An age which disliked effective government particularly disliked the excise, and the articles involved were in common use. Moreover, in order to reduce the land tax, Walpole not only proposed this extension of the excise system, but had also renewed the tax on salt, a necessity of life for all classes, after abolishing it two years earlier. Placards and pamphlets soon proclaimed that Walpole's scheme would grow until the poor were burdened by duties upon all the necessities of life and gangs of excise men invaded everyone's private life. The London mob was roused to shout 'Excise—Wooden Shoes' and demonstrate around Walpole's coach outside Parliament. The campaign had its effect. The country gentlemen, who would have had to pay less taxation, and the City merchants, whose trade would have benefited, were persuaded that the liberties of the subject were to be invaded. Walpole's majority in the Commons began to fall until he decided to withdraw the Bill; and after that he abandoned economic and financial reform.

Walpole disliked the merchants who opposed him and his foreign policy, but he realized that if the country enjoyed general economic prosperity, it would benefit everyone and promote the stability of the Hanoverian régime. From the start, therefore, Walpole concerned himself with the encouragement of trade and industry. His policy was laid down, in the King's speech in 1721 at the opening of the first Parliament after Walpole took office, as 'to make the exportation of our own manufactures, and the importation of the commodities used in manufacturing of them, as practicable

[1] Pp. 261-2.

and as easy as may be; by this means, the balance of our trade
may be preserved in our favour, our navigation increased, and
the greater numbers of our poor employed'.

These were mercantilist aims.[1] Walpole initiated important measures which removed obstructions upon commerce
and encouraged the growth of exports.   Early in his ministry
he abolished all duties on the export of farm produce and of
many manufactured articles, and he also gave bounties on the
export of gunpowder, silk, sail-cloth and refined sugar.   He
removed import duties on dyes, undressed flax, raw silk and
other materials needed by industries.   Between 1724 and 1731
he regulated the quality and size of such goods as broadcloth,
linen, sail-cloth and bricks and tiles to maintain their
standards in the export markets, while other regulations in
1721 and 1726 were designed to prevent high wages and
combinations of workmen.   Besides these efforts to encourage
manufacturers to sell their goods abroad, Walpole also
protected domestic industries by tariffs from foreign, Irish and
colonial competition, though the Molasses Act of 1733, passed
to satisfy West Indian planters, was not made effective.[2] 'I
have old England set against me', he said typically in 1739,
'do you think I will have new England likewise?'

Walpole's ministry was a period when British trade
flourished as never before, and it continued to flourish afterwards.[3]   Between 1723 and 1738 shipping grew by more than
a million tons and by over £2,000,000 in value.   The value
of exports increased between 1720 and 1738 from £6,910,998
to £9,993,232 and of imports from £6,090,083 to £7,273,513
so that the balance of trade improved from £820,816 to
£2,719,719.   Of course, Walpole was not responsible for this
economic progress, but his financial and economic policy
assisted it, and so did his foreign policy.

Foreign Policy (1721–39)

In his early political career, Walpole had been concerned
mainly with finance and taken little interest in foreign affairs.
In 1721 it seemed natural that Townshend, who had considerable diplomatic experience, should control foreign
policy.   It was inevitable, however, that if Walpole were to
establish his position in the ministry he would sooner or later

[1] P. 156.   [2] P. 157.   [3] P. 154.

have to assert himself in foreign affairs. He had eventually to attempt to bring foreign policy into line with his general aims. His efforts were to achieve great success and yet in the end they brought about his fall from office.

It was Carteret's aspirations that first drove Walpole to an active apprehension of the implications of foreign policy.[1] At first Carteret's presence in the ministry was useful to Walpole and Townshend since it reassured the French Regent Orleans that Stanhope's policy of alliance with France would be continued, but the death of Orleans in 1723 removed this need. Moreover, Carteret's love of bold action and desire to gain George I's favour had led him to suggest the dangerous plan of subsidizing Sweden and sending a British fleet into the Baltic to protect Hanover from the possible consequences of Peter the Great's policy. Walpole's fear of war combined with other circumstances to impel him to manœuvre Carteret out of office in 1724.

The elimination of Carteret left Walpole more ready to leave foreign policy to Townshend. In 1721 the territorial arrangements of the Quadruple Alliance had yet to be completed. After long delays, the European politicians met at the Congress of Cambrai in 1724, but failed to reach agreement. Dissatisfied with this indecision, Elizabeth Farnese opened secret negotiations with the Emperor Charles VI, which resulted in the signing of the First Treaty of Vienna in 1725. Spain recognized the Pragmatic Sanction guaranteeing the right of Charles VI's daughter, Maria Theresa, to succeed to the undivided Habsburg territories on his death;[2] and Austria recognized Don Carlos as heir to the Duchies of Parma and Tuscany and promised to Spain the recovery of Gibraltar and Minorca from Britain. The agreement alarmed Britain and France. British merchants were especially apprehensive because Spain had also granted commercial concessions to the Ostend Company which the Emperor had recently founded in an effort to secure Austrian participation in overseas trade.

The general hostility to Spain and Austria in Britain encouraged Townshend, who wanted a forceful foreign policy. He at once countered by negotiating the Treaty of Hanover between Britain, France and Prussia for the mutual

[1] P. 253.   [2] P. 267.

guarantee of their territories. This was intended to be the basis for other alliances; and he secured the accession of Holland, Denmark and Sweden and made a treaty with Hesse-Cassel for 12,000 troops. By 1726 Britain and Spain were engaged in warlike activity against each other. Spanish forces besieged Gibraltar, and a British fleet blockaded the West Indies to prevent the Spanish treasure fleet sailing.

By now the foreign situation seriously perturbed Walpole. He disliked the increase in the land tax which had become necessary, and he feared the outbreak of a general European war. Townshend was anti-Habsburg and even toyed with the idea of taking half the Austrian Netherlands for Britain; but Walpole believed that, with French help, Spain could be detached from Austria. Unknown to Townshend, who was then in Hanover, Walpole in 1729 negotiated the Treaty of Seville with France and Spain. By this, Spain promised to maintain Britain's trading privileges, and France agreed that Spain should garrison Parma and Tuscany. A year later Townshend resigned.[1] Walpole went on to make the Second Treaty of Vienna with the Emperor in 1731, by which Britain acknowledged the Pragmatic Sanction in return for Austrian recognition of the Italian claims of Don Carlos and the dissolution of the Ostend Company.

Walpole now had sole control of British foreign policy, and for nearly a decade he was able to secure peace for Britain. He considered this essential for the security of the Hanoverian dynasty, as war would alienate the country gentry by raising the land tax and would also gain foreign support for the Pretender, while peace would promote commercial growth and prosperity. He was assisted by Cardinal Fleury, Louis XV's principal minister from 1726 to 1743. Fleury also wanted peace, since he believed that war would bring financial ruin upon France. So the Franco-British alliance was maintained, and the peaceful lull in the rivalry between the two powers continued.

Walpole resisted Austrian efforts to draw Britain into the War of the Polish Succession (1733–8) against France. 'Fifty thousand men slain this year in Europe', he said to Queen Caroline in 1733, 'and not one Englishman'; but George II, Caroline, their Hanoverian advisers and even

P. 254.

Newcastle wanted war. They saw the French attack on Austria as an attempt to upset the Utrecht settlement and renew her dominance in Europe, and the threat seemed the more serious because France made the Family Compact with Spain in 1733 which gave her an ally in the War. As long as hostilities lasted, Fleury ably conducted lengthy, fruitless negotiations with Britain and then concluded the Third Treaty of Vienna with Austria in 1738 without British knowledge. This was an important diplomatic victory for France. Don Carlos became King of Naples and Sicily; France obtained the reversion of Lorraine. France had gained the initiative in European affairs, while Britain was dangerously isolated at a time when her armed forces had been allowed to decline.[1] In addition, there was unrelenting hostility between French and English colonists in North America and between the East India companies of the two nations. Public opinion was turning against Walpole's pacific policy, and the parliamentary opposition took full advantage of this.

The Growth of the Opposition (1725–9)

As Walpole remained in office year after year, an effective opposition to him in Parliament gradually came into being. However much patronage he tried to control, he could never have sufficient places at his disposal to satisfy everyone. The numbers of the dissatisfied and resentful grew and wanted only a leader to be able to threaten Walpole's position. This came with Pulteney's dismissal in 1725.[2] Resentment spurred him to turn his oratorical powers against Walpole in the Commons, and he immediately found a powerful ally outside Parliament in Bolingbroke, who had been dismissed from the Old Pretender's service soon after the 'Fifteen. Walpole was not able to prevent his pardon, which enabled him to return to England in 1723, nor the reversal of his attainder in 1725 (obtained by bribing the Duchess of Kendal), but he insisted upon his exclusion from the House of Lords. Nevertheless, Bolingbroke hoped to form an opposition to Walpole by uniting the Tories and the dissatisfied Whigs.

In 1726 Bolingbroke and Pulteney founded *The Craftsman*

[1] P. 190.   [2] P. 254.

(which continued until 1750) as a weekly opposition news-paper. Besides themselves, its contributors included Swift, Pope and Arbuthnot, whom the pamphleteers hired by Wal-pole found difficult to answer. In number after number it held up Walpole and his engrossing of patronage to ridicule and contempt and called for a 'reformation of government'. Ten thousand copies of a single number were sold, and squires and parsons in the country asked London friends to send it to them regularly. The opposition gained a valuable supporter when Frederick, Prince of Wales (1701–51), whom George I had kept in Hanover, came to England in 1728 and soon was estranged from his father. Once again Leicester House became the social centre of the opposition. And in 1730 Carteret resigned his Irish post to seek revenge upon Walpole through critical speeches in the House of Lords.

The opposition also had on its side the wealthy, influential merchant classes of the City of London, who were suspicious of Walpole and the Hanoverian connection and wanted a foreign policy that would promote their interests against France and Spain. As early as 1725 the erratic Duke of Wharton (1698–1731), a recent convert to Jacobitism, exploited their hostility through his ephemeral newspaper, *The True Briton*. Corruption and violence became prevalent in every City election. Government aldermanic candidates were defeated, and two Tories were returned as Members of Parliament for the City. Walpole's reply was to force through Parliament a bill disfranchising some 3,000 freemen and giving aldermen a veto of the Common Court's decisions. This gave Walpole control of the City's constitution, but its dominant classes remained a powerful stay of the opposition.

The year 1733 was a turning-point in Walpole's career. His Excise Bill gave the opposition its first serious chance to strike at him and its first real victory.[1] When the Bill was withdrawn, both opposition and City rejoiced; houses were illuminated and bonfires blazed. Yet Bolingbroke's hopes of replacing Walpole's ministry by a coalition came to nothing. The Whig moneyed classes mistrusted the Tory landed gentry, and the two groups differed about foreign affairs. Because of Newcastle's control of the smaller boroughs, Walpole main-tained his majority in the general election of 1734, though it

[1] P. 257.

fell to the dangerously low figure of fifty. Bolingbroke thought it wise the next year to retreat to France again, where he devoted himself to writing political philosophy.

In fact, Bolingbroke's plans could not have succeeded. A ministry containing Tories was still an impossibility, and the dissident Whigs had not the ability or influence to gain office. As this was so, the opposition could not seem like an alternative government. Nevertheless, the episode of the Excise Bill made the opposition a serious political force. Walpole dismissed from office the Duke of Bolton, the Earl of Chesterfield, Lord Cobham and other Whig peers who had opposed him. These were men of ability, wealth and influence, who could do more than skilfully exploit various discontents. They could put forward a rival policy and were ready to seize power whenever opportunity offered.

Moreover, both Walpole and George II were now elderly. Younger politicians, whose hopes lay in the future, naturally turned from them to the opposition. The most important of these were a group of young men, who called themselves 'Patriots', claiming to serve the public good, but whom Walpole derisively called the 'Boy Patriots' or 'Cobham's Cubs'. Cobham made his country seat, Stowe in Buckinghamshire, a rallying-point for aspiring young politicians whom he delighted in discovering and patronizing. Among them were George and Richard Grenville, George Lyttleton and William Pitt, who held a cornetcy in Lord Cobham's Horse and in 1735 entered Parliament, to be dismissed from the army for his first speech in which he ironically congratulated the King on the Prince of Wales's marriage.

Walpole clung determinedly to power. He had behind him royal favour, the power of patronage and bribery and a sufficiently large standing army. He increasingly raided the Sinking Fund to avoid higher taxation and would not consider reducing the interest on the National Debt. Events, however, were not on his side, and they reached a dramatic climax in 1737. The quarrel between the Prince of Wales and his father grew worse, to the opposition's advantage. Walpole's attempt to deal with the evils of gin-drinking – the Gin Act of 1736, imposing a duty of 20s. a gallon and fixing the cost of a licence to sell spirits at £50 – had provoked such serious riots in London that after a few months attempts

s

to enforce the Act had to be abandoned. In Scotland the Porteous Riots and the consequent fine of £2,000 imposed by Walpole on the city of Edinburgh cost him the support of the Scottish members.[1] The Playhouse Act of 1737, requiring the submission of plays to the Lord Chamberlain for approval, was Walpole's answer to the constant attacks made upon him by the playwrights (of whom Henry Fielding was the most effective). And, finally, Queen Caroline died, depriving Walpole of a constant supporter.

Throughout the later 1730's the opposition persisted in taking every opportunity to discredit Walpole, denouncing the corruption of his government, demanding the repeal of the Septennial Act and criticizing his foreign policy. Walpole, however, was in a strong enough position to hold out as long as no question arose with a sufficiently strong national appeal to turn the independent members against him. When it came, Walpole continued to struggle to retain power for a further three bitter years.

The Fall from Power (1739–42)

The issue which drove Walpole from power was raised by the long-standing dispute between Britain and Spain over trade in South American waters.[2] In 1738 a West Indian shipmaster, Captain Robert Jenkins, complained that seven years previously he had been mutilated by Spanish *guarda-costas*, who had pillaged his ship and tortured his crew, and he exhibited a cut-off ear preserved in a bottle of spirits to support his story. The opposition supported his case and stirred up feeling in the country. Jenkins's words that, when the Spaniards threatened him, he had 'committed his soul to God and his cause to his country' inflamed public opinion to a warlike pitch.

Walpole wished to arrange the matter peacefully, and so did the Spanish government. Early in 1739 negotiations at last produced the Convention of Pardo which, by offsetting British and Spanish claims against each other, assigned to Britain only the sum of £27,000 as compensation to merchants whose ships had been seized, and left the crucial question of the right of search for future discussion. Walpole believed that war after this settlement would be 'impolitic and

[1] P. 208.   [2] P. 163.

dishonourable', but he was widely denounced. The commercial classes thought that a successful war would expand their trade. Their case was voiced by Pitt, who asserted, 'The Convention of Pardo was a stipulation for national ignominy'; and in the ministry, Newcastle and others wanted Britain to take naval action against Spain. The South Sea Company refused to pay the claims made against it by the Spanish government, as required by the Convention of Pardo. Walpole had to give in. War was declared in October 1739. 'It is your war', he said to Newcastle, 'and I wish you joy of it.' George II would not let him resign; he kept himself in power, sick, embittered and able to do little. The first winter of the War was intensely cold (and there was not to be a worse one until 1963); the harvest was bad and there was much discontent. The Cabinet was divided, and the War went badly. It had to be a naval contest, but there were not enough ships or men to undertake it successfully. Admiral Vernon captured Porto Bello in 1739, and Anson sailed round the world between 1740 and 1744, capturing much Spanish treasure; but in 1741 Vernon made a disastrous raid on Cartagena, and the next year an expedition to Cuba was unsuccessful. Meanwhile, the Emperor Charles VI had died, and Frederick the Great of Prussia, ignoring the Pragmatic Sanction, had invaded Silesia.[1] It was now clear that sooner or later there would be a general war in Europe.

In such a situation the general election of 1741 was held. The Prince's electoral influence was turned against Walpole. His majority fell to about fourteen. The King, fearful of a French invasion of Hanover, tried to ensure the Electorate's neutrality.[2] Ever ready suspicions that British interests would be sacrificed were aroused. By January 1742 Walpole had been defeated seven times in the Commons, and he insisted upon the King accepting his resignation. He was raised to the peerage as Earl of Orford and died three years later.

Walpole's fall from office marked the end of an era. 'For twenty years', in Dr. Plumb's words, 'Walpole had just held in check those aspirations natural to a society which was faced with enormous possibilities of commercial expansion.' He had wished to avoid war because he believed the stability of

[1] P. 267.   [2] Pp. 268–9.

the country and its régime depended on the support of the landed gentry who wanted peace and low taxation, but he was increasingly criticized by ambitious traders and patriotic politicians. Both of these groups wanted a Britain that was strong, prosperous, commercial and imperial and believed that an aggressive policy was necessary to secure this position for her. The war that followed Walpole's defeat brought Britain comparatively few gains, but Pitt's direction of the war after that was to gain her spectacular overseas conquests and wealth.

XIII · THE WAR OF THE AUSTRIAN
SUCCESSION, 1740-8

Britain and the Opening of War (1740–2)

THE Emperor Charles VI's death in October 1740 ended the
male line of the Habsburg rulers of Austria, Bohemia, Hun-
gary, Silesia, the Netherlands and other hereditary territories,
who had also since 1411 been appointed by successive generations of German electoral princes to the position of Holy
Roman Emperor. Charles had foreseen that on his death
the Electors would choose a non-Habsburg prince as Emperor
(and this occurred in 1742 when they raised the Duke of
Bavaria to the Imperial throne as Charles VII); but he hoped
to secure the succession of his daughter, Maria Theresa, to
the hereditary Habsburg lands by promulgating a decree,
the Pragmatic Sanction, in 1717 that this should take place
if there were no male heir. During the following years the
main objective of his foreign policy was to secure the acceptance of this decree by all the important European states.
When he died, Bavaria alone had not accepted it.

Late in 1740, however, Frederick of Prussia, who had
recognized the Pragmatic Sanction in 1726, invaded and
occupied Silesia. The war-party in France was encouraged
to press for action against their country's long-standing
enemy, Austria. The aged Fleury was overruled, and in
1741 France formed a coalition with Spain, Bavaria, Saxony
and Sardinia, as well as with Prussia, which recognized
Frederick's conquest of Silesia, and began hostilities against
Austria. These allies also agreed to support Charles of
Bavaria's claim to the Imperial throne, and each coveted a
part of the Habsburg dominions.

By the time this general European conflict – the War of the
Austrian Succession – began, Britain had been at war with
Spain for over a year. Britain had recognized the Pragmatic
Sanction in 1731, and Maria Theresa at once asked her for
help. Walpole, anxious that Britain should not become
involved in further hostilities, urged that Maria Theresa

should be persuaded to make terms with Frederick, but public opinion sympathized with the defiant young Queen and believed that Britain would sooner or later have to fight an increasingly aggressive France; and the first reaction of George II was to see Prussian aggrandizement as a potential threat to Hanover.

Yielding to parliamentary and royal pressure, Walpole moved that a subsidy of £300,000 be voted to Maria Theresa. This was in April 1741, not long before Parliament was dissolved for the general election which seriously reduced Walpole's majority.[1] The war against Spain continued to go badly, and when French troops threatened in September to attack Hanover, George II declared his Electorate neutral and retained for its defence the Danish and Hessian troops in British pay which were to have assisted Austria. The next month Walpole persuaded Maria Theresa, so that she might have time to concentrate against France, to agree to the Convention of Klein-Schnellendorf by which Frederick was allowed to occupy the whole of Silesia in return for suspending operations against Austria. These events contributed to the undermining of Walpole's position which led to his resignation in January 1742.[2]

The Supremacy of Carteret (1742–4)

It has been commonly believed that Walpole was still powerful enough, through his influence with George II, to control largely the ministerial reconstruction which followed his resignation, but insufficient evidence about the accompanying negotiations has survived to indicate whether this was so or not. In the event, the Duke of Newcastle and his brother, Henry Pelham, remained in office. Pulteney accepted membership of the Cabinet, but sought to retain his independence by refusing office, only to lose all political influence and have to retire to the House of Lords as Earl of Bath; 'he was fixed in the House of Lords, that hospital of incurables', said Chesterfield, 'and his retreat to popularity was cut off'. Carteret regained his old office of Secretary of State, and the Earl of Hardwicke retained the Lord Chancellorship which he had held since 1737. Neither the Tories nor 'Cobham's Cubs' secured office. Pitt persuaded Parliament to set up a committee to investigate Walpole's past actions, but it was dissolved before doing anything. The King had been compelled to part with Walpole, but he was not prepared to give in to the opposition which had supported his son and denounced the Electorate.

Royal favour and supremacy in the ministry for almost three years belonged to Carteret, who was denounced by Pitt as the 'sole minister'. During his twelve years in opposition, he had devoted much time to the Greek and Latin classics and also to fine claret, but recently he had attacked Walpole's management of the war against Spain in masterly and vehement speeches. His knowledge of German brought him the same favour with George II as it had done with the King's father; his brilliance of intellect remained, and so did his desire for a spectacular conduct of foreign affairs.[1] He now came back to office expressing a wish to 'knock the heads of the kings of Europe together'.

At first the remodelled ministry could rely on a majority of about a hundred in the Commons, and Carteret himself enjoyed much popular support in 1742. The several British failures in the war against Spain and the growing likelihood of conflict with France seemed to call for vigorous strokes of policy. Carteret boldly wished to revive the conception of a Grand Alliance against France and Spain which the Whigs had pursued so successfully in the War of the Spanish Succession. He was not concerned with the dispute between Austria and Prussia, but only the threat of French aggrandizement. 'I will always', he said, 'traverse the views of France in place and out of place; for France will ruin this nation if it can.' Britain was not yet officially at war with France, but Carteret immediately made sure that circumstances should be as favourable as possible for her when the confrontation came.

The British subsidy to Maria Theresa was increased to £500,000, and George II was induced to abandon Hanover's neutrality on condition that Britain paid for her army. A treaty was signed with the Empress Elizabeth of Russia by which Britain would receive 12,000 Russian troops if a third power were to come to the support of Spain against her, while Britain would send twelve warships to the Baltic if Russia were attacked by a third power during the war she

[1] P. 259.

was then waging against Sweden. Maria Theresa was persuaded to sign the Treaty of Berlin with Frederick by which she ceded Silesia to him in return for Prussian neutrality. The appearance of a British fleet off Naples compelled Don Carlos under threat of bombardment to promise his neutrality; and Maria Theresa was also persuaded to sign the Treaty of Worms by which Sardinia became her ally through the promise of territorial concessions in the Milanese and a British subsidy of £200,000.

These achievements prepared the way for direct – though still unofficial – action against France in 1743. Carteret had already sent a British force to the Austrian Netherlands, and early in 1743 these troops, joined by Hanoverian and Austrian contingents, marched into Germany under the name of the Pragmatic Army. George II (acting as Elector of Hanover) came over to command it and won the Battle of Dettingen in Bavaria over a French army, the last battle in which a King of England was engaged. The French withdrew beyond the Rhine. Carteret looked forward to the rapid conversion of the War into a general attack on France by a coalition led by Britain.

The victory at Dettingen, however, was to mark the summit of Carteret's power and prestige. His very successes stirred up fresh trouble for his policy which moved from apparent triumph to collapse in 1744. Frederick could not feel safe while Maria Theresa took advantage of the Treaty of Berlin to strengthen her army; he again attacked Austria. France similarly felt that the threat to the Spanish position in Italy by Britain, Austria and Sardinia contained in the Treaty of Worms meant that she must take the offensive vigorously. She made a definite alliance with Spain and declared war on Britain. Her chief objective was now the invasion of the Austrian Netherlands, but she also made ready to support the Young Pretender in an attempt on the British throne. Moreover, a British fleet under Admiral Mathews failed to prevent a Franco-Spanish fleet leaving Toulon and reaching Spanish ports.[1]

Even before these events, Carteret's policy had encountered mounting criticism in Britain. The costly subsidies which it involved were resented. George II's part at Dettingen did

[1] Pp. 196, 278.

not allay suspicion that he only wanted British money and troops to further Hanover's interests, and Carteret, who had gone abroad with the King on his campaign, inevitably was accused of subservience to royal wishes. Pitt condemned him in the Commons as the 'Hanoverian troop-minister', who had degraded 'the great and powerful kingdom' to the position of 'a province to a despicable electorate'. As Carteret's hopes crumbled on the Continent, such criticism intensified at home, and his position became very vulnerable.

Being in the House of Lords, Carteret was at a disadvantage in not being able to reply to Pitt's speeches. Still more, his own character did much to make him defenceless. By nature proud and aloof, he was secretive with his colleagues and disdainful towards his supporters. Political management was not for him – 'What is it to me, who is a judge or who is a bishop? It is my business to make kings and emperors and to maintain the balance of Europe.' He believed that his foreign policy would secure him popular and parliamentary support and that his favour with the King would make him independent of the Cabinet. 'Give any man the crown on his side,' he asserted, 'and he can defy everything.' This was not the way to political survival in eighteenth-century conditions.

So far the Pelhams' skilful management of the Commons had saved the ministry, but alarmed now by Carteret's foreign policy and aware of his declining influence, they informed the King that either he must be dismissed or they would resign from office. George did not want to part with him. 'Surely when ministers disagree,' he said to Newcastle, 'it is hard if I may not determine amongst you'; but the Duke replied, 'To be sure, Sir, your Majesty ought, must and does, but then, as is the Constitution, your Majesty will have the goodness to excuse those from executing what they think wrong or not for your service.' The King could not support Carteret against the Pelhams because he would have no support in the Commons. In November 1743 George had to accept Carteret's resignation.

Though deficiencies in political ability and personal influence contributed towards it, Carteret's downfall came about mainly through the failure of his foreign policy. This was not because it was in any way subservient to Hanoverian interests.   Carteret's policy was entirely aimed at the defeat of France.   He saw that she was Britain's chief enemy and realized that the conflict in Germany must be brought to an end and an offensive organized against France, but his attempts to do this were over-ambitious.   His subsidies gained allies on the Continent, but the alliance was not adequate for the purpose.   When both France and Prussia turned determinedly against it, rapid collapse seemed likely, and Carteret's colleagues were faced with the prospect of British participation in an expensive yet fruitless European commitment.

The Rise of the Pelhams (1744–5)

Henry Pelham had already become First Lord of the Treasury in 1743, and Newcastle was still a Secretary of State.   In view of the difficulties likely to face the ministry at home and abroad, they now wanted to protect it from attacks from the opposition, such as both Walpole and Carteret had experienced, by bringing into it as many representatives of the different parliamentary groups as possible. They formed what became known as the Broad-Bottom Administration, which was to last for ten years until Henry Pelham's death in 1754.   In order to make room for all shades of Whig opinion, a number of 'new Whigs', who had joined the ministry with Carteret and Pulteney after Walpole's resignation, were removed.   Among those who replaced them were Chesterfield and some of the 'Patriots', including Cobham and two of his 'Cubs', George Grenville and Lyttleton, and also John Russell, Duke of Bedford (1710–71), the wealthy leader of the 'old Whigs'.   There were even some Tories.   The Pelhams were unable, however, to offer any place to Pitt, who had done most to rally the opposition against Carteret.   George II had not forgotten his remarks about Hanover and would not have him for a minister.   'Although I have been forced to part with those I like,' he said, 'I will never be induced to take those who are disagreeable to me.'

This ministerial reconstruction considerably strengthened the ascendancy of the Pelhams in Parliament, but serious difficulties still faced them.   At home public opinion was critical of the new administration, while the King was openly antagonistic towards it.   He resented the way in which he had been compelled to accept the resignation of Carteret (who had now become Earl Granville on his mother's death) and continued for some time to look to him for advice. The ministers had to try to gain his favour without arousing the anti-Hanoverian feelings of the Commons. As a start the direct payment of the Hanoverian troops by Britain was discontinued, but Maria Theresa was given an additional subsidy of £200,000 a year so that she could hire them and maintain them as before in the Netherlands. On the other hand, the administration did not now have to face the attacks of Pitt, who accepted its advent as a 'new dawn of salvation'; he ceased to frequent Leicester House and no longer attacked the granting of subsidies to Britain's allies on the Continent.

The cessation of Pitt's hostility was particularly welcome to the administration because the course of the war abroad went badly for Britain throughout 1744 and 1745. Austria was defeated by Frederick, and the Spanish triumphed in Italy. The command of the allied force in the Netherlands had been given to the King's youthful second son, William Augustus, Duke of Cumberland (1721–65). A French army under Marshal de Saxe was invading Flanders and in May 1745 threatened Tournai. Holland had at last reluctantly agreed to declare war on France, but the defence of the Netherlands devolved largely upon Britain. Cumberland advanced to relieve Tournai, but, fighting gallantly, was defeated by a French force twice the size of his own at Fontenoy. As a consequence, Saxe rapidly occupied Flanders, capturing not only Tournai, but also Ghent, Bruges, Oudenarde and Ostend, the last being the British base and the main port of supply from England. Another result of the Battle of Fontenoy was that George II signed the Convention of Hanover, which recognized Prussian possession of Silesia in return for an acknowledgement of Hanoverian neutrality. Though the British government were not concerned in this agreement, it confirmed the mistrust which Maria Theresa was already entertaining about her British ally.

These European events were hardly the new administration's fault. They were a legacy which it had inherited from Carteret's policy, but they served to deny it a favourable reception from British public opinion. Some ten weeks after the defeat at Fontenoy, however, a development occurred which was to unite the country behind the government and compel it to extricate its force from the Continental fighting. In July 1745 the Young Pretender arrived in Scotland, and by October Cumberland and most of the British troops had been withdrawn to England to counter the Jacobite revolt. Only 6,000 Hessians now formed the British contribution to the allied army.

The 'Forty-Five

The 'Forty-Five was essentially an episode of the War of the Austrian Succession. The Jacobites were stimulated to make another attempt by Britain's involvement in war with France, but they gained little, in fact, from the international situation. After an unsucessful attempt the year before, the French were now not very keen to assist their venture.[1] Fewer than a thousand French troops came, late in the day, to join the Young Pretender.

Without adequate French help, the 'Forty-Five had really no more chance of success than the previous rising. In Scotland several thousand Highlanders rallied to Charles Edward, but in England Jacobitism was a languishing cause. The romantic character of 'Bonny Prince Charlie' might attract some, but the actual claimant to the throne was his less appealing father, 'James III', who for the last twenty-seven years had lived a dreary, devout life at Rome, surrounded by bickering followers and receiving only occasional sums of English money from the Duke of Beaufort and a few others to augment his papal pension. This man and his associations had few admirers in England, even among those who were lukewarm towards the Hanoverian royal family. The landed gentry and clergy, the merchants and politicians, had no wish to exchange the security they enjoyed under the dynasty for a hazardous, unprofitable and reactionary rebellion.

Nevertheless, the rising in Scotland produced a sharp, if short-lived, emergency. The government, ill-informed about Scottish affairs, was caught unprepared when the news reached London in mid-August. The King was away in Hanover and did not return until the last day of the month. By then the streets of Newcastle-upon-Tyne were strangely deserted and the inns along the Great North Road full of

[1] P. 210.

refugees, while the militia was slowly assembling at Finchley to defend the capital.   George rudely berated his ministers as 'pitiful fellows' and continued to scheme with Granville. As the Pretender marched southwards into England, only a few individuals, like the energetic Thomas Herring, Archbishop of York, actively supported the government.   On the 'Black Friday' in December, when the Pretender was known to be in Derby, there was panic in London and a run on the banks.

Soon afterwards, however, Charles began to retreat northwards again.   The danger had been more apparent than real.   Only some three hundred Englishmen, mostly Roman Catholics in Lancashire, had joined his army.   His defeat by Cumberland's army at the Battle of Culloden came four months later.[1]   From now onwards Jacobitism ceased to be a political factor.   The Young Pretender spent the rest of his life on the Continent in wandering, intrigue and drunkenness. When he died in 1788, the Jacobite claim passed to his brother, Henry, by now a genial, scholarly and boring Cardinal and Bishop of Frascati.   When Napoleon's armies deprived him of his fortune, George II granted him a pension of £4,000 a year.   He died in 1807, bequeathing the crown jewels (taken away by James II) to George IV, who later gave 50 guineas towards Canova's monument in St. Peter's, Rome, to 'James III, Charles III and Henry IX'.

The Triumph of the Pelhams (1746–7)

Before the Jacobite defeat at Culloden, there had been a dramatic political crisis.   It was a conflict between the King and the administration which both welcomed.   The ministers still had to face George II's unconcealed hostility, which did not abate during the most dangerous days of the rebellion. His wish to restore Granville to power remained as firm as ever, and the ministers suspected Granville's influence at court.   In February 1746, conscious that the real threat from the rising was over and that they had strengthened their position in the country, the Pelhams and Hardwicke resigned. The King asked Granville to form a ministry, but after two days he had to confess himself unable to find colleagues ready to attempt to govern without the support of the Commons. He retired, laughing at the whole fiasco as an excellent joke,

[1] Pp. 211–12.

and henceforward exchanged political ambition for the pleasures to be found in books and bottles and also in the company of his young second wife.

The Pelhams had successfully demonstrated their power to the King and shown him that he could not govern without them.   He had to ask them to resume office, and they asked him to make such changes as they recommended, though these were few.   Having come to terms with Pitt, they wanted him to have office.[1]   George, however, would only agree that he should have the sinecure Vice-Paymastership of Ireland, which he was able to exchange three months later for the lucrative post of Paymaster of the Forces in England. Though Pitt was thus confined to minor office, since he was already popular in the country his presence in the administration and readiness to co-operate with its members added greatly to its prestige.

It was a real triumph for the Pelhams.   Henry Pelham steadily adopted the political methods and outlook of Walpole whose follower he was proud to be, and (also like Walpole) he owed much to the continued industrious borough-mongering and lobbying of Newcastle.   The Prince of Wales was now leading a new opposition, and he, as Pelham wrote, had 'as much to give in present as we have, and more in reversion'; but they got the King to dissolve Parliament in June 1747, a year earlier than expected, and the ensuing general election gave them a majority of at least 125 in the Commons.   They had made themselves indispensable to the King, drawn all the leading politicians on to their side and persuaded the electorate that their government was most likely to promote the best interests of the country.

The Maritime War (1744–8)

In 1745 Pelham wrote to the British envoy at The Hague, 'Our hasty engagements, three years ago, making ourselves principals of all the wars on the Continent, without any plan concerned, or any obligations from the parties we were serving, except it was to take our money and apply it as they pleased, have rendered this country incapable of doing what its inclination and interest always induce it to do.'   There were good grounds for this criticism of the consequences for

[1] P. 297.

Britain of Carteret's policy of widely-extended participation in the War. He had regarded the European struggle as the main theatre of war for Britain, but the system of alliances he had so expensively built up had proved ineffective. Subsidies had been augmented by the despatch of British troops to the Austrian Netherlands, but these had failed to prevent the advance of the French in this area of such traditional concern to the nation. A greater concentration of the war effort against the Bourbon powers was needed.

Despite the withdrawal of British troops from Flanders to deal with the 'Forty-Five, the government did not abandon the aim of defeating France on the Continent. As the price of continuing to subsidize Maria Theresa, it brought pressure on her to make peace with Frederick in December 1745 by the Treaty of Dresden in which she had reluctantly to recognize Prussian possession of Silesia; but the Austrian troops thus released joined with Sardinia to defeat the Spanish forces in northern Italy, and a British request that they should co-operate in invading France was refused. Meanwhile, Marshal de Saxe had swept on with his advance in the Netherlands. In 1746 he captured Brussels, Antwerp and Liège. 'A good peace is every man's wish,' said Pelham despondently, 'an indifferent one would be gladly accepted, a sad one, I am afraid, will be our lot.'

There was, however, another and brighter side to the picture – the maritime war. When the War of Jenkins's Ear had merged into the War of the Austrian Succession, Carteret's policy required the British navy to be used largely in the Continental conflict. An early task demanded of it was to prevent France and Spain from securing naval supremacy in the Mediterranean by joint action and so be able to protect the passage of military reinforcements to Italy. Admiral Thomas Mathews (1676–1751) was given control of the Mediterranean fleet with instructions to watch the combined French and Spanish fleets which lay in Toulon harbour; but though a large part of the British navy had been sent to his command, its numbers and efficiency had been impaired by inactivity and lack of maintenance during the years of peace, and it had yet to benefit from the reforms accomplished by Lord Anson after his return in 1744 from his voyage round the world. When the Franco-Spanish

fleet emerged from Toulon in 1744, Mathews' caution and
shortage of fast ships allowed the enemy to sail into Spanish
harbours without much damage.[1] Mathews was dismissed
from the service for failing in his duty; but the enemy made
no further attempt to convoy troop-ships to Italy.

Greater naval success was achieved off Britain's coasts.
When Marshal de Saxe planned to invade England in 1744,
the British government heard of his preparations and was able
to send a superior fleet commanded by Admiral Norris into
the Channel, which would probably have overwhelmed the
French expedition if it had not been crippled by strong easterly
gales.[2] The next year Prince Charles Edward, in the
absence of adequate French help, pawned his jewels and
borrowed money to fit out a battleship, the *Elizabeth*, and a
frigate, the *Du Tellier* (commonly known in Britain as the
Doutelle). The *Elizabeth* was intercepted by a British warship
and after a running fight of six hours was so badly battered
that she had to put back into a French port. The *Du Tellier*
evaded pursuit and sailed on to land the Prince in Scotland
with his few companions, but the *Elizabeth* had been carrying
his vital supplies of arms and ammunition.

In October, when the Prince had gained all Scotland and
advanced into England, the French government was now
prepared to send him military support, particularly as autumn
had ended the regular Continental campaigning season. Invasion craft had been collected again in several harbours and
15,000 troops were brought into Dunkirk by early December
when the victorious Highlanders were not much more than a
hundred miles from London; but the Brest fleet could not
enter the Channel to escort the expedition. Admiral Vernon
kept a strong fleet out to the westward together with sufficient
small squadrons in the Channel and the North Sea to prevent
the troop-ships from getting out.

Such incidents in home waters showed the need of naval
supremacy to protect Britain from invasion, but there were
also oceanic actions which revealed the growing importance
of sea power in deciding the outcome of a conflict. In June
1745 a squadron under Commodore Peter Warren, assisted
by militia from Massachusetts, captured the fortress of Louisbourg, built by the French in 1720 on Cape Breton Island at

[1] Pp. 196, 270.   [2] P. 210.

the mouth of the St. Lawrence.[1]   The French settlements of Canada were thus opened up to attack along the river. The French tried to send two military expeditions, escorted by warships, across the Atlantic to meet this threat. The first, which sailed in company with another convoy for India, was unrestrainedly chased in May 1747 by Anson with ships commanded by young officers trained by himself; the whole enemy fleet was captured in this first Battle of Cape Finisterre and triumphantly towed back to England.   The second expedition was overwhelmed almost as thoroughly five months later by Hawke in the second Battle of Cape Finisterre.   These two sea-battles destroyed French naval power in the Atlantic and brought French trade almost to a standstill, while British exports and imports continually increased during the War.   They also foreshadowed the gradual adoption of more aggressive British naval tactics within the next forty years.[2]

The reverse occurred in Indian waters.   There the commander of the British squadron was cautious and unenterprising and lacked a well-equipped base.   When the energetic Dupleix summoned a French fleet from Mauritius, it captured Madras in September 1746.   The British naval successes off Cape Finisterre, however, prevented the French sending sufficient military assistance to Dupleix to consolidate his position in India and made it possible for Britain to send large naval reinforcements under Admiral Boscawen in April 1748, which regained complete command of the sea.   Boscawen's first attempt to recapture Madras failed, and the War ended before he could make another.

British concentration on European hostilities had prevented her from giving more attention to naval and overseas undertakings during most of the War of the Austrian Succession. So many troops had been sent to Flanders that not until the last year of the War was a single contingent despatched for colonial operations.   Nevertheless, there were sufficient maritime operations to indicate their importance and especially the essential value of naval supremacy for Britain.   Louisbourg had been captured and held by sea power; Madras had been lost without it.   The way was prepared for Pitt's adoption in the next struggle against France of a strategy in

[1] P. 164.   [2] Pp. 196–7.

T

which control of the seas and conquest of the enemy's colonial possessions were to engage the greater part of Britain's war efforts and bring her decisive victories and wealthy territorial gains.

The Treaty of Aix-la-Chapelle (1748)

Although Marshal de Saxe by the end of 1746 possessed all the Austrian Netherlands, the British government was ready to continue the War, but the next year he invaded Holland, capturing the fortress-town of Bergen-op-Zoom on the border and defeating the allied army, again commanded by Cumberland.   Early in 1748 the Dutch government declared that it could only continue to fight with a substantial British loan. The Continental fighting depended on the Dutch, but Pelham knew that Parliament would refuse to add to Britain's subsidies which already amounted to £1,750,000. 'Dear brother, we are conquered', he wrote in a letter to Newcastle.

So peace negotiations had to be opened, and in October 1748 the Treaty of Aix-la-Chapelle was signed by Britain, France and Holland and later by Spain, Austria and Sardinia. It made few changes in the map of Europe.   France withdrew her troops from the Austrian Netherlands. Parma and Piacenza went to Don Philip, Elizabeth Farnese's younger son, and Savoy and Nice to Sardinia as the part of the Milanese which had been promised in 1743.   The Pragmatic Sanction was recognized by all the signatory powers, and so was the election of Maria Theresa's husband, Francis Stephen, as Holy Roman Emperor, which had taken place on Charles VII's death in 1745; but Prussia retained Silesia.

For Britain and France, the basis of the Treaty was a restitution of conquests. Louisbourg was exchanged for Madras. France once again recognized the Hanoverian succession to the British throne and promised to expel the Young Pretender from her territory.   She also undertook to dismantle the sea-defences of Dunkirk. The original cause of the war with Spain, the right of search in the Spanish Main, was not mentioned in the Treaty.   The South Sea Company's trading privileges, the annual ship and the *Asiento*, were merely renewed for four years and were, in fact, to be given up before then.[1]   War and the inclusion of many

[1] P. 245.

of the members of the opposition in the administration had stilled the slogans of 1739.

The Treaty of Aix-la-Chapelle settled neither of the two great European issues – the dispute between Prussia and Austria and the rivalry between France and Austria – which had brought about hostilities. Nor were the colonial rivalries between Britain and France resolved. Boundaries remained undefined in North America, and the two trading companies continued their contest in India. Such an uneasy balance in Europe and beyond made inevitable a renewed test of force in the future, and the Treaty could be no more than a truce.

XIV · THE PELHAMS IN POWER, 1748–56

Pelham and Domestic Policy

'You know', Pelham wrote to his brother as the treaty negotiations were bringing the War of the Austrian Succession to an end, 'I have had very little comfort in the great scene of business I have long been engaged in. I have no Court ambition and very little interest views; but I was in hopes, by a peace being soon made and by a proper economy in the administration of the government afterwards, to have been the author of such a plan as might, in the time to come, have relieved this nation from the vast load of debt it now labours under.' With the coming of peace, Pelham exercised a dominant influence in the management of domestic affairs and could, therefore, give his attention to this financial reorganization which he considered so necessary.

During the past nine years of warfare, though the British effort had been inconstant, the subsidies paid to allies had added to its cost in a way which many people felt was ruinous. By 1748 the National Debt had risen during the war years from £46,000,000 to £78,000,000, while the budget for the last year of the War amounted to £9,819,345. To Pelham the situation seemed as it had done to Walpole over twenty-five years previously. He believed that the country needed a period of peace during which government expenditure could be reduced by retrenchment and economy in the interest of national prosperity and social well-being.

Immediately the war ended, Pelham cut down drastically the size of the armed forces. In 1748 the number of seamen and marines was reduced from 51,550 to 17,000. The next year he brought it down to 10,000 and the year after that as low as 8,000, but protests from Newcastle, Pitt and other ministers compelled him to raise it again in 1751 to 10,000 and maintain it at that figure. The size of the standing army was similarly reduced from 50,000 to 18,850. The total paid in subsidies to foreign rulers was reduced to £30,000 by 1750. Pelham would have liked to have abolished these subsidies altogether, but Newcastle insisted that they were essential for his foreign policy, and from 1751 he even obtained Pelham's reluctant agreement to increase them.

By means of the economies in these items, which accounted for the largest part of the country's budget, combined with the retention of the duty on salt, the maintenance of the land tax at its wartime rate of 4s. in the pound and the transfer of £1,000,000 from the Sinking Fund, Pelham was able to prevent the government from running into further debt. At the same time he achieved another economy which Walpole had evaded in his later years – a conversion scheme for the National Debt. With the ready assistance of a great City financier, Sir John Barnard, he consolidated in 1751 all the various government stocks into a single stock bearing an interest of 3 per cent. These Consolidated Annuities became known as 'Consols' and were a popular investment, attracting considerable money from abroad, especially Holland. In this way the management of the National Debt was simplified, and by the time of Pelham's death in 1754 more than £270,000 had been saved in interest.

These measures brought about a steady decline in expenditure and a corresponding reduction in his budgets until in 1752 he was able to balance the budget at as low a figure as £2,628,356. This made it possible for him to reduce taxation from its high wartime level. Here also he followed Walpole's example by making the land tax lighter, bringing it down to 3s. in 1749 and even to 2s. in 1752. Besides seeking the support of the landed gentry in this way, Pelham also wished to placate the City of London and in 1746 restored to it some of the powers its Common Court had lost through Walpole's Act of 1725.

Besides his financial reorganization, Pelham was also associated with a number of salutary domestic reforms which made some attempt to deal with the social problems of the times. The first years of peace brought an even greater prevalence of disorder in London. Particularly alarmed by the brutal gangs which were terrorizing the streets of the capital after dark, Pelham discussed the possibility of measures against them with Henry Fielding, the novelist, who was a Justice of the Peace for Westminster, sitting in the court at Bow Street. As a result, Fielding organized the Bow Street Runners, the first regular police and detective force in London. When ill-health forced him to give up his post in 1753, he was succeeded by his blind half-brother, Sir John Fielding (d. 1780), who carried on his plans. There were two runners always on call at the Bow Street Court, and they were paid by the rewards they received as thief-takers. Though they could do comparatively little to check the vast amount of crime in London, they made a beginning. After they had broken up several gangs and arrested a number of notorious thieves and highwaymen, Sir John persuaded Newcastle in 1757 to make them a grant of £400 a year from the secret service money, and they became available for service outside Westminster. Their foot-patrols were merged with the Metropolitan Police Force when it was established in 1829 and their horse-patrols abolished ten years later.

Henry Fielding was also the first to attempt a constructive examination of the reasons for the spread of crime in London and in 1751 published his findings as a pamphlet, *An Enquiry into the Causes of the late Increase of Robberies, etc., with some Proposals for Remedying this Growing Evil.* Among the causes he gave was the gin mania, and in the same year Hogarth's *Gin Lane* came out to arouse the public conscience still more acutely by its bitter satire.[1] Since Walpole's failure to check the evil, sales of gin had gone on increasing, but now at last the government acted effectively. The Gin Act of 1751 forbade distillers to sell gin retail or to unlicensed retailers and strictly confined the issue of licences to reputable inn-keepers and vendors; its provisions were enforced by penalties of imprisonment, whipping or transportation. The consumption of gin fell from 8,495,000 gallons in 1751 to 5,946,000 in 1752 and 2,100,000 in 1760. The elimination of the notorious dram-shops by this measure gradually checked what clergymen, justices and doctors had agreed in describing as the worst evil of the times.

Another social problem faced by the government was the inadequacy of the laws about marriage. Though the law of the Church of England required the publication of banns or the obtaining of a licence before the celebration of a marriage an irregular marriage performed by any clergyman was still legal. This made possible the clandestine marriages

---

[1] P. 103.

romantically described (commonly after a dashing escape by the runaway couple) in novels about the eighteenth century.   It is true that parents expected to make matrimonial plans for their daughters and that a rebellious young woman might be beaten and confined to her room until she accepted a husband of their choice; but there were scandalous aspects to the situation.   In the words of a historian, 'The vision of a broken-down parson ready, without asking questions, to marry any man to any woman for a crown and a bottle was an ever-present terror to parents and guardians.'   Moreover, since marriage gave a husband complete control of his wife's money, heiresses were especially liable to the designs of unscrupulous men.   Or a designing woman might marry a drunken young heir and never live with him, allowing the man to marry bigamously a lady of birth, only to appear on his death to claim his estate and bastardize his children.   It was a case such as this which brought the marriage laws to the attention of the House of Lords during Pelham's administration.

The abuse was tackled by Lord Hardwicke.   He induced Parliament in 1753 to pass the Marriage Act associated with his name, which introduced for the first time the principle that marriage was a civil contract in which the State as well as the Church was concerned, though he was strongly opposed by Henry Fox, Secretary-at-War since 1746, who had eloped with the Duke of Richmond's daughter, and by Charles Townshend, who was considering a similar match.   The Act required marriages to be performed in a parish church by a clergyman after banns or licence and minors to obtain the consent of parents or guardians and for the first time provided that omission to observe these requirements invalidated a marriage.   It excepted the royal family, Jews and Quakers, but not Dissenters or Roman Catholics; they were only allowed to marry in their own chapels by Lord John Russell's Dissenters' Marriage Act of 1836, which also made provision for civil marriages in register offices.   The Act brought to an end in England irregular marriages performed in the chapels of the Fleet and other prisons by clergymen imprisoned there for debt and in private chapels built as a speculation for what they would earn in marriage fees, such as the notorious Mayfair Chapel in London; but it did not apply to Scotland so that Gretna Green, the nearest village over the border, became the resort of eloping couples, and the innkeepers of nearby Carlisle did well out of the provision of wedding breakfasts.

Among the changes made by the administration, the one which aroused most popular opposition was the reform of the calendar. Britain still followed the Julian or Old Style calendar, which had been introduced by Julius Caesar in 45 B.C., though superseded by the more accurate Gregorian or New Style calendar promulgated by Pope Gregory XIII in 1582. This change had been adopted first by Roman Catholic countries and later also by Protestant countries, so that by the eighteenth century the British calendar was eleven days behind those of other countries, and, in addition, each year began on 25th March instead of 1st January as on the Continent. Despite the opposition of Newcastle (through his usual concern for the government's popularity), Pelham supported Lord Chesterfield's measure in 1751, which adopted the New Style calendar, rectified the existing error by providing that the day following 2nd September should be reckoned as 14th September and ordering that the new year should begin on 1st January 1752. The quarter days, however, were left unchanged at the saints' days which came at intervals of three months from 25th March (Lady Day, 25th March; St. John the Baptist, 24th June; St. Michael, 29th September; Christmas, 25th December). The bill was duly passed by Parliament, but contemporary ignorance and conservatism produced much opposition in the country which was expressed in the popular cry, 'Give us back our eleven days!'

Perhaps the most permanent monument of Pelham's administration is the British Museum. In 1753 Sir Hans Sloane (1660–1753), the physician, bequeathed to the nation his books, manuscripts and museum collection for a payment of £20,000 to his heirs, and in the same year the government was offered for £10,000 books and manuscripts from the collection of the first and second Earls of Oxford. Pelham welcomed these offers and secured the passing of the British Museum Act of 1753, which raised by a public lottery enough money to buy these collections and also Montagu House, Great Russell Street, to house them. To them were added the library of Sir Robert Cotton (1571–1631), the antiquary, which the nation had already purchased in 1707. George II transferred the volumes and manuscripts collected by the Kings of England to the British Museum in 1757 and gave it the privilege of obtaining a free copy of every book published in Britain. The library of George III was acquired in 1823.

Not all the reforms supported by Pelham were successful. He gave his approval in 1751 to a bill for nationalizing foreign Protestants, but it aroused such opposition, especially from financial and commercial circles in the City of London, that he withdrew his support, and it was abandoned. Another measure, which he supported, the Jew Naturalization Bill, designed to facilitate the naturalization of Jews living in Britain, was passed in 1753. He argued that the country would benefit from the capital investments made by wealthy Jews, but here also those who feared their financial interests would suffer disliked the measure. They stirred up prejudice against it outside Parliament, and the reports of Newcastle's agents throughout the country so alarmed him, especially as a general election was imminent, that he persuaded Pelham to agree to its repeal the next year.

Henry Pelham died in April 1754 in his sixtieth year ending his period of office too soon for him to have really left his mark on the country. Chesterfield described him as 'an honourable man and a well-wishing minister' and also said, 'He wished well to the public and managed the finances with great care and personal purity'. He was, indeed, an able and an economical financier, his policy being that of a faithful follower of Walpole, whom he had rescued from a hostile, well-dressed mob in the lobby of the House of Commons after the last debate on the Excise Bill of 1733. Chesterfield thought he 'had good sense without either shining parts or any degree of literature'. He was not a man of commanding abilities or much strength of character. He might have become a great peacetime minister through his concern for enlightened social reforms, which were to be unique in the eighteenth century; but he held office during a period which was a mere truce between two wars, and his reduction of the army and navy for financial and political reasons was not in the national interest. For foreign policy, however, he had little responsibility. That was largely Newcastle's concern.

Newcastle and Foreign Policy

The Duke of Newcastle has suffered badly at the hands of historians. They have been too ready to accept the bitter words of Horace Walpole, who pursued him with unforgetting resentment because he considered he had deserted his father in 1742. Horace Walpole spoke with particular scorn of the way he displayed 'a constant hurry in his walk, a restlessness of place, a borrowed importance, a real insignificance', but this hurried, flustered manner has blinded historians to what Dr. J. B. Owen has recently called his 'good sense and judgement and excellent principles'. The Duke's ability as a manager of patronage is well known;[1] but foibles, such as his fear of draughts and the cold, which gave his enemies good opportunities to practise their wit at his expense, have obscured his real integrity and common sense. To hold, as he did, cabinet office almost continuously for forty-five years must suggest that he was not among the least able of the politicians of the eighteenth century.

His most serious political weakness was an ultimate sense of insecurity which made him wish to avoid the responsibility of taking decisions. Chesterfield spoke of him as 'exceeding timorous, both personally and politically, dreading the least innovation, and keeping with a scrupulous timidity in the beaten track of business as having the safest bottom'. This failing explains why he acted best as a subordinate in an administration led by a more determined politician. It can also be seen to have an effect upon his direction of British foreign policy during the complicated period of transition in European international relations from 1748 to 1756, which culminated in the reversal of alliances of the Diplomatic Revolution and a fresh outbreak of general warfare.

Newcastle was not as incapable or ignorant of foreign affairs as is sometimes supposed. His fault was an inability (shared by other politicans at the time) to realize the changing circumstances of European diplomacy during this period. He proposed to meet the likelihood of renewed war against France by continuing to follow the same system of Continental alliances which had contained France in the previous two wars when Britain had fought her. Unfortunately he failed

[1] P. 253.

to appreciate that the two countries – Holland and Austria – which had hitherto been the mainstay of this system were no longer willing to perform this rôle. Holland's days as a great power were over. She had suffered severely in her wars against France and had been reluctant to engage in the last war. Now she wished to keep out of any compromising British alliance. Austria had not forgotten how Britain had continually brought pressure on her to come to terms with Frederick, at the cost of Prussian retention of Silesia, so that hostilities might be concentrated against France. The contest between Britain and France for commercial and colonial superiority was of no concern to Maria Theresa, who was determined to renew her efforts to regain Silesia. Her new minister, Prince von Kaunitz (1711–94), had no difficulty in persuading her that a French alliance was likely to make a more effective contribution towards the recovery of her lost province than one with Britain.

While Kaunitz was preparing to direct Austrian foreign policy towards this new objective, Newcastle had evolved a plan, with George II's concurrence, to secure the election of Maria Theresa's son as King of the Romans, a device which the Habsburgs had adopted in the past to ensure their retention of the Imperial crown and which would now enable her son to succeed on the death of Maria Theresa's husband, the Emperor Francis I.[1] This required the bribery of the Electors, but Newcastle believed it would be worth while to cement Austria to Britain and Hanover. In 1750 and 1751 subsidies were paid, with the unwilling support of Pelham and Hardwicke, to the Electors of Cologne, Bavaria, Saxony and the Elector Palatine, but in 1752 Austria rejected the scheme. Maria Theresa's son, the future Emperor Joseph II, was to be chosen King of the Romans unanimously and without any bribery of the Electors in 1764.

From 1750 to 1753 Kaunitz was Austrian ambassador to the French court at Versailles and tried hard to get the French government to accept his plan, but without success. Louis XV and his ministers did not want to be involved in new Continental entanglement, and, when Kaunitz went back to Vienna in 1753 to become Chancellor, there seemed little prospect that he would ever manage to form an alliance with

[1] P. 280.

France. The situation was rapidly changed, however, by events in the struggle between Britain and France in North America which had not ended with the coming of peace in Europe. The French had begun to establish forts in the valley of the Ohio the year after the Treaty of Aix-la-Chapelle, and by 1753 were settled in this rich area and planned to link it with Louisiana and Canada.[1]

This was a challenge which no British government could have declined. It is not true that Newcastle was ignorant and unappreciative of Britain's interests in North America. Too much must not be made of stories about his surprised discovery, after its conquest, that Cape Breton was an island and not on the mainland or his enquiry as to the whereabouts of Annapolis after agreeing with a general's suggestion that it ought to be defended. He made it clear that he thought 'that the colonies must not be abandoned, that our rights and possessions in North America must be maintained and the French obliged to desist from their hostile attempts to dispossess us'. In the summer of 1753 the Cabinet instructed the colonial governors that encroachments on British territory were to be repelled by force. This led to the sending of the unsuccessful expedition under George Washington against the French in the Ohio in the spring of 1754, which was repeated the next year by the failure of a force of regular troops sent from Britain under General Braddock.[2] When the French government followed this by preparing to send more troops to Canada, Admiral Boscawen was ordered to attack the transports and their escorting fleet.[3]

Newcastle, however, wished to carry on a limited war as long as possible and avoid provoking France in Europe. He wanted time to achieve his diplomatic intentions which still seem to have been, as Basil Williams has said, 'to make so strong a system of Continental alliances against France that, unable to move in Europe, she would be obliged to confine herself to the overseas struggle, where she would be at a disadvantage owing to England's great superiority at sea'. He had also to consider the position of Hanover, for George II expected the government to provide for its defence.[4] Newcastle asked Austria to send troops to Hanover and increase

<hr>

[1] P. 166.   [2] P. 166.
[3] P. 302.   [4] Pp. 226–7.

her garrisons in the Netherlands as a precaution against a French attack, but Kaunitz would not reply definitely to either request. To Newcastle, this seemed to point to the necessity of extending his alliances still further. Approaches were made, therefore, to Russia, and in September 1755 a treaty was made with the Czarina Elizabeth by which she agreed to protect Hanover, if attacked, with 55,000 Russian troops in return for a British subsidy.

This treaty, though never to come into effect, had rapid consequences in the European situation. It was, in fact, the event which set off the Diplomatic Revolution. It alarmed Frederick the Great. The prospect of Russian troops in Germany was bound to appear menacing to him. So far he had retained his alignment with France and stayed aloof from Newcastle's attempts to extend his system of alliances on the Continent, but now he offered George II Prussian troops to defend Hanover. Newcastle welcomed this as an opportunity to gain yet another ally. So the Convention of Westminster was signed between Britain and Prussia in January 1756. It provided for Prussian protection of Hanover, as long as Britain did not call upon Russian troops, and both countries agreed jointly to resist the entry of foreign armies into Germany.

Newcastle regarded the Convention of Westminster as another extension of his system of alliances, which might prevent the outbreak of hostilities on the Continent, but the reactions it produced had warlike results. Since Prussia would now clearly be of no value to France as an ally in a war against Britain, the French government was more ready to consider an alliance with Austria, but hesitations remained, because a new Continental commitment might jeopardize French chances of a maritime victory over Britain. These, however, were soon dissipated by the action of the Czarina Elizabeth, who announced in April that she regarded the Convention of Westminster as bringing to an end her agreement with Britain and offered Maria Theresa to attack Prussia with 80,000 Russian troops with a promise not to make peace until Silesia was regained. As tension in Europe mounted, France was in danger of being left without an ally. At last Kaunitz's diplomatic plans succeeded. The next month France and Austria made an alliance, and at the same time

Holland declared her neutrality. The reversal of alliances was complete. The old system of alliances, which Newcastle had tried to maintain and enlarge, had collapsed. Britain had a powerful new ally, but one which faced grave danger from the threatening combination of France, Austria and Russia.

The Failure of Newcastle

The Pelhams had been able to concern themselves with their respective policies in domestic and foreign affairs during these years between the wars with comparatively little distraction because of the absence of a powerful political opposition. The Tories, further discredited by the 'Forty-Five, had become still weaker in numbers and influence, and Bolingbroke, who had hoped to remake them as a party, died in 1751. The Broad-Bottom administration continued to be comprehensive enough to include the leading members of all the important Whig groups. Still more effective in easing the position of the administration was the death of Frederick, Prince of Wales, also in 1751. Since the heir to the throne, Prince George, was only thirteen, and his mother seemed ready to adopt a friendly attitude towards her father-in-law, the most powerful rallying-point for an opposition disappeared from politics. Leicester House ceased to be a meeting-place for discontented politicians who received encouragement from the heir-apparent and in the hope that his succession to the throne would reverse their exclusion from office.

The last years of the Broad-Bottom administration were, therefore, especially peaceful, but its existence soon terminated with Henry Pelham's death in March 1754. 'Now I shall have no more peace' were George II's well-known words when he heard the news. More important were the consequences for the Duke of Newcastle. Lord Chesterfield, while considering that Henry Pelham 'had by no means an elevated or enterprising genius', judged him to have 'had a more manly and steady resolution than his brother'. He had succeeded in inducing Pitt and Henry Fox, both strong and ambitious men, to accept his leadership for several years. Newcastle, besides suffering from the disadvantage of being in the House of Lords, had not the character to exercise the same power.

On his brother's death, Newcastle succeeded him as First
Lord of the Treasury, through Hardwicke's representations
to George II. Pitt was still too strongly under royal dis-
favour to expect promotion, but Newcastle offered the post
of Secretary of State with the all-important leadership of the
House of Commons to Henry Fox, who had shown himself a
formidable debater in his attacks on Hardwicke's Marriage
Bill. Newcastle insisted, however, that he himself would
retain control of all patronage, and Fox refused the offer on
these terms. 'How shall I be able', he asked, 'to talk to
Members of Parliament when some might have received
gratifications and others not?' Newcastle therefore appointed
to the Secretaryship Sir Thomas Robinson (1695–1770), who
had been British ambassador at Vienna from 1730 to 1748
and had taken an important part in the negotiations leading
to the Treaty of Aix-la-Chapelle. Diplomatic experience
and ability made him well-suited for his new post, but he had
scant knowledge of the House of Commons and little chance
in debate against such seasoned parliamentarians as Fox and
Pitt.

At first, however, neither the Secretary-at-War nor the
Paymaster of the Forces troubled the administration, and
Newcastle won a sweeping victory in the general election
that summer; but when the parliamentary session began in
November both men, for the only time in their political
careers, joined together with the bitterness of frustrated
ambition in an open and formidable attack upon Newcastle
and his leading ministers.[1] They dwelt upon Robinson's
inadequacies, which were by now only too apparent; the
House of Commons was becoming, Pitt declared, 'a little
assembly, serving no other purpose than to register the
arbitrary edicts of one too powerful subject'. And they
gained further fuel for their oratory from Washington's defeat
in North America that May.[2]

Newcastle soon realized that his administration was in
great danger in the Commons. He decided to separate Fox
and Pitt by bringing one of them into the Cabinet. George
II was still hostile to Pitt, and Fox seemed likely to be more
co-operative in the ministry. Accordingly, in December
1754 the support of Fox was obtained by giving him a place in

<hr />

[1] P. 299.   [2] P. 290.

the Cabinet and in the Council of Regency when the King should go to Hanover for several months the next spring, but he was not offered the Secretaryship. This arrangement was not adequate for the administration's safety. Events continued to give the opposition grounds for attacking it. Braddock's expedition was overwhelmed before it got to Fort Duquesne, and Boscawen's fleet failed to prevent French reinforcements from reaching Canada.[1] Pitt attacked the agreement made with the Czarina Elizabeth of Russia as a wasteful diversion of money in the interests of Hanover which could not be defended and had no strategic value for Britain.[2] So Fox received further promotion in September 1755. He was given the Secretaryship of State and leadership of the Commons 'with a notification to be divulged, that he had power with the King, to help or hurt in the House of Commons', while Robinson was transferred to the lucrative sinecure of the Great Wardrobe.

Robinson's replacement by Fox led George II to comment, 'The Duke of Newcastle has turned out everybody else, and now he has turned out himself'. It soon proved to be so. The ministry could not be protected from the debilitating combination of Pitt's oratory and news of overseas defeats. Pitt's answer to Fox's promotion was even more devastating criticism of Newcastle's ministry, which he compared to 'a child driving a go-cart on the edge of a precipice' and accused it of subordinating 'the long injured, long neglected, long forgotten people of America' to Hanoverian interests in its foreign policy. Newcastle dismissed him from his Paymastership in November. By themselves Pitt's words made little impression on Newcastle's parliamentary majority, but in 1756 a series of widespread disasters shook the government – the French captured Minorca in the Mediterranean, Calcutta in India and Fort Oswego in North America.[3] The government hurriedly brought hired Hessian and Hanoverian troops over to England as a protection against invasion. Then in September, Frederick the Great attacked Saxony and began the war on the Continent which Newcastle's now defunct system of alliances had sought to avert. The final blow came in October with the resignation of Henry Fox, determined not 'to be treated like a dog' any longer. He had found

[1] Pp. 290, 302.   [2] P. 227.   [3] Pp. 303, 165, 166.

Newcastle unwilling to allow him any proper authority, and now he did not want to be identified with the government's unpopularity and to face renewed attacks from Pitt in the Commons.

Newcastle could go on no longer. His ministry by now was hesitant, irresolute and divided, quite unable to meet the demands of a world-wide war. He sought the support of Pitt, who had become the most popular man in the country and the rallying-point of the national desire for an effective answer to the French challenge. Pitt, however, was not prepared to serve with Newcastle, who he believed was not really ready to share authority with anyone. Newcastle had to resign. Though he had controlled Parliament for a generation, his own ministry had lasted little more than two years.

XV · THE ELDER PITT AND THE SEVEN YEARS' WAR, 1756–63

Pitt's Early Years

WILLIAM PITT came of a family which for generations had taken part in the local life of Hampshire and Dorset as clergymen and magistrates. Its first member to achieve wider fame was Pitt's grandfather, Thomas Pitt (1653–1726), often called 'Diamond Pitt'. The son of a Rector of Blandford, he made several successful voyages as an interloper in the East India trade until he made terms with the Company and was Governor of Madras from 1697 to 1709, during which time he kept a constant look-out for large diamonds; he obtained the great Pitt diamond from an Indian merchant and sold it for £135,000 to the Regent of France, and it still remains among the State jewels. With the proceeds, Thomas Pitt set up on his return to England as a landed gentleman with estates in Berkshire and Cornwall. He was haughty, violent, unstable and gouty, and these were characteristics inherited by his grandson.

William Pitt had an undistinguished father, Robert Pitt, but his mother, Lady Harriet Villiers, was sensible and graceful. He was a younger son, born in 1708. He was sent to Eton, which he hated, saying afterwards, 'a public school might suit a boy of turbulent forward disposition, but would not do where there was any gentleness'; he completed an undistinguished education at Oxford and Utrecht. Without personal wealth or influence, he was introduced by his friend, George Lyttleton, to Lord Cobham (1669?–1749), who gave him a cornetcy in his regiment and also his patronage.[1] The young Pitt's ambitions went beyond a military career; his mind was already turning towards politics. Four years later he entered Parliament for Old Sarum, the pocket borough which his grandfather had acquired and which now belonged to his elder brother.

Although his family already had political influence, Pitt

[1] P. 263.

did not care for the assiduous application necessary to culti-
vate it. Cobham's patronage, however, did something to
overcome this handicap. The connection brought him into
the opposition against Walpole and the Leicester House circle,
and in 1736 it cost him his cornetcy.[1] This only served,
however, to make him a hero of the opposition, who quickly
realized that they had a powerful young orator in their midst.
Pitt became a Groom of the Bedchamber to the Prince of
Wales in 1737, but he ironically displayed his poverty and
obscurity by ostentatiously driving about the streets of London
in a one-horse chaise without servants. In Parliament he
lost no chance of attacking Walpole and supporting the
Prince's cause; he also became an effective spokesman for the
trading interests of the country who disliked Walpole's pacific
policy, denouncing it in long-remembered sentences – 'When
trade is at stake it is your last retrenchment, you must defend
it or perish' – 'Sir, Spain knows the consequences of war in
America. Whoever gains, it must prove fatal to her.'

Walpole's downfall in 1742 did not bring Pitt or his friends
into office.[2] He now turned his attacks against Carteret's
foreign policy, alleging with particular vehemence that the
nation's interests were being subordinated to those of Hanover,
and the King's resentment at his language condemned him to
further exclusion from office on the formation of the Broad-
Bottom administration in 1744.[3] Pitt did not want to spend
the whole of his political career in factious opposition; he was
also prepared to give the Pelhams a chance to prove themselves
and believed that their administration might mean a change
for the better in policy. So he ceased to be a Groom of the
Bedchamber at Leicester House and throughout the anxious
days of 1744 and 1745 supported the Pelhams. Before long
they came to terms with him and were able early in 1746 to
persuade George II to appoint him to an office.[4] The King
would not agree to make him Secretary-at-War, since this
would involve his admission to the court. Pitt had to be
content at first with the Vice-Paymastership of Ireland and
soon afterwards the Paymastership of the Forces in England.
At the general election of 1747 his brother, who remained
loyal to the opposition, would not put Old Sarum at his

[1] P. 263.   [2] P. 268.
[3] P. 272.   [4] P. 276.

disposal; he was nominated instead for one of Newcastle's boroughs, Seaford, and Newcastle himself travelled down to sit beside Pitt at the hustings, scrutinizing the votes. This secured his election, but exposed him to the same sort of denunciations of ministerial tyranny and corruption from the parliamentary opposition as he himself had made in the past.

Though Pitt had achieved a post in the administration, it was not one that brought him any power. He approved the government's policy and wished to convince the King that he was not a mere champion of discontent. Pelham valued his support, writing of him in 1750, 'I think him the most useful, able and strictly honest man we have among us'; but he gained no political advancement. So he ceased to attend the Commons regularly and did not speak when he was there. He spent much of his time studying military questions, comparing British and French commercial statistics and cultivating the merchants of the City, to be ready for the time when he might get into power. He had frequent attacks of gout and was also to be seen at Bath and in country-houses, giving way to the reckless extravagance which was to condemn him to financial embarrassment all his life. This might have been relieved now by the customary perquisites of his office, among them a subsidy paid out to all foreign princes which was particularly lucrative at this time. Previous Paymasters had made large fortunes by such means. The Duke of Chandos, while Paymaster for most of the War of the Spanish Succession, was said to have gained from the profits of his office, £250,000 which he spent on the building of Canons, his magnificent mansion at Stanmore in Middlesex. Pitt, however, did not wish to lose, as other politicians had, the popularity he had earned in opposition by his conduct in office, particularly as he now seemed to be countenancing a Continental policy favourable to Hanover such as he had formerly denounced. With typical self-display, he refused to become enriched from his position and contented himself with his official salary. He established that reputation for honesty noticed by Pelham, a reputation which he was to retain throughout his career.

Pelham's death in 1754 still did not bring Pitt promotion.[1]

[1] P. 293.

'Pitt has no health', wrote Horace Walpole, 'no party and, what in this case is allowed to operate, the King's negative.' Pitt had set out from Bath for London immediately on hearing of Pelham's death, but at Marlborough he was struck down with that combination of gout and mental disorder which was often to afflict him in the future. That summer he was sunk in despairing depression, declaring, 'The weight of irremovable royal displeasure is a load too great to move under'. He was, indeed, now forty-six and had yet to hold a responsible political post.

Before the end of the year, however, Pitt's situation had changed. He had married Hester Grenville (1721–1803), the only sister of the two remarkable brothers with whom he had served in the 'Boy Patriots'.[1] The elder, Richard, was now Lord Temple, wealthy, ambitious and already forming his family into a formidable political force nicknamed 'The Cousinhood'. Pitt's marriage brought him new political strength and the support of a wife whom Thomas Coutts admired as 'the cleverest *man* of her time in politics and business'. Pitt's new happiness restored both his health and ambition. When Parliament assembled after the election which Newcastle had won, he combined with Henry Fox to launch a bitter onslaught on the administration.[2] It was now the turn of Newcastle and Robinson to attract the attention of Pitt's violent and forceful speeches from which Walpole and Carteret had previously suffered. Once again the Commons were dominated by this extraordinarily eloquent orator, the effect of whose controlled voice and accomplished gestures was increased by his lean figure, hawklike nose and piercing eyes.

The promotion of Fox, immediately to membership of the Cabinet and then to a Secretaryship of State as well, was Newcastle's response to this dangerous combination against him.[3] Assisted by worsening circumstances overseas, Pitt redoubled his attacks on Newcastle. He was finally dismissed from office in November 1755, after he had both ridiculed and vehemently denounced Newcastle. Fox now became the main target for Pitt's bitter tirades, but with little effect. As long as the administration could manage the Commons, its ministers appeared impregnable, while Pitt had lost his

[1] P. 263.   [2] P. 293.   [3] Pp. 293–4.

post and its salary and seemed further away from political power than ever.

The foreign situation, however, was such as to favour Pitt. The first months of 1756 brought further British defeats.[1]   A crisis was approaching for Newcastle.   War was inevitable, but the government was so unpopular in the country that there was doubt whether the Commons would vote the money it needed to fulfil its subsidy treaties.   Moreover, Pitt threatened to enquire into the past actions of the ministers. Newcastle even feared impeachment.   He hoped for 'something to be done at once until it could be seen what might be done'; but the only development was the resignation of the frustrated and insecure Fox in October.[2]   Newcastle told the King that he had no alternative but to approach Pitt.

Pitt, however, was aware of the strong position he now enjoyed.   Already he was becoming popularly known as the 'Great Commoner', and his following in the country was immense.   He would not agree to join Newcastle's ministry and ease his problems.   Since he could not make his views known personally to George II, he did so through the Countess of Yarmouth, the King's mistress.   The King insisted that the Duke of Devonshire, a political mediocrity but acceptable to both Fox and Cumberland (who as Commander-in-Chief of the army was powerful at court), should become First Lord of the Treasury, and Pitt agreed to become Secretary for the Southern Department.   In November Newcastle formally resigned, and Pitt's ministry took office.

Yet it could hardly be more than temporary.   Pitt lacked both royal favour and a solid parliamentary majority. Newcastle's words, 'he flung himself upon the people and the Tories', were largely true.   Though he was popular with the people, he had to rely in the Commons on the independent members, especially the country gentlemen; he did not possess the confidence of the 'Old Whigs' and their supporters. By the spring of 1757 Pitt had lost some popularity through the absence of good news from overseas and his courageous efforts to prevent Byng's execution.[3]   In April the King dismissed him and for eleven weeks, while the country was at war, tried to secure a ministry under Fox and Cumberland,

---

[1] Pp. 303, 165, 166.   [2] P. 294.   [3] P. 303.

but could not find politicians ready to assume the responsibility of office in such a situation.

Public opinion showed, however, that it was still really behind Pitt. During this period, in Horace Walpole's words, 'for some weeks it rained gold boxes', as first the City of London and then the corporations of eighteen other cities and towns all over the country made him a freeman to demonstrate their support for him. Eventually, secret negotiations were begun between Pitt and Newcastle which produced a compromise between the two men. Pitt had to relinquish the idea of being in complete command of the ministry, but was to be Secretary of State for the Southern Department again, with the implied control of war policy. Newcastle had to accept the political superiority this brought Pitt, but was himself to return as First Lord of the Treasury to the task of managing patronage and the House of Commons and also of providing the money for the war. 'Mr. Pitt did everything', it was said, 'while the Duke gave everything.' George II had to acquiesce in this arrangement. So Pitt at last gained real political power in June 1757, but it was at a time when hostilities on the Continent were going badly for Britain and her Prussian ally.

'I believe', said Pitt, 'that I can save this country and that no one else can.' And he was able to do this, since he was, in effect, sole war minister, often, for instance, issuing fleet orders himself without consulting the Admiralty. Moreover, he had not only the self-confidence necessary for a war minister, but also the equally necessary ability to inspire others. His patriotism and integrity continued to give him the confidence of the people. His oratory assured him the support of country gentlemen in Parliament who were too independent to be held by Newcastle's patronage. He could equally enhearten those with whom he worked. 'No man', said an officer, 'can enter his closet without coming out of it a braver man.' He also had the gift of choosing capable men, especially officers such as Hawke and Wolfe, and he knew what qualities he wanted from them – 'Others make difficulties', he said to Admiral Boscawen. 'You find expedients'. The unreliability, deviousness and even dishonesty which he had displayed in peacetime politics were overshadowed by his genuine patriotism and inspiring leadership. And, finally, he brought to his conduct of hostilities a strategy which, while not in itself revolutionary, was marked by a range and thoroughness of application which was new in British policy.

The Conduct of the War (1756–63)

Pitt had a firm conviction, probably derived from his grandfather's pioneering commercial activities in the East, that Britain should seek as great a share in the trade and wealth of the world as she could and that the government should support the efforts of her merchants uncompromisingly and to the extent of war if necessary against their French rivals. Moreover, he believed that when war came, Britain should fight it, not with large land forces for political objectives in Europe, but with sea power to destroy the enemy's overseas trade and acquire gains which would more than pay for the cost of hostilities. The strategical conception of such a policy had already been discussed in the country, and Pitt had made it the subject of the combined military and commercial studies to which he devoted himself, in consultation with his City friends, during his years in opposition. Now that he had, belatedly, come to power at the beginning of a great war, he wished immediately to put this policy into effect.

For four years Pitt was to conduct a world war that produced an unparalleled series of British victories and brought her the prospect of a monopoly of the world's commerce, and this after events which had hardly seemed to foretell such an outcome. Britain and France had drifted into hostilities against each other before the Seven Years' War began on the Continent. First there was the fighting in North America where the French successively defeated Washington and Braddock in 1754 and 1755.[1] Naval warfare followed when Boscawen, acting on the government's orders, tried in June 1755 to destroy a large French convoy taking reinforcements to Canada. He captured two French warships, but the convoy was saved by the fog so common in those waters and escaped to the protection of Louisbourg. During the following months the British navy seized more than three-hundred French merchant ships on the high seas.

French retaliation brought the war to Europe. In May 1756

[1] P. 290.

a French fleet attacked Minorca, which Admiral Byng failed to save. He displayed faults in battle, and his fleet was superior in numbers to the French, but he believed he was justified by the *Fighting Instructions* in not engaging the enemy.[1] National indignation, politicians, and the King, decided he was to blame for sailing away and leaving Minorca unprotected. Pitt, by then a Secretary of State, tried to save Byng after he had been condemned by a court martial, but he was shot at Portsmouth – '*pour encourager les autres*' in Voltaire's phrase. Meanwhile, the news of the landing in Minorca had led the British government to declare war on France in May 1756. Further reverses followed that summer – the capture of Calcutta in India and of Fort Oswego in North America.[2] And in September the Continental war broke out. Frederick the Great, anticipating Maria Theresa's intention to attack Prussia, invaded Austria's ally, Saxony, and called on Britain for aid.

It was not, therefore, a promising situation which Pitt inherited. It was already winter when he first took office, and he was dismissed by the King before the next year's campaigning could begin, and the season of 1757 was lost by the time he was restored and had real power. In June Frederick was defeated by an Austrian army at Kolin, thereby encouraging the French to send a force into northern Germany which defeated a greatly inferior force of Hanoverian and Hessian troops under Cumberland at the Battle of Hastenbeck in July and forced him to sign the Convention of Klosterseven binding him to disband his army and accept French occupation of Hanover for the duration of hostilities. For Britain the outlook overseas was no brighter. Even Pitt thought 'the Mediterranean lost and America itself precarious'. The French capture of Minorca had enabled them to send squadrons from their Mediterranean fleet to American and West Indian waters. Britain maintained a blockade of the Channel and Atlantic ports, but could not stop some further French ships slipping through.

Pitt set about reversing the tide of war by introducing new measures and conducting operations on a scale hitherto unattempted by any British government. The Hessian and Hanoverian troops brought over to England by Newcastle

[1] P. 196.   [2] Pp. 165, 166.

were returned to Germany and replaced by a more effective militia; the size of the regular army was increased more than sevenfold and the number of ships of the line in the navy fit for service fourfold.[1] Inevitably it was a more expensive war than any Britain had previously fought, and a heavy burden was imposed on the country. The land tax rose to 4s., and the taxes on malt, houses and windows increased. Over £11,000,000 a year was raised from a population of less than 6,000,000, many of whom were very poor; but by 1759 expenditure was some £20,000,000 a year. When the War ended, the National Debt had risen from £75,800,000 to £132,700,000.

The way for Pitt's four years of successes was prepared by Frederick the Great. Soon after the Convention of Kloster-seven, the Russians had entered East Prussia, and the Swedes had invaded Prussian Pomerania, while the Austrians advanced into Silesia and raided Berlin. The French, however, were slow to take advantage of the situation, and in November 1757 Frederick overwhelmed their army at Rossbach in Saxony. He then turned eastwards and defeated the Austrian army in Silesia at the Battle of Leuthen the next month. This change in the outlook enabled Pitt to repudiate the Convention of Klosterseven and make new plans for Britain's part in the Continental war.

Cumberland's command was given to Prince Ferdinand of Brunswick, one of Frederick's most able officers and a further example of Pitt's gift of making successful appointments. By the end of March 1758 Ferdinand, with the aid of some British troops, had driven the French out of Hanover and across the Rhine. Meanwhile, Pitt had entered into negotiations with Frederick who he recognized would have to bear the brunt of the struggle. He would not send him British troops or ships, but that April he agreed to give him an annual subsidy of £67,000. This arrangement remained the basis of Pitt's European policy. He supplemented it by raids on Rochefort in 1757 and St. Malo and Cherbourg in 1758, which may have kept some French troops from Germany at a critical time, but were so mishandled that they justified Fox's gibe that they were only 'breaking windows with guineas'.

While making his Continental arrangements, Pitt was also

[1] P. 190.

preparing his plans for the overseas war against France which he regarded as crucial. He had decided to make America the main theatre of war and to seek victory by the full use of sea-power. Warren's capture of Louisbourg in the previous war had impressed him. He resolved that Cape Breton Island should be attacked again. The trusted Admiral Boscawen was sent with a strong fleet to North American waters. At the same time, another fleet under Admiral Hawke was stationed off Brest and a third in the Mediterranean to prevent reinforcements being sent to Canada. The French could not get a single ship across the Atlantic to Louisbourg, but British troops under James Wolfe with naval support captured the fortress in 1758. In the same year the capture of Fort Duquesne (which was renamed Pittsburg) ended French control of the Ohio, and the capture of Fort Frontenac severed their communications between the St. Lawrence and the Great Lakes.

These successes were followed by Horace Walpole's 'glorious and ever-memorable year 1759', when, he said, 'Our bells are worn threadbare with ringing for victories'. Pitt's concentrated aggression in North America and full use of sea-power brought its rewards. The first success of the year was the conquest in May of Guadeloupe, the richest of the French islands in the West Indies, which was followed by the capture of the French posts of Senegal and Gorée in West Africa established to supply the sugar-plantations with slaves. On the North American mainland the taking of Quebec by Wolfe in September virtually gave Britain command of Canada. It was the most important part of a carefully-concerted plan of attack against the whole line of the French defence, which had previously seemed so impenetrable.[1] In itself it was an extremely successful combined action by the army and navy led by Wolfe with tenacity and courage. His dramatic death in the hour of triumph caught popular feeling at home, but the brilliance of the victory also established Pitt's reputation as a national leader.

Yet 1759 might have brought French recovery and triumph in Europe which would have nullified any overseas conquests. In Germany, when the year opened, Frederick was still unconquered, but the strain was beginning to tell seriously

[1] P. 168.

on his small country's military resources. The Russians resumed the offensive and in August completely defeated the Prussians at the Battle of Kunersdorf. Earlier in the year, the brilliant and courageous Duc de Choiseul had assumed control of French policy. He tried to reconquer Hanover. A French army drove Ferdinand's forces out of Hesse and up to the very borders of Hanover, but August brought also Ferdinand's victory over the French at the Battle of Minden. The French might well have been completely routed but for the incompetence of Lord George Sackville (1716–85), the commander of the British contingent in the battle, who was court martialled and dismissed from the army. Pitt had urged his promotion, and he was one of his few failures. Nevertheless, Minden by liberating Hanover and redeeming the German situation, brought much the same moral stimulation as the capture of Quebec.

Choiseul, however, had already decided on a bold plan to save French fortunes even at this late hour by an invasion of England. Flat-bottomed barges and troops were assembled at the French Channel ports and careful plans made; but British sea-power defeated this also. The blockade could not be broken even to unite the French fleets to cover the invasion. The Mediterranean fleet ran out of Toulon in July and tried to escape into the Atlantic, only to be pursued by Boscawen and destroyed off Lagos Bay on the Portuguese coast. The news of Minden made Choiseul decide to rely on the Brest fleet alone but, when it came out in November to join the transports in Quiberon Bay, it was boldly attacked and destroyed by Hawke amid treacherous shallows and rocks and despite a rising storm and the closing darkness of a winter night. Choiseul's last hope had gone. The threat of an invasion had caused anxiety in Britain, even amid the victories of 1759, and it was relief as well as exultation that greeted David Garrick's words in his *Heart of Oak*:

> Come, cheer up my lads! 'tis to glory we steer,
> To add something more to this wonderful year.

The next year brought the culmination of Pitt's triumphs in America. With the capture of Montreal, the whole of Canada came into British hands. Across the other side of the world, Franco-British rivalry in India, which had begun with reverses for Britain, now also brought her victory.[1] Though family tradition naturally made Pitt keenly interested in India, the British government was not immediately concerned in this contest between the two trading companies. When, however, the French threatened Madras in 1758, Pitt permitted the raising of a new regiment in England for service in India and granted the Company an annual subsidy of £20,000 for the rest of the War; and in 1760, when the French threat to invade England in 1759 was over, he sent out further reinforcements to India which assisted Eyre Coote in driving the French from the Carnatic.

The Fall of Pitt (1761)

In the midst of these continuing successes, however, while Pitt was making further plans for the prosecution of the War, an event occurred which was to bring about a new turn in the political story in Britain. Early one morning in October 1760 George II suddenly dropped down dead from a heart attack. The new monarch, George III, had been turned against Pitt deliberately by Bute.[2]   During the War, Leicester House had once again become the centre of opposition to the ministry. So strong had been the Prince of Wales's hatred of the war minister and his supporters that the splendid victories over France had aroused in him resentment instead of elation. After the fall of Montreal, a few months before his accession to the throne, he wrote to Bute, 'I can't help feeling that every such thing raises those I have no reason to love', and added that, Britain's 'popular man is a true snake in the grass'. Now as King he showed his hostility to Pitt in his first public act when he read his declaration to the Privy Council on his accession. This had been drawn up by Bute and spoke of his reign beginning 'in the midst of a bloody and expensive war'; Pitt succeeded in insisting that this should be changed to 'an expensive, but just and necessary war'.

George III's accession came at a very unfortunate time for Pitt. The new King's antagonism brought into the open a growing criticism of Pitt and a rising demand for peace which hitherto had been suppressed. Pitt still remained the idol of the City merchants. Earlier in the War, they had been divided in their views about his policy of seizing French trade

[1] P. 166.   [2] P. 45.

and so making it even more profitable for Britain. Some had feared that the taking of the French islands in the West Indies would lead to a glut of sugar and a reduction of its price; but Pitt believed that the American colonies could take as much sugar as these produced, and he was proved right. Within two years of the capture of Guadeloupe, the stimulation of a rising demand for sugar had doubled its production, and the rising yield of customs duties had already more than paid for the cost of the expedition which had conquered it. Similarly, the fall of Quebec had transferred the valuable French fur and fish trade to Britain, while the taking of Gorée and Senegal brought her a share in the gum and slave trade of Africa. As the seizure of these commercially desirable islands and forts produced their profits, the City firmly united behind him as the man who was bringing an unprecedented prosperity to the nation's trade and industry.

Other aspects of Pitt's policy, however, aroused growing opposition to him in the country and in the administration. One was its cost, which brought an increasing burden of debt and mounting taxation, especially for the landed classes.[1] There was now a feeling that its continuation was less and less justified. The successes in the overseas campaigns against France were producing misgivings. If France were thoroughly defeated and completely deprived of her commerce and colonies, it seemed likely that all Europe would be driven to unite against Britain and engage in further hostilities to destroy her dominant power. On the other hand, while adequate gains seemed to have been made overseas, there was stalemate on the Continent. After the Battle of Minden, Pitt had taken more German troops into British pay, increased the British contingent from ten to twenty thousand men and replaced the disgraced Sackville by the Marquis of Granby (1721–70), whose name and image on the signboards of English inns, together with that of the 'King of Prussia', was to be a lasting record of the War in the countryside; but the year 1760 produced no decision in Germany.

In face of the greatly superior numbers of the French, Austrian and Russian armies, Frederick and Ferdinand could do no more than hold their own. The British effort and money expended on the Continent seemed to be wasted.

[1] P. 304.

There was a strong demand for a separate peace with France. Israel Maudit, a rich woollen draper of Huguenot origin, attacked Pitt's policy along these lines in *Considerations on the Present German War*, which went through six editions within six months in 1760 and, according to Horace Walpole, exercised an enormous influence.

Opposition to Pitt appeared also in the Cabinet and divided the ministers. The Whig noblemen had always been inclined to resent him as an upstart whose family had not gained wealth and position from the Tudor dissolution of the monasteries, but from the profits of the Indian trade under Queen Anne. Nor did Pitt's aloofness from the arts of political persuasion and his proud and despotic character assist his hold on his colleagues. Relations had been particularly difficult between two such men of differing temperament as Pitt and Newcastle. As he struggled with the details of domestic policy, administration and patronage and (above all) the task of raising money for Pitt's subsidies and campaigns, Newcastle could not contain his resentment against the successful war minister. 'Such treatment', he told Hardwicke, 'from one whom I have nourished and served is not and cannot be borne.' Now, he inevitably sympathized with the growing outcry against the War and its cost, and so did the rich and influential Duke of Bedford, then Lord-Lieutenant of Ireland, who also expressed himself to Hardwicke, saying, 'The endeavouring to drive France entirely out of any naval power is fighting against nature and can tend to no one good to this country; but on the contrary must excite all the naval powers of Europe to enter into a confederacy against us'. The opposition to Pitt was further strengthened when George III made Bute a member of the Cabinet in the same month as his accession, and a Secretary of State early the next year, though the general election that year brought little change in the composition of Parliament.

The War continued in 1761. Pondicherry in India was captured and so was Dominica in the West Indies. Peace talks began in the spring on Choiseul's initiative, but Pitt was prepared to end hostilities only on his own terms. He persisted in his warlike plans, striking even at France herself in June when a naval expedition occupied Belle Isle in the Bay of Biscay to strengthen his hands in the negotiations. He was not prepared to allow any restoration of French power or interest in North America. As Choiseul found himself unable to get the concessions he wanted, particularly the restoration of French fishing-rights off Newfoundland, he paid increasing attention to the possibility of an alliance with Spain. Charles III, who had succeeded to the Spanish throne in 1759, was ready to join in the War in the hope of restoring Spain's greatness in Europe. A secret Franco-Spanish treaty of alliance was signed in August 1761; Spain was to enter the War on 1st May 1762 if peace had not been made by then.

Pitt knew about the treaty. His secret service had intercepted the Spanish ambassador's despatches. He wanted an immediate declaration of war on Spain so that the navy might seize the annual treasure-fleet bound from the Caribbean to Vigo and Cadiz which was so vital for the Spanish treasury. However, only his brother-in-law, Temple, supported him. Bedford, Newcastle and the rest of the Cabinet did not want the War extended as long as any chance remained that Spain would not be bound by the treaty. Even Pitt's own military and naval advisers opposed him, Anson insisting that 'our ships were not in condition to enter immediately into any material operations against Spain'. Pitt made it clear that either his policy must be accepted or he would resign. He made his famous claim to the Cabinet, 'Being responsible, I will direct and will be responsible for nothing that I do not direct'. George III and Bute could not have retained him even if they had wished to do so. Pitt and Temple resigned office in October 1761. Pitt had destroyed himself by his obstinancy. He lost power, not through any intrigue by George III or Bute, but because his war policy had failed to retain the confidence of the administration.

The Treaty of Paris (1763)

The hope that war with Spain might be averted proved to be vain. After the treasure-fleet had reached Spain safely, Bute demanded assurances from her as to her peaceful intentions towards Britain. When these were not obtained, war was declared on her in January 1762. Thanks to measures already planned by Pitt, Britain's victorious course was not halted. Early in 1762 the French West Indian islands of

Martinique, Grenada, St. Lucia and St. Vincent were captured.   Then British naval power struck at Spain in both West and East Indies.   Havana, the capital of Cuba, was captured, and so was Manila, the capital of the Philippine Islands; and in both these waters British warships took treasure-galleons, containing millions of pounds worth of bullion and jewels.

The extension of hostilities and the consequent expense (which included assistance for Britain's ally, Portugal) strengthened the case of those who disliked British partici-pation in the Continental war.   Moreover, the situation in Germany changed with dramatic suddenness early in 1762. When the year opened, Frederick the Great was in low straits.   Silesia and much of Saxony were held by the Austrians and Prussian Pomerania by the Russians.   His army was exhausted.   In January, however, the Czarina Elizabeth died.   Her successor, Peter III, fervently admired Frederick; he made peace and withdrew his troops from all occupied Prussian territory.   British ministers feared that Frederick, now relieved from the dangers to his state, would use their subsidies to prolong the War.   In the spring of 1762, therefore, Bute resolved to withhold Frederick's subsidy and reduce the assistance given to Ferdinand of Brunswick.   The decision brought about the resignation of Newcastle, who had increasingly resented the loss of power and adherents to the rising Bute, and now, though he had long disliked the expense of assisting Prussia, declared that the withdrawal of the sub-sidy might 'be interpreted as if the resolution were taken here to abandon *entirely* the German war'.

By now Bute had reopened peace negotiations with Choiseul.   Both wanted a speedy end to the War.   Bedford was sent to Paris to conduct the talks.   The Preliminaries were signed in October 1762.   Fox secured their acceptance by Parliament, despite Pitt's forceful criticisms in a speech of more than three hours which he came from a sick-bed to make.[1]   Horace Walpole alleged that Fox won over the Commons by widespread bribery, but this was not so.   There was a large vote for the government from the country gentle-men, who hastened up to town, determined to have peace, while the opposition were divided and unable or unwilling

[1] P. 313.

W

to condemn the proposals completely. There was much war-weariness in the country and dislike of high taxation; the idea of peace was popular, and the proposed gains seemed great. In February 1763 the Preliminaries became the Treaty of Paris between Britain, France and Spain and the basis of the Treaty of Hubertusburg between Prussia and Austria. So the Seven Years' War ended.

By the Treaty of Paris, Britain retained Canada, but restored to France her most valuable West Indian islands.[1] France was allowed to keep her fishing-rights off Newfoundland together with the islands of St. Pierre and Miquelon as a base for her fishing-boats. France also got back her factories in India, but was not allowed to fortify them. Britain kept Senegal, but restored Gorée to France. Britain regained Minorca in return for Belle Isle. Havana was exchanged for Florida and the right to cut logwood in Honduras, and Manila was returned to Spain in exchange for a ransom. France ceded Louisiana to Spain as compensation for the loss of Florida. France again agreed to demolish the fortifications of Dunkirk.

The parliamentary debates over the Preliminaries had revealed the differences of opinion about the terms which should be granted to France at the end of the War. Bedford and other supporters of the government repeated the diplomatic and strategic reasons against a complete weakening and humiliation of France which they had already used when attacking Pitt's policy in the last years of the War.[2] And the parliamentary majority they secured reflected a strong feeling in the country in favour of the Treaty. There was some debate about keeping Guadeloupe in preference to Canada;[3] but the Treaty as a whole found general approval because it was believed that France would not accept stricter terms. A prime British war aim had been to prevent French superiority in North America and India and, if this were achieved, most people saw no reason to risk the prolongation of the War or the speedy outbreak of another by retaining for Britain too many possessions. The Treaty satisfied their ambitions because it secured the original objects for making war and also seemed to place before the nation an immense commercial and colonial future.

[1] P. 168.   [2] P. 309.   [3] P. 168.

Burke, therefore, had some justification in sarcastically describing Pitt as the spokesman of 'a parcel of low toad-eaters' – the London merchants – who knew very little of the 'great extensive public'. The theme of Pitt's attack on the Treaty was 'we retain nothing, although we have conquered everything'. Britain, he considered, had so thoroughly subdued France that she could not have fought much longer. It seemed to him that Britain had sacrificed enormous future power and prosperity by returning to France such vital islands and trading concessions, and that since she had not been eliminated 'as a maritime and commercial power', she could seek revenge and would as soon as she could. 'By restoring to her all the valuable West Indian Islands and by our concessions in the Newfoundland fishery', he said, 'we have given her the means of recovering her prodigious losses and of becoming once more formidable to us at sea.'

Though public opinion at the time condemned him as an extremist, the future showed him to be right. The moderation of the Treaty of Paris did not placate France, and she intervened in the American War of Independence to gain revenge. Also Pitt was shown to have a clearer understanding of the problems of imperial defence than his contemporaries. The British peace-makers probably assumed that British naval supremacy would secure the Caribbean without the retention of the French and Spanish bases, but Pitt's forebodings were to be realized within his own lifetime. The French continued, in the 1770's and 1780's, to take many islands in the Leeward and Windward groups and to threaten the safety of the whole British West Indies.

The Treaty of Hubertusburg brought no changes in the boundaries of the states. Prussia retained Silesia which Maria Theresa had tried so hard to regain. Pitt and his followers were equally critical of the way Bute had ended the alliance with Frederick, and historians have commonly agreed with them. Basil Williams, for instance, stated that it 'created a distrust of us which . . . left us friendless when, barely more than ten years later, we had to fight for our empire'. Yet this was not really so. Britain was to be without allies in the American War of Independence, not because the rest of Europe accepted Frederick's charges against her of treachery and instability of policy through her parliamentary system of government, but because they had no mutual reasons for supporting her. France no longer seemed likely to seek European dominance, and the Continental states were not interested in events in North America.

Despite the defects of the Treaty of Paris, however, the war conducted by Pitt had brought Britain gains in territory, trade and prestige greater than she had made in any previous war. Two great territories seemed inevitably destined to be developed by her. The sea-power and maritime trade of a large part of the world belonged to her. Through Pitt's policy, she was now definitely committed to pursue overseas aims and interests as well as maintain her position in Europe; and this continued to be so, even although the first empire she established was to be disrupted by the American Revolution. Horace Walpole, by no means a sympathetic critic of Pitt, wrote in later years, 'Even the shameful Peace of Paris, concluded in defiance of him, could not rob the nation of all that he had acquired, nor could George III resign so much as Pitt had gained for George II. Half the empire of Hindustan, conquered under his administration by the spirit he had infused, still pours its treasures into the Thames. Canada was subdued by his councils, and Spain and France, that yet dread his name, attest the reality of his success.'

XVI · MINISTERIAL UNCERTAINTIES, 1760–70

The Accession of George III

THE political importance of George III's accession to the throne has been a matter of controversy for nearly a century. There have been varying interpretations of the new King's conception of his duties as a monarch and of the extent to which the relations between the Crown and its ministers differed during the first years of his reign from what they had been between 1714 and 1760. Recently the research inaugurated by Sir Lewis Namier has made possible a deeper understanding of these questions by putting forward a much more extensive and realistic view of the politics of the time. There are still differences of opinion and judgement about these issues, but the traditional interpretation of them, which resisted challenge for so long, can no longer be accepted without question.

This interpretation of George III's part in politics in the first years of his reign owes much in origin to Burke's *Some Thoughts on the Cause of the Present Discontents*, which he published in 1770.[1] It was taken up by nineteenth-century historians, to most of whom English political history appeared as a story of progress and liberty won for the people by the Whig party. These Whig historians looked at George III's policy in the light of their political sympathies. They too readily assumed that political conditions by the middle of the eighteenth century were substantially the same as those they knew in the nineteenth century. They thought that between 1715 and 1760 the Whig ministers had succeeded in reducing the first two Hanoverian kings to the position of constitutional monarchs and in establishing a system of responsible parliamentary government – even though parliamentary corruption took the place of a democratic electoral system. They, therefore, took it for granted that George III's policy was to recover the Crown's lost prerogatives and destroy the constitutional system of party

[1] Pp. 344–5.

government which had been achieved during the two previous reigns; and they saw him assisted in this attempt to make himself a personal or absolute monarch by a revived Tory party and resisted by the descendants of the old Whig olig-archy which had deprived the Crown of its traditional powers. Similarly, these Whig historians supposed that the struggle with the American colonies also came about through George III's desire to deprive them of the rights of self-government which they had come to enjoy.

The research of Namier and others had undermined the validity of this Whig view by showing that it was based on a misinterpretation of the condition of the constitution when George III became King. Burke's famous treatise is now seen to be, not an accurate account of cabinet and party government at that time, but rather a piece of political propaganda.[1] George III did not threaten responsible government because this, in the way it was to come into being during the nineteenth century, did not then exist. In fact, the Revolutionary Settlement of 1688 had left the Crown considerable powers, which were not intended to be merely formal and were still exercised by George II.[2] Since they had not been lost, George III could not have set out to regain them. Moreover, Namier's discovery of George III's letters to Bute has shown the falsity of attributing to the King at his accession a deep-laid scheme to upset the constitution. He was too young and inexperienced to be capable of this. His chief aim was the purely personal one of substituting his 'Dearest Friend', Bute, for Newcastle in the government of the country.

George III's background and personality partly explain what happened in the first years after 1760.[3] This was bound to bring about changes in the composition and outlook of the government, and it was expected that it would do so. During the long years of his reign, George II had been content to rely upon the Devonshires, Pelhams, Townshends, Russells and other great Whig families to rule the country and had allowed them to use the Crown's vast patronage in the way initiated by Walpole and perfected by Newcastle. When, therefore, George III came to the throne no one was surprised that he should wish to get rid of these ministers and

[1] P. 345.   [2] P. 48.   [3] P. 45.

replace them by an administration in which he could have personal confidence. The immediate promotion of his tutor and most intimate friend, Bute, to a place in the Cabinet seemed to contemporaries an entirely natural consequence.

It was not, however, just a matter of personal feelings. Differences about policy, and especially foreign policy, also had an effect. Bute's outlook on foreign affairs was that of the old Tories and included a strong hostility towards Hanover. George III shared this completely, and almost the whole country now supported him. Only the merchants did not want an end to the War and its foreign entanglements. George III had thus every reason to expect public support for his policy.

Again, George III believed that the Whig ministers of his father's reign had proved themselves self-seeking and corrupt. He was proud of England's political traditions and was also genuinely pious.[1] He was determined to be the saviour of his country and to effect a political, moral and religious revival. He was resolved not to be the slave of his ministers as his grandfather had been. He also objected to the idea of 'party' in politics and wished to abolish it; he wanted to have ministers appointed only for their honesty, ability and patriotism. These are typical amateur criticisms of politics. George III's intentions were well-meant, but they were undermined by his temperament. His self-righteousness made him incapable of self-examination or imagination. His obstinacy and narrowness of intellect, as Dr. Plumb has said, might have been forgiven, 'if only they had been exercised on the trivialities of politics – the promotion of ensigns, the appointment of deans or the ritual of the royal lives. But they were not. They were exercised on fundamental questions of policy and personalities.'

In wishing to replace the old Whig politicians by men who would govern in the true interests of Crown and nation, George proposed to use the Crown's patronage to achieve this instead of allowing politicians to use it to keep themselves in power, and he expected to have the support of public opinion here also. But he found himself unable to do this. He ousted the Whig group which Walpole and Newcastle had kept in power, but could not replace it. He tried for

[1] P. 18.

ten years with a succession of unstable ministries until Lord North was finally to establish a settled government, and it became clear that George III had to govern within the same framework of politics as his grandfather.

The way in which George III came to struggle vainly against the course of political development in the country was to provide support for the Whig interpretation of his policy, but there was a more immediate reason for its adoption. George came to the throne young, unmarried and likely to reign for a long time. There was now no royal heir likely to come to the throne within a foreseeable period and able to reward with power those dissatisfied, dispossessed politicians who had rallied around him. Since such politicians now had no such cause to uphold their desire for office, they had to evolve a new conception of the constitution in order to denigrate the administration and justify their opposition to it.

George III had been urged by his mother, according to the well-known story, to 'be a King', but this did not mean that when he came to the throne he wished to rule as a despotic monarch. His only intention was to use the power which he believed rightly belonged to him under the existing constitution, and he sought to use it in a way which would meet the political situation at the beginning of his reign and give him ministers whom he could trust. As Namier has said, his purpose was essentially to carry on 'to the best of his more-than-limited ability the system of government which he had inherited from his predecessors'. It was not this policy but the situation in which he sought to achieve it and his failure to do so that led to new political developments in the country.

The Dominance of Bute (1760–3)

John Stuart, third Earl of Bute (1713–92), belonged to a Whig family and succeeded his father to the Scottish earldom in 1723. In 1736 he relieved himself from penury by marrying Mary, the only daughter of Edward Wartley Montagu and heiress to an estate worth £1,500,000, and in 1737 he was elected a Scottish representative peer. For ten years, however, he took no part in politics, but devoted himself, in Bute, to his family and to literature and botany – he was later to secure a pension of £300 a year for Dr. Johnson and encourage George III to develop Kew Gardens.

In 1747 he gained an entry into the circle of Leicester House by making a fourth at cards when a cricket match, in which Frederick, Prince of Wales, was playing, had to be abandoned through rain. He continued to play cards and organize amateur theatricals for the Prince, who made him one of his Lords of the Bedchamber. After Frederick's sudden death in 1751, he became the intimate adviser of the widowed Princess, and her son's tutor. Though ignorant of affairs, he thirsted for political power, having experienced both impecuniousness and obscurity, and shrewdly used his opportunities. With the assistance of the Princess, he taught Prince George to mistrust the leading figures of the time in the administration and court.[1] He established a complete control over the young man, whose reverence for him, as a recent writer has said, was like 'the sort of adoring attachment which immature girls sometimes feel towards their schoolmistress'.

Bute's opportunity came with the accession of George III, who at once appointed him to the post of Groom of the Stole with a seat in the Cabinet. He was, he told Temple, 'not a bare Groom of the Stole. The King will have it otherwise.' The general election in March 1761 produced a House of Commons very similar to previous ones, but in that year Bute increased his political influence by becoming the leader of the forty-five Scottish Members of Parliament and sixteen peers and by gaining a fortune on his father-in-law's death. When the new Parliament met, the King had made Bute Secretary of State for the Northern Department and accepted Pitt's resignation.[2]

Bute had now achieved the place in the ministry intended for him by George III; he was now the royal successor to Pitt. Newcastle had been persuaded to join in opposing Pitt's desire for an immediate declaration of war against Spain, but resentment at Bute's ascendancy in the Cabinet, uneasiness at his own exclusion from the King's confidence and a belief that the Prussian alliance must be maintained led to his resignation in May 1762.[3] He went because he disagreed with his colleagues about policy and because he received no support from the King, who was very ready that the fall of the corrupting minister should follow that of the tyrannical minister.

Except for a short six months in 1756–7, Newcastle had

[1] P. 45.   [2] Pp. 309–10.   [3] P. 311.

been in the Cabinet for forty-five years, thirty-two as a
Secretary of State and eight as First Lord of the Treasury.
Old and unhappy, he went with reluctance and could not
believe that his departure from government was final, but
it was the end of his political career. He had not been a
distinguished statesman, but neither had he been as contemp-
tible as some of his contemporaries have suggested.[1] He left
office, as Horace Walpole said, 'a Duke without money', for
he had spent his large fortune in maintaining the alliance
between the executive and the landed nobility which had
given them power and also provided the country with stable
government. Hardwicke, his friend and adviser, also
resigned, and many of the younger members of the 'old
Whigs' went into opposition. It was the end of a chapter in
British politics.

Bute was now made First Lord of the Treasury. He headed
the ministry and had the King behind him, but he was ill-fitted
for the position. George II had said of him that he would
have made 'an excellent ambassador in any court where there
was nothing to do'. This was a harsh verdict, for Bute did,
in fact, display some diplomatic ability during the negotiations
for the establishment of peace; but his lack of political capacity
and administrative experience were to lead to his fall from
office within a few months.

Bute knew that Newcastle's departure left the administration without an effective organization to secure support in
the Commons. In October 1762, therefore, Henry Fox was
made the leader of the court party in the Commons, with the
immediate task of securing acceptance of the Preliminaries
of the peace treaty which had just been signed. Fox had
much experience of the House of Commons, but he was
unpopular as a politician. Since 1757 he had been Paymaster of the Forces and (unlike Pitt before him) had been
amassing wealth from the perquisites of office during the war
years. He obtained a vote of 319 against 65 in favour of the
peace terms. Then he took his reward. He went to the
Lords as Lord Holland, holding the Paymastership for two
more years to complete his family fortune, but his reputation
had declined still further through his association with Bute.

The year 1763 should have brought Bute's hour of triumph.

[1] P. 288.

The long-awaited ending of the War was at hand, and there followed the 'massacre of the Pelhamite Innocents', the dismissal from office of Newcastle's supporters who had voted against the government; but Bute was extremely unpopular. Though most people wanted peace, his opponents were able to arouse a virulent attack on the settlement and its author, and a further outburst against him came when the administration, in an effort to find new sources of revenue in face of the wartime increase in national indebtedness, proposed to extend the hated excise system by a cider tax. Bute was abused as 'The Northern Thane' or 'Sir Pertinax Mac-Sycophant'. The press libelled him, dwelling with derisive innuendo and satire on his relations with the Dowager Princess of Wales, and the *North Briton* was but an extreme example of this campaign.[1] Mobs attacked his carriage, hanged him in effigy, broke the windows of his house and serenaded him with bawdy songs. The Cider Bill was passed, but Bute's health gave way, and his government was divided. He lacked the political stamina to hold out. His nerve failed him, and, as Chesterfield wrote, 'in this odd situation, unpopular without guilt, fearing without danger, presumptuous without resolution, and proud without being respectable or respected, he on a sudden, and to the universal surprise of the public, quitted his post' in April 1763.

George III assured his successor, Grenville, and subsequent ministers that he would have nothing more to do with Bute, but for some time he did not keep that promise. Bute remained as friendly and influential with the King as before and even more unpopular as a 'minister behind the curtain'. Gradually, however, his influence declined, and marriage gave the King greater self-reliance.[2] Finally, George decided in the summer of 1766 to break with Bute, whose advice seemed to be increasingly valueless. He cut off all relationship with him, freeing his ministers from continual grounds for annoyance and himself from the most serious embarrassment to his personal prestige.

Grenville, the North Briton *and the Stamp Act (1763–5)*

When Bute resigned office in 1763, he comforted himself with the assurance that as he had steered the ship of state through the billows into harbour, 'it could be handed over to a freshwater pilot'; but for George III, who now began his period of personal government, the situation was not an easy one. The lesson of Bute's short-lived administration was that the King, like his grandfather, must have a minister with experience, self-confidence and parliamentary support. Such men, however, after the long supremacy of the Pelhams were few. Through Bute's agency, Pitt and then Fox were approached, but both refused, and George III was determined not to have a ministry of the Newcastle Whigs, who had preserved their unity as a 'party'. He wanted only Bute as his minister, but if he could not have him, he would 'support those who will act for me and without regret change my tools whenever they act contrary to my service'.

The only possibility seemed to be George Grenville (1712–70), who was free of party allegiance. He was Pitt's brother-in-law and a member, therefore, of 'the Family', though he had earned Pitt's bitter enmity for deserting it. Having resigned the Treasurership of the Navy on the dismissal of Pitt and Newcastle in 1756, he had held it again from 1757 to 1762 in their ministry, being admitted to the Cabinet in 1761. He retained power under Bute and served as Secretary of State for the Northern Department and First Lord of the Admiralty. He had, therefore, the necessary parliamentary and administrative experience, and his administration was strengthened by the accession of the Russell connection through the appointment of the Duke of Bedford as Lord President of the Council.

Grenville's opponents nicknamed him the 'Gentle Shepherd' in allusion to Pitt's mocking reference to a song of the time, *Gentle Shepherd, tell me where*, during a debate in which Grenville had defended the Cider Tax and asked where there was another source of revenue. He was a shallow, humourless, verbose man, but had strength of will and was a careful organizer. When he became First Lord of the Treasury in 1763, he told the King he 'came into his service to preserve the constitution of my country and to prevent any undue and unwarrantable force being put upon the Crown', but his relations with George were not easy. Realizing that to retain power he must possess the King's confidence and control all patronage, he demanded that George should not communicate with Bute, but this was not observed by the King; and his insistence that 'he must be known to have the patronage, or the whole must break' was to contribute towards his downfall.[1]

Grenville's administration was soon involved in a political furore when, in another effort to safeguard its future, it decided to take action against John Wilkes (1727–97), who had been prominent in the recent violent campaign against Bute. Wilkes was the son of a prosperous Clerkenwell distiller, who married him to an elderly heiress. The marriage did not last long, but he made free use of his wife's fortune to become a country gentleman, enter the profligate, dissolute society of fashionable young noblemen (including Sir Francis Dashwood who initiated him into the secret debauches of the fraternity of Medmenham Abbey) and in 1757 purchase a seat in Parliament. In rebellion against his middle-class origins, he associated politically with Temple and Pitt and sought prominence, prestige and popularity. Bute's unpopularity gave him an opportunity. He founded in June the *North Briton* in opposition to Bute's newspaper, *The Briton*, edited by Smollett. In this he brilliantly attacked, ridiculed and abused Bute and the administration. It appealed to the growing newspaper-reading public of the time, who wished to know about current political issues.[2]

In April 1763 the King's Speech at the opening of Parliament praised the peace settlement as 'honourable to my Crown and beneficial to my people'. Wilkes immediately wrote in reply the famous Number 45 of the *North Briton*. He was careful to make it clear in his opening sentence that he did not wish to insult the King personally – 'The King's Speech has always been considered by the Legislature, and by the public at large, as the Speech of the Minister'; he went on to denounce the speech as 'the most abandoned instance of ministerial effrontery'. By this time Bute had resigned, but the leading members of the Cabinet were still the same, and George considered he had been accused of lying. The ministers felt they could not ignore this challenge which signified that they were to be attacked as severely as the former administration. Morever, they hoped it was a chance to discredit the opposition and distract public attention from the controversy over the peace treaty.

[1] P. 325.   [2] P. 101.

They decided to proceed by way of a general warrant, that is one which mentioned no names. Issued in the name of Lord Halifax, Secretary of State for the Southern Department, it ordered the arrest of 'the authors, printers and publishers of a seditious and treasonable paper, entitled the *North Briton*, Number XLV'. Wilkes and forty-eight others involved in its publication were arrested, Wilkes himself being committed to the Tower. In doing this the government raised an issue which was to disturb British politics for several years. Wilkes seems to have wanted to provoke the ministers into acting in a way that would give him cause to fight them, and they had played into his hand. Although general warrants had been issued in the past, their legality was doubtful; Wilkes was ready to test it, and the opposition were with him. Temple secured a writ of Habeas Corpus in the Court of Common Pleas, carefully choosing a sympathetic judge in Chief Justice Pratt, who held that Wilkes was protected by his privilege as a Member of Parliament. The decision raised 'a loud huzza in Westminster Hall'. Further legal action by Wilkes secured a ruling from Pratt that general warrants were 'unconstitutional, illegal and absolutely void', and he was awarded £4,000 in damages against Halifax for wrongful arrest. Wherever Wilkes went, the crowd greeted him with shouts of 'Wilkes and Liberty!', a cry which was to be heard in the London streets for many a year.

Wilkes had gained a spectacular victory. George and his ministers were determined to retrieve their prestige by parliamentary action. Many of the opposition were now anxious about being identified with a man like Wilkes, who had claimed at his first trial that he stood for the liberties of all, including 'the middling and inferior sort of people, who stand most in need of protection'. When Parliament reassembled in November, the Commons declared by 237 votes to 111 that the number 45 of the *North Briton* was a 'false, seditious and scandalous libel'. Wilkes had discredited himself by light-heartedly printing for private circulation that autumn an obscene poem, *An Essay on Woman*. Wilkes lost much moderate support in the country; he was challenged to a duel by another member of the Commons and so badly wounded that he could not attend the House in December when it voted that parliamentary privilege did not cover seditious libel. To escape prosecution in the courts, Wilkes fled to France. The next year he was expelled from the Commons and outlawed by the Court of King's Bench. His disappearance strengthened the opposition. They could concentrate upon the issue of general warrants which the country gentlemen, who disliked Wilkes and his popular support, suspected as an extension of executive authority. They proposed a motion that general warrants were illegal, which was defeated by a bare majority of fourteen. Grenville and the King hoped that no more would be heard of Wilkes and that by their determination they had preserved their parliamentary position.

Though it was to have grave consequences, there was general support for Grenville's financial policy which aimed at avoiding new taxation. The legacy of the recent war was a heavy increase in government expenditure and the National Debt.[1] This alarmed politicians, and country gentlemen resented the continuance of the land tax at 4s. in the pound. Grenville retrenched government expenditure drastically, especially on the army and navy;[2] but this was not enough. He decided, therefore, to increase the imperial contribution to the national revenue by means of the Sugar Act of 1764 and the Stamp Act of 1765.[3] Opinion at home supported these measures, feeling it only right that the colonies, which were so expensive to defend, should pay their share of taxation. None foresaw the immediate uproar which the Stamp Act aroused in America.

Rockingham, the Declaratory Act and the 'King's Friends' (1765–6)

Grenville, indeed, was out of office when the disturbing American news reached England. In the spring of 1765 George III had his first attack of mental illness. His illness was only brief, but he wanted a Council of Regency to be appointed in case it recurred. The ministers agreed to introduce a Regency Bill, but angered the King by insisting, in order to protect themselves from a repetition of the scandalous imputations which had broken Bute, that his mother must be excluded from the Council. George still resented Grenville's determination to control patronage; and the minister's insistence

---

[1] P. 304.   [2] Pp. 190, 199.   [3] Pp. 170–1.

on economies in his new Buckingham Palace provided him with a further grievance; and finally the opposition in the Commons embarrassed him by wishing to include his mother in the Council of Regency. He was determined to dismiss Grenville and asked his uncle, the Duke of Cumberland, to find him a new ministry.

Cumberland persuaded the Marquess of Rockingham (1732–82) to become First Lord of the Treasury and head a new ministry. As a boy Rockingham had won a reputation for spirit, which he did not later sustain, by running away from Westminster School to join Cumberland's army as it went to fight the Young Pretender. He had great territorial influence as a wealthy landowner in Yorkshire and belonged to the old Whig aristocracy, which could have gained him political importance, but his interests were his estates and the racecourse. He had only entered politics because he felt that in his position he should do so, but he lacked ability and experience and rarely spoke in the Lords – 'A silent First Minister', said Horace Walpole, 'was a phenomenon unknown since Parliaments had borne so great a share in the revolutions of government.' His own attractive and blameless character won him the support of a group of Whigs, but his ministry was weak. The King accepted him reluctantly, and Pitt would not join him as a subordinate. This deprived him of Pitt's followers, while ambitious politicians did not want to identify themselves with such an unpromising administration. Yet, short-lived though his government proved to be, his group of supporters was to outlast it in importance, for he appointed as his private secretary Edmund Burke, who became its mouthpiece and gave a new meaning to the Whigs as a party and, indeed, to the whole idea of the party system.[1]

Rockingham inherited the extremely difficult situation caused by American resistance to the Stamp Act. The trading classes wanted the Act repealed because they were already suffering from the 'non-importation' movement in the colonies, but most country gentlemen disliked the idea of yielding to colonial violence and still wanted them to share in the cost of imperial defence. By 1766 Rockingham was convinced of the need for repeal, and he was emboldened both by a speech attacking the Act from Pitt, which contained

[1] Pp. 344–5.

the famous pronouncement, 'I rejoice that America has resisted. Three millions of people so dead to all the feelings of liberty, as voluntarily to submit to be slaves, would have been fit instruments to make slaves of the rest', and by the response of a body of London merchants, who afterwards removed the horses from Pitt's coach and dragged him triumphantly home. The Stamp Act was repealed in 1766, but the opposition had to be won over by simultaneously passing the Declaratory Act proclaiming that Parliament 'had, hath and ought to have full power and authority to make laws to bind the colonies in all cases whatsoever'.

The ministers further sought popularity by abandoning the right of cider excisemen to search private houses and declaring general warrants illegal; but the administration, already weakened by Cumberland's death in the atuumn of 1765, was nearing its end. Charles Townshend had compared it to a fashionable glossy silk fabric in calling it 'a lutestring ministry, fit only for summer wear', meaning that it would not last when it had to face Parliament, and now the stresses of debate had split the Cabinet and weakened the confidence of its supporters. Pitt had opposed the Declaratory Act, saying scornfully that Parliament had 'voted the right in order not to exercise it', while over fifty members had voted in the Commons against the repeal of the Stamp Act.

Among these members opposing Rockingham were a group who had acquired the name of the 'King's Friends'. A number of them had met in the spring of 1766 to discuss the continued ministerial instability which seemed particularly dangerous for the country in view of the disquieting developments in America. They decided that the King should rise above all 'groups' and 'factions' and form a government which would be stable and act in the national interest – 'His Majesty should have the free choice of his own servants and that he should not put the management of his affairs unconditionally into the hands of the leader of any party'. They shared George III's dislike of 'party' and believed that the present situation was due to partisan behaviour, but they also thought that most Members of Parliament were such as themselves, who 'have always hitherto acted upon the sole principle of attachment to the Crown' and would be able to form a government under a great national leader. Of these

x

'King's Friends', some aspired after office and became permanent placemen – 'embryonic civil servants' some modern historians have called them – who gave their support unswervingly to the Crown, so providing continuity of office and more efficient administration.   Others were 'independent and unconnected' country gentlemen, not bound to any particularly leader or group, but having, in Namier's words, 'a conception of parliamentary duties radically different from our own: such members did not deem it a function of Parliament to provide a government – the government to them was the King's.   Their duty was to support it as long as they honestly could.'[1]   To Rockingham's group, the 'King's Friends' were 'hired royal mercenaries', and nineteenth-century historians were inclined to accept this view of their activities, but their importance as a political force and their subservience to the King have both been exaggerated.

George III, indeed, made no attempt to assist the opposition to the Rockingham government.   He had approved it in 1765 as the best Cumberland could secure, but he knew that its increasing weakness and disunity would embarrass him, and he did not wish, therefore, to exert his influence in an effort to keep it in office.   He believed the time had come to look for a new administration under another minister.

The Chatham Administration (1766–8)

George III had now come to believe that only Pitt's leadership could give him a secure government.   Pitt's popularity in the City had made him ever since 1761 the most formidable statesman in opposition to the Crown.   He would be a powerful man to have in office.   Moreover, he respected the Crown, mistrusted the Whig oligarchy and was detached from all political groups in Parliament.   George III, therefore, opened negotiations with Pitt, who accepted office and pleased him by announcing that, since he intended to be as supreme in this administration as he had been in that of 1757, he would 'dissolve all faction' and form his government on the principles of 'measures not men'.

Pitt's return to power was greeted with widespread pleasure. George III had a minister of his own choice and not one whom he had been forced to accept by political circumstances.   He

[1] P. 59.

was prepared to support Pitt and believed that he could secure for the Crown the popular approval that it needed. In Parliament, although Pitt had not got a political group behind him, he could rely on the independent country gentlemen. The City merchants still trusted him, and the American colonists believed he sympathized with them. Pitt himself had again come to power on his own terms, while his self-confidence was undiminished. His ministry seemed likely to provide the country with a much-needed resumption of stable and popular government and win for it the renown, security and prosperity which the Seven Years' War had not yet achieved.

Nevertheless, this ministry, from which so much was expected, suffered from crippling handicaps which doomed it to failure. There was no return to the great days of Pitt's first ministry. At the outset, Pitt decided to accept a peerage as Earl of Chatham and take the post of Lord Privy Seal. There were sound reasons for doing this. The peerage was a public sign of immediate royal confidence in him; his post enabled him, as in his previous government, to lead his ministers and formulate policy without the distraction of considerable administrative duties. Also, there were advantages in his transference to the Lords, since the leaders of the Whig oligarchy sat there, and he would be relieved from the strain of the more exacting attendance required in the Commons. On the other hand, his pride was partly responsible for the decision. The dignity of a peerage attracted him, particularly as an admirer had bequeathed him the estate of Burton Pynsent in Somerset, which he hoped, with his usual financial recklessness, to develop into an outstanding landed property. The new honour, however, lowered severely the reputation of the 'Great Commoner', who so deliberately had avoided any suggestion of corruption in the past. Still more, his disappearance from the Commons destroyed the hold over the independent members and placemen which he had been able to exercise so effectively by his oratory. Choiseul compared him as a peer to Samson without his hair.

This unpopularity and weakness in the Commons might not have lasted if Chatham's ministry had indeed been a stable one, but his attempt to ignore all political groups produced a divided Cabinet described by Burke as 'a diversified piece of mosaic'. The Rockingham group soon relinquished their places. The First Lord of the Treasury was also in the Lords. He was the Duke of Grafton (1735–1811), a devoted supporter of Chatham, but unable to bear the responsibility now placed upon him; he frequently neglected business for racing at Newmarket or love-making in a cottage. The ablest minister was perhaps Charles Townshend (1725–67), Chancellor of the Exchequer and Leader of the Commons, who was a grandson of Walpole's colleague and rival. He had charm and great eloquence; he was nicknamed the 'Weathercock' and was said to be insincere and unprincipled, but his behaviour may rather have been due to a shallowness of mind and an inclination for devising expedients for their own sake. Moreover, Chatham's self-confidence had now degenerated into megalomania. Not only did he scorn the support of a party, but was unable to co-operate with his colleagues. 'Lord Chatham has just shown us what inferior animals we are', sneered Townshend after he had lectured and commanded them at a cabinet meeting. In this way he destroyed all sense of loyalty and cohesion among them. Grafton and Townshend soon acted more like rivals than colleagues, and hope of harmony in the ministry disappeared.

This situation caused Chatham to suffer a complete mental and physical collapse in January 1767. Psychosomatic illness, aggravated by gout and probably Bright's disease, brought him to the verge of insanity. He tried to travel back from Bath to London, but only got as far as Marlborough, where he shut himself up in a room in the Castle Inn and insisted on all the inn's ostlers and potboys wearing his livery of blue and silver. When he reached London in March, he took refuge for days in a darkened room, unable to endure even to see his wife, or sat at an upper window staring out vacantly hour after hour. Between these bouts of profound melancholia, he sought distraction in fantastic building schemes. He planned to add thirty-four bedrooms to his house at Hampstead, but a month later repurchased his previous house at Hayes for almost £6,000 more than he had sold it on inheriting Burton Pynsent. His colleagues could not even see him, and their urgent requests for advice were ignored. The Cabinet's drift towards disintegration was unarrested. The Duke of Bedford, now going blind, resigned office; his followers were still an important group, but Chatham had not gained them, and they went into opposition.

In such circumstances, Townshend was able to defy his colleagues and induce Parliament to accept his American Import Duties Act of 1767, which imposed duties on lead, glass, paper, painters' colours and tea.[1] All these articles were legally importable only from Britain, and the duties were to be collected by British agents in American ports. It was a measure typical of Townshend's ingenuity. He insisted that, since these were 'external taxes', part of the system for regulating trade which the colonists had said they accepted, the American financial contribution should now be secured with ease. He did not live to see his chop-logic fail for he died of a 'putrid fever', probably typhoid, in the early autumn of 1767.

Grafton and the Middlesex Election (1768–9)

In October 1768 Chatham aroused himself sufficiently from his torpor to resign from office, despite the King's opposition. This made little practical difference to the government, but it lost all pretence of being an independent ministry led by a great national statesman trusted by the Crown. Grafton stayed in office, however, impelled by a sense of loyalty to the King and incapable of appreciating how slight in reality was his influence with his colleagues. Moreover, he was too proud to withdraw from the political crisis precipitated by the reappearance of John Wilkes.

Wilkes had no intention of staying abroad, and by now the demands of his French creditors were pressing. He decided to come home and seek to return to public life at the general election of 1768. The political situation seemed to be in his favour. So did the considerable economic distress caused by the disruption of trade with America, a bad harvest and severe winter, high food prices and unemployment. There had been rioting, particularly among the Spitalfields silk weavers, probably the largest single group of skilled workmen in London, whose employment was made irregular by surplus Irish immigrant labour. Wilkes stood first for the City of London, only to be at the bottom of the poll; but when he

[1] P. 171.

went on to stand for the county of Middlesex, his fortune was reversed, and his demagogic appeal brought him to the top of the poll. The result set off nearly two days of celebratory rioting in London and Westminster. Little damage was done, but citizens were forced to light up their windows at night or have them broken, and every door from Temple Bar to Hyde Park was said to be chalked with 'No. 45', despite the efforts of Alexander Cruden, driven mad by the labour of compiling his *Biblical Concordance*, who followed the Wilkesites, muttering and erasing the figures with a wet sponge.

The Cabinet were divided between those who wished to take action against Wilkes and those who wished to temporize; Grafton, much to George III's annoyance, wished to ignore him. Wilkes was able again, therefore, to seize the initiative as he carefully did by complete submission to the law. He surrendered to the courts on the sentence of outlawry imposed on him in 1764. This was quashed on a technicality, but on the original charge of libel he was sentenced to a fine of £1,000 and twenty-two month's imprisonment. There were renewed demonstrations, this time more violent and widespread. Riots were continuous for almost a fortnight and culminated in a clash outside Wilkes's prison in St. George's Fields when troops shot down half a dozen of the mob.

Wilkes was to remain in prison until April 1770, but he was neither idle nor silenced. Eighteenth-century prison conditions allowed him to live in comfortable style, keep an open table and receive leaders of the opposition groups. He wrote a pamphlet accusing the government of responsibility for the 'Massacre of St. George's Fields' and petitioned the Commons, claiming his privileges against further imprisonment; and in January 1769 he was elected an alderman of the City of London. The government could no longer ignore his challenges, and the King was determined to get him out of Parliament. The struggle to do this brought Wilkes his greatest popularity. Between February and April there took place in rapid succession his expulsion from the Commons; his readoption by the Middlesex electors and unopposed return; his further disqualification by the Commons; his third unopposed election and its annulment by the House; and finally his fourth election by Middlesex with a majority of 1,043 votes to 296 over a candidate put up by the ministry, a Colonel Luttrell, whom the Commons accepted as the true member for the constituency.

Far from concluding the matter, however, such action enlarged it into a vital constitutional question. To many people Parliament was revealed by its attitude to be corrupt, unrepresentative and ready to make a spiteful and tyrannous misuse of its power of expulsion to deny electors their free choice of representation. The importance of these issues led the supporters of Wilkes early in 1769 to direct the struggle against the government by the establishment of an organization that brought new methods into politics. With the help of a radical clergyman, John Horne Tooke (1736–1812), they formed the Society of Supporters of the Bill of Rights. Their immediate purpose, while Wilkes was in prison, was to pay his large debts and supply him with wine, salmon, game, tobacco and other luxuries; and they then intended to restore him to Parliament. Their objects also were 'to maintain and defend the legal, constitutional liberty of the subject'. It was characteristic of English political life at the time that they called the society by a name which appealed to the past and expressed their intentions in such general, conservative terms, but their plans were revolutionary, and they proceeded to campaign for an enlarged franchise and shorter parliaments in novel ways. They introduced the practice of issuing instructions to Members of Parliament favourable to their cause. Still more, they employed paid agents to hold public meetings all over the country, get letters and articles printed in the provincial press and organize petitions by freeholders and burghers. Between May 1769 and January 1770 the King received dozens of petitions, containing altogether about 60,000 signatures, about a quarter of the voting population of the country. To their support in London, they added especially strong gains among merchants in Bristol and Liverpool, who feared the economic consequences of the government's American policy. Moreover, the unprecedented attack they launched upon the government marked the real inauguration of Radicalism as a movement with social and political demands, prominent among them being parliamentary reform.

The administration had meanwhile become the butt of the fiercest political satire of the century in the *Letters of Junius*. Seventy in number, these appeared in the *Public Advertiser* between November 1768 and January 1772, though only the later ones actually appeared above the name of Junius. It is generally thought that their author was Sir Philip Francis (1740–1818), then a clerk at the War Office and later to be the relentless enemy of Warren Hastings.[1] Certainly these letters were marked by the same bitter antagonism and fanatical hatred which he displayed against the Governor-General. Ranging himself on the Wilkesite side in the Middlesex election dispute, he castigated the government's inefficiency and disregard of law and took a malign pleasure in holding up the King and his ministers to popular hatred. He warned George III, 'While he plumes himself upon the security of his title to the Crown, [he] should remember that, as it was acquired by one revolution, it may be lost by another'. He told Grafton, 'I do not give you to posterity as a pattern to imitate, but as an example to deter', and asked of his policy, 'Is this the wisdom of a great minister? or is it the ominous vibration of a pendulum?'. And by insisting that 'the right of election is the very essence of the constitution', he did much to persuade his educated readers that the King's ministers actually were threatening the constitution and the liberty of the people.

Together with these attacks, the ministry now had to face an offensive from Chatham, who had recovered sufficiently to return from his seclusion to politics in the summer of 1769. He denounced with vigour its handling of affairs. In January 1770 he opposed in the Lords the address to the Crown with a speech that was among his best. 'What then', he asked, 'are all the generous efforts of our ancestors that instead of the arbitrary power of the King we must submit to the arbitrary power of the House of Commons?' He asserted, 'It contradicts Magna Carta and the Bill of Rights, by which it is provided that no subject shall be deprived of his freehold, unless by the judgement of his peers or the law of the land'. And he concluded, 'Unlimited power is apt to corrupt the minds of those who possess it; and this I know, that where law ends, there tyranny begins'. This challenge finally broke the ministry. Soon afterwards Grafton, wearied of the abuse he had suffered and mistrustful of his fellow-ministers, insisted that the King must accept his resignation.

[1] P. 179.

XVII · LORD NORTH'S ADMINISTRATION
1770–82

The Establishment of the Ministry (1770–4)

AFTER Grafton's fall, George III turned to Frederick, Lord North (1732–92), son of the first Earl of Guilford, one of his boyhood playmates and now a man of considerable political experience. He had served in both the Grenville and Chatham governments and in 1767, on Townshend's death, had become Chancellor of the Exchequer and Leader of the House of Commons, in which dual capacity he had shown himself a skilful financier and an able debater in and manager of the Commons. He had maintained his reputation amid the disintegration of Grafton's administration, and he possessed a personal charm and pleasant wit which overcame the disadvantages of his grotesquely ugly appearance and attracted men to him. Writers have since dealt harshly with him, partly because of the declamations of Burke and Chatham against him and partly because of the part he played in the loss of the American colonies. Yet in happier circumstances his fame might well have been higher. Burke described him as 'a man of admirable parts, of general knowledge, of a versatile understanding, fitted for all sorts of business', but he added that North lacked 'something of the vigilance and spirit of command that the time required'. In fact, North would probably have been a competent peacetime minister, but his misfortune was to hold office during the American Revolution and War.

In 1770, however, all that lay in the unrealized future. Then it seemed natural that George III should appoint him to take over from Grafton the post of First Lord of the Treasury and the leadership of the ministry. Moreover, the King, who had experienced six administrations during the first ten years of his reign, at last had a minister after his own heart, one prepared in the fullest sense to be the King's minister and also able to manage the Commons. During this period George III ruled as well as reigned in a way never true of George II, and his persistance in keeping North in power brought the period of ministerial uncertainty to an end and gave the country twelve years of settled government such as it had not known since the time of Walpole and George II.

It did not take many months for North to establish himself in a strong position. The government majority in the Commons, which had fallen to 40 in January, rose to 163 in March. He had not lost his skill in managing the Commons. Still more, the Crown's patronage was at his disposal, and he possessed the King's confidence. Eventually even this combination was not to keep him in power in face of a national crisis, but at first he seemed unshakeable. He had gained the support of the old Bedford group. Not even a combined opposition could have upset him, and the opposition at this juncture was disunited and diminishing. It had been weakened by the reaction which followed the violent emergence of Radicalism. An important political issue might have stimulated and reunited it, but North was careful to avoid this. Even the American issue seemed to have subsided after the repeal of Townshend's customs duties (with one exception).[1]

The opposition's weakness was shown by the ease with which the Royal Marriage Act of 1772 was passed. The marriage of the royal Dukes of Gloucester and Cumberland to commoners had so angered George III that he insisted on legislation to prevent members of the royal family marrying in future without the sovereign's consent. This might seem a matter of principle, and the vesting by statute of such a right of veto in the Crown provoked criticism in Parliament. 'The doctrine', Chatham said, 'is new-fangled and impudent, and the extent of the powers given wanton and tyrannical.' Charles James Fox resigned from the administration to attack the measure.[2] The efforts of the opposition, however, to accuse the ministry of subservience to the Crown failed, and it was passed without difficulty.

The government also passed two important statutes making provision for the administration of British overseases possessions – the Regulating Act for India of 1773 and the Quebec Act of 1774.[3] The latter was bitterly criticised by groups in in opposition, but it was a realistic and tolerant approach towards a recently-conquered, alien people and gained liberal

---

[1] P. 172.   [2] P. 346.   [3] Pp. 178, 173.

sympathy for the government.   By 1774, indeed, Lord North seemed to have succeeded in securing a broad basis of support for his power; and in the general election of that year the administration's majority was increased.

The last of Wilkes (1770–74)

Nor had the ministry been shaken by another political incident in which Wilkes was intimately involved.   On his emergence from prison in 1770, Wilkes wanted revenge and another contest with the government to uphold his popularity. He chose as an issue the reporting of parliamentary debates. Parliament had long held this to be a preach of privilege, but in the eighteenth century the efforts of newspapers to satisfy the interest of their readers in parliamentary proceedings had led to clashes with reporters.   Wilkes now instigated several printers to publish reports of debates without the customary precaution of disguising the names of the speakers.   The Commons sent a messenger to arrest two of them, but Wilkes, as a London alderman and magistrate, arrested the messenger for violating the City's privileges.   The Commons ordered Wilkes and two other magistrates (who were also Members of Parliament) to appear at the bar of the House.   Wilkes refused, unless he were allowed to take his seat; the others obeyed and were committed to the Tower for the rest of the session.   This was a matter of crucial constitutional importance, since Parliament could hardly claim to represent the people if they were not allowed to read its debates; but the opposition were embarrassed by Wilkes's demagogic connections and could only agree upon a proposal to pay a formal visit to the prisoners in the Tower.

The release of the prisoners was greeted by a great popular demonstration which made their progress from the Tower to the City a triumphal march.   This was another victory for Wilkes.   The Commons formally reaffirmed the publication of debates to be a breach of privilege, but henceforward made no attempt to enforce its order.   These events coincided with another period of food shortage; the London crowd was bitterly hostile to the Commons, and ministers were hissed in the streets, but a common dislike among members of Wilkes and 'Junius' and their ideas assured the government of strong parliamentary support.

When the general election of 1774 came, Wilkes was returned unopposed for Middlesex, and this time no effort was made to exclude him, but he had fought his last great political battle. He was now middle-aged, and once in Parliament his ardour for noisy crusading disappeared. For a few years he spoke in favour of the rights of the American colonies, parliamentary reform and religious toleration, but made no effort to identify the 'inferior set of people' with these causes. Wilkesism disappeared when he commanded the guard which fired into the mob before the Bank of England during the Gordon Riots of 1780.[1] Thereafter he rarely addressed the Commons, and when he retired from Parliament in 1789 described himself as 'an extinct volcano'. The events of the French Revolution left him shocked and uncomprehending. He spent the years that remained, until he died in 1797, enjoying his aldermanic dignity and duties as a magistrate in the course of which he sought to moderate the punishment of apprentices and maidservants by their employers.[2]

Although its founder was an almost forgotten figure at his death, the Wilkesite movement played a very important part in British political history. It gained notable victories for political liberties – the end of general warrants, the right of parliamentary voters to elect whom they chose and the freedom of the press to publish parliamentary proceedings. In addition, it contributed to the development of Radicalism as a national movement. George Rudé's recent researches into the composition of the Wilkesite mobs have shown that they did not consist merely of labourers and journeymen, but included also numerous small tradesmen, shopkeepers and householders, who were also, as the majority of the freemen of Middlesex, the voters who insisted on returning Wilkes to Parliament; and those in the provinces who signed the petitions organized by the Society of Supporters of the Bill of Rights in 1769 were usually of a rather higher class. It was a new achievement to unite these classes in a political movement. Though the violence of the Gordon Riots scared middle-class Radicals away from further approaches to the lower classes throughout the 1780's, the outbreak of the French Revolution stimulated a revival Radical movement which found new and wider support in the growing industrial towns of the North and Midlands.[1]

The American War of Independence (1775–83)

The quiet years from 1771 to 1774 had enabled North's administration to settle down and offered the opposition few questions upon which it could receive independent support, but this period of comparative political calm was now to be broken by events in America which were beginning to move towards armed colonial resistance. Though the outbreak of war did not immediately affect the government's position at all seriously nor seem likely to have much effect upon the development of the political groups, the course of hostilities made a great impact on British domestic politics and produced a dramatic change in the operation of the eighteenth-century constitution.

The renewal of serious trouble in America was itself largely unexpected. North's almost complete abandonment of Townshend's duties had produced a lull in the American controversy. The Boston Massacre and the *Gaspée* affair were ugly acts of violence, but they could be regarded as isolated incidents. The period of quiescence was brought to an abrupt end, however, by the Boston Tea Party late in 1773 and the administration's retaliatory 'Intolerable Acts' the next year.[2] This time there was to be no retreat in Parliament as had occurred previously in the face of American resistance to the Stamp Act and Townshend's customs. The government was now determined to stand firm. This was partly because, as an American historian has recently shown, the ministers got most of their information about American affairs from the governors, judges, tax-collectors and other royal officials in the colonies who were prime objects of American hostility and naturally urged vigorous action against all manifestations of colonial insubordination. Moreover, loyalists were in the large majority among the colonists even after the fighting actually began;[3] and the government's attitude was also due to a not unwarranted feeling that the extreme minority in the colonies took advantage of every concession made by Britain and must sooner or later be faced by a show of severity. George III approved of North's

[1] P. 373.   [2] P. 173.   [3] P. 170.

policy. 'The die is now cast', he wrote to him in the autumn of 1773; 'the colonies must either submit or triumph. We must either master them or totally leave them to themselves and treat them as aliens.'

George III has, indeed, been widely accused of personal responsibility for the outbreak of the American War of Independence. Historians have tended to accept this view, based on the arguments of contemporary opponents of the King, that the American colonists were provoked into rebellion because they were the first to suffer from his determination to rule absolutely and destroy political freedom throughout his dominions. Sir George Otto Trevelyan, for instance, described their rising as 'a defensive movement, undertaken on behalf of essential English institutions (genuine national self-government and real ministerial responsibility) against the purpose and effort of a monarch to defeat the political progress of the race', and he went on to argue that their victory in war prevented the King from making a similar attempt in Britain. It is not accepted nowadays, however, that George III wished to upset the constitution and govern as an unparliamentary monarch.[1] Moreover, if he had really set out to do this, the American colonies would have been his obvious allies for they were largely beyond parliamentary control and wished to remain so. In fact, he persistently and obstinately advocated the cause of the full sovereignty of Parliament over his entire overseas empire. If he contributed to the loss of America, it was because he consistently maintained this attitude towards the question throughout the period from 1760 to 1783 and supported the efforts of his ministers to assert their authority over the colonies.

In the course of the American War of Independence, George III perhaps showed himself more stubborn than most of his people in his insistence that the colonies must submit before any fresh attempt could be made towards reconciliation. Nevertheless, there is no doubt that when hostilities began, his outlook was general both in Parliament and the country at large. In the autumn of 1775, when fighting had already taken place at Lexington and Bunker Hill, Rockingham wrote to Burke, 'The violent measures towards America are fairly adopted and countenanced by a majority

[1] Pp. 315–18.

of all individuals of all ranks, professions or occupations in this country'. The idea of war had appalled many but, when it came, there was a general outburst of patriotic feeling in its favour. Most people agreed that the time had come to compel the Americans to accept the British government's authority. The country gentry, the universities and the clergy were especially ardent, while the Dissenters were powerfully influenced by Wesley's anti-American attitude. Adam Smith and Gibbon agreed that Parliament's legal supremacy must be asserted. Even the trading classes, who had previously urged conciliation, now thought there could be no security for commerce until the colonies were delivered from the danger of anarchy. Burke's constituency of Bristol gave its freedom to the Cabinet ministers.

Indeed, given the outlook of the time, war between Britain and America was almost inevitable. The idea of rebellion and independence in the colonies outraged King, politicians and people in Britain. To them the Americans were merely rebels who must be subdued and punished. Hardly anyone realized that the situation had now gone beyond this. The extremists in America had come to aim at complete independence from Britain, and they were assisted by the publication of Tom Paine's *Common Sense*.[1] By setting aside all the legal and historical arguments hitherto used and by depicting emotionally the controversy as a struggle for freedom and independence against the tyrannical George III, he stimulated a spirit of idealism and converted many moderates to the idea that reconciliation was no longer desirable. So far the colonists had claimed the 'rights of Englishmen' against Parliament's encroachments, but when Thomas Jefferson drafted the Declaration of Independence he asserted their 'natural rights' against the repressive British monarchy. The American leaders now regarded themselves as champions of an independent nation, but few in Britain, from the King downwards, recognized what a difference this appeal to a new sense of nationality made to the situation.

The early days of the conflict brought little to sustain the parliamentary opposition. The Rockingham group of Whigs persistently opposed the passage through both Houses of the 'Intolerable Acts', and Chatham made a rare visit to the

[1] P. 174.

Lords to protest against the severity of the measures against Boston. They were sympathetic towards the colonists because they disliked George III and North and because of their own part in the repeal of the Stamp Act; but while the Rockingham Whigs believed in Britain's right of taxation but thought it might be inexpedient to use it, Chatham and his friends distinguished between the right of Parliament to legislate for the colonies – which they admitted – and its right to tax – which they denied. Both groups believed, however, in contradiction to the expectation of the ministry and of most people that colonial resistance would speedily collapse once Britain resorted to force, that the conquest of America was impossible from the start and the attempt would end in disaster. 'The generality of the nation are aiding and assisting in their own destruction', said Rockingham in 1775; 'and I conceive that nothing but a degree of experience of the evils can bring about a right judgement in the public at large.' Chatham, Burke and Fox all argued that it would be wise not to insist on rights which could not be enforced. Historians have lauded them for the accuracy of their gloomy prognostications, but to contemporaries their attitude seemed completely negative and unacceptable.

The opposition politicians at least saw that the dilemma facing Britain over the American question was one of conquest or conciliation; but they were no more cognizant of the true nature of the American situation than most other people in Britain. They still thought of the colonists as Englishmen struggling to maintain their historic liberties. 'An Englishman is the unfittest person on earth to argue another Englishman into slavery', said Burke. He wished to undo all the mischief occasioned by the legalistic dispute over taxation and parliamentary rights and return to the previous relationship of unsuspecting confidence between the mother country and the colonies.[1] He typically based his arguments on expediency and not principle. 'My hold of the colonies', he declared, 'is in the close affection which grows from common names, from kindred blood, from similar privileges and equal protection. These are ties, which, though light as air, are as strong as links of iron.' But two are needed for conciliation. He did not realize that such a situation was now impossible.

[1] P. 96.

The repeal of the controversial legislation would not have bound the American colonies closer to Britain, but rather have enabled them to gain that virtual independence which they now wanted. British public opinion would not have been satisfied with a mere nominal sovereignty over the colonies, and nor would Burke, who believed that Britain could retain commercial control over them.

Similarly, Chatham continued to sympathize with American views and express himself as exuberantly as ever, declaring in 1777, 'If I were an American, as I am an Englishman, while a foreign troop was landed in my country, I would never lay down my arms – never – never – never!'. He had suggested in 1775 that the newly-established Continental Congress should be accorded taxing and legislative powers in America, but only on condition that it explicitly acknowledged Parliament's supremacy. Had he been in control he would sooner or later have had to fight the Americans. He was for conciliation, not surrender, and when Rockingham's friend, the Duke of Richmond, proposed in April 1778 a motion in the Lords for granting American independence, he performed the last great dramatic and theatrical act of his life as, gaunt and leaning on crutches, he struggled to attend the debate, collapsed while speaking and died a month later.

By then the government's prestige was gravely weakened, but it was not the opposition's arguments which brought it low. 'The opposition seem to have lost all spirit', wrote Horace Walpole in January 1776. Later that year Rockingham decided to desist from parliamentary activity, and the next year Burke agreed with him. Gradually, however, the succession of bad news which came from America during the fighting seasons of 1775, 1776 and 1777 had their effect at home.[1] The conditions of this far-distant war made direction by the Cabinet extremely difficult. The commanders on the spot had to be given considerable latitude, and the War was lost in the American wilderness and not in Whitehall, but failure to gain the expected rapid victory eroded inexorably the government's support. The politicians began to desert North, and, more serious, the independents also were losing confidence in him. And not only did the disastrous

[1] Pp. 173–4.

Y

outcome of the American contest add to the opposition's numbers. It also gave them the chance of overthrowing the government, and they possessed two men able to take advantage of the situation.

Burke and Fox

By the end of 1777, when news of Burgoyne's surrender at Saratoga reached England and made the country first realize seriously the possibility of defeat, one of the government's most formidable parliamentary opponents was Edmund Burke (1748-97), the son of an Irish attorney and from 1759 the editor of the *Annual Register*, which he made influential as an impartial survey of contemporary events. His rising reputation had brought him foundation membership of Dr. Johnson's Literary Club and also the acquaintance of Rockingham, who made him his private secretary, when he became First Lord of the Treasury in 1765, and got him into Parliament as a member for the pocket borough of Wendover. Burke soon distinguished himself in the Commons despite the dual handicap of lacking English birth and private means. Red-headed and nearly six feet tall, he was an impressive figure, but was never a good speaker. He soon, however, became a skilful debater, particularly as his journalistic work gave him (in an observer's words) 'a comprehensive knowledge in all our exterior and interior politics and commercial interests'. He was the chief spokesman of his group in the Commons, particularly during the years in opposition after the short-lived Rockingham ministry.

His most important achievement during this time, however, was the publication in 1770 of his *Some Thoughts on the Cause of the Present Discontents*, one of the most influential political pamphlets ever written. It appeared in the midst of the tumult about Wilkes and the publication of parliamentary debates. There was, as Christopher Hobhouse pointed out, much of the mystic in Burke; when he took up a cause, he did so with passionate devotion. His political studies had convinced him of the excellence of the British constitution.[1] He had been attracted to the Rockingham Whigs because of the claim by the group of great landowners who led it to be the upholders of the principles of 1688 and to be above all

[1] P. 39.

political corruption; and now he was alarmed by the conflict between Parliament and public opinion aroused by Wilkes, which had deprived 'rank and office and title and all the solemn plausibilities of the world' of their reverence and effect. He found George III's intervention in politics to be the reason for this loss of confidence. The country was discontented because they suspected that the Crown was seeking to regain its former powers by using its vast patronage to form a group of King's Friends whom it could control as ministers for its own ends – 'The power of the Crown, almost dead and rotten as prerogative, has grown up anew, with much more strength and far less odium, under the name of influence.' Burke's solution was to uphold the idea of 'party' which the King's Friends had denigrated.[1] They, Burke insisted, were really a faction, motivated merely by personal connections and interests: but to be stable a ministry must rest on public opinion and act for the public good, and it could only do this if its members were drawn from a party, which he defined as 'a body of men united for promoting by their joint efforts the national interest upon some principle in which they are all agreed'. Burke further claimed that the Rockingham Whigs, being such a party, alone could restore to British politics its lost confidence and harmony, and because George III had denied them his support in 1766, he had wrongly tried to rule 'without party' and affronted public opinion

Burke's interpretation in this pamphlet of George III's part in contemporary politics is not now accepted as accurate by historians, who see it rather as a piece of political propaganda designed to assist the Rockingham Whigs.[2] They needed the active support of a party. In the absence of a young heir to the throne around which an opposition could rally, they had to justify their resistance to a ministry in a new way. So Burke gave them a cause, and he also gave them strength since, in D. A. Winstanley's words, 'without the organization which the party system alone could give, the unreformed House of Commons lay at the mercy of the occupant of the throne'. Burke also did more than this. He laid the foundation for the Whig interpretation of the political developments of this period which was long to be the traditional view accepted by historians.[3]

[1] P. 327.   [2] P. 316.   [3] P. 315.

When *Some Thoughts on the Cause of the Present Discontents*
appeared, the opposition's prospects were not bright.   Burke
gained a personal victory in the general election of 1774.
Forced to find a new seat, he contested Bristol, traditionally
Tory but now hard-hit by the American ban on British trade;
he was elected on a pledge to protect British commerce and
reconcile British constitutional rights with the American
demand for liberty.   He returned to a Parliament, however,
in which the government was strengthened, the opposition were
despondent, and his own speeches on the American question
made no impression.   It was important, therefore, that at
this juncture he received the powerful support of a new ally.

This was Charles James Fox (1749-1806), second son of the
first Lord Holland.[1]   At an early age he was distinguished
for his ability, but his father indulged him, encouraging him
while he was still at Eton and Oxford to spend his vacations in
dissipation in London and Paris.   As a young man, he was
notorious for his reckless gambling and expensive diversions,
but at the age of nineteen his father got him into Parliament
as a member for Midhurst, and he made an instant mark.   He
was not a graceful orator.   He spoke too quickly and did not
arrange his matter carefully, but his vehemence and facility
of argument, his idealism and sympathetic manner, held the
attention of the House, while his capacity for charm and
affability, which the Younger Pitt called 'the wand of the
magician', won him many friends.   Not yet apparent were
the serious absence of application and reckless lack of judgement, due to an indiscipline fundamental to his nature and
encouraged by the defects of his upbringing, which were to prevent such a man of enduring vitality and dazzling talents from
exercising a greater influence on the political history of his time.

His father's dislike of Chatham was largely responsible for
making Fox a supporter of North when he entered Parliament
in 1768.   He first gained attention by his anti-Wilkesite
speeches.   Anxious to bind such a formidable speaker to the
administration, North made him a Junior Lord of the
Admiralty when he was barely twenty-one.   It was characteristic of him that his attendance at the Board of Admiralty
was irregular and that he resigned his office in order to lead
an attack on the Royal Marriage Act of 1772, thereby

[1] Pp. 285, 293-4, 320.

incurring the enmity of George III, who already detested him for his dissolute life. He was, however, still too valuable to be lost to the opposition, and before the end of the year North had made him a Lord of the Treasury, but his tenure of this post was again short. In 1774 a quarrel with North over a personal matter led him to vote against the government until one morning a door-keeper of the Commons handed him the the famous note: 'Mr. Fox, His Majesty has thought proper to order a new Commission of the Treasury to be made out, in which I do not see your name. North.'

Fox, therefore, broke finally with North just when the American question was again becoming serious. Soon he associated himself with the Rockingham Whigs and spoke against the government's policy in North America. To Burke's monumental, literary speeches, he added his own magically persuasive fluency. He spoke mainly about the impossibility of defeating the colonists and the incompetence of the ministers in conducting hostilities; he accused the King of obstinately prolonging the War and urged it should be ended at once by granting independence to the colonies; and he also insisted that the Americans were in reality defending the liberty of the British people as well as their own rights, and sought to associate the Whig party with this view. In 1776 and 1777, when Rockingham and Burke desisted from opposition, Fox continued to attack the government and added greatly to his reputation.

By then Fox had come to be recognized as one of the leading opponents of the government. He had also done much to make it seem that the cause of the colonists transformed the opposition from a mere politically-ambitious faction into men with a genuine principle to uphold, particularly as (with no justification in fact) he insisted that the government depended for its majority upon the Crown's corrupt influence. Nevertheless, success did not come easily to the opposition. During the following years, they exploited the worsening situation in America, but the government remained in power until after the military catastrophe of Yorktown.

The End of the Ministry (1778–82)

The news of the capitulation at Saratoga unnerved Lord North. His will became increasingly paralysed, and his control of the Cabinet virtually disappeared. Early in 1778 he asked the King to allow him to resign, saying, 'Capital punishment itself is, in Lord North's opinion, preferable to that constant anguish of mind which he feels from the consideration that his continuance in office is ruining His Majesty's affairs'; but George III believed that his resignation would generally be taken as a sign of weakness in prosecuting the War which he was still determined should be continued vigorously. So North remained in office during the following months which brought the entry of France and Spain into the War and the formation of the League of Armed Neutrality.[1]

Events in Ireland added to the government's difficulties.[2] The Rockingham Whigs exploited Irish difficulties. Burke received the freedom of Londonderry; Fox even incited the the Irish Volunteers to take up 'arms in order to obtain deliverance'. It was partly to break this alliance between the Irish patriots and the parliamentary opposition that North introduced the measures abolishing in 1779 many of the restrictions on Irish commerce. These concessions brought only temporary satisfaction in Ireland, but they afforded the government a lull in which it could face the activities of a fresh movement for Radical reform in England.

Parliament's maladroit handling of the trouble over Wilkes and the administration's failure to achieve success in America had produced growing dissatisfaction and criticism of the way the country was governed. In 1776, the year of the American Declaration of Independence, four publications appeared which epitomized the outlook of the various reformers of this time. Adam Smith's *Wealth of Nations* represented the views of economists who believed that mercantilism was ruining the country's prosperity.[3] Jeremy Bentham, then only twenty-eight, in his first published work, the *Fragment on Government*, criticized Blackstone's eulogistic view of the British constitution and advocated changes in it such as were wanted by Radical thinkers, who were already adopting the ideas of utilitarianism.[4] Richard Price, an Independent preacher, expressed in his *Observations on Civil Liberty* the desire of Dissenters, educated in their academies, for a form of government in which all would enjoy equal

[1] Pp. 174, 187.   [2] P. 216.
[3] Pp. 159–60.   [4] P. 97.

political rights.   And, finally, John Cartwright, a major of the militia, published a pamphlet, *Take Your Choice*, advocating for the first time in England such future Radical and Chartist demands as annual parliaments, voting by ballot and manhood suffrage, which he sought to secure by organizing in 1780 a Society for Promoting Constitutional Information.

To these publications were added the effect of speeches and writings by opposition politicians and journalists accusing the government of incompetence and corruption.   Many country gentlemen, already dismayed by the continual disasters in America and the mounting National Debt which now stood at over £167,000,000, were becoming aware of such ideas. They were stirred into action in Yorkshire by Christopher Wyvill (1740–1822), an energetic clergyman who owned considerable property in the county.   Late in 1779 he arranged a mass-meeting of freeholders at York who were induced to form a representative Yorkshire Association to organize a petition against high taxation and government extravagance and 'to support that laudable reform . . . as may conduce to restore the freedom of Parliament'.   This was the beginning of the petitioning movement.   County associations were formed in several parts of the country to get further petitions organized.   By March 1780 these had sent representatives to a central committee in London, under Wyvil's chairmanship, which demanded strict economy, a hundred more county members in the Commons (as they were thought to be the most independent) and annual parliaments.

The organization of this movement owed much to the earlier Wilkesite campaign, but now for the first time the high taxation and national uncertainty and humiliation of the political situation drove the country gentlemen to join the protest.   To be really dangerous to the government, however, it needed leadership from the parliamentary opposition. Lord Shelburne, the Chathamites' new leader, welcomed it.[1] Fox, too, with typical opportunism rushed wholeheartedly to its support.   While he had said disdainfully in 1771, 'I pay no regard whatever to the voice of the people', now he declared that, 'when the representative body did speak the sense of the constituent, the voice of the latter was constitutional and conclusive'.   He exchanged his red-heeled

[1] Pp. 354–5.

shoes, blue hair-powder and dandified clothes for the plain blue coat and buff waistcoast associated with Washington's army.   To the King's further disgust, he took the chair at Radical meetings in Westminster and avowed himself in favour of annual parliaments and a reform of the franchise. At first it seemed as if the rest of the opposition would join with them and at last achieve unity, but soon the Rockingham Whigs backed away.   Radical proposals to reduce the landed gentry's borough influence and make the representative system more democratic alarmed them.   For them, reform meant a limitation of the Crown's influence which would leave Parliament firmly under aristocratic control.

Burke's own plan – 'economical reform' – was designed to satisfy Radical aspirations, meet the widespread public dislike of the expenses of the War and wrest for the parliamentary opposition the control of patronage from North and the King. By representing this as a vital attack on corruption and administrative inefficiency, he hoped to reduce the Crown's numerous perquisites without making concession to the popular agitation for parliamentary reform.   In February 1780 he introduced a bill proposing the suppression of many useless offices, the sale of most of the Crown lands, a reform of the pension list and various government departments and the abolition of the ancient separate jurisdictions of Wales, Lancaster, Chester and Cornwall.

It did not, however, succeed in bringing down North.   The cry of 'economy' attracted the country members, but they were not prepared to upset the balance of the constitution, and North managed to defeat Burke's proposals one by one in committee; only the motion to abolish the Board of Trade was carried against the government.   The turn of events was the same in April when John Dunning proposed his famous (though hardly accurate) motion 'that the influence of the Crown has increased, is increasing and ought to be diminished'.   It was carried by 233 votes to 215 because members wished to protest against the inefficiency of the King's ministry, but they did not really want to replace North by some leader of the opposition who might sympathize with the petitioning movement's revolutionary ideas.   North had no difficulty in reasserting his authority in the Commons.

By the early summer of 1780 the reform movement was

declining, and this was completed by the outbreak of the
Gordon Riots. Influenced largely by the need to obtain
more men for the army, the government had carried in 1778,
with the support of the Rockingham Whigs, a Roman Catholic
Relief Act which abolished all religious oaths required from
recruits in favour of a simple oath of allegiance to the Crown.
A Protestant Association was formed under the presidency
of the eccentric Lord George Gordon (1751–93) to demand
its repeal. In June 1780, accompanied by a crowd some
60,000 strong, he presented a petition to Parliament against
the measure. In the evening, rioting broke out and continued for six days. Roman Catholic chapels and dwelling
houses, breweries and distilleries were sacked. Newgate and
other prisons were attacked and the prisoners freed. The
parish constables were helpless and the authorities afraid to
act. Eventually George III himself insisted that troops must
be called in. An assault on the Bank of England was repulsed
and the rioting suppressed. Perhaps about 500 people lost
their lives in the disturbances, and rather more than 100
private buildings were destroyed. Twenty-five rioters were
later hanged, but Gordon himself was found not guilty of
high treason.

There is no evidence that either Gordon or the Protestant
Association deliberately planned the outbreak of the riots.
Rather they unintentionally set off the uncontrollable readiness to resort to public violence so common during this
period.[1] Nevertheless, 'No Popery' feeling, stimulated by
the entry of France and Spain into the War and mistrust of
the government, played an important part in the course of
events. Most of the houses attacked belonged to Roman
Catholics or magistrates and others suspected of sympathizing
with them. At the same time, there seems to have been a
strong element of social protest as well. The violence against
Roman Catholics was not indiscriminate. The main sufferers
were not poor, immigrant Irishmen, but persons of some
substance. As George Rudé has pointed out, most of the
rioters tried were hitherto respectable working-men – journeymen and apprentices, servants and small tradesmen – who
were influenced by 'a groping desire to settle accounts with
the rich, if only for a day'.

[1] Pp. 11–12.

The immediate effect of the Gordon Riots was to cripple the reform movement and drive the Whigs further away from the Radicals. The country gentlemen renewed their support of the government, which was further strengthened by the news of British successes in Georgia and South Carolina.[1] North was induced to hold a general election in the early autumn of 1780, which seemed to promise him a new lease of power. The riots were also destined to have more lasting results. Opposition politicians lost their readiness to use the London mob against a government, and the governing classes acquired a horror of popular violence, and a suspicion of reform movements, which was to influence Parliament's attitude towards domestic discontent during the time of the French Revolution and afterwards.

The improvement in North's position lasted for just over a year. Victory in America still seemed possible, and he attempted a calm and even self-assured attitude both towards the King and in public. The situation was transformed, however, in November 1781 when news came of the surrender of Cornwallis at Yorktown. A member of the Cabinet was asked how North took the news. 'As he would have taken a cannon-ball in his breast', was the reply. 'He opened his arms, exclaiming wildly, as he paced up and down the room, "O God, it is all over!".' It was indeed the end. Although Washington's army could launch no further offensive, and Britain still possessed New York, Charleston, Savannah and other strong-points and rapidly regained control of the sea, French, Spanish and Dutch hostility frustrated the possibility of further attempts to coerce America. Britain could no longer direct her efforts towards the reconquest of the mainland colonies, but had to concentrate on meeting the French efforts to recapture the West Indies and India and the Spanish and French siege of Gibraltar and on raiding convoys, in the hope of bringing the War to as favourable a conclusion as possible.

North saw that he would have to go. He fell again into despondency and inactivity. He asked George III to accept his resignation. The King obstinately tried to avoid defeat, but confidence in North's foreign policy had gone, and the country gentry were deserting him. The opposition pressed

[1] P. 174.

him hard. Their numerous votes of censure and resolutions in favour of peace were defeated by increasingly small majorities. Only in March 1781, however, when the government survived a vote of censure by a mere 10 votes and a group of country gentlemen asserted their resolve to withdraw their support completely from the government, did George reluctantly agree to North's resignation. 'At last the fatal day has come', the King wrote to him, 'which the misfortunes of the times and the sudden change of sentiments of the House of Commons have drove me to.' North announced his resignation to a House which had assembled expecting a long debate, and all the members had to wait for their carriages on a cold, snowy evening except North who had not dismissed his coachman. 'Gentlemen', he said smilingly, as he drove off, 'you see the advantage of being in the secret.' He did not expect ever to be back in office.

XVIII · THE YOUNGER PITT AND NATIONAL RECONSTRUCTION, 1782–93

Renewed Uncertainties (*1782–84*)

WHEN North's resignation could no longer be avoided, George III asked the Lord Chancellor, Lord Thurlow (1731–1806), to negotiate the formation of a new ministry. The great Whig families, who had been in opposition so long, had preserved their unity and were resolved to use that unity to return to power. Thurlow reported that only 'Lord Rockingham and Lord Shelburne with their parties' were able and willing to undertake an administration, and the King unwillingly had to accept this surrender to party government. Rockingham became First Lord of the Treasury, while Burke was Paymaster to the Forces, a post which did not bring him membership of the Cabinet. The two Secretaryships were now renamed.[1] Shelburne became Home Secretary, and Fox Foreign Secretary. Shelburne would have liked William Pitt (1759–1806), Chatham's younger son, to be included in the ministry, but he was considered too young for an important post, and he would not accept 'a subordinate situation'.

The new ministry contained several men whom George III disliked. Rockingham's recent activities in opposition had not improved the King's estimate of him, and Burke shared this mistrust, while Fox's attacks in debate on the Crown's influence and encouragement of the Prince of Wales into dissolute ways through his growing friendship with him, had aroused further royal anger. The man most acceptable to George III, apart from Thurlow, who by remaining Lord Chancellor was his only friend to remain in office, was the Earl of Shelburne (1737–1805), one of the most enigmatic eighteenth-century politicians. His political career had begun in unfortunate circumstances. He had been employed in 1760, while a newly-elected member for the family borough of High Wycombe (and less than a year before succeeding

---

[1] P. 53.

his father in the earldom), as an intermediary between Lord Bute and Henry Fox in the negotiations then being made to gather a party to support Bute.   Since neither Bute nor Fox trusted or behaved openly towards the other, Shelburne gained an unmerited reputation for deceit, and his later connection with Bute opened him to damaging, though false, accusations of support for royal power and disloyalty to the principles of the Glorious Revolution.   This start and his appointment as a Secretary of State in Chatham's second administration prevented him gaining co-operation from the Rockingham group in common opposition to North's ministry. Moreover, Shelburne's own character told against him in political circles.   He was talented and industrious, witty and cultured; he maintained a staff of clerks at his princely houses – Bowood and Lansdowne House, Berkeley Square – who kept him better informed about diplomatic and financial matters than any minister in power.   Also he patronized the leading thinkers of the time, particularly Richard Price, Joseph Priestley and Jeremy Bentham, who turned his mind to ideas of parliamentary reform.   Yet he had no gifts of leadership and failed in his personal relations with others in politics.   George III called him the 'Jesuit of Berkeley Square', and the newspapers nicknamed him 'Malagrida'. As a follower of Chatham, however, he shared some of his old leader's respect for the monarchy, which won him the King's favourable regard, but only increased the mistrust of others for him.

With so many men whom he disliked in office, George III only regarded the ministry as temporary, and this, indeed, seemed likely.   Besides royal hostility, it suffered from disunity.   In particular, Shelburne and Fox intrigued against each other, especially over negotiating a treaty to end the American War.   Their temperamental differences soon led to mutual mistrust and hostility.   Unable to agree whether America was still a colony or had become a foreign country, both insisted that peace negotiations concerned their own office.

Nevertheless, the ministry succeeded in undertaking some reforms.   The Rockingham Whigs wished to apply to Ireland the policy of conciliation which they believed would have succeeded in America; and Parliament was persuaded to

repeal Poynings' Act and the Declaratory Act.[1]   Burke's Act
of 1783 made possible improvements in military administration.[2]   And Burke was able to take some steps towards
reducing the Crown's influence and putting into effect some
of his ideas of economical reform, though the strong opposition he aroused made the measures less comprehensive than
he would have wished.   Government contractors were forbidden to sit in Parliament, some thousands of revenue officers
and excise men were disfranchised, more than forty valuable
offices in the King's gift were abolished, and the pension list
and secret service money were reduced.   The diminution of
the Crown's patronage in sinecures and places and its pressure
on those in its service or holding government contracts affected
considerably the court's political influence, but the reduction
of the pension list and civil-servant money was not so effective.
Burke was wrong in supposing that large sums had gone in
corruption from these sources.[3]   His actions were those of a
political theorizer rather than a practical administrator.
Patronage could only really be checked by a regular examination of the working of such public offices as was undertaken
by the Younger Pitt.   Nevertheless, Burke's measures were
an advance towards securing parliamentary control over
public finance.

Like the Elder Pitt in 1746, Burke wished, while he was
Paymaster, to demonstrate his own incorruptibility; he
secured measures to regulate the Paymaster's salary and prevent him putting balances in the Pay Office to his own use.
Yet, at the same time as he was seeking to put his ideas of
economical reform into practice, Burke was also obtaining
sinecures for his family and friends.   Other supporters of the
government did the same.   Even Dunning, the author of the
famous resolution of April 1780 calling for the reduction of
the Crown's influence, secured the remunerative Chancellorship of the Duchy of Lancaster, which the Whigs had originally proposed to abolish.   They did not want to abolish the
system of patronage, which they considered politically
necessary, but to prevent it from acting as a means of royal
power.

The Rockingham ministry lasted barely three months.
Rockingham, whose health had never been robust, died from

---

[1] Pp. 206, 215, 217.   [2] P. 202.   [3] P. 58.

influenza in July 1782. The King appointed Shelburne as First Lord of the Treasury. Fox, Burke and several others immediately resigned their posts. Shelburne's position was weak since his own supporters in the Commons were fewer than those of Fox and North combined. He hoped, however, for the support of many of the independent members, and he secured an able spokesman in the Commons by persuading Pitt to become Chancellor of the Exchequer.

Shelburne also hoped to gain public support by a por-gramme of administrative reform. His ideas were not the same as those of Burke and his Rockingham allies. He had been particularly influenced in this matter by Joseph Priestley, who, as John Norris has pointed out, 'made Shelburne a utilitarian', a believer in the idea (later associated with Jeremy Bentham) that the value of all institutions must be measured by their utility. So, while Burke's 'economical reform' meant almost entirely limiting a largely-imaginary bugbear, 'the influence of the Crown', Shelburne's conception of reform was primarily aimed at obtaining administrative efficiency and preserving the national resources. During his short period in office, he began to tackle these problems by reforming the civil list, reducing fees, redistributing offices, overhauling methods of accounting and simplifying taxation. Pitt's later achievements along these lines owed much (without acknowledgement) to his pioneering work.

Shelburne's reforms were the more remarkable since he was at the same time himself directing the final negotiations for peace. He needed a settlement acceptable to most of Parliament and the country. Fortunately, the last part of the War had brought British successes. Gibraltar had withstood a siege by combined Spanish and French forces from 1779 to 1783. The French fleet had been contained in the Indian Ocean. Rodney's victory over De Grasse at the Battle of the Saints in 1782 had thwarted the French naval threat to the West Indies and re-established British control of the Atlantic. Shelburne was able, therefore, to secure terms which made the Treaty of Versailles in 1783 more favourable to Britain than had once seemed likely.[1]

Apart from the failure to obtain alleviation of the sufferings of the Loyalists in America, the terms of the Treaty provided

[1] P. 174.

the opposition with few plausible reasons for criticism; but while the Preliminaries were still being debated in Parliament, Fox and North made an alliance to drive Shelburne from power. They could not win the confidence of most of the independent country gentry, but most of the courtiers, place-men, government contractors and serving officers, who feared Shelburne's attack on the patronage system, voted against the ministry. After defeats in the Commons, Shelburne insisted on resigning in February 1783. Although he was only forty-five, he disappeared from public life. His brief attempts at reform had made him mistrusted by the King, the Whigs and the country gentlemen. He continued, however, to gather advanced thinkers around him at Bowood, and encouraged the development of the new ideas which were to be increasingly important in the politics of the next century and were to overthrow the patronage system which had defeated him.

After Shelburne went, George III had no alternative but to accept a Whig coalition ministry. Its nominal leader was the Duke of Portland with North as Home Secretary and Fox as Foreign Secretary. George was furious. To him the manœuvre of Fox and North was 'the most daring and unprincipled act that the annals of this kingdom ever pro-duced'. George's anger was particularly intense against Fox, who believed that he had succeeded in depriving the Crown of its voice in the selection of ministers and excluding it from politics. Fox even boasted that he had effected 'a complete change in the constitution'. This, however, was an impossibly unreal belief, contrary to generally accepted political conceptions and unacceptable to all but extreme Foxites. It did a great deal to undermine Fox's reputation in the country.

Even more damaging to Fox was his alliance with North, which lost him the confidence of many independent members in the Commons. To them he seemed no longer a man of principle but rather a mere political self-seeker. Now that he was in power he appeared to be countenancing the very things for which he had vehemently attacked the previous administration right up to the time of its fall. The ratifica-tion of the Treaty of Versailles in March on the same terms as Shelburne had obtained, though probably inevitable, added to his unpopularity. The ministry might yet have survived if Fox had been content with quiet uncontroversial government and set out to placate the most important groups in Parliament and the City, but instead he embarked upon legislation on a contentious matter in a way which suggested an obvious political manœuvre.

Burke had by now turned his attention to India, and he persuaded Fox to attempt the reform of British rule in the sub-continent. Chronic problems had been created by the division of authority between the East India Company and the British government by Lord North's Regulating Act of 1773.[1] An India Bill was introduced in December 1783, which had been drafted by Burke and was described by Fox as 'vigorous and hazardous'. It proposed that the entire management of the Company's territory and all the appointments that went with it should be handed over to seven commissioners, appointed in the first instance by the government for four years and subsequently by the shareholders. These proposals alienated the City and the returned 'nabobs', but the greatest outcry came with the publication of the names of the new commissioners, who were revealed as four Foxites and three supporters of North, including his own son. No one had been more outspoken than Fox between 1780 and 1782 in denouncing the use of patronage for political purposes, yet now it seemed to the opposition that he was making arrangements to ensure that within the four years at their disposal the commissioners would be able to secure such a monopoly of Indian patronage for the Foxites that the shareholders would not dare to oppose them.

This outcry presented George III with his opportunity. He had already weakened the coalition by refusing to create peerages while it was in office. Now he might destroy it. The Commons passed the India Bill, but before it reached the Lords the King let it be known, by means of a note written by Thurlow and handed to Temple, that 'whoever voted for the India Bill was not only not his friend, but would be considered by him as an enemy'. The Lords defeated the Bill. The ministers were immediately dismissed by the King.

George III had taken the step of bringing the last of these short-lived coalitions to such an abrupt end because he believed

[1] Pp. 178–80.

z

he had a new minister and administration to hand.   Pitt was
prepared to take office, and his prospects of support seemed
good.   Less than a week before Christmas he was appointed
First Lord of the Treasury.

The Younger Pitt's Accession to Power

William Pitt was born in 1759, the 'Year of Victories' when
British successes were at their height in the struggle against
France which his father was conducting.[1]   When the Elder
Pitt fell from office in 1761, he turned his attention to his
family and particularly to William, his second son, who
seemed the most promising.   The boy's constitution was not
strong, and he was afflicted with hereditary gout for which the
family physician prescribed early hours, daily horse-riding
and – with later unfortunate consequences – port wine.
Because of his bad health and his father's views about public
schools, he was educated privately until he went up to Cambridge, at the early age of fourteen.   Here he worked hard,
studying the classics and mathematics and revealing that
reserved, aloof and self-controlled character which he was
to display all his life.   He also read modern writers, being
particularly influenced by Adam Smith's views, and among
the few undergraduates with whom he established a life-long
friendship was William Wilberforce (1759–1833).   After his
father's death, he read law at Lincoln's Inn, but he was
determined to realize his ambition, held since boyhood, of
entering Parliament.

He stood for the University of Cambridge in 1780, only to be
at the bottom of the poll, but soon afterwards he became a
member for Appleby, the county town of Westmorland and
one of the nine pocket boroughs on the northern estates of Sir
James Lowther, afterwards Lord Lonsdale, who was known
as the 'Cat-o'-Nine-Tails of Parliament'.   When Pitt entered
the Commons, North's ministry seemed as securely in power
as ever.   Pitt not unnaturally attached himself to the Shelburne Whigs.   His maiden speech was in support of Burke's
economical reform, and Burke exclaimed, 'He's not a chip
off the old block; it's the old block itself'.   In other speeches
he advocated parliamentary reform and denounced the War
as 'most accursed, wicked, barbarous, cruel, unnatural, unjust

[1] P. 305.

and diabolical'. His fluent delivery and clear, resonant voice made an immediate impression, and the opposition welcomed him as a worthy successor to his father.

When North fell in 1782, Pitt showed that he also possessed his father's self-confidence by declining a minor post under Rockingham, but he accepted the Chancellorship of the Exchequer from Shelburne later in the year.[1] When that short-lived administration came to an end, Pitt played his part so skilfully in opposition that he rapidly acquired the confidence of both King and country as the man who could give the nation stable government. After only three years in Parliament and at the age of twenty-four he was placed at the head of an administration, a post he was to hold with only a brief interlude for the remaining twenty-three years of his life.

When Pitt first took office in December 1783, however, his chances of a long and stable period of power seemed far from good. He had the King's support as a man above faction and party, and the reformers believed he sympathized with their cause, but the Fox-North opposition enjoyed a majority of some 40 or 50 against him in the Commons, and he encountered great difficulties in getting together a Cabinet, difficulties which he himself increased by excluding Shelburne to safeguard his independence. His period of office seemed destined to be brief. The opposition called him the 'schoolboy minister', while Fox mocked his 'mince-pie administration' which would fall when the Christmas festivities were over.

Yet Fox's position was not, in fact, as strong as it appeared. His obvious course was to demand a general election, but he could not be certain that an appeal to the country would go in his favour. In the first few weeks of the new year Fox carried fourteen motions against Pitt, but without avail. Pitt again displayed excellent parliamentary tactics. His policy was to hang on, win supporters and discredit the opposition. He carefully declared his continued support for parliamentary reform. He introduced an India Bill of his own which sought reform without transference of patronage; and its defeat did the opposition no good. Instead, as Pitt remained in power so the opposition became less attractive for independent

[1] P. 354.

members, and they began to go over to an administration which could rely on royal favour and patronage. The majority against the government steadily fell until in less than three months it was down to one vote, and Fox had failed to carry out his threat to stop supplies. At the same time reports from the country told of public opinion turning more and more in favour of the government. In March 1784 Pitt advised the King to dissolve Parliament.

In the general election which followed the next month, the opposition again had the support of the heir to the throne. The Prince of Wales declared for Fox and opened Carlton House to his followers. Fox fought a vigorous campaign in Westminster with the assistance of Georgiana, Duchess of Devonshire, and other aristocratic Whig beauties, but he was only returned as second member for the constituency, while Pitt headed the poll for the University of Cambridge. Pitt and the King had correctly judged the result of the election as a whole. The returns were, the King said, 'more favourable than the most sanguine could have expected'. Pitt secured a working majority of over 200. About 80 of Fox's friends – mockingly designated 'Fox's martyrs' – were defeated.

Pitt enjoyed the assistance of the Crown's influence and patronage in the traditional manner, but his striking victory was not entirely due to this. He had the support of the moneyed classes, who feared that Fox's East India Bill presaged an attack on their chartered privileges. There were also signs that political issues were beginning to pass from local to national affairs in a way that foretold future developments. Fox's alliance with North, his desertion of the cause of reform and his seeming desire to perpetuate his power by the organization of Indian patronage were all used in a nationwide campaign against him, while his supporters retaliated vainly with attacks on Pitt's refusal to acknowledge parliamentary defeat for three months and the dissolution of a Parliament which lasted for less than half the maximum time prescribed by the Septennial Act. Wilberforce's eloquence and the adherence to him of the old petitioning movement secured his unopposed return for the county of Yorkshire, even though Fox had friends among the great landed families there.[1] The extent to which the advocates of radical reform

[1] P. 61.

had changed sides was shown by Wyvill's comment on the result – a victory for the Fox–North coalition, he wrote to a friend, would 'have changed our limited monarchy into a mere aristocratical republic'. The unusual combination of these factors told strongly in Pitt's favour and made the election unique in eighteenth-century politics.

Peacetime Government (1784–89)

The election of 1784, which relegated Fox so disastrously to the opposition, increased his implacable hostility towards his opponent. He embarked upon a turbulent and unscrupulous campaign against Pitt, and the rivalry between the two men was to last until Pitt's death. It might have seemed that they had so much in common that they could have worked together. Both favoured economic and political reform, government control of the East India Company, greater freedom for Ireland and the suppression of the slave trade; but such agreement in principle could not undo the division imposed upon them by past events and differences of temperament. Fox never forgave Pitt for his opposition to him in 1783 and his acceptance of the King's call to form a ministry on the fall of the coalition, while the affable, sociable, ebullient Fox was far removed in character from the cold, lofty, solitary Pitt. Throughout the long period of Pitt's tenure of power, Fox was condemned to the political wilderness. The experience affected them both. The responsibilities of office made Pitt cautious and calculating; the frustrations of parliamentary opposition increasingly submerged Fox's passionate idealism under a readiness to resort to factious behaviour.

Despite the great victory he had won over Fox, Pitt's difficulties were by no means over in 1784. He had little connection with the great landed families, and yet until 1789 he was the only member of the Cabinet who belonged to the Commons. In 1788, in a House of 558 members, only 52 were described as his regular followers, but Fox was credited with 138. Pitt depended for a majority on the votes of the 185 members of the Crown party or some of the remaining 183 who were independents or usually supporters of the existing government. Pitt's major support came, therefore, from the King and such royal patronage as remained after the abolition of the sinecures. The election of 1784 had been essentially a triumph for the Crown.   George III had got the minister of his choice, who would govern according to his interpretation of the constitution and reverse what he regarded as the coalition's attempt to deprive him of his just prerogatives.   This meant that the King was to some extent dependent on Pitt, for if he went it would be difficult to resist a return of Fox to power, but in normal circumstances Pitt would have to act as the King's minister and also as one standing for a national, patriotic party to convince the ordinary Members of Parliament that he deserved their support.   These conditions under which he held office inevitably exerted a strong influence on his policy and his actions.

This was clearly shown in his attitude towards measures which Wilberforce and other reformers hoped he would accomplish when he took office.   He had previously advocated parliamentary reform, despite the King's dislike of it.   In 1785 he introduced a bill to abolish thirty-six rotten boroughs, paying £1,000,000 compensation to their patrons, and transfer their seats to the counties, where the franchise was to be enlarged by augmenting the 40s. freeholder by 40s. copyholders and some leaseholders; but the King would not countenance it, and many of the Crown party voted against it, defeating it by 248 votes to 174, and Pitt took no further action.   Similarly, when in 1793 Wilberforce moved resolutions for ending the slave trade, Pitt supported him with a fine speech, but acquiesced in the House's refusal to take action.   On both these occasions, his attitude was based on his belief that he should not go against either the King's wishes or a parliamentary majority.

Pitt was prepared, however, to use the King's favour towards him to gain further support for himself.   An unprecedented number of new peers was created during his ministry to provide followers to vote for him against the Whig aristocracy in the Lords.[1]   The old orders of chivalry were also enlarged to provide knighthoods which would gain him adherents elsewhere.   Many of these honours were bestowed on newly-enriched City men, upon whom he came to depend increasingly to fortify himself against the great landed nobility's opposition.

[1] P. 53.

Indeed, Pitt's need to acquire their support and also act as a national minister, played an important part in shaping his legislative enactments. Public opinion was now highly critical of Indian affairs and was to accept the charges made against Hastings.[1] Pitt's India Act of 1784 attempted to combine a reform of Indian administration with the preservation of the East Indian Company's patronage. This and the subsequent Act of 1786 strengthened the Governor-General's power in India and created an administrative system which remained in operation until 1858, but the maintenance of dual control placed such a strain on the Company that it had eventually to relinquish its trading activities.[2] Similarly, Pitt's other piece of imperial reorganization, the Canada Constitutional Act of 1791, was designed to safeguard the new Protestant settlers from subjection to the French Roman Catholics, to give to each representative assemblies, and yet also to safeguard the British government's control of Canadian administration; but it separated power from responsibility and set up growing tensions which culminated in rebellions in 1837.[3]

Pitt's reputation as a great peacetime minister rests largely on the financial and commercial reforms which did so much to assist the country's economic revival after the American War. His position also demanded that he should do this. He inherited a difficult financial situation. The cost of the American War had aroused widespread discontent. It had added over £100,000,000 to the National Debt, raising it by 1784 to a total of almost £243,000,000, the interest on which amounted to nearly £9,000,000 a year out of a total income of £18,506,000. There was an annual deficit in the revenue of about £2,000,000, and Consols stood at only 56. The debt had to be reduced and the revenue increased, but at the same time the public expected economies in expenditure and reforms in taxation. Pitt built on the previous achievements of Pelham, Grenville and Burke and was also assisted by the findings of a commission on the public accounts set up by Lord North in 1781.

To begin a reduction of the National Debt, Pitt resorted to Walpole's plan of a Sinking Fund, but his was too inalienable and inviolable to save it from the ill-fortune of Walpole's

fund.[1] His scheme owed much to the ideas of Dr. Richard
Price, a Dissenting minister and a member of Shelburne's
circle of Radicals at Bowood, which Pitt often visited. In
1786 he set up a Sinking Fund, administered by six independent commissioners, who were to receive £1,000,000 each
year from the revenue to purchase national stock and re-invest
the interest. To prevent later Chancellors of the Exchequer
from diverting the fund to meet government expenditure,
Pitt made the commissioners responsible solely to Parliament.
The scheme restored public faith in the government's financial
integrity, and by 1793 the National Debt had been reduced
by £10,000,000, but it depended for its success on an annual
surplus in the national revenue. When war against France
changed this into a deficit, since Pitt believed hostilities would
be short and was determined to maintain the inviolability of
the fund, money was borrowed unintelligently at high rates
of interest to reduce a debt at a lower rate. His scheme
was abandoned in 1828.

   Pitt's Sinking Fund required a surplus of at least £1,000,000
a year, but there had been a deficit since the outbreak of the
American War, and no minister had succeeded in devising
means of taxation which would give the government a fair
share of the country's growing wealth. Customs duties were
still largely evaded by smuggling, and the land tax was
resented by the gentry. Pitt showed great ingenuity in seeking fresh taxes, mostly on luxury items. These included
horses, personal servants, hackney coaches, windows, hats,
ribbons, candles, bricks, dogs, clocks and watches. By 1792
Pitt could claim in his budget speech that these new imposts
had added about £1,000,000 to the revenue, but as a whole
such fragmented taxes were unpopular, hard to enforce and
costly to collect. Not until 1798, when he imposed income
tax as a wartime measure, did Pitt really introduce a new
source of revenue which was uniform, elastic and adapted to
modern conditions.[2]

   Pitt added about another £1,000,000 to the revenue by his
administrative and financial reforms. Burke's work in
abolishing sinecures was completed, and the old perquisites
and fees of many office-holders were replaced by official
salaries. By 1789 over 700 posts had been abolished in the

revenue service alone. A proper system of auditing the public accounts was introduced in 1785 and another of inspection to eliminate fraud among tax-collectors which greatly increased the yield of taxation. Pitt also succeeded in improving the revenue obtained from customs duties. To take the profit out of smuggling, the several duties on tea which amounted to about 119 per cent were replaced by a single duty of 12½ per cent collected through the East India Company. The excise system was extended, as Walpole had planned in 1733, to wines and tobacco.[1] Finally, Pitt reformed the complicated system of taxation, which had grown up over the past and resulted in a single article often having to pay as many as a dozen duties. He imposed a single duty on each article and in 1787 set up a single 'Consolidated Fund' into which the customs and excise duties were to be paid instead of into numerous separate funds. Dr. Binney's recent researches have established the enormous simplication of accounting procedure and consequent saving of money which this achieved. Unfortunately Pitt failed to see that this system ought to be applied to future financial provisions; and because new duties were not always put to the credit of the Consolidated Fund, eight new separate accounts had to be reconsolidated in 1803.

The amount added to the revenue by Pitt's new imposts and reforms was equalled by the greater yield of taxation produced by increasing national prosperity. Pitt realized that flourishing trade was essential for the success of his financial policy. Adam Smith had convinced him that this would best be assisted by removing restrictions on commercial intercourse. In 1785 he introduced a bill to admit Ireland into free trade with Britain and the colonies, only to have to abandon it in the face of opposition from both English and Irish merchants, each nervous of competition from the other. The next year he negotiated a commercial treaty with France, which reduced British duties on French wines and brandy and gained equivalent benefits from France for British textiles, pottery and hardware, but this had hardly time to take effect before the outbreak of the Revolutionary War nullified it.

Fox had unscrupulously stirred up feeling on both sides of the Irish sea to defeat Pitt's free trade proposals for Ireland,

[1] P. 257.

and he had as energetically, though unsuccessfully, opposed the French commercial treaty. In 1788 the opposition engaged in fresh contention – the impeachment of Warren Hastings.[1] Burke was moved by the fate of the 'undone millions' of India to take up the case; he was supported by the eloquence of Fox and his devoted friend and parliamentary adherent, Richard Brinsley Sheridan (1751–1816), the dramatist. Pitt supported the charges against Hastings. He could hardly have done otherwise. Public opinion was hostile to Hastings, and the opposition's accusations were plausible. Politically the trial harmed the opposition. It diverted their attention from Parliament and the government, and it seemed to develop into a personal feud between Hastings and Burke, whose speeches were, as his modern biographer has tactfully expressed it, 'marred by extravagant abuse and lapses of taste'. Sympathy for Hastings grew. The fashionable world ceased to flock to Westminster Hall. The impeachment became boring and unpopular. Long before it was over in 1795, Sheridan wished, he said, that Hastings would fly the country with Burke howling and gesticulating at his heels. The opposition had not emerged as the champions of freedom and justice against official tyranny and corruption.

In the same year as the trial of Hastings began, another event occurred which was exploited by the opposition but only served to weaken it. George III got out of his carriage in Windsor Great Park and greeted an oak tree as the King of Prussia. His illness had returned; he rapidly became depressed and violent. Fox was exultant. He insisted that the Prince of Wales, with whom he was still on terms of intimate friendship, had the hereditary right to be appointed Regent immediately with complete royal authority. Under such patronage, the Foxites might hope for a long and secure tenure of office. Pitt insisted that it was Parliament's right to nominate a Regent by legislation and define his powers, but at the same time he prepared to return to the bar. The opposition drew up its ministry, and several members of the government prepared to go over to Fox, but early in the next year the King recovered. Pitt induced him to remove from office the ministers (including, eventually, Thurlow in 1792) who had made overtures to Fox, and the opposition was left

[1] P. 180.

weakened, embittered and divided. When the King's mind finally gave way in 1810, Parliament accepted Pitt's original contention. By the Regency Act of 1811, the Prince was made Regent, but his powers were limited in such matters as the creation of peerages and the granting of offices.

Though the Regency crisis of 1788 revealed the extent to which Pitt's power was limited by his dependence on royal favour, nevertheless its outcome served to strengthen Pitt's ascendancy. From the formation of his ministry, his own indispensability to the King had enabled him to exercise an unprecedented personal supervision over policy and departmental administration which put him above the rest of the Cabinet. Now the dismissal of the ministers who had not supported him over the Regency question was a move towards greater Cabinet solidarity; and thereafter the King suffered from periods of bad health which prevented him taking his customary interest in parliamentary and governmental business. On such occasions Pitt assumed full administrative responsibility, and during the perilous years after 1789 the concentration of authority in his person grew. These developments make it possible to regard Pitt as the first Prime Minister and as the originator of something appreciably like the modern system of Cabinet government.

Pitt's peacetime achievements were cut short by a war which accentuated the imperfections of his financial measures and the defects of his foreign policy. A sense of incompleteness, indeed, hangs over his domestic policy of these years, despite its undoubted attainments. Nor is this entirely due to the outbreak of war. Pitt's reforms were largely inspired by the ideas of others, and he left behind no body of doctrine. He established no party, and at the end of his first seventeen years of office his personal followers were fewer than sixty in number. Yet he did bequeath to British political life a sense of efficient administration, which was maintained by Huskisson, Canning and other younger men who first took office under him and later professed themselves guided by his example.

The French Revolution and War (1789–93)

The French Revolution broke out in the summer of 1789 when the trial of Hastings was already wearying London.

At first the general reaction among English people towards the storming of the Bastille, the abolition of the French nobility's feudal immunities and the establishment of a new constitutional monarchy was one of sympathetic approval. For long popular opinion had regarded France as a notorious example of outworn tyranny and unfair privilege. It was the land of 'Popery, wooden shoes and black bread'. Now it seemed that the French were at last emulating the Glorious Revolution of 1688. Writers and poets especially welcomed it, believing that the powerful example of France would spread the great ideas of 'liberty, equality and fraternity' to other countries and bring about a new age of happiness for mankind.[1] William Blake assumed a red cap of liberty when he walked about London; Robert Burns, then an excise officer, sent firearms to the Convention in Paris; and the youthful William Wordsworth went himself to Paris and rejoiced at

> France standing on the top of golden hours
> And human nature seeming born again.

The French Revolution aroused the parliamentary opposition. Its leaders were ready to put themselves at the head of a popular movement in favour of political liberty. Fox, after perusing a few newspapers, wrote of the fall of the Bastille, 'How much the greatest event it is that ever happened in the world! and how much the best!'. And later he described the new French constitution of 1791 as 'the most stupendous and glorious edifice of liberty which has been erected on the foundation of human integrity in any time or country'. He also changed his costume yet again to express his sympathies.[2] Outside Parliament, the Revolution was enthusiastically acclaimed by the Radical members of the reform movement which had been languishing since the Gordon Riots.[3] Horne Tooke revived in 1791 the Society for Promoting Constitutional Information, which had suspended activities since 1784.[4] This was supported by other societies, some newly-founded to celebrate the centenary of the Glorious Revolution. The membership of these societies, however, was still largely from 'men of rank and consequence' – idealistic or eccentric

[1] P. 99.   [2] P. 31.
[3] P. 352.   [4] P. 349.

noblemen, rationalist middle-class intellectuals, businessmen tired of royal and aristocratic misgovernment and Dissenters whose civil disabilities made them insistent upon political reform.

In November 1789 one of these societies, the London Revolution Society, met to commemorate the landing of William of Orange in England and heard a sermon by the veteran Dissenting minister, Richard Price, in which he described the French Revolution as fulfilling the principles of the Glorious Revolution. Then the English had secured the right 'to choose our own governors; to cashier them for misconduct; and to frame a government for ourselves'. Now the French were doing the same, and oppressors everywhere must tremble and 'consent to the correction of abuses'.

In answer to this sermon, which encouraged the reforming societies to urge the relevance of the French revolutionary ideas to domestic politics, Burke published his *Reflections on the French Revolution* the next year.[1] Burke had supported the American Revolution because he regarded it as a conservative revolution, led by men of his own class and outlook, who were animated by true English political principles and opposed by the repressive legalism of the British government. He now attacked the French Revolution because its leaders were extremists, inspired by dangerous abstractions and out to attack all established institutions and private property. It was, therefore, something very different from the English Revolution of 1688, which had taken its place in the evolution of the British constitution. The French were destroying their ancient monarchy, aristocracy and Church and breaking completely with all that linked them with the past in a way that had destroyed all vestiges of law and ordered society and would, he prophetically foretold, lead them to anarchy, tyranny and war. 'Good order', he insisted, 'is the foundation of all things' and only to be achieved by gradualism, restraint and orderly development in politics.

When the *Reflections on the Fremch Revolution* appeared, Louis XVI and the royal family were virtual prisoners in Paris, châteaux had been burned, the French Church was despoiled and *émigré* noblemen and priests were sailing into Eastbourne and Rye in open boats. People of 'substance and respectability' in England were increasingly upset by the turn of

---

[1] P. 96.

events in France and what Burke called 'the proceedings of certain societies in London'. Burke's book expressed their views. Published at five shillings, it attained the unprecedented sale of 32,000 copies in a year. 'It is a book which every gentleman ought to read', George III declared. The famous passage, in which Burke described how he had seen Queen Marie Antionette at Versailles 'full of life and splendour and joy' and now wondered that he 'should have lived to see such disasters fallen upon her in a nation of gallant men', was described by his friend, Sir Philip Francis, as 'pure foppery', but its sentiment appealed to a reading public alarmed by the French Revolution.

Burke was quickly answered by Radical writers, the best-known being Thomas Paine, whose *The Rights of Man* appeared in two parts in 1791 and 1792. This was a masterly tract written in language which artisans and small shop-keepers could readily understand. Paine accused Burke of indifference to the French people's sufferings, because he was 'not affected by the validity of distress touching his heart, but by the showy resemblance of it touching his imagination. He pities the plumage, but forgets the dying bird.' The first part of the book defended the French Revolution and claimed the right of all the British people to elect their government; the second part demanded social reforms, which included universal education, children's allowances and old-age pensions, to be financed by a progressive income tax rising to 20s. in the pound on the highest incomes.

The Rights of Man was a turning-point in the reform movement. So also was the foundation of the London Corresponding Society in January 1792 by Thomas Hardy, a shoemaker, which soon became the largest Radical organization and pioneered working-class reform politics in England. It attained a membership of over 3,000 within a few months of its existence. Its subscription was a penny a week (compared with the London Revolution Society's entrance-fee of half-a-guinea), and its members were mainly lower middle-class and working-men. It was organized throughout the country in 'sections' of thirty members each, which exchanged 'constitutional information' by correspondence and sent delegates to a 'national convention' in Edinburgh in December 1792. Its manifesto called for annual parliaments and manhood suffrage. Its chief activities were printing pamphlets and holding meetings and discussions. By such means the ideas of the Radicals and the French revolutionaries were made known to weavers and cottagers, artisans and labourers all over the country.

By this time, the increasingly violent and republican trend of the French Revolution was intensifying passions in England. Pitt's hold on the country was increased at the general election of 1790. Burke and Fox broke for ever in 1791; Burke went over to the government and was gradually followed by the most prominent of Fox's supporters. The Radical movement, despite its energy and enthusiasm, attracted only a very small minority even of the working-class, which remained largely indifferent to its ideas. Mobs were still easily stirred by talk of sedition and French plots. There were scenes of violence in several parts of the country, including the two days' rioting in Birmingham which caused Priestley to leave the country permanently for America.[1] The next year, a government proclamation urged magistrates to control rigorously riotous meetings and seditious publications, and it was decided to prosecute Paine for 'scandalous, seditious and malicious libel', but he was able to escape to France.

Meanwhile, Pitt was having to devote increasing attention to foreign affairs. When he took office in December 1783 the foreign situation was not promising for Britain. After the American War of Independence she remained isolated in a Europe which resented her commercial and colonial supremacy. Pitt feared that France might take advantage of this isolation to pursue an aggressive policy again. He wished to prevent this and maintain international peace, which he realized was essential if his financial policy was to continue to benefit the business and trading community. His management of foreign affairs, however, was not marked with much skill or success in the years before the outbreak of the French Revolution. His greatest diplomatic triumph was the establishment of a Triple Alliance between Britain, Prussia and Holland in 1788. He valued this as a means of securing the balance of power in Europe, but it was resented in France and contributed to the hostile attitude of the revolutionary government towards Britain.

Pitt did not, however, believe that the French Revolution would mean war. Rather he thought that France would long be weakened by her internal disorders and afterwards might become less aggressive than she formerly had been under her old rulers. Early in 1790 he said, 'The present convulsions in France must sooner or later terminate in general harmony and regular order, and though the fortunate arrangements of such a situation may make her more formidable, they may also render her less obnoxious as a neighbour.'

As events in France unfolded, Pitt's attitude to foreign affairs was based on this assumption. When a Spanish expedition in 1790 ejected a British settlement from Nootka Sound, Vancouver Island, Pitt asserted Britain's possession of the Pacific coast of Canada, and Spain, failing to get support from revolutionary France, had to yield. The next year, however, when, in an effort to check the great increase of Russian power in Europe brought about by her victories over the Turks, he tried to prevent Catherine the Great annexing the key Turkish fortress of Ochakoff, he was ignominiously rebuffed. All the while he steadily maintained his belief that there would not be war between Britain and France. In February 1792 he reduced the naval estimates and said, 'Unquestionably there never was a time in the history of this country when from the situation in Europe we might more reasonably expect fifteen years of peace than at the present moment'

Soon afterwards, however, France declared war on Austria and Prussia and sent an army into the Austrian Netherlands. Pitt held that this did not warrant British intervention, but public opinion was alarmed. Later that year the deposition of Louis XVI and the September massacres hardened feeling against France. In November the French government committed two further actions which Pitt could not ignore. It issued the Edict of Fraternity, proclaiming its war a revolutionary struggle to liberate the people of every state from their tyrannical rulers; and it opened the Scheldt estuary to the shipping of all nations, in violation of the Treaty of Westphalia of 1648 which had granted exclusive navigation of the river to the Dutch, an action which also seemed likely to damage London's commercial importance. When France threatened to invade Holland, Pitt stated that this would be considered by Britain as a hostile act. The annexation of the Austrian Netherlands and the execution of Louis XVI followed. The French envoy in London was dismissed. In February the French government declared war on Britain and Holland.

XIX · THE REVOLUTIONARY WAR, 1793–1802

The War of the First Coalition (1793–97)

PITT thought of the war against revolutionary France as having the same limited objectives as the previous contests of the eighteenth century. To him it seemed that France was undermining the European balance of power and consequently threatening Britain's security. He wished to establish normal relations with her revolutionary government, but also to make it accept 'the natural frontiers of France'. He spoke, therefore, in terms of checking French aggression and inflicting military defeat on her, but others wanted the destruction of the republic and the restoration of the monarchy. George III said there would soon be no kings in Europe if this were not done, while Burke, deriding a war for the Scheldt as a war for a chamber-pot, called for the proclamation of a moral crusade, and an important part of the Cabinet also thought along these lines. Pitt was ready to give assistance to counter-revolutionary movements in France, but he insisted that the war should be fought with the same methods and aims as his father had employed.[1] 'It will be a short war,' he declared, 'and certainly ended in one to two campaigns.' He believed that the French economy would soon collapse through inflation, and in 1793 he maintained both taxation and the armed forces at their previous level.

So Britain entered the War ill-fitted to endure the long and costly conflict into which it was to develop. Unlike his father, Pitt was not an oustanding war minister and could not evolve an overall strategic plan for victory; he failed to appreciate the real threat presented by the virulent nationalism of revolutionary France; his armed forces were inadequate, and he failed to make the best use of them. Yet at first it looked as if he would be successful. France's aggressive policy secured him the Continental allies he needed. By the end of August 1793 he had formed the First Coalition of fifteen states, which

[1] P. 186.

included Britain, Austria, Russia, Holland, Spain, the Papal
States and Piedmont, and subsidized it with 'Pitt's gold'.   An
ill-equipped expeditionary force of 5,000 British troops was
raised with difficulty and sent under the Duke of York to
help the Dutch.   It joined a veteran Austrian army in the
Netherlands which compelled the French to retreat, invaded
France and invested Dunkirk.   The Spaniards penetrated
south-western France, and in the east the Prussians invaded
Alsace.   There was a royalist rising in Toulon, and Pitt was
persuaded to send Admiral Hood with the Mediterranean
fleet to take possession of the port.

The allied triumphs, however, were short-lived.   The
French government, through the *levée en masse*, adopted universal military conscription, a new development in warfare, and
organized mass armies which could overwhelm the smaller
professional forces of their opponents.   The allies also
suffered from the disadvantage of fighting on external lines,
lacked a common plan of campaign and were divided by
jealousies and suspicions.   By the end of 1793 the French
had relieved Dunkirk and driven the Austrians and Prussians
from their territory; their artillery, commanded by young
Napoleon Bonaparte, had forced the British to abandon
Toulon, while other royalist risings in La Vendée and Brittany
had been suppressed before British troops could intervene.
The next year French armies repulsed the Spaniards and
invaded Catalonia, overran the Austrian Netherlands and
advanced into Holland, which was organized under French
domination as the Batavian Republic.   The remnants of the
Duke of York's force were brought back home from Bremen.
In March 1795 Prussia made a separate peace, followed in
June by Spain, which later became an ally of France.   The
greatest French triumph came when Bonaparte embarked
upon his Italian campaign in the spring of 1796.   He overran
Piedmont, Naples and the Papal States and in October 1797
forced Austria to accept the Treaty of Campo Formio.
France now had her boundary on the Rhine and effective
control over the entire Netherlands and northern Italy.   No
army had been able to withstand the tactics and spirit of the
new French revolutionary forces and the genius of the man
who had now become their leader.   The First Coalition was
destroyed, and only Britain remained in the War.

There was little Pitt could have done to prevent the collapse of his Continental allies, but he added to Britain's reverses by a lavish dispersal of her war effort.   In accordance with his father's strategy and supported by West Indian interests, he withheld troops from Holland, Toulon and La Vendée and used British naval power to attempt the conquest of the French West Indies.   Admiral Jervis took a force across the Atlantic which occupied Tobago and St. Pierre and Miquelon in 1793, and reinforcements captured Martinique, St. Lucia and Guadeloupe and temporarily occupied Haiti the next year, but their losses were very heavy.   A hurricane destroyed many ships, and by 1796 some 40,000 troops had died, mostly from yellow fever, and about the same number had been permanently discharged from the army.   These were greater casualties than the British forces were to sustain in the Peninsular campaign.   The Dutch and Spanish submissions to France made possible more profitable British colonial gains – Ceylon, the Cape of Good Hope and the East Indies from Holland in 1795 and Trinidad and Demerara from Spain in 1797.   The conquests from Holland weakened the French efforts to intrigue with the rulers of Mysore and the Deccan against the British in India;[1] but none of these successes made any contribution to the defeat of France in the vital European theatre of war.   George III himself warned Pitt, 'The misfortune of our situation is that we have too many objects to attend to, and our forces consequently must be too weak at each place'.

The British navy had been maintained at fair strength since the end of the American War.[2]   It blockaded the French coast so successfully that by the summer of 1794 the country was beginning to experience a food shortage, and the main Brest fleet was sent out of port to escort a vital grain convoy from America.   It was defeated with heavy losses by Admiral Howe in the first important engagement of the War – the Glorious First of June off Ushant.   The news was acclaimed with rejoicing at home, but the grain ships finally got safely into Brest; and the use made of British naval supremacy in the Channel the next year, the landing of a force of French royalist refugees in Quiberon Bay in Brittany, ended in disaster and massacre.   Indeed, the dispersal of the British

[1] P. 181.   [2] P. 190.

war effort strained the navy's resources too much for the country's safety. Spain's declaration of war on Britain in October 1796 brought France control of the Spanish as well as the Dutch fleets, and the Mediterranean had to be abandoned. At the end of that year another French fleet sailed from Brest with troops for an invasion of Ireland, and only bad weather prevented their landing.[1]

The navy now was no longer employed, as earlier in the War, to support raids on the French coast, but had to guard against a French invasion of England. In February 1797 the danger seemed to be lightened by a daring naval battle at Cape St. Vincent. Admiral Jervis with fifteen sail of the line sighted a Spanish fleet nearly twice the size making for Cadiz. He immediately attacked them, and Commodore Nelson broke from the line to prevent their escape. The result was a victory which removed, for the time being, the threat from the Spanish navy. Two months later, however, came the naval mutinies, first at Spithead and then at the Nore.[2] The Spithead mutiny was quickly settled by Howe, but the Nore mutiny, under Parker's leadership, was more serious. Only two ships remained faithful to duty, and with these Admiral Duncan bluffed the Dutch fleet at Texel into believing that he was continuing to blockade them. Order was restored by July. Parker and his leading 'delegates' were hanged, others were flogged or imprisoned, and some grievances were redressed. This same fleet in October crippled the Dutch fleet at the hard-fought Battle of Camperdown, which prevented any but small-scale French intervention in Ireland when rebellion broke out there in the next year.[3] The War was at a stalemate. Britain had survived great perils, but France remained undefeated and dominant on the Continent.

Domestic Problems (1793–1800)

The trials of these years of war tested Pitt's character, but his stubborn self-confidence and calm did not fail. Once he had come to a decision, he was not the man to change his mind, however many setbacks were encountered. He imposed on the country the burden of continuing losses through his persistence in the West Indian campaigns, but he also built up a sense of unity and purpose among the people

[1] P. 218.   [2] P. 195.   [3] P. 219.

which could survive repeated defeats. He could do little to control events, but he encouraged the country still to look to the future. 'It matters little whether the disasters which have arisen are to be ascribed to the weakness of generals, the intrigues of camps or the jealousies of cabinets,' he told the Commons in 1794; 'the fact is they exist, and that we must anew commence the salvation of Europe.' Such determination, combined with the reputation for integrity and industry which he had gained in peacetime, made him increasingly accepted as a national leader.

Nevertheless, the strain suffered by Pitt was very severe. In addition to the difficulties of presiding over the management of a country at war, he was during these years beset with an unhappy love affair, family bereavement and the financial embarrassment from which he was only rescued by the kindness of friends. His devotion to duty remained, however, unshaken. He spent long hours poring over War Office maps in Downing Street, interviewing other Cabinet ministers, reading official correspondence and sorting out material himself. From 1796 his health began to give way, but he kept his afflictions to himself, as he kept so much else.

The burden of office was made heavier for Pitt by the problems he had to face at home during this time when the situation abroad was so threatening. The first years of hostilities coincided with a series of poor summers and bad harvests which had financial repercussions. The year in which war began brought as many as 1,926 failures, twenty-six being those of country banks. This added to Pitt's difficulties in raising money for the increased expenditure of war. He was prepared to secure much of this by loans, particularly when he still hoped that the War would be short. He had reduced the National Debt to about £233,000,000 in 1793; it had risen to £456,100,000 by 1800, part of which was due to unintelligent continuance of his Sinking Fund.[1] In 1796, when the country's finances seemed to have improved, he issued a 'Loyalty Loan' of £18,000,000 which was soon fully subscribed; but the bad news of the next year produced a financial panic, and the Bank of England suspended cash payments, which were not resumed for twenty-two years.

This convinced Pitt that some way must be found of

[1] P. 366.

increasing the government's income by taxation, especially as trade was continuing to expand and bringing new wealth to those who shared its profits.   He had already trebled the existing assessed taxes on such items as windows, servants and carriages to draw money from the wealthy, but this was not enough.   In December 1798 he introduced, as a temporary wartime measure, an income tax, which had first been suggested by Godolphin early in the century.   Pitt's tax was imposed on all who earned more than £60 a year.   Those whose incomes were between £60 and £65 paid at the rate of 2d. in the pound, and the proportion rose until it reached 2s. in the pound for incomes of £200 and more.   This was an important new change in the fiscal system and succeeded in making Britain's growing economic prosperity contribute towards the supplies and subsidies needed to fight the War. The government's revenue, which had fallen to £19,000,000 in 1795, rose to £33,000,000 by the conclusion of the Treaty of Amiens in 1802.   There was an immediate outcry that the income tax was inquisitorial, unfair and likely to discourage individual effort, but feelings were not stirred as they previously had been over the excise.   It bore most heavily on the upper and moneyed classes, and they had been wholeheartedly behind the government since the fall of the French monarchy.

The excesses of the French Revolution, the possibility of invasion and the rise of Napoleon Bonaparte served, indeed, to unite the greater part of the people in support of the War; but governing circles remained alarmed by the activities of the Radical movement.   On the outbreak of hostilities, the campaign against its activities was intensified.   The Aliens Act established control and supervision over foreign immigration; and a number of Radicals were put on trial.   The judges acted most severely in Scotland, where heavy sentences of transportation were imposed.[1]   In England a member of the London Corresponding Society was sentenced so six months' imprisonment and an hour in the pillory, but Thomas Hardy, Horne Tooke and other Radical leaders were acquitted of high treason.

This made Pitt decide upon stronger measures.   Between 1794 and 1801 the Habeas Corpus Act was suspended, so that

[1] P. 212.

political prisoners could be detained without trial. This did not, however, achieve its desired effect. The harvest of 1794 was bad and the following summer wet and cold; food prices were high and trade was upset. Agitators were able to attract large meetings. There were bread riots in Nottingham, Coventry and in Sussex. The King was shot at on his way to the state opening of Parliament in October, and a mob attacked his coach with cries of 'No war! No famine! No Pitt! No King!', while the windows of 10 Downing Street were broken.

Parliament in 1795, therefore, passed two further acts to deal with the situation. The Treasonable Practices Act made it treason to plot against the King, to plan to help invaders or to try to coerce Parliament, and anyone who denounced the British constitution could be transported for seven years. The Seditious Meetings Act required, for the next three years, meetings of more than fifty people and all lectures (except in schools and universities) to be licensed by the local magistrates.

The naval mutinies of 1797 further alarmed the government, and the next year there was considerable industrial discontent owing to the dislocation by the War of some manufactures. The Newspaper Publication Act of 1797 placed publishers under close supervision by the magistrates. The Corresponding Societies Act of 1799 suppressed the London Corresponding Society and other similar organizations. And the Combination Acts of 1799 and 1800 declared illegal all societies imposing secret oaths or with branches throughout the country and forbade all collaboration to secure shorter working hours or more pay; offenders could be tried summarily by magistrates and imprisoned for three months.

Pitt has since been widely condemned for his wartime repressive acts. Subsequent Radicals thought of him as 'that bloody-handed tool of tyranny, William Pitt', and many historians seem to have agreed with them. It is true that the unrest of these years was probably caused by bad harvests, high food prices and distress rather than by the corresponding societies and French propaganda, but the real question is not whether a country-wide revolutionary conspiracy actually flourished in England. Pitt knew that, especially in times of stress and economic difficulties, a few unscrupulous agitators could use the aspirations of reformers to foment discontent and treason, disorder and violence. People had seen how the Gordon Riots of 1780 had inexplicably given London over to six days of mob violence similar to the scenes later enacted in Paris. To Pitt, 'malice domestic' appeared as threatening as 'foreign levy'. To historians in the later, peaceful years of the nineteenth century this seemed illusory, but the two wars of this century have been a reminder that governments have to take security precautions at home in time of war against intrigue from within.

Indeed, England under Pitt in these years was far from being governed by a reactionary despotism. The ordinary processes of law largely continued. At Horne Tooke's trial, Pitt himself was summoned as a witness to testify to his own part in the reform movement of the 1780's. Even the most criticized of the measures, the Combination Acts, were directed more against the corresponding societies than against combinations by artisans, and historians such as Professor T. S. Ashton have held that they have been over-emphasized in working-class history since they were rarely enforced. In fact, the application of all the measures varied greatly throughout the country. The government continued to rely on the Justices of the Peace, whose powers they increased. Some were severe, others lenient. The Duke of Portland, who was Home Secretary from 1794 to 1801, was not the man to attempt a uniform system of national repression. In any event, such was not the government's policy, nor could it have been since emergency action by the army was the only way it had of asserting its authority.

Throughout these first years of hostilities, Fox continued in unremitting opposition to Pitt. He refused to identify himself with the popular mood; he criticized the conduct of the War, urged that no occasion for making peace should be lost and condemned the security precautions as fatal to liberty in Britain. 'Say at once', he exclaimed during the debates on the legislation of 1795, 'that a free constitution is no longer suitable to us, but do not mock the understandings and the feelings of mankind by telling the world that you are free.' No doubt there was sincerity in this. It was a sign of the same strain of idealism which had made him welcome the

French Revolution with such rapidity and was to lead him in time of war to support the efforts of Grey for parliamentary reform and of Wilberforce for the abolition of the slave trade.[1] He had also taken an important step towards protecting political liberty by the Libel Act, passed through his advocacy and with Pitt's approval in 1792, which enabled juries in libel cases to decide, not merely whether the accused had originated the publication in question, but whether it was libellous or not. This afforded protection to many Radical writers who were accused before the courts of seditious libel during these years.

Yet Fox's attitude was also factious. At the end of 1792 he had 'declared with an oath, that there was no address at this moment Pitt could frame, he would not propose an amendment to, and divide the House upon', and this continued to be his attitude. Also in his attack upon Pitt's security legislation, Fox was self-deluded, and his criticisms and insinuations were exaggerated. Pitt was supported by many of Fox's former associates, some of whom had championed Wilkes and the London printers when Fox himself was engaged in measures against them. These men believed that the situation demanded action such as the government had taken, and most people agreed with them. The Foxites remained in the political wilderness, and in 1797 Fox withdrew from Parliament to escape the frustrations of politics and married, leaving criticism of the government and opposition to the War to the more restrained Sheridan.

Indeed, as the War continued, official and political opinion increasingly regarded it as an anti-revolutionary crusade. The accession of Burke's friends, the Portland Whigs, to the ministry in 1794 hastened the process. Some 8,000 royalist refugees were welcomed and assisted. Funds were raised for their support by parliamentary grants and private subscriptions. There was a great increase in the number of readers in the British Museum in Montagu House in 1795, when nearly half of those admitted were *émigré* bishops, abbés and noblemen, their names mingling with such as Walter Scott, Sydney Smith, Charles Lamb and Henry Brougham. The arrival of French clergymen and the transference of the English seminaries from France to England gave many people

[1] P. 82.

their first acquaintance with Roman Catholicism. French noblewomen opened fashionable boarding-schools for young ladies, while Burke's principal occupation during the last months of his life was the supervision of the school established near Beaconsfield for French refugee boys in which he hoped 'to give them a good dash of English education'.[1]

The War of the Second Coalition (1798–1801)

The defeat of the Spanish and Dutch navies in 1797 made it possible for Britain to reassert her naval power in the Mediterranean, and a fleet was sent there under Nelson the next year. The step was taken at a fortunate moment. When it seemed that an invasion of Britain was unlikely to succeed, Napoleon set sail from Toulon with a formidable fleet and an army destined for Egypt; his government had instructed him 'to drive England from all their possessions in the East, and above all destroy their entrepôts in the Red Sea, and to ensure the free and exclusive possession of the Red Sea for the French Republic'. He evaded Nelson, captured Malta from the Knights of St. John, landed in Egypt and defeated a Turkish army in the Battle of the Pyramids. Then Nelson, who had been sailing up and down the Mediterranean, annihilated the French fleet in the Battle of the Nile. He found the French ships anchored in Aboukir Bay, skilfully eluded the protecting shoals and sent some of his ships between the enemy and the shore to effect such a complete surprise attack from both sides that only two of them escaped capture or destruction. Britain had gained naval supremacy in the Mediterranean and proceeded to occupy Minorca. Napoleon tried to advance into Syria, but was held up at Acre by a British naval brigade under Sir Sidney Smith. In August 1799 he returned to France, leaving his army in Egypt.

The Battle of the Nile was the first serious defeat suffered by France. It enabled Pitt in December 1798, though broken in health, to induce Russia, Austria, Naples, Portugal and Turkey to join with Britain in forming the Second Coalition and receive subsidies raised by his new income tax. Britain herself sent an expedition to Holland which had soon to be withdrawn without any success except the British seizure of the Dutch fleet. While Napoleon was still in Egypt, the

[1] Pp. 16–17.

Austrians and Russians drove the French from Italy, but disputes between them led to Russia's withdrawal from the alliance in October 1799. On his return to Europe, Napoleon inflicted two decisive defeats on the Austrians at Marengo and Hohenlinden in 1800. Since Pitt had repeated his previous strategic mistakes in organizing descents upon Belle Isle, Ferrol and elsewhere, the available British forces were too widely dispersed to intervene effectively in Italy. Resistance to France on the Continent came to an end when Austria, Naples and Turkey made peace in 1800, and Spain, still allied to France, defeated Portugal.

Britain was now, therefore, again left alone against France. Napoleon sought a way of striking at Britain's omnipotent sea-power. The British blockade of France had again aroused neutral resentment by her claim to the right to search all vessels on the high seas for contraband goods, which Napoleon in 1800 exploited to persuade Denmark, Sweden, Prussia and Russia to revive the League of Armed Neutrality of 1780.[1] He hoped this would exclude British commerce from the Baltic and so deprive her of much-needed naval stores and corn. The scheme was thwarted, however, by Nelson's daring destruction of the Danish fleet at Copenhagen in the spring of 1801. Meanwhile, the British had captured Malta in August 1800, and a year later the French army in Egypt surrendered to a force landed at Aboukir Bay under Sir Ralph Abercrombie.

Pitt, Addington and Peace (1801–3)

By this time, Pitt was no longer in power. He had resigned in March 1801 on the question of Roman Catholic emancipation.[2] Pitt believed that political equality for Roman Catholics was vital for a successful union of Ireland with Britain, but he failed to carry the whole Cabinet with him and so was not in a strong position to persuade George III to overcome his emotional objection to the idea. The threat of resignation did not shake the King's obstinancy because he now had an alternative minister in Henry Addington (1757–1844), the Speaker of the House of Commons. So Pitt went out of office after seventeen years, and Addington became Prime Minister.

[1] P. 187.   [2] P. 221.

Addington was able to secure support for his ministry in Parliament not merely because he opposed political emancipation for Roman Catholics, but also war-weariness had been growing in the country and among the back-benchers of the Commons. The independent country gentlemen were determined to uphold the rights of the Established Church as part of the constitution and also wanted the War to end. They welcomed Addington as the champion of Crown and country against Pitt's reforming ideas and supporters. They welcomed him also as one who would end Pitt's determined continuance of the War which now seemed mistaken. The worst excesses of the Revolution seemed to be over, and Napoleon was establishing firm government in France, while the War was once again in an apparently hopeless condition of stalemate. At home, the harvest of 1799 had been very poor; bread was scarce and dear; riots had occurred; corn and timber supplies from the Baltic were threatened; taxation was high and a financial crisis seemed likely in the City. Many wanted, therefore, a minister who would make a reasonable peace, reduce official expenditure and govern the country without innovations.

Napoleon also wanted peace in order to have an opportunity to reorganize the government of France, but to satisfy his army it must be on as favourable terms as possible. When negotiations began, so strong was the British desire for peace that he was able to get a settlement very satisfactory for France. The Treaty of Amiens was signed in March 1802, bringing the Revolutionary War to an end. Britain was to restore all her conquests to France, Spain and Holland except Trinidad and Ceylon and also to restore Malta to the Knights of St. John. British troops were to be withdrawn from Egypt and French troops from the Papal States and Naples. France was to retain the Netherlands and the left bank of the Rhine and to maintain her vassal republics in Holland, Switzerland and northern Italy.

Addington described the settlement as 'a genuine reconciliation between the two first nations of the world', but Sheridan called it 'a peace which all men are glad of, but no man can be proud of'. Most English people, however, were only too relieved to have peace after nine years of war. Young men who were of suitable age seized their chance eagerly to enjoy the Grand Tour which was now again possible. Others of the upper classes were glad to be able to go to France again by the Dover and Calais packets. The new fashions there amazed English ladies, who looked old-fashioned to the French;[1] and they did not find the manners of the new society to their taste, for the postilions peered into their coaches and remarked, '*Diable, au moins elles sont jolies*'. Fox went to Paris and could not resist meeting Napoleon who, he afterwards declared, was 'the fittest person to be master'.

[1] P. 30.

XX · THE NAPOLEONIC WAR, 1803–15

Renewed War and Pitt's Return (1803–5)

HOPES that the peace would soon become lasting were seen to be without foundation. Napoleon had not really abandoned his policy of conquest. Within a few months, he annexed Piedmont and Elba, occupied Switzerland and intervened in Germany; he kept Dutch ports closed to British trade and imposed a heavy tariff on British goods. A rumour that he was preparing a new Egyptian expedition made the British government decide not to evacuate Malta. Napoleon rejected a British ultimatum demanding Malta for ten years and French evacuation of Holland and Switzerland; Britain rejected Napoleon's suggestion of Russian mediation; and the Napoleonic War began in May 1803. Some of the young English gentlemen did not hurry back from their Grand Tour in time, and were interned at Verdun to pass away their idleness in dissipation.

Having emboldened himself to make war, Addington however, showed himself incompetent to wage it, though he did his best. The general election of June 1802 had strengthened his hold on the Commons, but now he steadily lost its confidence. Fox, Grenville and Canning led the opposition to him. Yet his government lasted almost a year after the renewal of hostilities, for the King had a recurrence of his illness for several months, and Pitt, unwilling to join a ministry unless he were its undisputed head, refused to intervene, devoting himself to his military duties in Kent as Lord Warden of the Cinque Ports. Eventually Addington resigned, and Pitt was called to office again. He wished to form a ministry, he told the King, based on 'as large a proportion as possible of the weight of talents and connections, drawn without exception from parties of all descriptions'. He offered Fox the post of Foreign Secretary, but George III would not have him, and Grenville would not accept office without him. This badly weakened Pitt's ministry, and some mockingly called it the 'Cabinet of Billy and Pitt', but his respect for the monarchy would not allow him to join with Fox and Grenville in trying to coerce George III, who by now had gained much affection from the country. Above all, Pitt believed it was his duty to take up the burden of directing the war again, even though his health was still precarious.

Meanwhile, Napoleon, who had proclaimed himself Emperor of the French in March 1804, had decided to attempt an invasion of England. He brought to the Pas de Calais his Grand Army of over 100,000 seasoned troops who had vanquished every Continental force; he set about concentrating in Boulogne and the small ports on either side a fleet of 2,000 flat-bottomed barges and also a flotilla of small armed vessels to attack the patrolling British frigates. In anticipation of success, a Parisian coiner struck a commemorative medal inscribed '*Frappé à Londres en 1804*'.

On a fine day, the people of Dover could see the white tents of the military encampments across the Channel, and English mothers reinforced the rod with tales of Bonaparte to terrify their ill-behaved children. There were some 52,000 regular troops in England. The county militia forces were called out for training, which raised about another 120,000 men. In addition, about 350,000 men enrolled themselves in part-time, volunteer regiments, though they were armed only with pikes, and some never received either weapons or training. Martello towers, modelled on a small fort in Corsica which had strongly resisted a British attack, were built along the low-lying coasts of south-eastern England. Semaphores were set up on hilltops, and at night there were beacons. If the enemy landed, London was to be defended at all costs. The King was determined to lead the defending forces himself. The Queen and her daughters were to be sent to Worcester, together with the gold from the Bank and the crown jewels which were to be stored in the cathedral, while the artillery and stores from Woolwich Arsenal were to be taken to the Midlands along the Grand Junction Canal.

Despite these preparations, however, it was realized that Britain's main safeguard was the navy, which by the summer of 1804 had forced Napoleon to change his invasion plans. He had to abandon his original idea of a speedy crossing in a single night, for his harbour facilities required five or six tides to embark his troops on the barges, during which time the

British ships of the line would have been able to come up to support the frigates in the Channel. His plan now was that the French fleet, under Admiral Villeneuve, should slip out of Toulon, elude the British blockade, join up with the Spanish fleet from Cadiz, entice Nelson's fleet to the West Indies and then double back to protect the invasion barges in the Channel. The first part of the plan was achieved early in 1805, but on his return Villeneuve went to Cadiz to refit instead of going straight to Brest. Napoleon was indignant, but he had already begun to move the Grand Army eastwards to meet the threat of a new European coalition formed by Pitt. Meanwhile, Nelson had also returned, and when Napoleon ordered Villeneuve to take his fleet to the Mediterranean to support the French forces in Italy, he gave chase and defeated the enemy on 21st October off Cape Trafalgar, dying himself in the hour of victory.[1]

The War of the Third Coalition (1805–7)

Since Britain had not the military resources to mount a direct attack upon France as a counter-stroke to Napoleon's threatened invasion, Pitt employed diplomacy to create a diversion by forming yet another Continental alliance. Lengthy negotiations produced the Third Coalition with Austria, Russia and Sweden who were to provide 500,000 men; Britain was to supply £1,250,000 a year for every 100,000 men engaged against France. Pitt hoped for great things from the alliance, but the day before the Battle of Trafalgar an Austrian army had to surrender at Ulm on the Danube to Napoleon's Grand Army which he had rushed to Central Europe. Pitt remained optimistic, and at the Lord Mayor's banquet in November he made his shortest and most famous speech, 'I return you many thanks for the honour you have done me; but Europe is not to be saved by any single man. England has saved herself by her exertions and will, as I trust, save Europe by her example.'

It was not, however, to be so. Before the end of the year, Napoleon had occupied Vienna, defeated a combined Austrian and Russian army at Austerlitz in Moravia and compelled Austria to accept peace at Pressburg. The news shattered Pitt. The strain of the previous twelve months

[1] P. 197.

had exhausted him, and his gout could not be relieved. He now bore what Wilberforce described as 'the Austerlitz look'. He was only forty-six when he died in January 1806. Parliament paid his debts and buried him next to his father in Westminster Abbey.

So Pitt died against a background of disaster and defeat. Whatever his failings as a war minister, he had become the symbol and spearhead of the nation's resistance to the enemy when other states had crumbled. This was the tribute that had been paid to him by Canning in the well-known lines which hailed him as 'the pilot who weathered the storm'. Yet Pitt did even more than save the country from collapse and despair. Both during his peacetime ministry and in the years of war, he preserved the stability and constitutional framework of the country amid the strains which threatened it. He made his contribution not only to Britain's final victory in war, but also to her freedom from the revolutionary upheavals which convulsed other countries. On these counts, he deserved the commendation of his friend Wilberforce that 'for personal purity, disinterestedness and love of his country, I have never known his equal'.

Though Ulm and Austerlitz had dealt a virtual death-blow to the Third Coalition, resistance on the Continent to Napoleon lasted for another eighteen months after Pitt's death. Prussia joined the Coalition in the middle of 1806, only to be crushingly defeated at Jena and Auerstädt and compelled to sue for peace. The Russians held out until July 1807, when the Czar Alexander I and Napoleon signed the Treaty of Tilsit which recognized French hegemony in Central and West Europe. Napoleon was now at the height of his power, and Britain once more remained alone in the War.

When Pitt died, there was no single war minister to take his place, and the next six years of the War were also a period of impermanent government at home. The weak ministry over which Pitt had presided immediately collapsed in disunity. The King was forced to turn to Grenville, who formed a Cabinet which was predominantly Foxite, despite the presence of Addington, now Lord Sidmouth, in it. He called it the 'Ministry of All the Talents', but the exclusion from it of all who had supported Pitt meant that many of the most talented men in the Commons, including Castlereagh, Canning and

Spencer Perceval, were now in opposition. Fox, who had led his followers to vote against a state funeral for Pitt, was Foreign Secretary, though he knew that he had not long to live. He wished to devote the rest of his life to the attainment of two objects for which he had long contended – the ending of the slave trade and the conclusion of peace. The slave trade was abolished in 1807;[1] but he found himself mistaken in supposing that the traditional diplomatic processes could achieve peace with an aggressive France and her successful military dictator. The attempt had already failed when he died in September 1806.

In October Grenville persuaded George III to dissolve Parliament in the hope of improving his majority in the Commons. He won some forty borough seats in the election, and he hoped to win further support by vigorous prosecution of the War. An important step had already been taken towards army reform by abolishing enlistment for life in 1806.[2] Grenville and the Cabinet now wished to take a further measure to improve recruiting by allowing Roman Catholics to hold commissions, but George III suspected that this was a first move towards Roman Catholic emancipation and demanded from the ministers a written pledge not to raise the matter again. Grenville refused to do this, and the ministry resigned in March 1807. The elderly Duke of Portland was ready, however, to give such an assurance, and he formed a new and weak administration, though among its younger members were Canning as Foreign Secretary and Castlereagh as Minister for War.

Portland had been a Foxite, but in 1794 had joined Pitt and was now a firm supporter of the King. By this time a change was taking place in the party system.[3] The Foxites, the supporters of the French Revolution and parliamentary reform, had gone into opposition again, but they had appropriated the name 'Whig' for themselves and were engaged in fastening the name 'Tory' on their opponents. Pitt and his friends never regarded themselves as Tories, but Canning now occasionally used the name, and the modern two-party system was evolving.

Though the Portland ministry won a general election in 1807, increasing its majority considerably, it remained weak,

dominated by the personal animosity of Canning and Castlereagh and dogged by military reverses.[1] In 1809 Portland
had a fit and died; Canning challenged Castlereagh to a duel,
and when both men retired from office Spencer Perceval,
the Chancellor of the Exchequer, took over. He was not in
a position to secure a strong government, but he hung on,
and when he was shot on his way to Parliament by an insane
bankrupt in May 1812, the tide of War had turned in the
Peninsula. The way was prepared for the restoration of
ministerial stability by the Earl of Liverpool (1770–1828),
who was to be in power for nearly fifteen years.

The Continental System (1806–12)

After the Battle of Trafalgar had destroyed Napoleon's
hope of conquering Britain by invasion, he attempted
economic warfare against her on a large scale. The British
naval blockade had already driven French trade off the high
seas, and France had retaliated as best she could by privateering attacks on British merchantmen. Napoleon now intended
to take advantage of his control of so much of the European
coastline to enforce a Continental blockade on Britain. He
could not stop ships going into the enemy's ports, but he
would stop ships coming into his own ports with enemy goods.
He believed that the Continent was still economically self-
sufficient, while Britain had become dependent on exporting
manufactured goods in return for imports of food and raw
materials. By depriving Britain of her markets, he hoped to
destroy this trade which made possible both her naval
strength and the subsidies to allies upon which her power was
based.

From Germany, Napoleon issued his Berlin Decrees of 1806
which declared the British Isles to be in a state of blockade
and forbade all his dependent countries to trade with them.
The British government retaliated with a series of Orders in
Council issued in 1806 and 1807 which declared a blockade
of France and her allies, forbade neutral ships to sail to the
Continent and ordered those on their way to be diverted to
British ports. Napoleon replied from Italy with the Milan
Decrees of 1807 commanding that all ships calling at British
ports were to be confiscated and that all British merchandise

[1] P. 397.

on the Continent was to be seized. This completed the Continental System, which Napoleon extended to Russia after the Treaty of Tilsit in 1807 and to Spain and Portugal in 1808.

Napoleon's decrees were by no means without effect in Britain. Such French naval squadrons and privateers as eluded the blockade sank about 480 merchant ships a year, but the British navy seized almost eight times as many neutral vessels. Britain suffered most from a shortage of exports, particularly wool from Spain and Germany, timber from Scandinavia and corn from the Baltic. To these were added raw cotton when the United States in 1807 imposed a retaliatory embargo on trade with both belligerents. There was particular hardship and suffering in the years from 1809 to 1812 when disastrous harvests sent the price of corn up from 75s. to 130s. a quarter. The consequent starvation, unemployment and reduction of wages produced the Luddite Riots of this period, when tumultuous mobs smashed the power looms and other machinery of the textile industries, which they blamed for their plight. Dragoons had to be used to disperse demonstrating weavers in Manchester, and early in 1812 the government made frame-breaking a capital offence.

If the Continental System had been applied strictly during these years, Britain might have collapsed, but ideas of economic warfare were rudimentary. Napoleon yielded to the wishes of French farmers and allowed corn exports to Britain, even believing that if she had to pay for these in gold she would suffer from disastrous inflation. Moreover, Napoleon could not devise an efficient administrative system to prevent the smuggling of British goods into Europe. A huge establishment was erected at Malta as a base for smuggling operations in the Mediterranean countries, and in 1809 Britain obtained Heligoland for the same purpose in the North Sea. Nor could France and her dependencies do without British manufactured goods and such colonial products as cotton, tobacco, sugar and coffee. Napoleon relaxed prohibitions at times and issued licences allowing French merchants to trade with the enemy. 'Undoubtedly we must harm our foes', he said, 'but above all we must live.' At the same time, British manufacturers met with considerable successes in finding new markets overseas, especially in

South and Central America.[1] All in all, the Continental System did not have any significant effect upon British trade.[2] It had resumed its expansion by 1812 when Liverpool cancelled the Orders in Council and Napoleon removed the embargo on British goods in favour of high customs duties to bring him much-needed revenue.

Britain's use of her sea-power to combat the Continental System involved her in further offensive action. A report that Napoleon intended to occupy Denmark and seize her fleet resulted in a second British naval expedition to Copenhagen in 1807, when the city was bombarded and the Danish warships taken back to England. British confiscation of American cargoes and interference with her trade precipitated the outbreak of war between Britain and the United States in 1812, though the demand for war came not from New England shipping interests, but primarily from the aggressive frontiersmen of the West who dreamed of conquering Canada. Hostilities lasted until 1814 and were inconclusive. Britain's efforts remained concentrated upon the main war against France. The Americans won some single-ship actions on the high seas, but failed to diminish the overwhelming superiority of the British fleet, which blockaded the American coast and brought trade almost to a standstill.

The Peninsular War (1808–13)

The Continental System was also responsible for a development in the War which at last provided Britain with an opportunity of engaging French forces by successful intervention on the Continent instead of by wasteful, unimportant colonial expeditions. In order to make his blockade more effective, Napoleon resolved to gain control of Spain and Portugal. French troops were sent across the frontier, and the Spanish royal family was ejected, Napoleon's brother, Joseph, being made King of Spain. This provoked, however, a national rising against the invader in May 1808, and a deputation soon afterwards arrived in England from Spain to ask for help.

Canning at once realized the importance of the situation. He said, 'We shall proceed upon the principle that any nation of Europe which starts up with determination to oppose a power, which is the common enemy of all nations, becomes instantly our essential ally'; and he was assisted in his purpose by the popular sympathy which the Spanish revolt aroused in Britain. Even Sheridan, who had taken over from Fox the leadership of Whig opposition to the War, called for 'a bold stroke for the rescue of the world'. And an immediate advantage the situation brought Britain was the establishment of closer commercial ties with the Spanish and Portuguese colonies in South and Central America to which British exports increased from £1,326,000 in 1807 to £6,382,000 by 1809.

British military intervention in Spain was not at first, however, very successful. Sir Arthur Wellesley (afterwards Duke of Wellington) arrived in Lisbon with 12,000 men in July 1808 and defeated a French force at Vimiero, but was then induced to accept the Convention of Cintra which allowed the French to evacuate Portugal. Napoleon came from Central Europe with veteran French troops and compelled the British army, now commanded by Sir John Moore, to retreat to Corunna, where it was safely evacuated by sea, though Moore was killed, in January 1809. Ill-success seemed to descend upon the British cause again. As soon as Napoleon had to hurry back to France, Wellington returned to Portugal, but when trying to advance into Spain was checked at the bloody Battle of Talavera in July 1809. In that month also, Britain attempted a diversionary expedition to assist Austria who had re-entered the War. A force of 40,000 men occupied the swampy Isle of Walcheren in the Scheldt estuary for an attack on Antwerp, but through mismanagement it had to be withdrawn after accomplishing nothing and losing nearly half its men from fever. By that time Austria had been defeated and forced again to submit to Napoleon, who seemed to be as invincible on land as ever.

Wellington, however, had persevered in the Peninsula, despite demands from some politicians that British troops should be withdrawn from this isolated campaign. In 1810 he established an impregnable base for himself by protecting Lisbon with the lines of Torres Vedras.[1] Secure behind these, he could engage in summer campaigns against the French forces which endured constant shortages of food and

[1] P. 203.

forage through their practice of living off the land, a practice which had previously made them so mobile during Continental campaigns. His troops at first lacked experience of European fighting, but he built them up into an effective fighting force which finally drove the French out of Spain by the summer of 1813 and in the next spring entered France from the south.

Many European historians suggest that British writers have placed too high a value upon the contribution made by the Peninsular War to Napoleon's downfall. It is true that if his Grand Army had not perished in the snows of Russia, it is doubtful whether it could ever have been defeated in the field, but the Peninsular campaign did seriously sap French military strength. The British forces kept a large number of Frenchmen in the Peninsula, and it is a tribute to Wellington's insight and strategic ability that he rejected the myth of Napoleon's invincibility and realized so effectively the part that British troops could play in this theatre of war.

The War of the Fourth Coalition (1813–14)

In 1812 came the turning-point of the War. Since the Treaty of Tilsit, relations between Napoleon and the Czar had deteriorated and Napoleon now prepared to attack Russia. His ostensible reason was Russia's refusal to restrict her trade with Britain as required by the Continental System, but the real cause for enmity between the two empires was mutual fears and suspicions about each other's designs in the Mediterranean and the Near East. In June 1812 Napoleon invaded Russia with an army of about 430,000 men of whom perhaps two-thirds were not Frenchmen. The Russians refused to negotiate or fight in the open. The French supply system revealed the same defects as in the Peninsula, this time with catastrophic results. By December the retreat from Moscow had practically destroyed the Grand Army. Early the next year Prussia, which had now recovered from its disastrous defeat by Napoleon in 1806, declared war on France.

These events encouraged Castlereagh, who had become Foreign Secretary in the summer of 1812, to form the Fourth Coalition. Russia, Prussia and Austria accepted subsidies from Britain, and the alliance was established in June 1813.

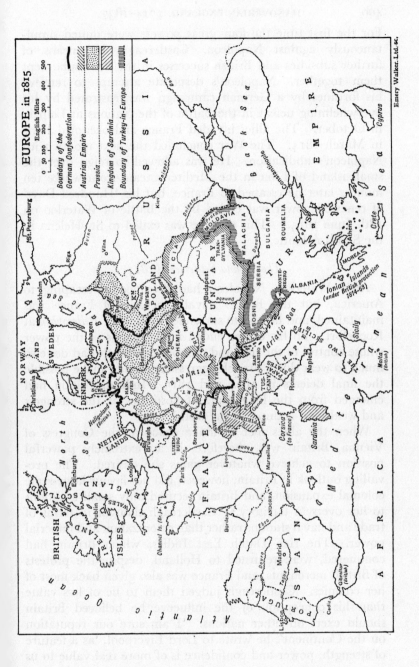

For the first time the four great powers were united simultaneously against Napoleon. Castlereagh, by means of
further subsidies and British successes in the Peninsula, kept
them together. Napoleon's desperate attempt to retrieve
his fortunes by a German campaign was frustrated by his
overwhelming defeat in the Battle of the Nations at Leipzig
in October. The allies invaded France and occupied Paris
in March 1814. The War concluded the next month with
Napoleon's abdication. He was allowed to reign over the
small island of Elba in the Mediterranean, from where ten
months later he escaped to France, but his 'Hundred Days'
of renewed power was ended by the Battle of Waterloo on
18th June 1815.[1] This time he was exiled to St. Helena in
the South Atlantic.

The Vienna Settlement (1815)

After Waterloo, Napoleon had dreamed of escaping to
America, but the British naval blockade of France was
maintained, and he had to surrender to H.M.S. *Bellerophon* at
Rochefort. So his career ended in the hands of the power
whose control of the seas and economic strength had done so
much to wear down French aggressiveness and make possible
the final defeats in 1814 and 1815. Indeed, Britain had
emerged from the long years of hostilities as the strongest
and wealthiest country in the world.

When the allies met to make peace at the Congress of
Vienna, Britain was, therefore, in an extremely powerful
position to achieve whatever gains she desired. The prevailing outlook in Britain, however, did not favour large-scale
colonial expansion, and Britain secured only small additions
to her overseas territory.[2] Castlereagh thought in terms of
trade and naval stations rather than colonization and imperial
power. The rich Dutch East Indies, which Britain had
conquered, were returned to Holland, despite the protests
of British merchants, and France was also given back most of
her colonies. Castlereagh judged them to be of less value
than his conception of the influence he believed Britain
should exert on other nations. 'I am sure our reputation
on the Continent', he wrote to Lord Liverpool, 'as a feature
of strength, power and confidence is of more real value to us

[1] P. 204.   [2] P 182.

than any acquisition thus made.' To compensate Holland for the loss of Ceylon and the Cape of Good Hope, which Britain kept, she received £6,000,000 to be spent on fortifying the new frontier between the Netherlands and France, which was in accordance with Castlereagh's wish to enable colonial questions to influence the wider European situation.

Castlereagh devoted much labour at Vienna to the questions of the great European rivers and the slave trade. The powers were persuaded to agree to the principle of freedom of navigation on the Rhine and the Meuse, and the closure of the Scheldt, enforced by the Treaty of Utrecht, was not renewed.[1] He was unable, however, to persuade the other powers to follow Britain's example in abolishing the slave trade. All he could secure from them was a pronouncement that its universal abolition was 'a measure particularly worthy of their attention', but even this was subject to the reservation that 'this general declaration cannot prejudge the period that each particular power may consider as most advisable for the definite abolition of the slave trade'. Philanthropic opinion in Britain was very dissatisfied.

There was also dissatisfaction in Britain with the European settlement made in Vienna. France was treated generously, being restored to her boundaries of 1790, and Castlereagh resisted Prussian proposals that she should yield territory to the new united Kingdom of the Netherlands (formed of Belgium, Holland and Luxembourg), even though he considered British security required its creation; but following a principle of 'legitimacy' the Bourbons were restored to the French throne as well as similar 'rightful' rulers in other countries, and neither Germany nor Italy were granted the unity that their nationalists wanted. This angered liberal sentiment in Britain. Wordsworth regretted that the Italians were 'transferred to Austria, to the King of Sardinia and the rest of those vile tyrants'. Byron wrote, 'Here we are retrograding to the full, stupid old system – balance of Europe – posing straws upon Kings' noses instead of wringing them off', while Shelley spoke of the despots of Europe crawling out again into the open air as insects when a stone is lifted.

Yet Castlereagh was not a reactionary. 'It is impossible not to believe', he wrote in 1814, 'a great moral change is

[1] P. 374.

coming on in Europe, and that the principles of freedom are in full operation.   The danger is that the transition may be too sudden to ripen into anything likely to make the world better or happier.   We have new constitutions launched in France, Spain, Holland and Sicily.   Let us see the result before we encourage further attempts.'   He wished to secure a balance between the old legitimate régimes and the new ideas which he considered 'most hazardous'.   After years of war, he regarded liberal thought as productive of insurrection and aggression, and he felt strongly Europe's need of 'repose'. The settlement, he hoped, would establish this, and the Congress System would maintain it.[1]   Though Europe did enjoy half a century of comparative peace, his optimism was not to be justified.   Metternich and the Czar Alexander I were not the men to allow liberal, nationalist movements to develop either in their own empires or outside.   Castlereagh's critics were never silenced, and were assisted by his own indifference to parliamentary and public opinion and also by the mood of isolationism which rapidly spread in Britain with the coming of peace.

[1] P. 412.

XXI · LORD LIVERPOOL'S ADMINISTRATION
1812-27

The Ministry

WHEN Perceval's assassination brought Liverpool to power in 1812, he came to it with extensive political experience. From Oxford he had gone on the Grand Tour and while in Paris witnessed the storming of the Bastille, which left him with a lasting fear that the 'incendiary lava' of mob violence would spread to England. On his return, he entered Parliament as a member for the Younger Pitt's pocket-borough of Appleby. He was Foreign Secretary under Addington (and negotiated the Treaty of Amiens), Home Secretary under Pitt and Secretary for War under Perceval (being responsible for supplying Wellington in the Peninsular War). The tide of war was turning in Britain's favour when Liverpool became Prime Minister, but there were still troubles to face: the country was drifting into war with America, trade was bad and bread dear, and the Luddite Riots were raging in the North. Liverpool was not daunted; nor did he attempt anything spectacular. He supported Wellington in continuing his successes in the field and Castlereagh in following Pitt's tradition in forming a final coalition until victory was gained.

When peace came, Liverpool's attitude remained the same. He encouraged and assisted his colleagues. He never lost his nerve and never considered comprehensive schemes of reform. His faith lay in what he called 'the gradual effect of the general policy of the government', a belief that sound and continuous administration would restore public confidence and stability. He has been condemned as a narrow-minded reactionary, but recent historians have pointed out that he was in advance of many of his party and exerted a reconciliatory influence in politics. Keith Feiling regards him as unjustly blamed 'for severities in which he was overborne by Eldon, for omissions which he shared with Peel', while W. R. Brock suggests, 'He seems at one moment to be looking back to the eighteenth century, at another to have set his face towards the prosperous commercial world of the high nineteenth century'. Indeed, in his speeches he honoured both engineers and landowners as contributors to the national well-being, and he understood the importance of trade and industry, though as a disciple of Adam Smith he believed the government should not legislate on economic matters. In his own lifetime, Liverpool's colleagues admired his 'pure and unquestioned integrity'. His tact and patience composed Cabinet quarrels, especially between Castlereagh and Canning, and enabled him to hold his ministry together for so long.

Liverpool particularly needed these qualities. His ministry contained diverse and opposing personalities and representatives of conflicting groups which had fought each other in the previous decade. The Earl of Eldon (1751–1838), who had been Lord Chancellor almost continuously since 1801, had made his way from humble parentage.[1] He believed that a lawyer should live like a hermit and work like a horse, and his mind was bounded by the contemporary outlook of his profession. Though tolerant and sympathetic by disposition, he unyieldingly upheld the penal code's severities and resisted any relief for Dissenters or Roman Catholics. Sidmouth, the Home Secretary, was, like Liverpool, a follower of Adam Smith; on taking office in 1812, he wrote, 'Man cannot create abundance where Providence has inflicted scarcity'. His last speech in the Lords was to be against Roman Catholic emancipation in 1829 and his last vote against the Reform Bill of 1832. In the popular mind, he was identified with the government's unpopular domestic measures, but it is unlikely that he had, in fact, sufficient standing to have initiated them.

Lord Castlereagh (1769–1822), an Irishman by birth, as Foreign Secretary and Leader of the House of Commons, was the Cabinet's most distinguished member, but he combined outstanding gifts of character and political ability with little oratorical and social skill. 'He is so cold that nothing can warm him', said Cornwallis; and he himself suspected popularity and declared that 'unpopularity is the more convenient and gentlemanlike'. This lack of the competency and desire to gain popularity brought down upon

[1] P. 33.

Castlereagh public vituperation and the unjust, ignorant rhymes of Byron and Shelley. As Leader of the Commons he introduced the government's repressive legislation and accepted responsibility for it, but his main interest was in foreign affairs, and here also his aloofness and reserve led to popular misunderstanding of his policy.

The most brilliant and eloquent of Pitt's disciples, George Canning (1770–1827), only joined the administration in 1816 and then merely as President of the India Board. As Foreign Secretary from 1807 to 1809 he had been largely responsible for the second attack on Copenhagen and intervention in the Peninsula, but his duel with Castlereagh was followed by a long deprivation of political power. The party magnates were prejudiced against him because his mother had been an actress, and they disliked his acid wit, obvious ambition and delight in publicity. Another later addition to the government was Wellington, who became Master-General of the Ordnance with a seat in the Cabinet in 1818; he was as great a politician as a general, and he was actuated by a high sense of duty and added prestige to the government. Liverpool also gained the support in minor posts of promising young men like Palmerston, Peel and Huskisson, who were later to become well known. The weakest member of the government was Lord Vansittart (1766–1851), who unfortunately held the important post of Chancellor of the Exchequer.

The leading members of Liverpool's ministry had much in common. They came neither from the old aristocracy nor (except Eldon) from the newer nobility of recent years, but from the more numerous country gentry. They had mostly been educated at public schools, gone on foreign travel and gained experience as landlords, magistrates and yeomanry officers, but this was limited to the rural southern England and did not extend to the northern industrial regions. They had also mostly entered the Commons for pocket-boroughs and served their political apprenticeship under the Younger Pitt's tutelage. These factors strongly influenced their policy. They were guided by the abandonment of reform and resort to repression, in the face of threatened insurrection, which had marked Pitt's wartime ministries, and they relied for the keeping of the peace mainly on the local system established under the Tudors, which was becoming inadequate as the wealth, population and industry of Hanoverian England grew.[1]

The ministry had little to fear in the early post-war years from the opposition which still suffered from the unpopularity its attitude during the wars had produced in the country. It was divided and confused. The nominal leader was Earl Grey (1764-1845), but he now spent most of his time on his estates and had been virtually replaced by Henry Brougham (1778-1868) who had already acquired a parliamentary reputation as an advocate of reform, but was mistrusted for his instability and lack of judgement. The opposition might have won popularity by advocating extensive parliamentary reform, but it could not reach agreement on this. In fact, most members belonged to the same class as the government and shared its outlook and limitations.

The Post-War Years (1815-22)

The sudden cessation of the war against France produced immediate economic difficulties for Britain. The government ceased to spend about £50,000,000 a year on war supplies and cancelled its contracts for guns, ammunition, uniforms and other military needs. Hopes that these would be replaced by foreign exports were not fulfilled. Britain's allies withdrew their own orders for war material. The Continent as a whole was too impoverished to buy her normal products, and some countries wished to establish and protect their own industries. This was now more serious for Britain than it had ever been before. She was no longer self-sufficient in food. During the war years corn imports had averaged over 500,000 quarters a year; this was bound to rise, and exports were needed to pay for it. Moreover, Britain's expanding industries were dependent on foreign markets. By 1815 every man, woman and child in the country would have had to spend £3 10s. if all that was sold abroad were sold at home instead; and a large part of the population could not afford to increase their purchases.

When, therefore, British exports between 1815 and 1819 declined by 16 per cent and imports by nearly 20 per cent, the consequences were soon felt. There was a serious fall in the price of industrial raw materials: copper fell from £180 to £80 a ton and iron from £20 to £8. The slump also

[1] P. 64.

reacted on coal-mining and the textile industries. At the same time, about 500,000 men were demobilized from the armed forces in 1815. There followed increased unemployment, widespread bankruptcies and further sporadic outbreaks of Luddite rioting and rick-burning.

Unfortunately, the government's immediate actions hardly benefited the mass of the people who suffered most from the post-war situation. The Corn Law of 1815 assisted the farmers, but agricultural wages remained low, and the price of bread rose in the towns.[1] Similar consequences arose over the income tax which Pitt had initiated as a wartime impost.[2] In 1816 Vansittart proposed only to halve the tax (because of his need for revenue) instead of redeeming Pitt's pledge to abolish it. The National Debt was now as high as £820,000,000 (which was probably nearly as large, in relation to the country's wealth, as it is today), and the service of it exhausted about half the total revenue; expenditure was still high, the army and navy estimates, for instance, coming to £29,000,000; and there was a deficit of over £30,000,000.

Vansittart's proposal, however, brought in petitions from all over the country demanding the repeal of the tax. Brougham led the parliamentary agitation against it, and the Commons insisted on repeal by 238 votes to 231. It was a triumph for both the moneyed classes and the country gentlemen. The income tax had brought in £15,000,000 in 1815. The government had to borrow £11,000,000 from the Bank of England and increase the duties on common articles like tea, sugar, tobacco, beer, paper, soap and candles, which fell on both rich and poor.

This economic disorder and social distress came at a time when many men of varying position and ability believed that the coming of peace must bring about urgent political and social changes in the country. Some of them belonged to the Radical movement, submerged by the anti-Jacobin reaction of the wars against France but now seeking to assert itself again, though without hope of increasing its representation in the unreformed House of Commons. The most influential Radicals were probably the Benthamites.[3] Bentham was a remote figure, who did not address meetings or lead demonstrations, but he provided Radicalism with ideas which gained

[1] Pp. 127–8.   [2] P. 381.   [3] P. 97.

a ready popularity in these years. He insisted that the greatest happiness of the greatest number would be achieved if individuals were left to pursue it with as little interference as possible. Restrictive measures, like the Corn Law, which failed this test of utility, should be abolished; and under the influence of his greatest disciple, James Mill, Bentham had come to believe that utilitarian reform could only be accomplished by a democratically elected parliament. To all those excluded from political power and subjected to legislation designed to assist the ruling landed classes, Bentham's philosophy made a strong appeal.

The most active Radical in London was Francis Place (1771–1854), who had been a journeyman and was now a successful master-tailor in Charing Cross. Behind his shop, where he discussed plans with reformers he had a large library of Radical literature. He had a hard, clear, practical mind, and in 1807 set out to gain the election of Sir Francis Burdett (1770–1844), a wealthy Radical and disciple of Horne Tooke, for the borough of Westminster in which Fox had won his triumphs. To the general surprise, he succeeded in getting Burdett elected by a handsome majority. It was an important stage in the revival of the reform movement, though Burdett himself became increasingly conservative in his views after 1815.

More prominent as Radical speakers and writers were Henry Hunt (1773–1835) and William Cobbett (1762–1835). 'Orator' Hunt, the son of a prosperous farmer, had adopted Radical views after meeting Horne Tooke and others. He was a born mob-orator and delighted in swaying large audiences with such slogans as 'Universal suffrage – or nothing!'. He spread the message of reform among the working-classes, but his vanity, extremism and invective aroused alarm among 'men of consequence'. Cobbett was the son of a small farmer in Surrey. He ran away from the drudgery of a ploughboy's life to become first a lawyer's clerk and then a soldier, serving for eight years in Canada. Discharged in 1791, he thought it wise, after writing a provocative pamphlet on army discipline, to flee to France and later to the United States, where he became a prominent journalist. On his return to England in 1800, he started two years later his *Weekly Political Register*, which at first was anti-Jacobin but by 1806 had become uncompromisingly Radical. In 1812 he was imprisoned for two years for an attack on flogging in the army, but after the Napoleonic War his influence increased immensely, and his *Register*, which he boldly reduced from 1*s*. to 2*d*., gained a circulation of 60,000 a week. Cobbett's conversion to Radicalism had come about through his sympathy with the agricultural labourers' plight; he looked back to an idealistic old England which had been destroyed by manufacturers, profiteers, grasping landlords, nabobs and Methodists, all of whom he loathed. He had no knowledge of politics or economics (pouring scorn on 'feelosophers') and was no revolutionary. Because Parliament had allowed his rural England to be destroyed, he held it must be reformed. His prejudices found popular acceptance, and his violent writing aroused official alarm, but the *Register* always advocated constitutional action and peaceful means in politics.

Behind these men were other Radical figures. There was Major Cartwright whose connection with the reform movement went back to pre-Revolutionary times.[1] When Horne Tooke and others had despaired in the 1790's he had maintained his faith in the cause. In 1811 he and Burdett founded Hampden Clubs to carry on the work of the suppressed Radical societies. Their membership was confined to men of substance, but in 1816 their subscription was reduced to a penny a week, and working-class clubs were set up throughout the country. There were also the Spenceans, members of the Society of Spencean Philanthropists, who wished to put into operation the ideas of Thomas Spence (1750–1814), a Tyneside bookseller, about the rights of man, phonetic spelling and parochial communism in land. They met in East London taverns to discuss these 'subjects calculated to enlighten the human understanding', but within their unlikely ranks were Arthur Thistlewood and other desperate, half-crazy characters who dreamt of plots and violence against the government.

From the summer of 1816 the Hampden Clubs and the Spencean Society held reform meetings up and down the country and prepared to petition the Prince Regent. In December 1816 a large meeting, addressed by Hunt, at Spa Fields, London, ended in a riot, and the next month a stone

[1] P. 349.

was thrown at the Regent on his way to Parliament. Early in 1817 some spinners and weavers from Manchester, where there was a bad slump, set out to present a petition to the Regent. As they carried blankets for the night, they became known as the Blanketeers. They were quickly dispersed by troops at Derby and their leaders imprisoned without trial.

Such disturbances were spasmodic and mostly due to local discontent; the demonstrations were generally peaceful, and the leaders had no clear plans for a revolution; but the government was alarmed, partly because it largely relied on the information of paid informers (in the absence of detectives) whose stories were often exaggerated. When a number of magistrates wrote to Sidmouth asking for increased powers, Parliament passed the 'Gagging Acts' in the spring of 1817. These suspended the Habeas Corpus Act, forbade all public meetings except under licence from the magistrates and increased the penalties for seditious speeches or writings and attempts to weaken the loyalty of the troops. Some Radical leaders were arrested, and Cobbett thought it advisable to flee to America.

The autumn of 1817 brought a better harvest and a temporary trade revival. Unrest declined. The government ended the suspension of the Habeas Corpus Act, while revelations by the Whig opposition in Parliament discredited the use of informers. Tension gradually relaxed, and in the general election of 1818 the government maintained its majority over the divided opposition. It looked as if the troubles were over, but it was only a short lull. There was another bad harvest and an industrial slump, especially in the textile trade. Vansittart still had difficulty in balancing his budgets and in 1819 further increased the duties on a number of foodstuffs. The restoration of Habeas Corpus had released the agitators, and Cobbett returned from America. Large meetings, particularly in Manchester, demanded higher wages, parliamentary reform and the repeal of the Corn Law. Hunt organized demonstrations at Birmingham, Leeds and other towns. In August 1819 an orderly crowd of about 60,000 people assembled at a reform meeting at St. Peter's Fields, Manchester (now the site of the Free Trade Hall). While Hunt was addressing them, the magistrates lost their nerve and ordered the yeomanry to arrest him.   A general panic followed in which eleven people, among them two women, were killed and some 400 injured. The Regent and Sidmouth both congratulated the magistrates on their action, but many protest meetings were held, violent Radical newsheets appeared, and the event was sardonically called the 'Battle of Peterloo'.   It had the effect of aggravating both fear in official circles and resentment against the government among Radicals and the working classes.

Sidmouth and Eldon were alarmed, and so also were Canning and Grey.   Parliament passed the Six Acts amid general approval in the autumn of 1819.   They prohibited private military training, enabled magistrates in disturbed counties to search for arms, prevented delay in bringing cases of misdemeanour to trial, checked and punished seditious libels, forbade the holding of public meetings of more than fifty persons and extended to cheap pamphlets the stamp duty already paid by newspapers.   The government's attitude seemed to be vindicated the next February by the 'Cato Street Conspiracy'.   The excitement over Peterloo stirred Thistlewood and his companions to plan the assassination of the whole Cabinet while they dined with Lord Harrowby, but they were betrayed by an informer and surprised by the Bow Street Runners in a house in Cato Street in Marylebone. Thistlewood and five others were hanged and five transported for life.   Meanwhile, Hunt had been imprisoned for two years for his part at Peterloo.

It would be wrong, however, to regard the government's policy during these months as one of unrelieved reaction. Several reforms were initiated.   In 1818 a number of important naval and military posts were opened to Roman Catholics.   The Cotton Factory Act of 1819 was an attempt to protect factory children;[1] and the Truck Act of 1820 initiated efforts to control the much abused practice of paying wages otherwise than in money.   Moreover, the government's repressive policy culminated with the Six Acts, and the powers conferred on the magistrates to search for arms were in force for only two years and the restrictions on public meetings for five years.

From 1820 protest and unrest steadily diminished.   The leaders of the Radical movements were not capable of conducting a sustained agitation, and public opinion was diverted

[1] P. 145.

between June and November 1820 by the vain attempt of George IV, who had become King that year, to divorce Queen Caroline.[1] Above all, trade began to revive. This was assisted by the Bullion Act of 1820, the work of Robert Peel and William Huskisson, which resumed cash payments by the Bank of England, so stabilizing the country and restoring financial confidence. By 1820 prices were already rising, and within a year it was clear that the post-war economic difficulties were over. In the Midlands, the Black Country and Lancashire, industry expanded, unemployment declined, and discontent died down. 'I defy you to agitate a fellow with a full stomach', said Cobbett.

Castlereagh's Foreign Policy (1812–22)

The first three years of Castlereagh's period of office as Foreign Secretary were also his greatest. Though as Secretary for War under Portland he had been deeply committed in the disastrous fiasco of the Walcheren expedition in 1809,[2] he had by 1812 seen that victory could only be sought by concentrated attack where the enemy was weakest, and his consistent support for Wellington made success possible in the Peninsula. He established and preserved the unity of the triumphant Fourth Coalition, and from it came after the War the conception of a Quadruple Alliance of Britain, Russia, Prussia and Austria to preserve European peace against any renewed French aggression. It was Castlereagh who got its members to agree 'to renew their meetings at fixed periods for the purpose of consulting upon their common interests, and for the consideration of the measures which at each of these periods shall be considered the most salutary for the repose and prosperity of nations and for the maintenance of the peace of Europe.'

Castlereagh thought that British policy should perform, as it had in wartime, a unifying, mediatorial purpose among the European states to preserve international harmony. In December 1815 he wrote, 'In the present state of Europe it is the province of Great Britain to turn the confidence she has acquired to the account of peace, by exercising a conciliatory influence between the powers rather than put herself at the head of any combination of courts to keep others in check'.

[1] P. 47.   [2] P. 397.

This objective, however, presented him with seven years of harrassing difficulties which contributed towards his insanity and death. His countrymen did not believe that their future peace and security depended on this policy; they wished to withdraw from co-operation with the Continental despotisms in alliance with whom the War had been won. The restored and reprieved monarchies themselves wanted to ensure that their position would never again be threatened by outbreaks of liberalism or nationalism anywhere. The danger of such an outlook was underlined when the Czar Alexander put forward his idea of a Holy Alliance of Kings which threatened to identify the upholding of monarchical absolutism with the principles of the Christian religion. Every monarch in Europe joined it, except George III who was prevented by his illness. The Cabinet declared the Regent constitutionally unable to sign treaties, but he expressed concurrence in its 'sacred maxims'.

Castlereagh privately called the Holy Alliance 'a piece of sublime mysticism and nonsense', but publicly he had to use the language of diplomatic courtesy and accord. British public opinion failed to appreciate the distinction, and he made no attempt to enlighten it.[1] He embodied a tradition of aristocratic statesmanship and detachment which was fast becoming obsolete in an age when a critical House of Commons and a popular press were making it necessary for a minister to explain and justify his policy. His inability and unwillingness to do this brought Castlereagh crippling embarrassment and unpopularity.

The first meeting of the Quadruple Alliance was at the Congress of Aix-la-Chapelle in 1818. The allied armies of occupation were withdrawn from France, which was admitted into the alliance, henceforward called the Quintuple Alliance. The alliance, however, had lost its original purpose of preventing renewed French aggression. The Emperor Alexander proposed it should have a new aim; he wanted every ruler to be secured in his throne and territory. Castlereagh successfully opposed this, and the members of the alliance expressed 'their invariable resolution never to depart either among themselves, or in their relations with other states, from the strictest observation of the principles of the rights of nations'.

[1] P. 404.

Castlereagh was not, however, able to restrain the Continental powers much longer. In 1820 and 1821 there were liberal revolts against the absolute rulers of Spain, Portugal, Piedmont and Naples. Prince Metternich, the Austrian Chancellor, wished the allies to intervene jointly to suppress these risings, and he was supported by the Czar and Louis XVIII of France. Castlereagh had no sympathy with the revolutions, but he was opposed to general agreements to intervene in the affairs of independent states. He expressed his ideas in his State Paper of May 1820, which has been described as 'the most famous State Paper in British history'. In it he explained the dangers of despotic efforts to extend and pervert the terms of the alliance – 'In this Alliance, as in all other human arrangements, nothing is more likely to impair or even to destroy its real utility than any attempt to push its duties and obligations beyond the sphere which its original conception and understood principles warrant.' British foreign policy, he insisted, must always be influenced by its representative system of government – 'The King of Great Britain, from the nature of our constitution, . . . must well know that if he embarked on a war, which the voice of the country does not support, the efforts of the strongest administration which ever served the Crown would soon be unequal to the prosecution of the contest.' And he concluded, 'We shall be found in our place when actual danger menaces the situation of Europe, but this country cannot and will not act upon abstract and speculative principles of precaution'.

The allies next met at the Congress of Troppau in October 1820. Castlereagh sent his half-brother, Lord Stewart, as an observer only. Metternich, with the concurrence of the Russian and Prussian governments, issued the Protocol of Troppau claiming that any state that had succumbed to a revolution had, *ipso facto*, ceased to be a member of the Alliance and that the other powers had a duty to coerce such a state 'back to the bosom of the Alliance'. The British government publicly repudiated the Protocol, and the Congress adjourned in some confusion to Laibach. A general policy of intervention was prevented by the outbreak of the Greek revolt in 1821;[1] but Austria sent troops to subdue Naples and Piedmont.

[1] P. 421.

Another Congress was arranged for Verona in October 1822, but before it met Castlereagh was dead. That summer he had committed suicide, worn out by overwork, weakened by bad medical treatment and depressed by parliamentary and popular hostility which identified him with the government's repressive measures and regarded his refusal to withdraw Britain from the Alliance as tantamount to countenancing the reactionary policies of the Continental despotisms. And added to this was his disenchantment with the Congress system and realization that attempts to establish a stable concert of Europe, in which Britain could participate, had failed.

'Liberal Toryism' (1822–7)

Castlereagh's death and burial amid cheers from the crowd outside Westminster Abbey hastened a reconstruction of the ministry which Liverpool had already begun. The previous January Sidmouth had resigned as Home Secretary and was succeeded by Robert Peel (1788–1850), the son of a Lancashire cotton-manufacturer who had pioneered factory reform.[1] Now Canning became Foreign Secretary and Leader of the House of Commons. Then, at the beginning of the following year, Frederick John ('Prosperity') Robinson (1782–1859) replaced Vansittart as Chancellor of the Exchequer, while William Huskisson (1770–1830) became President of the Board of Trade. These changes prepared the way for the 'Liberal Toryism' of the last years of the administration, when a beginning was made with the introduction of reforms demanded by the mounting social and economic changes of the times. Now that discontent and disorder had died down, Liverpool was ready to give a new lease of life to his government by admitting to it men who were all members of the new middle class, capable administrators and aware of the need for policies amenable to the wishes of public opinion and contemporary needs.

Peel was very much a member of this new class. His father, the first baronet, who had made a fortune in the cotton industry, intended that his son should have a parliamentary career. He sent him to Harrow and Oxford and in 1809 purchased him a seat for an Irish borough. His father's

[1] P. 144.

influence and his own abilities secured Peel's appointment as Chief Secretary for Ireland in 1812; he often worked for twelve hours a day in his office and obtained valuable administrative experience in dealing with the difficulties presented by O'Connell's campaign for Roman Catholic emancipation.[1] He was sensitive to British public opinion, and in 1820 asked a friend whether he did not think it was 'more liberal – to use an odious but intelligible phrase – than the policy of the government'. As soon as he became Home Secretary, he abolished the use of government informers and the prosecution of the press for political reasons and turned his attention to important legal and penal reforms.

The harshness and confusion of the punishments imposed by the English law were notorious.[2] Evangelicals and humanitarians, Radicals and Utilitarians were demanding a less barbarous penal code. A committee of the House of Commons, set up in 1819, had recommended the repeal of the death penalty for many offences. Peel succeeded in carrying five acts in 1823 which abolished capital punishment for about a hundred felonies. Public opinion supported him. Further abolitions of the death penalty followed, so that by the end of the Hanoverian period its use was in practice confined to cases of murder.

Public opinion was also demanding prison reform. Agitation had begun in the late eighteenth century, being first led by John Howard (1726–90), who, on becoming Sheriff of Bedfordshire in 1773, was responsible for inspecting the county gaol and was so shocked by the conditions there that he devoted the rest of his life to an extensive investigation of prisons. His reports describing how those offenders of all types and ages, even those untried and often both men and women, were crowded together in dirt and neglect and at the mercy of their gaolers, led to some improvements; but here, as elsewhere, the long wars interrupted reform, and overcrowding increased as, after transportation to America ceased, imprisonment became more common as a punishment. Howard's work was taken up by a Quaker woman, Elizabeth Fry (1780–1845), who from 1812 visited Newgate prison to minister to the women prisoners. Her example was followed by pious men and women in many towns, and

[1] Pp. 15–16.   [2] Pp. 15–16.

their revelations made many aware of the conditions existing in prisons. By the Gaols Act of 1823, Peel ordered that the gaols in London, Westminster and seventeen provincial towns were to be administered by the local magistrates, who were to inspect them regularly and send quarterly reports on their condition to the Home Secretary. In addition, gaolers were to be paid and were not to extort fees from prisoners; women warders were to control female prisoners; prisons were to have chaplains and surgeons provided; and prisoners were to be graded for work and to receive elementary education and religious instruction. These measures remedied the worst abuses in the larger prisons, but did not apply to debtors' prisons and prisons in smaller towns, and, moreover, Peel's successors at the Home Office were very slow in taking his first measures of reform any further.

Peel's own attention in his last years of office was increasingly devoted to the establishment of an effective police force. The general traditional fear that such a force would allow a government to destroy individual liberty had been diminished by the Gordon Riots and the more recent occurrences at Spa Fields and 'Peterloo'. Peel hoped to form a civilian force which would no longer make it necessary for the authorities to rely on the military; when Chief Secretary for Ireland, he had already established a similar force in Dublin, which was to become the Royal Irish Constabulary.[1] His plans were delayed by Liverpool's seizure and Canning's death, but in 1829 the Metropolitan Police Act set up a regular police force for London under the direct control of the Home Office. It was immediately successful – there was no rioting in London during the Reform Bill struggle – but the establishment of police forces in the provinces had only just begun when Victoria came to the throne.

Peel's administrative efficiency and enlightened outlook at the Home Office were matched by the financial reputation which Huskisson brought to the Board of Trade. He was a convinced free trader, wishing to continue the commercial policy of Walpole and the Younger Pitt. As early as 1810 he had stated in a pamphlet that the interests of every country were 'most effectually consulted by leaving . . . every part of the world to raise those productions for which soil and

[1] P. 221.

climate were best adapted'; and now British traders were themselves turning against commercial restrictions.[1]   Huskisson's ideas were shared by Robinson, the Chancellor of the Exchequer, and their collaboration brought Britain much nearer to free trade.   His great abilities made Huskisson the more influential of the two ministers; Robinson was content to support with financial measures Huskisson's plans for the freeing of trade.

First consideration was given to the Navigation Acts, which were now provoking considerable retaliation from Continental states.   The Reciprocity of Duties Act of 1823 empowered the government to negotiate commercial treaties with foreign powers which provided mutual reductions of duties and restrictions.   By 1829 fifteen such treaties had been concluded, and British shipping had increased by 50 per cent.   In 1824 the first budget of the century to lower tariffs reduced the import duties on raw wool and silk and replaced the prohibition on imported silk goods by a tax of 30 per cent. Later the reductions were extended to linen, cotton, china, copper, lead, zinc, glass and books.   The duty on general manufactures (goods not subject to a specific tariff) was reduced from 50 to 20 per cent and on raw materials from 20 to 10 per cent.

These reforms were probably the most that could have been achieved without arousing the opposition of old-fashioned industrialists.   Moreover, the continued absence of an income tax made some import duties necessary for revenue purposes, and since receipts from taxation were less than £60,000,000, of which about half was still spent on the service of the National Debt and a quarter on the armed forces, little economy in government expenditure was possible. Huskisson was suspected by country gentlemen of wishing to abolish the Corn Law.   He denied this, but did modify it in 1828 by the introduction of a sliding scale.[2]

The growing acceptance of *laissez-faire* in commerce encouraged the Radicals to open a campaign against the Combination Acts.[3]   It was led by Francis Place, who insisted that the laws of economics required that wages should find their own level as the result of the operation of supply and demand.   He prompted Joseph Hume (1777–1855), a

---

[1] Pp. 160–1.   [2] P. 126.   [3] P. 382.

Radical politician, to obtain the appointment of a parliamentary committee in 1824 to enquire into the position. Hume was chairman, and Place prepared the evidence and witnesses so effectively that it condemned the Acts. Huskisson accepted its report, and the Acts were repealed the same year. Trade was still flourishing and prices rising. Trade unions were immediately formed in many industries all over the country. There were strikes, some of which were accompanied by far-reaching demands and violence. Employers were alarmed, and consequently Parliament in 1825 passed an act which forbade strikers to 'molest' or 'obstruct' either employers or other workmen and forced them to confine their activities to questions of wages and hours of labour. This maintained, however, the legality of combinations and made possible the growth of the trade union movement during the century.

Canning's Foreign Policy (1822–27)

While Peel and Huskisson were implementing their important reforms with much administrative efficiency, the minister who dominated the Cabinet and appealed most to public opinion as 'liberal' was Canning. So much had he abandoned hope of returning to power that he had accepted the Governor-Generalship of India when Castlereagh's suicide unexpectedly brought him back to the Foreign Office. His appointment led to no break in British foreign policy. His aims were essentially identical with those of Castlereagh but his rapidity of mind and tenacity in action made him bolder and more adventurous than his predecessor. At the same time he understood, as Castlereagh had not, the importance of public opinion. The most outstanding orator since Fox, his speeches in the Commons gave him complete control of the House, while he was the first Foreign Secretary to explain his policy at meetings outside Parliament and arrange for the immediate publication of his despatches. He also realized that his countrymen wanted a foreign policy which seemed to be more in accordance with national interests. 'For Europe', he said, 'I shall be desirous now and then to read England', and he was applauded for such remarks. The resilience of his personality carried him through difficulties, which he faced with gusto and even enjoyment. Wellington commented in 1823, 'There are some people who like to fish in troubled waters, and Mr. C. is one of them'.

When the Congress of Verona met, it proved to be the last attended by Britain. Russia and Austria supported the despatch of a French force to quell the Spanish revolt. Canning instructed the British delegate, Wellington, to protest and withdraw from the Congress. He could not stop French troops entering Spanish territory the next year without risking a war he did not wish to wage, but he strengthened the navy and announced in Parliament that the British government would not allow the permanent military occupation of Spain, the violation of Portuguese territory or the annexation of any of the Spanish colonies in South America (which had been in revolt since 1809).

Canning's South American policy gained him his greatest triumph and speedily won him the support of commercial circles and informed opinion. Canning, who had been brought up by a banker uncle and represented Liverpool in Parliament from 1812 to 1822, knew more about mercantile aspirations than either his predecessor or cabinet colleagues. He knew the value of the increasing trade with South America and the strong sympathy felt in Britain for the colonists. Moreover, this was a situation which could be controlled by British naval power. Canning entered into negotiations with the United States, which resulted in President Monroe's message to Congress in 1823 that 'the American continents . . . are henceforth not to be considered as subjects for future colonization by any European powers' and that any such attempt would be regarded as 'the manifestation of an unfriendly disposition to the United States'; but the Monroe Doctrine contained in this statement could only be asserted by the American government because the British navy could enforce it. After a long struggle in the Cabinet, Canning secured British recognition of the independence of the republics of Mexico, Columbia and the Argentine in 1824 though George IV refused to read the royal speech at the opening of Parliament proclaiming this step (saying he had gout and had lost his false teeth), and Eldon, who had opposed it, read the speech unenthusiastically. The next year the recognition of Brazil's independence crowned Canning's success in South America. His own well-known claim was typical and premature – 'I resolved that if France had Spain, it should not be Spain with the Indies; I called the New World into existence to redress the balance of the Old'.

Canning also made use of British naval power in his policy towards Portugal. In 1821 the King of Portugal, John VI, died. His elder son, Dom Pedro, after acting as his Regent in Brazil, had proclaimed himself Emperor of an independent Brazil in 1822 and had been recognized by his father three years later through British mediation. Dom Pedro now claimed the Portuguese throne, but was opposed by his younger brother, Dom Miguel. Pedro's response was to abdicate in favour of his eight-year-old daughter, Donna Maria, and propose that a papal dispensation should be sought to permit her marriage to Miguel; he also granted the kingdom a liberal constitution. But Miguel, who was absolutist in outlook, was supported by the reactionary party, who continued to try, with unofficial Spanish help, to get him on the throne. The constitutionalists appealed to Canning, who sent a fleet and 4,000 troops to Lisbon. The Spanish government withdrew, and the Portuguese constitution was preserved. Portugal's maritime situation had enabled Canning to act and prevent the sending of a Continental army into the country.

Meanwhile, Canning had been struggling with the much more complex problem of the Greek War of Independence, which he had inherited from Castlereagh. The Greeks rose against their Turkish overlords in 1821 and proclaimed their independence the next year. The Turks tried to quell the revolt by terrorizing Greeks in Constantinople and Asia Minor. On Easter Day 1821 the Patriarch and three archbishops were murdered in the Greek Cathedral in Constantinople, and the next year over three-quarters of the people of the island of Chios were slaughtered or enslaved. There were dangerous international possibilities in the situation. Russia had designs on Constantinople and by the Treaty of Kutchuk Kainardji in 1774 had acquired an undefined position as protector of the Sultan's Christian subjects. Other nations, including Britain, did not wish to see Russian influence in the Near East extended. With Castlereagh's support, Metternich induced the Czar Alexander not to intervene.

Though the Greeks replied by taking no prisoners, the

Turkish atrocities aroused indignation in Britain, where there was strong sympathy for the rebels. Liberal politicians, Romantic poets and Evangelical preachers saw the savage peasants of the Morea as descendants of the ancient Greeks struggling against the barbarous Turks to establish a free, Christian state. Byron's death from rheumatic fever in 1824 in the swamps of Missolonghi gave the Greek cause a martyr. In addition, much trade in the eastern Mediterranean, including British trade, was in the hands of Greeks, and British financial houses had made loans to them. On becoming Foreign Secretary, Canning's first action with regard to Greece was to recognize them as belligerents in 1823, but he would do no more. He suspected Russia and was unwilling to arouse Turkish hostility. He did not want a war for 'Epaminondas or St. Paul'.

Greek shipping gave them command of local waters. The Turks could not supply or reinforce their forces. Greek successes seemed to assure their independence; but in 1825 two events changed the situation. In February the Sultan secured help from his vassal, Mehemet Ali, Pasha of Egypt, whose powerful fleet and army quickly inflicted serious losses on the Greeks, and in December the Czar Alexander was succeeded by Nicholas I, who did not believe that Russia should withhold assistance from the Greeks. Canning wished to prevent the new Czar from intervening alone. Wellington was sent to St. Petersburg, and Canning went to Paris. By July 1827, during his brief period as Prime Minister, Russia and France signed with Britain the Treaty of London by which they agreed that Greece should become autonomous, and to enforce this settlement on Turkey by naval action, if necessary. In October allied squadrons sailed into Navarino Bay, where they faced the Turkish and Egyptian fleets and, in an unintended battle, destroyed them.

Canning had died that August. Wellington was now Prime Minister. He had mistrusted Canning's policy. He believed that Turkey should be maintained as a bulwark against Russian designs, and Navarino alarmed him. To him it was an 'untoward event', and the King's speech at the opening of Parliament 'lamented deeply the conflict with the naval forces of an ancient ally'. The initiative passed to Russia and France. Russian troops forced Turkey to accept the Treaty of Adrianople in 1829, granting Greece autonomy; French troops expelled the Egyptian army from the Morea. Wellington believed that complete independence for Greece was necessary as an assurance against Russian intervention, but this issue was not resolved until his government had fallen and Palmerston was Foreign Secretary.[1]

'The ministry of Mr. Canning marked an era in the history of England and Europe', Metternich bitterly said as late as 1831. In fact, however, Canning had inherited as Foreign Secretary an international situation which was changing inexorably. The attempt to regulate Europe by the Congress System was already failing, and the fears of the other powers about Russian intervention in Greece served to preserve the possibility of concerted action for only a few years longer. The policy adopted by Canning of concern for British interests and support for European nationalism and liberalism, coupled with a refusal to persist in an alliance with the despotic monarchies, satisfied British public opinion and was to be continued by the most remarkable Foreign Secretary of the century.

[1] P. 435.

XXII · PARTY POLITICS, 1827–37

The Break-Up of the Tory Party (1827–30)

IN the summer of 1826 a general election returned Liverpool's supporters to Parliament with an increased majority, while several of his leading critics lost their seats, but on a February morning in the next year he was found lying paralysed on his study floor, and at once it became clear how much the success of his ministry had depended on his ability to keep its members together. Though he did not die until the end of the following year, it was soon apparent that he would never transact public business again, and that his colleagues would have to find a successor. By now Jacobinism seemed a distant danger, and the Tory party's cohesion, which had been forged in fear, was increasingly strained as that fear diminished. Canning and his fellow-liberals were turning towards new policies of reform, which seemed likely to win fresh support in the country, but to Wellington and other conservatives, who mistakenly believed that the party was now safe, these ideas were abhorrent. They regarded Canning's foreign policy as dangerously irresponsible, disliked Huskisson's changes in the Corn Law and feared the outcome of O'Connell's campaign in Ireland for Roman Catholic emancipation.[1] 'The real opposition of the present day,' wrote Palmerston in 1826, 'sit behind the Treasury Bench.'

After eight weeks of manœuvring, George IV had to overcome his personal dislike of Canning for supporting Queen Caroline's cause in 1820 and recognize that he alone could attempt to govern. Canning, therefore, became Prime Minister in April. Six cabinet ministers, including Wellington, Peel and Eldon, resigned; and Wellington even gave up the command of the army as well. Altogether, there were forty-two resignations from the government and royal household. Without Wellington's action, the defection would not have been so large, and his responsibility was great. The collapse of the Tory party of Pitt and Liverpool was fore-

[1] Pp. 419–23, 126, 222.

424

shadowed, but Canning himself was spared the final crisis. His health was failing, and he died in August, in the same house where Charles James Fox (who also had only survived for a few months the attainment of the office he had desired for years) had died in 1806. The King asked Lord Goderich (as Robinson had now become) to assume the premiership, which he did for six months proving himself so weak and ineffective that his resignation had to be accepted in January 1828.

George IV persuaded Wellington to become Prime Minister. He tried to restore the political balance of Liverpool's ministry and obtain the support of the King and the propertied classes, especially the landed gentry. He showed good judgement in selecting his ministers. He omitted Eldon and other former conservative colleagues; he restored the Home Secretaryship to Peel, who persuaded him to include Huskisson and three other Canningites in the Cabinet. He also showed some political dexterity, for when the Canningites offered to resign after a dispute over parliamentary reform, he allowed them to go, knowing that their brief service under him had destroyed the dangerous alliance they had made with the Whigs on Canning's death. So with the opposition divided and coherence possible in his administration, he might hope that the future would bring a period of settled government.

Wellington was not, however, to be allowed the respite from political contention necessary to make this possible. Events moved beyond his control. In February 1828 Lord John Russell introduced a bill for the repeal of the Corporation and Test Acts in so far as they excluded Protestant Dissenters from office, and, after at first opposing it, Wellington and Peel allowed it to become law. This strengthened the case for Roman Catholic emancipation, and O'Connell took advantage of it.[1] By the midsummer of 1828, Wellington and Peel believed that the choice for the government had become emancipation or civil war, and they chose emancipation. They could not resign to allow emancipation to be carried by the Whigs, who had long supported it, since they alone could overcome the opposition of George IV and the Lords. The Catholic Emancipation Act was passed in March 1829.

[1] P. 222.

Its passing, nevertheless, cost Wellington the support of many of the independent country gentlemen in the Commons who believed that emancipation had undermined the established constitution in Church and State. Yet his position was by no means unfavourable. Since Grey also had supported Queen Caroline, George IV, as long as he lived, would never permit him to form a Whig ministry, and Wellington believed that time and prosperity would regain him the natural adherence of the landed gentry. In 1830, however, he lost both these advantages. George IV died in June, His brother and successor, William IV, had no dislike of Grey and wanted to restore the Crown's lost popularity. And the winter of 1830 brought an agricultural slump and rural distress.[1]

The general election, necessitated by a new monarch's accession, was conducted in the autumn of 1830 in traditional manner. Only about a quarter of the seats were contested, and local issues and loyalties swayed the electors more than the renewed demands of the parliamentary reformers, who had been encouraged by Roman Catholic emancipation, or the July Revolution in France, which had overthrown the absolutist Bourbons and put Louis Philippe, the 'citizen king', on the throne. Wellington lost, on balance, about thirty votes in the Commons. The long-term prospects for his ministry were not hopeless, but he threw them away by his lack of political skill. When the new Parliament met in October, he went out of his way to reject all idea of parliamentary reform, saying that 'the system of representation possessed the full and entire confidence of the country'. Whigs, Radicals and Canningites were angered, and many of his moderate supporters were upset, while the country members, whose resentment at the condition of agriculture had kept alive their mistrust of him, were not placated. Within a fortnight the government was defeated on a motion concerning the civil list and Wellington decided to resign.

The long-term reasons for the break-up of the Tory party lay in the changing economic and social structure of society. It had come into power fifty years previously and stayed in power all that time because of the dangerous uncertainties arising from the French Revolution, the long wars and the

[1] P. 129.

first troubled years of peace. As more settled conditions returned in the 1820's, Liverpool's reconciling ability had enabled the party's liberals, such as Peel and Huskisson, to introduce gradually reforms to meet the needs of the circumstances. If that policy had continued after his death, the Tory party might have survived, but Wellington alone had sufficient authority to take his place, and he was a man of the eighteenth century. He still feared the country might lapse into civil war and anarchy, and he believed that his primary duty as a minister of the Crown was to prevent this. His eyes were on the present and could not see into the future. He contributed much to the immediate causes of the break-up of the Tory party, which had begun with his precipitate resignation in 1827 and was completed now by his equal lack of political judgement in opposing parliamentary reform so directly.

Lord Grey's Ministry (1830–4)

Lord Grey, whom William IV made Prime Minister, had as a young man joined with Fox and Sheridan against Grenville and Pitt, supporting parliamentary reform and opposing war with republican France. With the establishment of the Consulate, however, he had begun to support the War and succeeded Fox as Foreign Secretary in the brief ministry which came to an end in 1807 on the question of Roman Catholic emancipation.[1] For the next twenty-three years Grey was out of office. While opposing the government's post-war oppressive measures, he gave little thought in opposition to the cause of parliamentary reform.[2]

In 1830 Grey's concern for reform was not really much stronger. He described himself as 'aristocratic both by position and by nature' and confessed 'a predilection for old institutions'. It is true that he had made the acceptance of a reform bill a condition of forming his ministry, but his motive was to admit the new propertied classes to a share of political power in order to preserve the traditional constitution; he believed that such a settlement would 'afford sure ground of resistance to further innovation'. His Cabinet was the most aristocratic of the century. All but four of its thirteen members were in the Lords. Six or seven of his own relatives

[1] P. 393.   [2] P. 406.

were members of the administration. The Canningites supported him, but their importance had declined since the death of Huskisson, at the opening of the Liverpool and Manchester Railway, had deprived them of their ablest member. The support of the Radicals embarrassed Grey, and only with difficulty did Henry Brougham become Lord Chancellor. In fact, the leadership of the ministry was formerly in the hands of the old Whig magnates, whose attitude towards popular discontent was shown in their severe repression of the agrarian disturbances before the end of the year.[1]

The Whigs had inherited their support for parliamentary reform from the earlier movement of Wilkes and Pitt and Fox, which had been stifled by the French wars.[2] The distribution of seats and the franchise remained in their antiquated and anomalous condition.[3] Indeed, the spread of industrialism steadily increased the size of the manufacturing towns and the proportion of the population living in the North and Midlands. Reform was urged in the post-war years by Bentham, Cobbett and the Radical societies on constitutional lines, but working-class leaders continued to advocate Jacobinical ideas of direct action.[4] Whig party banners still demanded reform together with 'retrenchment', 'civil and religious liberty' and 'the abolition of colonial slavery', but in Parliament it was taken up actively only by a few politicians, notably Brougham, the Earl of Durham (1792–1840) and Lord John Russell (1792–1878), nicknamed 'Radical Jack'. Russell wanted large towns and counties to have the seats of boroughs found guilty of corruption. He succeeded in 1821 in getting Grampound's two seats transferred to Yorkshire, but failed in 1830 to obtain those of East Retford for Birmingham.

By 1830, however, politicians had to recognize that opinion in the country had inclined more strongly towards reform. After Peterloo and the Cato Street Conspiracy, the lower classes moved with high hopes to electoral reform as the means of gaining political power and the ability to redress their grievances. The middle classes also now wanted changes in the constitution. As the fear of Jacobinism declined, reform

[1] P. 129.   [2] Pp. 333, 364, 393.
[3] Pp. 54-5.   [4] Pp. 407-10.

lost its perils for them, and the recurrence of economic depression in the later 1820's induced them to believe that their interests were not best safeguarded by a Parliament dominated by the landed classes. In Parliament, most Whigs had come to share Grey's views about the necessity of reform. Few Tories agreed with them. They argued that reform would upset disastrously the balance of the constitution, leading to further demands for change and attacks on property by the masses. Even Peel said that he was unwilling to open a door which he saw no prospect of being able to close.

The Reform Bill was introduced in the Commons in March 1831 by Russell, though he was not a member of the Cabinet. It proposed to disfranchise 60 boroughs with less than 2,000 inhabitants and returning 119 members, to take one seat from 47 boroughs with between 2,000 and 4,000 inhabitants and to reduce the representation of the combined boroughs of Weymouth and Melcombe Regis from four to two seats. This meant the abolition of a total of 168 seats. In their place, seven large English towns, including Manchester, Leeds and Birmingham, and four London districts – Finsbury, Marylebone, Tower Hamlets and Lambeth – were each to receive two seats; 20 towns were to have one seat each; 26 counties were to have their representation doubled, while Yorkshire was to have six instead of four seats; and the Isle of Wight was to have one seat. In addition, Wales was to have one new seat, Scotland five and Ireland three. This made a total of 106 new seats, so the total membership of the House of Commons was to be considerably reduced. The proposals about voting maintained a distinction between the boroughs and the counties. In the boroughs a uniform franchise was to be possessed by the £10 householder – the man who occupied as owner or tenant a building of an annual value of at least £10; in the counties the franchise was to be retained by the forty-shilling freeholder and extended to the £10 copyholder and the £50 long leaseholder.

The Bill disappointed Radicals, who had hoped for a wider suffrage, shorter parliaments and voting by ballot, but it went much further than the Tories had anticipated, one of their speakers in the debate calling it 'a revolution that will overturn all the natural influence of rank and property'. The second reading of the Bill passed the Commons by a majority of one vote in the largest recorded division of the unreformed House.   But in the next month it was defeated in the committee stage.   The Cabinet wanted a dissolution, and William IV reluctantly agreed.   Unlike that of the previous year, the general election of 1831 was fought entirely on a single issue – the question of reform.   The excitement of the hour gave the reformers nearly all the large and popular constituencies: 76 of the 82 county members were pledged to the Bill.

A new Reform Bill was introduced in the Commons in June 1831.   The government had to accept an amendment, instigated by the Marquis of Chandos, further extending the county franchise to the £50 tenant-at-will.   The Bill then passed the Commons by large majorities, only to be defeated by the Lords in October.   Their defiance brought excitement in the country to still greater heights.   Political unions, organized in London and the manufacturing towns, held meetings and demonstrations at which the slogan, 'The Bill, the whole Bill and nothing but the Bill', was chanted.   Elsewhere there were violent scenes.   Peers and bishops were insulted in the streets.   Mobs destroyed Nottingham Castle, Derby gaol and the Bishop's palace at Bristol.   An outbreak of cholera added to the alarm and excitement.

The government introduced yet another Reform Bill in December which contained a few concessions designed to win over moderate Tories.   Fifty-six boroughs, returning 111 members, were to be abolished and only thirty-one to lose one seat.   These changes were made possible by abandoning the proposal to reduce the numbers of the House of Commons.   This Bill got through the Commons and passed its second reading in the Lords by a majority of nine votes in April 1832, but in the committee stage a motion, which postponed the abolition of the rotten boroughs, was carried. Grey asked William IV to create fifty new Whig peers to secure a majority for the government, but the King refused, and Grey resigned.   Yet again excitement mounted in the country, though without the previous disorder.   The political unions considered a scheme for a collective refusal to pay taxes, while Francis Place suggested a run on the banks to create a financial panic and placarded London with the slogan, 'To stop the Duke, go for gold!'.

The King had, meanwhile, asked Wellington to form a ministry. Loyal to his notion of duty to the Crown, he was ready to do this and even to introduce a measure of reform himself, but Peel, with a greater sense of political reality, would not support him. After a week, the King had to recall Grey and agree to create the peers if necessary. When the Reform Bill once more reached the Lords, Wellington persuaded the majority of his party to allow it to pass. It received the royal assent in June 1832. The news was greeted throughout the country by blazing bonfires, illuminated windows, toasts, acclamations and speeches. Like a much earlier constitutional enactment, Magna Carta, the Reform Bill was both an event and a document, and it was the manner of its passing which really aroused such rejoicing. The contents and immediate consequences of the Bill hardly justified the fervent claims and dire prophecies which had attended its troubled enactment.

In 1830 the number of voters had been about 435,000 or just over a tenth of the total adult male population of four million. The Bill added only 217,000 to the electorate to raise it to a total of 652,000 or a sixth of the adult male population. Considerable changes were made in the distribution of seats. Cornwall's representation was reduced from 44 to 13; most of the boroughs which lost one or both of their members were in the South; and the growing industrial towns in the North and Midlands were prominent among the newly-created boroughs. Yet a comparatively small start had been made in equalizing the distribution of seats. The 345,000 English county voters elected 114 members; the 275,000 borough voters 327 members. Counties and boroughs north of the Wash and Severn returned 120 members; those south of that line returned 371 members. The agricultural South was still over-represented to the disadvantage of the North and even more of London.

The changes in the franchise, since they were not accompanied by secret voting, did not destroy the dominance of the landed interest in most of the counties and small boroughs. Indeed, the Chandos clause further protected it since the newly-enfranchised tenants-at-will could have little political independence. Twenty of the twenty-one electors in the parish of Rattery in South Devon were Sir Walter Carew's tenants, who joined him in voting Whig in 1832, but when he became a Tory three years later, all except one did the same. There were still boroughs with a small electorate — five had less than 200. In these bribery and corruption, influence and patronage continued. Of the 1,000 voters at Stafford in the election of 1832, for instance, it was estimated that 850 had been bought. Pocket boroughs remained, and even new ones were created by the Bill. The Grosvenor interest was retained at Chester and the Lansdowne interest at Calne, while the hitherto open borough of Leominster rapidly succumbed to the influence of the Arkwright family. The landlords as a class were still over-represented, but the Bill was deliberately intended to maintain the social and political power of the great landed families in the rural areas. It was agreed that this system should be preserved, and the Act would not have got through Parliament if it had not done this.

The Reform Bill required for the first time that there must be official lists of voters. The overseers of the poor, who compiled the rate-books, were to keep the lists, and voters had to pay a registration fee of a shilling to have their names included. Registration societies were soon organized to encourage registration. The Carlton Club, founded in 1831, began to scrutinize electoral registers for the Tories, and in 1835 the Reform Association, established the previous year by Lord Durham, set up a registration office in London and opened branches in the country. These bodies added their supporters to the list and removed opponents by legal ruses; but it would be premature to regard them as the forerunners of party organization in the constituencies. Family interests, local loyalties and influence in many forms still controlled politics, and independent members predominated in Parliament.

Wellington said of the Parliament elected in 1832 after the Reform Bill, 'I never saw so many shocking bad hats in my life', but that was prejudice. The Bill made no immediate change in the social composition of the Commons.[1] Financiers, manufacturers and merchants were gradually elected for the northern towns, but they remained a small minority for a generation after the Bill when the members on both

[1] P. 434.

sides of the Commons still mostly belonged to the landed classes.

It has been sometimes said that the Bill gave political power to the middle class. But this was not so. Rather, as G. M. Trevelyan has said, 'Power which had previously resided in a privileged section of the landlords was now divided between all the landlords on one side and a portion of the middle class on the other'. The £10 householder had the vote only in the boroughs, and their numbers depended on the level of rents throughout the country. The national average of £10 houses was between a third and a quarter, but Russell himself had to admit that it was as high as a half in some towns and as low as a sixth in others. Only in London and several northern towns were rents high enough to give some working-class householders the vote. Generally clerks and other lower middle class tradesmen were not enfranchised. Moreover, it was estimated in 1832 that two-thirds of the new voters had houses valued at more than £15. Indeed, the £10 borough franchise was intended, as a Whig speaker in the parliamentary debate on the Bill said, to extend the vote only to those 'connected with the property of the country, having a valuable stake amongst us and deeply interested in our institutions'. Only such a franchise could then have been passed into law. An amendment in favour of household suffrage obtained only one vote in the last debate in the Commons when the Bill was carried by a majority of 136.

Those who had the vote under the old privileges did not lose their right at once, but it died with them, and the non-residential franchises in a few boroughs, like Preston, were at once abolished.[1] So in these towns a working-class franchise disappeared, and the electorate, though larger, was confined to a narrower section of the nation. Some Whigs idealized the £10 householder as the 'solid and intelligent' part of the community and held that the Bill was a final readjustment of the constitution. Among these was Russell, who soon became known as 'Finality Jack'; but Cobbett, Place and the Radicals had supported the Bill as an assertion of the popular will and an earnest of the possibility of further change. They realized that the newly-enfranchised merchants, manufacturers, shopkeepers and farmers had really more in common

[1] P. 55.

with the classes inferior to them than with the landed
gentry who had made concessions to them, and that in time
they would demand an enlargement of the franchise so as to
get more political power themselves.   Meanwhile, working-
class opinion, already embittered by the government's
suppression of the agrarian disturbances, was disenchanted
by their exclusion from the franchise and turned to trade
unionism and other forms of economic action.[1]

The general election of December 1832 brought Grey back
in triumph with a nominal majority of about a hundred.   On
both sides of the Commons were almost unbroken ranks of
country gentlemen.   There were 217 sons of peers or baronets
among them, while 115 members still sat for boroughs with
fewer than 500 voters.   Cobbett had been returned for
Oldham and John Gully, a prize-fighter and horse-racer, for
Pontefract, but they were oddities, and fears that the House
would be invaded by a horde of Dissenters and businessmen
were not realized.   'A reformed parliament turns out to be
very much like every other parliament', said Charles Grenville.

Despite its prestige and majority, Grey's largely aristocratic
ministry was not in a strong position and lacked cohesion.
The ministers disagreed about Ireland, and there was
antagonism between Whigs and Radicals who wanted further
parliamentary reform.   Just as Roman Catholic emancipation had broken up the old Tory party, so the Reform Act
seemed likely to break up the Whigs.   The government's
majority steadily declined, and so did its support in the
country.   These circumstances placed great power in the
hands of Peel, who led the opposition and dominated politics
in the 1830's.   As befitted a new industrial magnate's son,
Peel was more adaptable than most of the politicians in both
parties.   He appreciated, as Grey did not, the difficulties of
a reformed parliament in an industrial nation and the policies
it ought to follow.   He belonged to the new era in politics
brought in by the Reform Bill.   The new electorate wanted
moderate reforms, but feared Radicalism.   Peel set out
successfully to induce his party to adopt a reforming yet anti-
Radical policy, and to persuade the electorate that the Tories
would satisfy them better than the Whigs.

[1] Pp. 441–2.

Nevertheless, three reforms, urged by various bodies of opinion, were accomplished during 1833, which was Grey's first and last complete year of office in the reformed Parliament. Slavery, against which the Evangelicals had so long campaigned, was abolished throughout the British Empire.[1] Shaftesbury and his friends secured the passing of the first effective Factory Act.[2] And, encouraged by Brougham, the government instituted an annual grant of £20,000 'for the purpose of education' to be divided between the two societies which maintained schools for poor children.[3]

Palmerston's Foreign Policy (1830–7)

When Wellington's government was defeated in November 1830, Grey made Lord Palmerston (1784–1865) his Foreign Secretary. Except during the short ministry formed by Peel in 1834, Palmerston held this post for the rest of the Hanoverian period and beyond. He was, in fact, to exercise a dominant influence over British foreign policy for the next thirty-five years. The son of an Irish viscount (like Castlereagh), he was elected to Parliament in 1807 and became Secretary for War in 1809, a post which he retained through successive administrations for nearly twenty years. During this long tenure of office he revealed his outstanding energy, unremitting industry and gift of mastering difficult questions. He resigned in 1828 with the other Canningite ministers from Wellington's government.[4] He typically likened to cartridge paper the minds of the ministers who succeeded him.

Indeed, though Palmerston's greatest fame as Foreign Secretary was to come later in the century, it was by this time foreshadowed by his character and policy during these years when he first directed British foreign policy. Already his words and actions showed how close a successor he was to Canning, not only in his principles but also in his personality. He told the Commons in 1832, 'The independence of constitutional states can never be a matter of indifference to the British Parliament' and asserted that the government should accept the idea of 'non-interference by force of arms in the affairs of any other country'. At the same time, he believed this should be combined with a continual concern for Britain's

[1] P. 82.   [2] P. 145.
[3] P. 38.   [4] P. 425.

interests and reputation. 'Our desire for peace', he said in
1830, 'will never lead us to submit to affront either in language
or in act.' Although he was not a good speaker like Canning,
he shared his belief in publicity, particularly through the
growing national press in which he himself wrote leading
articles. His buoyant manner, outspoken language and
mistrust of foreigners gained him a popularity in the 1830's
which was a foretaste of the triumphs he was later to enjoy.

In 1830, however, he was still a relatively little-known
figure, and it was neither intended nor expected that he would
make his name at the Foreign Office. Grey had retained an
interest in foreign affairs since the distant days when he had
been Foreign Secretary and intended to conduct foreign
policy himself; all he wanted was a competent subordinate in
the Commons. Palmerston was living with Lady Cowper,
a married sister of Melbourne, whose influence got him the
Foreign Secretaryship.

As with Canning, Palmerston came to the Foreign Office at
a difficult time. Europe was changing. Liberals and
nationalists were subjecting the settlement of 1815 to increasing criticism and hostility. Before he took office, the July
Revolution in France (which he welcomed) had affected the
Kingdom of the Netherlands, which had not achieved
harmony and stability in the fifteen years since its foundation.
Belgian resentment against the domination of the Dutch
government in the union had steadily grown; the news of the
Revolution in Paris caused a rising in Brussels; and soon afterwards a national congress declared the country to be independent of Holland. One of the last acts of Wellington's government was to recognize Belgian independence.

Grey's government wished Belgium to establish her
independence without having to cede territory to France or
fight Holland, which would probably receive Prussian and
Austrian help. Before the end of 1830, Palmerston had
induced the European powers at a conference held in London
to agree to the separation of Belgium and Holland. When
the French government suggested that its support for Belgian
independence deserved territorial compensation, Palmerston
made it clear that British friendship with France depended on
'the supposition that she contents herself with the finest
territory in Europe and does not mean to open a new chapter

of encroachment and conquest'. There were further difficulties with France, however. Early in 1831 the Belgians
offered the throne of their new state to the Duke of Nemours,
a son of Louis Philippe, who had to be persuaded to decline
it in favour of Leopold Saxe-Coburg; but the Dutch would
not accept the arrangement and that summer invaded
Belgium. The British government had to agree to the use
of French troops to drive them out, but insisted that they
must be withdrawn when this was accomplished. Palmerston's language on this occasion was less diplomatic but more
typical. France, he said, should not gain even 'a cabbage-
garden or a vine-yard' in Belgium.

Not until 1839 was the question settled finally and peacefully when Britain, France, Russia, Prussia and Austria signed
the Treaty of London which recognized the independence
and neutrality of Belgium. The new state had been established without war. Palmerston had achieved his first share
of public attention, but Grey had concerned himself closely
in all the negotiations, and the ultimate solution was as much
a triumph for him as for Palmerston. When the Hanoverian
period ended, Palmerston's dazzling successes in foreign
policy still lay in the wars and crises of the future.

Lord Melbourne's Ministry (1834-7)

Grey resigned office in the summer of 1834. The
differences in the Cabinet over Irish affairs had continued.
The Irish bishoprics had been suppressed;[1] but an attempt to
settle the question of tithes precipitated a crisis. Russell
insisted that part of the revenues of the Irish Church should
be diverted to secular purposes, and the Cabinet broke up in
disagreement. As Lord Stanley, the Colonial Secretary,
said, 'Johnny Russell has upset the coach'. Grey went
willingly. He was old and tired. He had assumed office
solely to reform Parliament in a way which would maintain
the traditional system of government, and now he wished to
retire to his estate in Northumberland.

William IV offered the premiership to the Home Secretary,
Viscount Melbourne (1779-1848), the most conservative of
the Whig ministers. He accepted office unwillingly, but the
longer he held it the more attractive he found it. Yet he

[1] P. 86.

cared little for the public questions of the day. He was contemptuous of 'improvement' and condemned the new middle classes as 'all affectation and conceit and pretence and concealment'. In his character he combined kindness and charm with cynicism and lethargy. He was not the man to give his administration strong and effective leadership or pursue an active policy. The controversies of the period bored him. His preference was for doing nothing at a time when there was much to do.

Melbourne could not, however, check further reform. Russell wanted it, and the Benthamites, whom Melbourne particularly despised, were influential. Jeremy Bentham had died in 1832, on the day before the Reform Bill became law, but he had left active and able disciples. Among these were Edwin Chadwick (1800–90), who had lived in Bentham's house and received a legacy from him. He took a large part in getting a royal commission set up in 1832 to investigate the administration of poor relief. The commission met against the background of growing concern over the effects of the Speenhamland System.[1] In particular, poor rates, even after a period of falling prices, were still nearly as high as in the immediate post-war years. There was a general desire to reduce expenditure on poor relief and also to remedy the 'pauperizing' consequences of the way it was granted.

The major recommendations of the commission were embodied in the Poor Law Amendment Act of 1834. This laid it down that outdoor assistance was to be continued only for sick and aged paupers and no longer given to the able-bodied poor, who would have to seek relief by entering a workhouse. There conditions were to be made as unattractive as possible in pursuance of the dictum of the commission's report – 'Every penny bestowed that tends to render the condition of the pauper more eligible than that of the independent labourer is a bounty on indolence and vice'. To carry out this policy, the local variations and independence of the old parochial system were replaced by grouping parishes into 643 unions, each with a workhouse, administered by elected Boards of Guardians and centrally supervised by three Poor Law Commissioners appointed by the government.

[1] Pp. 125–6.

These changes were supported in Parliament by Melbourne and Brougham, Wellington and Peel as likely to secure administrative efficiency and economy, but public opinion and the newspapers were more inclined to see the Act as a cruel and tyrannical attack on the traditional rights of the people. It aroused Cobbett's wrath in the last year of his life. 'What is a pauper?' he enquired angrily. 'Only a very poor man!' The whole question typified the disagreements that were to be aroused by attempts to solve the urgent problems of the mid-years of the nineteenth century.

At first, however, there was little popular resistance to the Act. Chadwick was appointed Secretary of the Poor Law Commissioners and drove them with ruthless efficiency to apply the new system. They began in the agrarian South of England, where the abuses of outdoor relief under the magistrates had been worse. The harvests between 1834 and 1836 were good, and railway-building was providing more employment. Poor rates fell, and the demoralization of the rural labourer was halted. When, however, attempts were made to extend the provisions of the Act to the industrial areas, the same alleviating circumstances did not exist. Here under the old system there had not been large-scale subsidizing of wages out of the poor rates, but rather relief for the considerable number of unemployed, especially in bad years. Chadwick claimed that the new Poor Law was 'the first great piece of legislation based upon scientific or economical principles', but it was soon clear that its principles might be applied to the old agrarian society but not to its new industrial successor. So great was the immediate outcry among factory workers that the complete abolition of outdoor relief proved impossible.

Popular hatred was concentrated upon the union workhouses, the new 'Bastilles'. The royal commission had wanted separate workhouses for able-bodied, elderly, sick, lunatic, criminal and juvenile paupers, but the Poor Law Commissioners, for financial reasons, did not insist on this. They wanted each class of pauper to be housed in different parts of the same building, but even this was not carried out. Respectable men found themselves living with criminals and women with prostitutes. During the first years, the regulations which they made for the conduct of the workhouses, in

EI

pursuance of the determination to make them unattractive, were brutally unfeeling. Married couples were not allowed to live together; parents had no right to see their own children: meals had to be taken in silence; smoking was forbidden, and so were visits outside the workhouse. Such regulations were harshest for the aged and sick and, still more, for the children, whose cause was taken up by Charles Dickens in *Oliver Twist*, published in 1838. Widespread resentment brought changes in workhouse conditions during the early years of Victoria's reign, but the shame attached to the institutions in working-class minds long remained.

After the Poor Law Amendment Act had received the royal assent, Melbourne described his difficulties in a still-divided Cabinet to William IV, who took advantage of this to dismiss the ministry in November. He was determined to maintain his right to choose his ministers and suspected Whig intentions towards Ireland. Peel accepted the King's invitation to form a government, and a general election followed in January 1835. Peel issued an address to his constituents at Tamworth, which was intended for wider consumption. This was the Tamworth Manifesto, commonly regarded as initiating the establishment of the Conservative party. In it he declared in favour of 'combining with the firm maintenance of established rights the correction of proved abuses and the redress of real grievances'. It was an important assertion of his conception of his party's policy as one of sensible, temperate change, which increasingly drew votes from the Whigs. By now not only had many old reformers become Conservatives but, more significantly, the younger members of traditionally Whig families were also going over to them.

The Tamworth Manifesto was accompanied by an effort on the part of Peel's followers to improve their party organization in a way which made it an important stage in the development of the party system. Their most striking achievement was the spread of local Conservative associations throughout the country. Peel won about a hundred seats in the election, but did not secure a majority in the Commons. He held office for six weeks, but was outvoted by Whig, Radical and Irish members. The King had no choice but to recall Melbourne, who headed a new ministry which was to survive growing difficulties until 1841. His position was no stronger than before, and his dislike of reform was unabated.

The only important reform accomplished in this period by Melbourne's government was that of the local government of the boroughs. The Radicals had secured the establishment of a royal commission in 1833 to enquire into their condition. Its report was biased, in that it suggested that all popularly controlled boroughs were efficient and attributed to the rest the corruption of a few, ignoring the achievements of such oligarchic corporations as that of Liverpool; but the general inadequacy of the boroughs was obvious.[1] The Municipal Corporations Act of 1835, which both Melbourne and Peel saw themselves bound to support, dissolved over 200 old corporations and replaced them by 178 municipal boroughs with a uniform system of government. Each was to have a town council, consisting of councillors elected by the ratepayers for three years (a third of them retiring annually), together with a mayor, elected annually by the council, and aldermen elected by the council for six years (a half retiring triennially). These new municipal corporations were compelled to sell the patronage of any ecclesiastical benefices they possessed, many of which were bought by Simeon's trustees;[2] but they were to take over the powers of improvement commissioners and were allowed to regulate markets, establish a police force and organize public health services. The Radicals, however, had been more interested in establishing household suffrage in the towns than in improving local government, and the middle classes, who had gained municipal power, were tardy in wishing the councils to exercise their powers. Consequently conditions of life in many towns were to be slow in improving.

The Municipal Corporations Act brought no benefit to the working classes and increased the dissatisfaction they already felt after their failure to obtain the vote in 1832. Economic action and co-operation seemed to be the best way of securing their rights, and they were encouraged by Robert Owen, who brought to the situation his latest utopian idea. In January 1834 he persuaded a number of trade unions, representing both skilled and unskilled workers, to unite in forming the Grand National Consolidated Trades Union, which he

[1] P. 65.   [2] P. 80.

hoped would revolutionize society by setting up co-operative workshops and a system of exchanging their products with each other instead of selling them for profit. Working-class leaders, however, did not share his idealism. They were more interested in organizing strikes for better wages and shorter working-hours.

The talk of such men was often wild and violent. The government was alarmed, especially when the Consolidated Union grew rapidly and may have temporarily numbered as many as half a million members. In March 1834 Melbourne, who was then Home Secretary, decided to make an example of six farm labourers who had formed a branch of the Consolidated Union in the village of Tolpuddle in Dorset. With his connivance, they were sentenced at Dorchester to transportation for seven years because they had administered oaths contrary to an act of 1797 (passed during the Nore Mutiny). As Prime Minister, Melbourne rejected a petition of protest with a quarter of a million signatures presented to him by a long procession of trade unionists marching behind banners. The men were sent to Australia until public opinion obtained a pardon for them in 1836.

By 1835 the Consolidated Union had collapsed. Most of its funds were exhausted, and its treasurer absconded with the rest. Its constituent bodies had been various, including a friendly society of agricultural labourers, lodges of 'industrious females' and even groups of sympathisers from the professions, and these had sent delegates to a meeting in February 1834, but they had quarrelled among themselves. A few unions called futile strikes, but the skilled better-paid workers, not wishing to risk their jobs any further, withdrew from it, and worsening trade conditions hastened its end. The attempt to achieve working-class aims by economic action seemed to have failed, but the discontent did not diminish. Many intelligent working-men turned to politics, and the Radical societies were revived. One of these was the London Working Men's Association, founded by skilled craftsmen in 1836 to secure 'equal political and social rights' for all classes. Its leader was William Lovett (1800–77), a cabinet-maker, and its chief adviser the veteran Francis Place. From it was to spring Chartism, the next working class movement of the century.

William IV died in June 1837 and was succeeded by his eighteen-year-old niece, Victoria. Melbourne found a new and important task in acting as adviser to the young, inexperienced Queen. His government survived the general election of 1837, but the Conservatives routed the Radicals, which increased working-class discontent. Among the new Members of Parliament was Benjamin Disraeli, who defeated a Radical at Maidstone. The Victorians were taking over the issues and problems bequeathed them by the Hanoverian age.

BIBLIOGRAPHY

GENERAL

Asa Briggs, *The Age of Improvement 1783–1867* (1959).
V. H. H. Green, *The Hanoverians 1714–1815* (1948).
D. Jarrett, *Britain 1688–1815* (1965).
Dorothy Marshall, *England in the Eighteenth Century* (1962).
J. H. Plumb, *England in the Eighteenth Century* (Pelican History of England, 1963).
W. T. Selley, *England in the Eighteenth Century* (2nd ed., 1957).
D. Thomson, *England in the Nineteenth Century* (Pelican History of England, 1950).
G. M. Trevelyan, *British History in the Nineteenth Century* (2nd ed., 1937).
J. Steven Watson, *The Reign of George III 1760–1815* (Oxford History of England, 1960).
Basil Williams, *The Whig Supremacy 1714–1760* (Oxford History of England, 2nd ed., 1962).
E. L. Woodward, *The Age of Reform 1815–1870* (Oxford History of England, 2nd ed., 1962).

SOCIAL

Rosamund Bayne-Powell, *English Country Life in the Eighteenth Century* (1935).
M. D. George, *London Life in the Eighteenth Century* (1925).
Dorothy Marshall, *English People in the Eighteenth Century* (1956).
G. M. Trevelyan, *Illustrated Social History* (Vols. 3 and 4, 1951).
A. S. Turberville, ed., *Johnson's England* (2 vols., 1933).
T. H. White, *The Age of Scandal* (1950).

COSTUME

I. Brooke, *English Costume* (3rd ed., 1949).
C. W. and P. Cunnington, *A Picture History of English Costume* (1960).
J. Laver, *Seventeenth and Eighteenth Century Costume* (1951).
C. H. Gibbs Smith, *English Fashions of the Nineteenth Century* (1960).

EDUCATION

H. C. Barnard, *A Short History of English Education 1760–1944* (1947).
A. D. Godley, *Oxford in the Eighteenth Century* (1908).
N. Hans, *New Trends in Education in the Eighteenth Century* (1951).
M. G. Jones, *The Charity School Movement* (1938).
Josephine Kamm, *Hope Deferred: Girls' Education in English History* (1965).

H. McClachan, *English Education under the Test Acts* (1931).
D. A. Winstanley, *The University of Cambridge in the Eighteenth Century* (1922).
D. A. Winstanley, *Unreformed Cambridge* (1935).

CONSTITUTIONAL

J. E. D. Binney, *British Public Finance and Administration 1774–92* (1958).
Keith Feiling, *The Second Tory Party 1714–1832* (1938).
D. L. Keir, *The Constitutional History of Modern Britain* (6th ed., 1961).
Betty Kemp, *King and Commons 1660–1832* (1959).
S. Maccoby, *English Radicalism 1762–1832* (2 vols., 1955).
L. B. Namier, *England in the Age of the American Revolution* (2nd ed., 1961).
L. B. Namier, *The Structure of Politics at the Accession of George III* (2nd ed., 1957).
R. Pares, *George III and the Politicians* (1953).
M. A. Thomson, *The Secretaries of State 1681–1782* (1932).
W. R. Ward, *The English Land Tax in the Eighteenth Century* (1953).
S. and B. Webb, *English Local Government* (11 vols., 1963).
E. N. Williams, *The Eighteenth Century Constitution 1688–1815: Documents and a Commentary* (1960).

ECCLESIASTICAL

C. J. Abbey and J. H. Overton, *The English Church in the Eighteenth Century* (2 vols., 1878).
C. J. Abbey, *The English Church and its Bishops 1700–1800* (1887).
E. D. Bebb, *Nonconformity and Social and Economic Life 1660–1800* (1935).
S. C. Carpenter, *Eighteenth-Century Church and People* (1959).
L. W. Cowie, *Henry Newman* (1956).
R. Coupland, *Wilberforce: a Narrative* (1923).
J. M. Creed and J. S. Boys-Smith, *Religious Thought in the Eighteenth Century* (1934).
Horton Davies, *Worship and Theology in England 1690–1850* (1961).
E. M. Howse, *Saints in Politics* (1952). [The Clapham Sect].
W. L. Mathieson, *English Church Reform 1815–40* (1923).
J. H. Overton, *The Evangelical Revival in the Eighteenth Century* (1886).
J. S. Simon, *John Wesley* (5 vols., 1927).
C. H. E. Smyth, *Simeon and Church Order* (1940).
Norman Sykes, *Church and State in the Eighteenth Century* (1935).
W. J. Warner, *The Wesleyan Movement and the Industrial Revolution* (1930).
A. B. Webster, *Joshua Watson* (1954).

SCIENCE

H. Butterfield, *The Origins of Modern Science* (2nd ed., 1957).
A. Castigioni, *History of Medicine* (1947).

A. R. Hall, *The Scientific Revolution 1500–1800* (1954).
C. Singer, *Short History of Scientific Ideas to 1900* (1959).
A. Woolf, *History of Science, Technology and Philosophy in the Sixteenth, Seventeenth and Eighteenth Centuries* (1950).

THE ARTS

C. H. Collins Baker, *British Painting* (1933).
R. S. Dutton, *The English Country House* (1935).
M. H. Grant, *Old English Landscape Painters, Sixteenth to Nineteenth Centuries* (3 vols., 1957).
J. Lees Milne, *The Age of Adam* (1947).
George Sampson, *Concise Cambridge History of English Literature* (1941).
H. C. Smith, *English Furniture Illustrated* (1950).
J. N. Summerson, *Architecture in Britain 1530 to 1830* (1953).
E. Walker, *History of Music in Britain* (1924).

ECONOMIC

T. S. Ashton, *The Industrial Revolution 1760–1830* (1948).
T. S. Ashton, *Iron and Steel in the Industrial Revolution* (1951).
T. S. Ashton, *Economic Fluctuations 1700–1800* (1959).
T. S. Ashton, *An Economic History of England: the Eighteenth Century* (1961).
G. D. H. Cole, *Robert Owen* (1925).
G. D. H. Cole and R. Postgate, *The Common People 1746–1946* (2nd ed., 1956).
C. R. Fay, *Great Britain from Adam Smith to the Present Day* (5th ed. 1950).
M. W. Flinn, *An Economic and Social History of Britain since 1700* (1963).
G. T. Griffiths, *Population Problems in the Age of Malthus* (1926).
P. Mantoux, *The Industrial Revolution in the Eighteenth Century* (1961).
C. S. Orwin, *A History of English Farming* (1949).
C. I. Savage, *An Economic History of Transport* (1959).
W. Schlote, *British Overseas Trade from 1700 to the 1930's* (1952).
W. R. Scott, *Adam Smith* (1929).

COLONIAL

R. G. Adams, *Political Ideas of the American Revolution* (1922).
J. R. Alden, *The American Revolution 1775–83* (1954).
G. L. Beer, *British Colonial Policy 1754–65* (1907).
O. M. Dickerson, *The Navigation Acts and the American Revolution* (1951).
L. H. Gipson, *The British Empire before the American Revolution* (1958).
C. S. Graham, *Canada* (1950).
V. Harlow, *The Founding of the Second British Empire 1763–93* (2 vols., 1952 and 1964).
J. C. Miller, *The Origins of the American Revolution* (1959).
E. P. Moon, *Warren Hastings and British India* (1947).
A. P. Newton, *The British Empire to 1783* (1935).

C. H. Philips, *India* (1948).
L. S. Sutherland, *The East India Company in Eighteenth Century Politics* (1952).
J. A. Williamson, *A Short History of British Expansion* (4th ed., 1953).

DIPLOMACY AND WARFARE

R. Aldington, *Wellington* (1946).
G. Callender and F. H. Hinsley, *The Naval Side of British History 1485-1945* (1952).
G. Davies, *Wellington and his Army* (1954).
James Joll, *Britain and Europe: Pitt to Churchill 1793-1940* (2nd ed. 1961).
M. Lewis, *The Navy of Britain* (1948).
C. Lloyd, *Ships and Seamen* (1961).
P. Mackesy, *The War for America 1775-83* (1964).
P. Mackesy, *The War in the Mediterranean 1803-10* (1957).
G. E. Manwaring and B. Dobree, *The Floating Republic* (1935). [The 1797 Mutinies].
C. Oman, *Nelson* (4th ed., 1954).
A. J. P. Taylor, *The Troublemakers, Dissent over Foreign Policy* (1957).
H. Temperley, *The Foreign Policy of Canning 1822-7* (1925).
A. W. Ward and G. P. Gooch, eds., *The Cambridge History of British Foreign Policy* (1922).
O. Warner, *A Portrait of Lord Nelson* (1958).
C. K. Webster, *The Foreign Policy of Castlereagh* (2 vols., 1931).
J. A. Williamson, *The Ocean in English History* (1941).

POLITICAL 1714-1760

J. P. Carswell, *The South Sea Bubble* (1960).
A. S. Foord, *His Majesty's Opposition 1714-1830* (1964).
J. B. Owen, *The Rise of the Pelhams* (1957).
W. B. Pemberton, *Carteret, the Brilliant Failure of the Eighteenth Century* (1936).
J. H. Plumb, *Sir Robert Walpole* (2 vols., 1956 and 1960).
J. H. Plumb, *Chatham* (1953).
B. Tunstall, *William Pitt, Earl of Chatham* (1938).
C. B. Realey, *Early Opposition to Sir Robert Walpole* (1931).
Basil Williams, *Life of William Pitt, Earl of Chatham* (2 vols., 1913).
Basil Williams, *Stanhope* (1932).
Basil Williams, *Carteret and Newcastle* (1943).

POLITICAL 1760-1815

H. Bleackley, *Life of John Wilkes* (1917).
J. Brooke, *The Chatham Administration 1766-68* (1956).
A. Bryant, *The Years of Endurance 1793-1802* (1942).
A. Bryant, *The Years of Victory 1802-12* (1944).
A. Bryant, *The Age of Elegance 1812-22* (1950).
H. Butterfield, *George III and the Historians* (1958).
H. Butterfield, *George III, Lord North and the People 1779-80* (1949).

I. R. Christie, *The End of North's Ministry 1780–82* (1958).
I. R. Christie, *Wilkes, Wyvill and Reform* (1962).
A. Cobban, *The Debate on the French Revolution* (2nd ed., 1960).
J. W. Derry, *The Regency Crisis and the Whigs 1788–89* (1963).
J. W. Derry, *William Pitt* (1962).
D. Gray, *Spencer Perceval, the Evangelical Prime Minister 1762–1812* (1963).
C. Hobhouse, *Fox* (1934).
P. Magnus, *Edmund Burke* (1939).
J. Norris, *Shelburne and Reform* (1963).
R. Pares, *George III and the Politicians* (1953).
W. B. Pemberton, *Lord North* (1938).
Michael Roberts, *The Whig Party 1807–12* (1939).
G. Rudé, *Wilkes and Liberty* (1962).

POLITICAL 1815–37

A. A. Aspinall, *Lord Brougham and the Whig Party* (1927).
H. C. Bell, *Lord Palmerston* (1936).
A. Brady, *William Huskisson and Liberal Reform* (1928).
W. R. Brock, *Lord Liverpool and Liberal Toryism* (1941).
J. R. M. Butler, *Passing of the Great Reform Bill* (1914).
Lord David Cecil, *The Young Melbourne* (1954).
Lord David Cecil, *Lord M* (1954).
G. Kitson Clark, *Peel and the Conservative Party* (2nd ed., 1964).
F. O. Darvall, *Popular Disturbance and Public Order in Regency England* (1934).
S. E. Finer, *Life and Times of Sir Edwin Chadwick* (1952).
Norman Gash, *Politics in the Age of Peel* (1953).
D. Read, *Peterloo* (1958).
G. M. Trevelyan, *Lord Grey of the Reform Bill* (1914).
R. J. White, *Waterloo to Peterloo* (1957).

INDEX

Adam, James (d. 1794) and Robert (1728–92), 10, 105, 107–8
Adams, Samuel (1722–1803), 170–3
Addington, Henry (1757–1844), 386–9, 392–3, 404, 411
Addison, Joseph (1672–1719), 94
Additional Curates Society, 85
Adrianople, Treaty of (1829), 423
Aix-la-Chapelle, Congress of (1818), 413–4
— Treaty of (1748), 164, 280–1
Alexander I, Czar (1801–25), 402, 413
America, North, trade with, 154–9; British colonies in, 161–2, 169–70; Anglo-French rivalry in, 162–3, 164–6, 290, 305. *See also* Canada, United States of America
—, South, Anglo-Spanish rivalry in, 163, 264–5; trade with, 396–7; revolutions in, 188, 420–1
American Import Duties Act (1767), 171, 331
— War of Independence, 158–60, 169–75, 186–7, 313, 339–44
Amiens, Treaty of (1802), 387–8
Amusements, 12–13, 18, 25, 148
Anne, Queen (1702–14), 43, 48, 228
Anson, George (1697–1762), 193, 196–7, 227, 279
Apprenticeship, 4, 27, 37
Arcot, 11, 165
Arkwright, Richard (1732–92), 132, 139, 141
Armed Neutrality, League of (1780), 187; (1800), 386
Army, 48, 198–202; in Peninsular War, 203–4, 397–8
Arne, Thomas (1710–78), 102
Arnold, Thomas (1795–1842), 38
Asiento, 163, 242, 280
Astronomy, 87–9
Atterbury, Francis (1663–1732), 228–9, 252
Augusta, Princess of Wales, 45, 318–19, 321
Austen, Jane (1775–1815), 71, 100.
Australia, 93, 182
Austria, and Treaty of Utrecht, 240–1; Britain and, 259–61; and Diplomatic Revolution, 289–62; in Revolutionary War, 374–5, 377, 385–6; in Napoleonic War, 391–2, 398–400; and Vienna Settlement, 401–2; and Congress System, 412, 413. *See also* Kaunitz, Metternich
Austrian Succession, War of the (1740–80), 163–4, 266–81
Bakewell, Robert (1725–95), 112
Ball, Hannah (1934–92), 37
'Bangorian Controversy', 69
Bath, 12, 83
Bear-baiting, 12, 18
Beckford, William (1760–1844), 98, 107
Bedford, John Russell, Duke of (1710–71), 272, 309–11, 331
Bell, Henry (1767–1830), 153
Belgium, 401, 436–7
Bengal, 164–6, 176–8
Bentham, Jeremy (1748–1832), 97, 348, 357, 407–8, 438
Bentinck, Lord William (1744–1839), 181–2
Berlin Decrees (1806), 394
Bernstorff, Andreas Gottlieb von (1649–1726), 43, 224
Birmingham, 7, 38, 55, 147
Birth-rate, 4
Black, Joseph (1728–99), 91
Blackstone, Sir William (1723–80), 39
Blake, William (1757–1832), 98, 370
Blomfield, Charles James (1786–1857), 83
Bolingbroke, Viscount (1678–1751), 228, 232, 261–3
Bombay, 164
Boroughs, and parliamentary representation, 55, 234, 297–8, 429; and local government, 65, 441
Boston, Mass, 172–4, 339
Boscawen, Edward (1711–61), 193, 279, 290, 294, 301–2, 305–6

Boswell, James (1740–95), 95, 137, 147
Bothmer, Baron von (1656–1732), 43, 224, 229
Boulton, Matthew (1728–1809), 91, 136–7
Bow Street Runners, 283–4, 411
Bradley, James (1693–1762), 87–8
Bramah, Joseph (1748–1814), 135
Brighton, 7, 12, 47, 64, 83
Brindley, James (1716–72), 149–50
Bristol, 7, 11, 24, 58, 65, 70, 147, 341, 346, 430
British and Foreign Bible Society, 81
British and Foreign School Society, 38
British Museum, 286–7, 384
Brougham, Henry (1778–1868), 406, 428, 435
Brown, Lancelot (1715–83), 10, 105–6
Brummel, George (1778–1840), 31
Bull-baiting, 12, 18, 25
Bunker Hill, Battle of (1775), 173, 340
Burdett, Sir Francis (1770—1844), 408–9
Burgoyne, John (1723–92), 174
Burke, Edmund (1729–97), career, 326, 344–7; and the constitution, 21–2, 41; and America, 96, 342–3; and the French Revolution, 96–7, 371–3, 376, 384; economical reform, 49, 350, 356; and India, 359, 362; and education, 17, 385; *Thoughts on the Cause of the Present Discontents*, 315–16, 344
Burns, Robert (1759–96), 98, 370
Bute, Earl of (1713–92), 45, 307–10, 316–27, 323
Butler, Joseph (1692–1752), 68
Butler, Samuel (1774–1839), 38
Buxar, Battle of (1764), 176
Byng, John (1704–57), 196, 303
Byron, Lord (1788–1824), 11, 100, 401, 405, 422
Cabinet, development of the, 50–3, 255
Calcutta, 164–5, 294
Calendar, reform of the, 88, 286
Cambridge, 11, 33–4, 38, 65, 79, 247, 360, 362
Camperdown, Battle of (1797), 220
Campo Formio, Treaty of (1797), 377
Canada, French in, 162, 290; British conquest of, 168, 305; government of, 175–6. *See also* Quebec Act
— Constitutional Act (1791), 175, 365
Canals, 6, 122, 149–52
Canning, George (1770–1827), 11, 125; career, 389, 393–4, 405, 419; and the Peninsular War, 396–7, 405; and South America, 188, 420–1; and Portugal, 421; and Greek independence, 188, 421–3
Cape Breton Island, 162, 278, 290
Carlisle, 211, 286
Carnatic, the, 164, 166, 179, 307
Caroline, Queen (1683–1737), wife of George II, 17, 43–5, 146, 251, 254, 264
Caroline, Queen (1768–1821), wife of George IV, 47, 412
Carteret, John (1690–1763), 52, 275; his foreign policy, 225–6, 238; his dismissal, 253, 259; his supremacy, 268–72; his downfall, 273, 52
Cartwright, Edmund (1743–1823), 140
Cartwright, John (1740–1824), 349, 409
Castlereagh, Lord (1769–1822), 11, 392–4; and Fourth Coalition, 398–400; and Vienna Settlement, 400–2; unpopularity, 100, 404–5; foreign policy, 188, 412–5
'Cato Street Conspiracy' (1820), 411.
Cavendish, Henry (1731–1816), 90–1
Ceylon, 181–2, 378, 401
Chadwick, Edwin (1800–90), 438–9
Chandernagore, 164
Charlotte, Queen (1744–1818), wife of George IV, 45
Charles Edward Stuart (1720–88), the Young Pretender, 210–12
Chatham, Earl of, *see* Pitt, William the Elder
Chathamites, 349
Chemistry, 91
Chesapeake Bay, Battle of (1781), 196

Chesterfield, Earl of (1694–1773), 44, 250, 268, 288, 292, 321; his dismissal, 263
Children, employment of, 128, 143–5; costumes of, 29; punishment of, 17–18, 30, 122, 148, 390. *See also* Schools
Chippendale, Thomas (1718?–79), 108
Clarkson, Thomas (1760–1848), 82
Church of England, condition of, 66–72; and Methodism, 72–8; Whig domination of, 235; and education, 33–4, 37. *See also* Evangelicalism, Tractarianism
— Missionary Society, 81, 85
— Pastoral Aid Society, 81, 85
'Clapham Sect', 80
Classicism, 93–4, 103, 104–6
Clive, Robert (1725–75), 165–6, 176–8
Coaches, 147–8, 153
Coal, 6, 135–6, 213, 406
Coal-gas, 91
Coalition, First (1793), 376–7; Second (1798–1800), 385–6; Third (1805–7), 391–2; Fourth (1813–14), 398–400, 412
Cobbett, William (1762–1835), 408–9, 410–12, 433–4
Cobham, Lord (1669?–1749), 263, 272, 296–7
Cock-fighting, 12, 18, 25
Coke, Thomas William (1752–1842), 112–13
Coleridge, Samuel Taylor (1772–1834), 85, 99–100
Collingwood, Cuthbert (1750–1810), 33, 191
Collins, William (1721–59), 95
Combination Acts (1799, 1800), 382, 418–19
Constable, John (1776–1837), 104
Continental Congresses (1774, 1775), 173, 343
Continental System, 158, 394–6
Cook, James (1728–79), 93, 182
Coote, Sir Eyre (1726–83), 166, 307
Cope, Sir John (d. 1760), 210.
Copenhagen, British fleet and (1801), 386; (1807), 396
Copper, 6, 406
Coram, Thomas (1668?–1751), 81
Corn Law, 47, 126–7, 407, 418
Cornwallis, Charles (1738–1805), 174, 352
Cornwallis, Frederick (1713–83), Archbishop of Canterbury, 18, 46
Corporation Act (1661), 66, 235, 251; repeal of (1828), 65, 85, 425
Corresponding Societies Act (1799), 382
Cort, Henry (1740–1800), 134
Costume, 28–31, 148, 388
Cotton, 138–45
— Factory Act (1819), 145, 411
Cowper, William (1731–1800), 79, 98
Counties, and parliamentary representation, 56, 429; and local government, 63–5
Crabbe, George (1754–1832), 98
Crompton, Samuel (1753–1827), 139
Colloden, Battle of (1746), 212, 275
Cumberland, Duke of (1721–65), and army reform, 202; and the War of the Austrian Succession, 273; and the Seven Years' War, 227, 303; and the 'Forty-Five, 212, 275; political influence of, 300; and George III, 45, 326–7
Dalton, John (1766–1844), 92
Darby, Abraham (1677–1717), 119, 133
Darby, Abraham II (1711–63), 133
Darby, Abraham III (1750–91), 134
Death-rate, 3–5
Deccan, the, 164, 378
Declaratory Act (1719), 215, 217; (1765), 171, 327
Defoe, Daniel (1660–1731), 6, 94
Deism, 68, 71, 93
Dettingen, Battle of (1743), 202, 270
Devonshire, Duke of (1720–64), 300
Devonshire, Georgiana, Duchess of (1757–1806), 13, 18, 362
Dibdin, Charles (1745–1814), 102
Disarming Act (1725), 210; (1746), 212.
Dissenters, numbers of, 67, 77; political disabilities of, 66; and education, 33, 37, 107;

and French Revolution, 371; and Radicals, 85. *See also* Methodism
Dissenters' Marriage Act (1836), 285
Dissenting Academies, 33–4
Domestic System, 26, 140, 142–3
Drummond, Robert (1711–76), Archbishop of York, 70
Dryden, John (1631–1700), 93
Dublin, 218
Dunkirk, 240, 280, 312
Dupleix, Joseph Francois (1697–1763), 164–5, 279
Duquesne, Fort, 166, 168, 294, 305
Durham, Earl of (1792–1840), 184, 429, 432
East India Company, 164–6, 176–82, 307, 363, 365
Ecclesiastical Commission, 83
Edinburgh, 34, 92, 147, 208, 210
Education, 12, 17, 31–8, 122–3, 385, 435. *See also* Schools, Universities
Egypt, 385, 422
Eldon, Earl of (1751–1838), 33, 404, 411, 420, 425
Elections, expense of, 56; issues in, 61–2; in 1715, 231; 1722, 252; 1727, 262; 1734, 262–3; 1741, 265; 1747, 276; 1754, 299; 1760, 309, 319; 1768, 331; 1774, 338; 1780, 352; 1784, 362–4; 1790, 373; 1802, 389; 1807, 393–4, 408; 1818, 410; 1826, 424; 1830, 426; 1831, 430; 1832, 434; 1827, 443.
Electricity, 89–90
Enclosures, 11, 26, 111, 114–21
England, population of, 2–9; classes in, 21–8; constitution of, 39–42; science in, 87–93; literature in, 93–101; music in, 101–2; painting in, 102–4; architecture in, 104–8; agriculture in, 109–29; industry in, 130–53; trade of, 154–61; foreign policy of, 185–8
Eton, 12, 32, 247, 296
Evangelicalism, 78–84
Excise Bill (1733), 11, 42, 256–7, 262, 287
Faraday, Michael (1791–1867), 90
Factories, growth of, 141–2; conditions in, 37, 142–4; legislation, 37, 144–5
Factory Act (1833), 145
Farnese, Elizabeth, 240–1, 259–61
Fashion, *see* Costume
Ferdinand, Duke of Brunswick (1721–92), 187
Fielding, Henry (1707–54), 13, 71, 96, 264, 283–4
Fielding, Sir John (d. 1780), 284
'Fifteen (1715), 209–10, 231–4
Finisterre, Battles of (1747), 164, 188, 279
Fletcher, John (1729–85), 79
Fleury, Cardinal (1653–1743), 260, 267
Flood, Henry (1732–91), 216
Fontenoy, Battle of (1745), 202, 210, 273
'Forty-Five (1745), 210–12, 274–5
Fox, Charles James (1749–1806), his character, 15, 346, 383–4; his clothes, 31, 349–50, 370; and George III, 45, 47, 346–7, 354, 389–90; and Lord North, 346–50, 358–9; and Younger Pitt, 361–3, 367–8, 383–4; and Royal Marriage Act, 336, 347; his India Bill, 359; and slave-trade, 82, 384, 393; and American colonies, 342; and French Revolution, 370, 373, 384, 399; death, 393
Fox, Henry, Baron Holland (1705–74), Secretary at War, 285, 292–4; and Marriage Act, 285; Secretary of State, 299–300, 311; and Elder Pitt, 304; Paymaster of the Forces, 320
Foxites, 61, 362–3, 384, 393
France, in America, 162–3, 166–8, 290; in India, 164–6; navy, 190–2, 277–9, 302–3, 306; English claim to, 205–6; invasion attempts by, 218–20, 278, 390; French Revolution, 369 f
Francis, Sir Philip (1740–1818), 179–80, 334
Franklin, Benjamin (1706–90), 89–90, 157, 170
Frederick II of Prussia (1740–86), 187, 265, 270, 291, 304–13
Frederick, Prince of Wales (1701–51), 45, 262, 297, 319

Gage, General Thomas (1721–87), 173
'Gagging Acts' (1817), 410
Gainsborough, Thomas (1727–88), 103
Gambling, 13, 346
Gaols Act (1823), 417
Gaspée, 172, 339
George I (1714–27), character 43–4, 201–2, 230; and Hanover, 224; and Walpole, 44, 250; death, 254
George II (1727–60), character, 43–5, 293; and Hanover, 224, 269; as Prince of Wales, 43, 236; and Walpole, 250, 254; death, 307
George III (1760–1820), character, 18, 45–6, 82, 315–18; and Hanover, 46; accession of, 307, 315–18; and Elder Pitt, 46, 307–10, 328, 331; and Bute, 46, 307, 309, 321; personal government of, 322–4, 327–8, 334; and Lord North, 334–6, 358; and American colonies, 340; illness of, 325, 368–9; and Gordon Riots, 351; and Roman Catholic Emancipation, 386; death, 412
George IV (1820–30), 31, 362, 412, 426
Georgia, 74–5, 81, 161
Gibbon, Edward (1737–94), 97, 100
Gibraltar, 185, 260, 357
Gilbert's Act (1782), 28
Gin-mania, 9, 13, 284
Glasgow, 7, 91, 208, 212–13
Godwin, William (1756–1836), 97
Goldsmith, Oliver (1730–74), 95
Good Hope, Cape of, 181–2, 378, 401
Gordon Riots (1780), 11, 67, 263, 338, 351–2
Gorée, 168, 305, 308, 312
Gothicism, 98, 107–8
Grafton, Duke of (1735–1811), 330–4
Grand Tour, 34–5, 107, 387–8
Grasse, Admiral de (1722–88), 196–7, 357
Grattan, Henry (1746–1820), 217
Gray, Stephen (d. 1736), 89
Gray, Thomas (1716–71), 95
Great Northern War (1700–21), 226
Greek War of Independence (1821–9), 198, 414
Grenville, George (1712–70), 299; and Broad-Bottom administration, 272; and George III, 322, 325–6, 393; and Wilkes affair, 323–4; his colonial measures, 110, 325; and Younger Pitt, 389–90; his 'Ministry of All the Talents', 392–3
Grenville, Richard, see Temple, Lord
Grey, Earl (1764–1845), 18, 406, 426; and Parliamentary reform, 427–34; and foreign policy, 435–7; resignation, 437
Grimshaw, William (1708–63), 79
'Hackney Phlanx', 84
Halley, Edmund (1656–1742), 87
Handel, George Frederick (1685–1759), 101–2
Hanging, 15–16, 416
Hanover, 43, 207, 223–7, 269
Hardy, Thomas (1752–1832), 372, 381
Hardwicke, Earl of (1690–1764), 227, 289, 293, 309; Lord Chancellor, 268; his Marriage Act, 285–6; resignation, 320
Harley, Robert, Earl of Oxford (1661–1724), 228, 232, 248
Harrison, John (1693–1776), 89
Harrow, 12, 32
Harvests, 5, 114–15, 126–7, 395, 407, 410, 439
Hastings, Lady Elizabeth (1682–1739), 71
Hastings, Warren (1738–1818), 178–80, 368
Hawke, Edward (1705–81), 193, 197, 279, 301, 305–6
Hauksbee, Francis (1687–1736), 89
Health and Morals of Apprentices Act (1802), 37, 144
Heligoland, 395
Heppelwhite, George (d. 1786), 92
Herring, Thomas (1693–1757), Archbishop of Canterbury, 70
Herschel, William (1738–1822), 88–9
High Wycombe, 12, 37, 202, 354
Hoadley, Benjamin (1676–1761), 69, 235
Hogarth, William (1697–1764), 13, 103

Holland, 273, 280, 282, 289, 374–5, 377–8, 385, 387, 401–2, 436–7
Holland, Lord, see Fox, Henry
Holy Alliance (1815), 413
Hood, Samuel (1724–1816), 197
Hospitals, 3, 34, 92
Howard, John (1726–90), 81
Howe, Richard (1726–99), 195
Howe, Vicount (1729–1814), 174, 202
Hubertusburg, Treaty of (1763), 312–13
Hume, Joseph (1777–1855), 418–19
Hunt, Henry (1773–1835), 408–11
Hunter, John (1728–93), 92
Huskisson, William (1770–1830), 405, 412, 417–18, 428
Income Tax, 366, 381, 407
India, Anglo-French rivalry in, 164–6, 176–81; government of, 61, 176, 178, 180, 359, 365. See also East India Company
— Act (1784), 180, 365
— Bill (1783), 61, 359
'Intolerable Acts' (1774), 172–3, 341
Ionian Isles, 182
Ireland, population of, 2, 221; English connection with, 206–7, 213–14; Protestant ascendancy in, 214–16; and American War of Independence, 216–17; prosperity under Pitt, 217–18; and French Revolution, 218–19; union with England, 220–1, 386; Roman Catholic emancipation, 221–2, 424–6
Iron, 6, 130, 132–5, 213, 406
Jacobites, on Anne's death, 228; 1715 rising, 209–10, 231–4; 1722 conspiracy, 252; 1745 rising, 210–12, 274–5
James Edward Stuart (1688–1766), the Old Pretender, 209–10, 228–9, 232–4, 274
Jenkins's Ear, War of (1739–43), 163–4, 264–5
Jenner, Edward (1749–1823), 92
Jervis, John, Earl of St. Vincent (1735–1823), 378–9
Jews, 11, 287
Johnson, Dr. Samuel (1709–84), 33, 35, 44, 69, 71, 95, 147, 249, 318
Junius, Letters of, 333–4, 337
Justices of the Peace, social class of, 22, 25, 63, 110, 405; powers of, 28, 63–4; and poor relief, 28, 124–5, 128; and factory laws, 145; under Younger Pitt, 383; under Lord Liverpool, 405
Kay, John (d. 1764), 139
Kaunitz, Prince von (1711–94), 289–92
Keats, John (1795–1821), 100
Keble, John (1792–1866), 86
Kendal, Duchess of (1667–1743), 43, 253, 261
Kent, William (1684–1748), 104, 249
King's College, London, 7
'King's Friends', 61, 327–8, 345
Lagos Bay, Battle of (1759), 306
Lancashire, 6, 27, 138
Land Tax, 256, 283, 304, 325
Lavoisier, Antoine (1743–94), 91–2
Lawrence, Sir Thomas (1769–1832), 103–4
Leeds, 55, 65
Leicester House, 236, 262, 273, 292, 297, 307, 319
Lewis, Matthew Gregory (1775–1818), 98
Lexington, 173, 340
Libel Act (1792), 384
Lind, James (1736–1812), 93
Liverpool, 7, 56, 65, 147, 149
Liverpool, Earl of (1770–1828), character of, 403–4; Prime Minister, 394; control of Cabinet, 52, 424; 'Liberal Toryism', 62, 415; and Church reform 83; death, 424
Local Government, 22, 62–5, 110, 406
Locke, John (1632–1704), 39–41
London, importance of, 8–9; population, 8–10; living conditions, 3–4, 14; expansion; 8, 106; bridges, 146; mob, 11, 257, 263–3, 283, 332, 351–2
— Corresponding Society, 372–3, 381–2
—, Treaty of (1839), 437
— Working Mens' Association 442,

Louisbourg, 162, 164, 188, 278, 280, 302, 305
Louisiana, 290, 312
Lovett, William (1800–77), 442
Luddites, 12, 395
Lyttleton, George (1709–73), 263, 272, 296
Macadam, John (1756–1836), 146
Macaulay, Lord (1800–59), 80, 100
Macaulay, Zachary (1768–1838), 80–1, 82
Macclesfield, Earl of (1697–1764), 88
Madras, 164, 189, 279–80, 296
Malta, 182, 385–6, 389, 395
Manchester, 7, 36, 55, 64, 141, 147, 149, 211, 233, 395. *See also* 'Peterloo'
Mar, Earl of (1675–1732), 209, 233
Maria Theresa, Empress (1740–80), 267–8, 269, 280, 289–92
Marlborough, Duke of (1650–1722), 185, 232
Marriage Act (1753), 284–6, 293
Martyn, Henry (1781–1812), 81
Massachusetts, 164, 171–3, 278
Mathews, Thomas (1676–1751), 196, 270, 277–8
Maudslay, Henry (1771–1831), 135
Mauritius, 279
Melbourne, Viscount (1779–1848), 17, character of, 437–8; Prime Minister, 437, 440; and 'Tolpuddle Martyrs', 442; and Queen Victoria, 443
Metcalf, John (1717–1810), 146
Methodism, origins of, 72–4; spread of 75–7; separation from Church, 77; divisions in, 76–7; and politics, 78
Metropolitan Police Force, 19, 417
Metternich, Prince (1773–1859), 402, 414
Milan Decrees (1807), 394–5
Militia Act (1757), 201
Mill, James (1773–1838), 408
Minden, Battle of (1759), 202, 306
Minorca, 185, 196, 294, 303, 312
Mississippi, 162, 168
Molasses Act (1733), 157, 170, 258
Monarchy, powers of, 47–50; George III and, 54–6, 315–18, 345
Montagu, Lady Mary Wortley (1689–1762), 44, 92
Montcalm, Marquis de (1712–59), 166–7
Montreal, 162, 168, 306
Moore, Tom (1779–1852), 102
More, Hannah (1745–1833), 37, 80
Municipal Corporations Act (1835), 65, 441
Murdock, William (1758–1839), 91
Mutiny Acts, 48, 198–9
Mysore, 179–80, 181, 378
Napoleon I (1769–1821), 204, 377 f
Napoleonic War (1803–15), 187–8, 197, 203, 389 f
Nash, John (1752–1835), 106
National Society, 38, 81, 84
National Debt, 9, 242, 255–6, 418; in 1714, 237; 1748, 282; 1763, 304; 1779, 349; 1784, 365; 1793, 380; 1800, 380; 1815, 407
Navigation, 20
— Act (1660), 156, 418
Navy, 188–98; size of, 190–1, 193–4, 282, 374; in War of the Austrian Succession, 210, 276–80; in Seven Years' War, 195, 305–7; in American War of Independence, 174–5, 190, 352; in Revolutionary War, 379, 385–6; in Napoleonic War, 197, 390–1, 394–6, 397–8, 400; and new inventions, 87–9, 192; in peacetime, 197–8, 420–2
Nelson, Viscount (1758–1805), 195, 197, 379, 385–6, 391
Netherlands, Austrian, 270, 280, 374, 377. *See also* Belgium, Holland
Newcastle, Sir Thomas Pelham-Holles, Duke of (1693–1768), 51; his patronage, 57–8, 253; and Walpole, 253–4; and Elder Pitt, 268, 297–8, 299–301, 309–10; and his brother, Pelham, 272–4, 275–6; his foreign policy, 288–92; his failure, 292–5; his resignation, 319–20
Newcastle-upon-Tyne, 7, 33, 61, 274
Newcomen, Thomas (1663–1729), 91, 133, 136–7

Newfoundland, 162
Newman, Henry (1670–1743), 81
Newman, John Henry (1801–90), 72, 85–6
Newton, Sir Isaac (1642–1727), 87–9, 244
Newton, John (1725–1807), 79
Newspapers, 94, 101, 148
Newspaper Publication Act (1797), 382
New York, 164, 171, 174
New Zealand, 182
Nile, Battle of the (1798), 11, 385
Nobility, 21–3, 34, 364
Nonconformists, *see* Dissenters
Nore Mutiny (1797), 195, 379
Nonjurors, 67–8, 252
Norris, Henry (1771–1850), 85
North, Lord (1732–92), 52; his ministry, 335–6; and Wilkes, 337–9; and American colonies, 172, 339–47; end of his ministry, 347–53; Home Secretary, 358–9
North Briton, 101, 321, 323–4
Norwich, 7, 12, 16, 24, 58, 65
Nystad, Treaty of (1721), 226
Occasional Conformity Act (1711), 66, 234–5
O'Connell, Daniel (1775–1847), 221–2, 425
Oglethorpe, James (1696–1785), 81
Ohio, 162, 166, 170, 173, 290
Olive Branch Petition, 173
Onslow, Arthur (1691–1768), 234, 253
Orange Order, 220
Ormonde, Duke of (1665–1745), 229, 232–3
Ostend Company, 259–60
Oswego, Fort, 168, 294
Otis, James (1725–83), 170–1
Owen, Robert (1771–1858), 144–5, 441–2
Oxford, 33–4, 38, 65, 73–4, 79, 86, 233
Oxford, Earl of, *see* Harley, Robert
Paine, Thomas (1737–1809), 97, 174, 341, 372
Palmerston, Lord (1784–1865), 17, 23, 405; foreign policy, 11, 188, 423, 435–7
Pardo, Convention of (1739), 264–5
Paris, Treaty of (1763), 166, 168, 310–14
Parliament, composition of, 53–4; electoral system, 54–6; Scots M.P.s, 207–8, 212, House of Lords, 53–4; House of Commons; 58–9, 251–2; parliamentary reform, 42, 62, 333, 349, 364, 428–34
Patronage, 56–8, 250, 297–8, 356, 366–7
Paupers, 28, 36–7, 143–5, 438–40.
Peel, Sir Robert, senior (1750–1830), 119, 141, 144–5
Peel, Sir Robert (1788–1850), 405; character, 415–16; penal reform, 416; and Metropolitan Police, 417; Church reform, 83; and Roman Catholic emancipation, 425; and Reform Bill, 431, 434; his Tamworth Manifesto, 440–1
Peerage Bill (1720), 53, 236
Pelham, Henry (1695?–1754), 52, 253, 268, 271; his rise to power, 272–4; his triumph, 275–6; domestic policy, 282–7; death, 298
Peninsular War (1808–13), 203, 396–8, 412
Perceval, Spencer (1762–1812), 393–4
'Peterloo' (1819), 410–11, 428
Pitt, Thomas (1653–1726), 109, 164, 296
Pitt, William the Elder, Earl of Chatham (1708–78), 32, 52; and the 'Patriots', 263, 296; in opposition, 265, 271, 297; and the Pelhams, 273; Paymaster of the Forces, 276, 297–8; and Newcastle, 292–5, 299–300; conduct of Seven Years' War, 186–7, 301–7, 314; fall from power, 307–10; and Treaty of Paris, 313; and American colonies, 326–7, 341–3; return to power, 328–31; resignation, 331; death, 343
Pitt, William the Younger (1759–1806), character, 354, 360–1; his administration, 52, 361–2; his new majority, 49, 362–3; and parliamentary reform, 364; India Act, 180, 365; financial reform, 365–7; and French Revolution, 369–74; and First Coalition, 376–9; wartime measures, 379–83; taxation, 380–1; and Second Coalition, 385–6; union

Pitt, William the Younger—*contd.*
with Ireland, 217–20, 386; his resignation, 386; resumption of office, 389–90; and invasion threat, 390–1; and Third Coalition, 391–2; death, 392
Pittsburg, *see* Duquesne, Fort
Place, Francis (1771–1854), 408, 418–19, 430, 433, 442
Plassey, Battle of (1757), 165–6
Playhouse Act (1737), 264
Poaching, 123–4
Polish Succession, War of the (1733–8), 260
Pondicherry, 164, 309
Poor Law Act (1601), 28
— Amendement Act (1834), 28, 42, 129, 438–40
Pope, Alexander (1688–1744), 93–4, 262
Population, 2–9, 27, 120–1, 127–8, 131
Porteus Riots (1737), 208, 264
Portland, Duke of (1738–1809), 358, 383, 393–4
Porto Bello, 163, 188
Portugal, 397, 421
Pragmatic Sanction, 259, 265, 280
Prestonpans, Battle of (1745), 211
Price, Richard (1723–91), 33, 348, 366, 371
Priestley, Joseph (1733–1804), 29, 90–1, 357, 373
Prime Minister, development of office, 51–2, 251
Prisons, 15, 81, 332, 416–17
Pulteney, William (1684–1764), 254, 261–2, 268
Pusey, Edward Bouverie (1800–82), 86
Punishment, of criminals, 15–16, 19; of women, 13, 15, 18, 19, 123; of children, 12, 16–17, 18, 30, 122, 148, 233; of servants, 17; of paupers, 28; of poachers, 124; in factories, 13–14, 143–4; naval, 194; military, 200
Quadruple Alliance (1718), 241, 259; (1815), 412–13
Quebec, 162, 168, 202, 305
— Act (1774), 173, 175, 336
Queen Anne's Bounty, 70–1, 84
Quiberon Bay, Battle of (1759), 306
Quintuple Alliance (1818), 413
Quota Acts (1795), 194
Radcliffe, Anne (1764–1823), 98
Radicalism, 39, 45; in Wilkesite movement, 333, 338; and American Revolution, 349–50; and French Revolution, 381; post-war movement, 407–12; and parliamentary reform, 429, 433–4; defeated by Conservatives, 443
Raikes, Robert (1735–1811), 37
Railways, 152–3
Reform Bill (1832), 42, 49, 85, 429–34
Regency Act (1811), 369
Regulating Act (1773), 178, 336
Revolutionary War (1793–1802), 187–8, 376 f
Rennie, John (1760–1821), 146–7
Reynolds, Sir Joshua (1723–92), 103
Rhode Island, 172, 174
Richardson, Samuel (1689–1761), 95–6
Riot Act (1715), 232
Roads, 6, 145–7
Roberthon, Jean de (d. 1722), 224
Robinson, Frederick John (1782–1859), 415, 425
Robinson, Sir Thomas (1695–1770), 293, 299
Rockingham, Lord (1732–82), character, 326; first ministry, 326; and Stamp Act, 326–7; out of office, 328; opposition to North, 342, 354; second ministry, 354–6; death, 356
Rockinghamites, 61, 327–8, 355
Rodney, George (1719–92), 193, 197, 357
Roebuck, John (1718–94), 91, 134, 136
Roman Catholics, in England, 67, 252, 275, 351, 385; in Scotland, 209; in Ireland, 214; in Canada, 173
Roman Catholic Emancipation, 49, 61, 85, 222, 386, 425
Romanticism, 30–1, 98–9, 107–8
Royal Irish Constabulary, 221, 417
Royal Marriage Act (1772), 46, 336, 346
Royal Society, 90, 93
Russell, Lord John (1792–1878), 285, 437–8; and Reform Bill, 428–9, 433
Russia, relations with Britain, 238–9, 291, 374;

in War of the Austrian Succession, 269–70; in Revolutionary War, 377, 385–6; in Napoleonic War, 391–2, 295, 398; and Congress System, 412–14, 421;3
Saints, Battle of the (1782), 197, 357
Saratoga, 174, 347
Savery, Thomas (1650?–1715), 91, 136
Scheldt, 374–5, 401
Schism Act (1714), 33, 66, 234–5
Schools, public, 12, 32, 296; grammar, 32–3; girls, 29–30, 35–6, 385; charity, 29–30, 35–6, 233; factory, 37; Sunday, 37, 80; British, 38; National, 38, 81
Schulenburg, Ehrengard von der, *see* Kendal, Duchess of
Scotland, population of, 2; union with England, 206–8; 1715 revolt in, 209–10; 1745 revolt in, 210–12; French Revolution and, 212; 'Athenian Age' of, 212–13, economic changes in, 213
Scott, Sir Walter (1771–1832), 39, 85–6, 100, 213
Secretaries of State, functions of, 52–3
Seditious Meetings Act (1795), 382
Senegal, 168, 305, 308, 312
Septennial Act (1716), 234
Settlement Act (1662), 28
Seville, Treaty of (1726), 254, 260
Seven Years' War (1756–63), 165–6, 168, 186
Shaftesbury, Lord (1801–85), 81, 84, 145
Sharp, Granville (1735–1813), 80–1, 82
Sheriffmuir, Battle of (1715), 209
Shelburne, Earl of (1737–1805), 349; character, 354–5; successor to Rockingham, 356; ideas of reform, 357; his resignation, 358
Shelley, Percy Bysshe (1792–1822), 100, 405
Sheridan, Richard Brinsley (1751–1816), 368, 384, 397
Sheriton, Thomas (1751–1806), 108
Shrewsbury, Duke of (1660–1718), 51, 228, 232
Sidmouth, Viscount, *see* Addington, Henry
Simeon, Charles (1759–1836), 80, 441
Sinking Fund (1717), 242, 255–6, 263, 283; (1786), 365–6, 380
Six Acts (1819), 411
Slave Trade, 13, 61, 155, 163; abolition of, 82, 364, 401
Smith, Adam (1723–90), 213, 360, 404; *Wealth of Nations*, 97, 159–60, 348
Smith, Sydney (1771–1845), 80, 83
Smollett, Tobias (1721–71), 96, 323
Smuggling, 16, 19, 256, 367
Society for Promoting Christian Knowledge, 36, 81
— for Promoting Constitutional Information, 349, 370
— for the Propagation of the Gospel, 81, 85
— of Supporters of the Bill of Rights, 333, 338
Societies for the Reformation of Manners, 25, 73, 81
South Sea Company, formation of, 241–2; and *Asiento*, 163, 242, 280; and National Debt, 242–3; its temporary success, 243–4; its failure, 244–5; Walpole and, 245–6, 248–9; later history of, 245, 280
Spain, relations with England, 163, 210, 240–1, 259–60; in War of the Austrian Succession, 267–81 *passim*; in Revolutionary War, 374, 377; in Napoleonic War, 203, 395, 396–7; and Congress System, 414, 420
Speenhamland System, 26, 28, 64, 124–5, 128, 438
Spithead mutiny (1797), 195, 379
Stamp Act (1765), 170–1, 325, 327
Stanhope, Earl of (1673–1721), character, 231; George I and, 230; and Hanover, 234; and Whig ministry, 234–7; foreign policy, 235, 237–41
Steam power, 90–1, 133
Steamships, 153, 198
Steele, Richard (1672–1729), 71, 94, 136–7
Stephenson, George (1781–1848), 153
Stevens, William (1732–1807), 84

Strutt, Jedediah (1726–97), 119, 139
Sunderland, Earl of (1674–1722), 236, 242, 245–6, 249
Sugar Act (1764), 170–1, 325
Surajah Dowlah, 165–6
Sussex, 6, 19, 132–3
Sweden, 225–6, 237
Swift, Joanathan (1667–1745), 94, 216, 229, 253, 262
Tamworth Manifesto (1823), 62, 440–1
Tea Acts (1773), 172
Telford, Thomas (1757–1834), 146–7
Temple, Lord (1711–79), 299, 310, 319, 323
Test Act (1673), 66, 235, 251; repeal of, 65, 85, 425
'Theorists of 1830', 20, 184
Thompson, James (1700–48), 95
Thornton, Henry (1760–1815), 80
Thurlow, Lord (1731–1806), 355, 359, 368
Tillotson, John (1630–94), Archbishop of Canterbury, 68
Tithe Commutation Act (1836), 129
'Tolpuddle Martyrs' (1834), 442
Tone, Wolfe (1763–98), 218–20
Tooke, John Horne (1736–1812), 333, 370
Toplady, Augustus Montague (1740–78), 76
Tories, origins of, 59–60; decline of, 60, 229–30; George I and, 60, 234; Walpole and, 234, 252; revival of, 62, 393; break-up of, 424–7; Peel and, 429, 434, 440
Toulon, Battle of (1744), 196
Townshend, Viscount Charles (1674–1738), character, 231; and Whig ministry, 224, 230; dismissal, 236; George I and, 236–7; and Walpole, 254, 259–60; foreign policy, 235, 259–60; resignation, 254, 260; as agriculturist, 112, 254
Townshend, Charles (1725–67), 171, 327, 330–1
Tractarianism, 67, 84–6, 100
Trade, its increasing importance, 154–5, 158–9; mercantilism and, 155–8; effect of Napoleonic War on, 158–9; opposition to control of, 159–161
Trade Unions, 144, 148, 441–2
Trafalgar, Battle of (1805), 197, 391
Transport, 6; by road, 146–9; by canal, 149–52; by railway, 152–3; by sea, 153
Transportation, 15
Treasonable Practices Act (1795), 382
Trevithick, Richard (1771–1833), 152
Trichinopoly, 165
Triple Alliance (1717), 240; (1788), 373
Troppau, Congress of (1820), 414
Truck Act (1820), 411
Tull, Jethro (1674–1741), 112
Turner, J. M. W. (1775–1851), 104
Turnpikes, 6, 11, 146
Ulster, 215 220
United Empire Loyalists, 175, 357
United Irishmen, Society of, 218–20
United States of America, independence of, 174; relations with England, 175, 395–6, 420; trade with, 158
Universities, 33–4, 38
University College, London, 38, 107
Utilitarianism, 19, 97, 348, 407
Utrecht, Treaty of (1713), 161–2, 163, 185, 231, 237
Vanburgh, John (1664–1726), 104–5
Vansittart, Lord (1766–1851), 405, 407
Virginia, 172
Venn, Henry (1725–95), 79
Venn, John (1759–1813), 80
Vernon, Edward (1684–1757), 188
Verona, Congress of (1822), 415
Versailles, Treaty of (1783), 174, 357
Vienna, Congress of (1815), 20, 400–2
—, First Treaty of (1725), 259; Second Treaty of (1729), 260; Third Treaty of (1738), 261
Wages, 26–7, 122–3, 125
Wakefield, Edward Gibbon (1796–1862), 184

Walpole, Horace (1717–97), 17, 39, 44, 46, 309, 311, 326, 343; and Gothicism, 98, 107; and Duke of Newcastle, 288, 320; and Elder Pitt, 301, 305, 314
Walpole, Sir Robert (1676–1745), character, 247, 249–51; his estates, 112, 249–50; and Whig ministry, 235–7, 248; and South Sea Bubble, 245, 248; rise to power, 248–9; and Queen Caroline, 44, 49; and Stanhope, 234; and Townshend, 253, 254–5, 259–60; and Carteret, 253, 259; and Duke of Newcastle, 253; financial and economic policy, 242, 255–8; foreign policy, 258–61, 267–8; and Cabinet, 52, 252–3; opposition to, 261–4; fall from power, 264–6, 297
Wandewash, Battle of (1760), 166, 307
Washington, George (1732–99), 166, 173–5, 290
Waterloo, Battle of (1815), 204, 400
Watson, Joshua (1771–1855), 84
Watson, Richard (1737–1816), Bishop of Llandaff, 40, 42
Watt, James (1736–1819), 91, 132, 136–7
Wedgwood, Josiah (1730–95), 142, 149
Wellesley, Lord (1760–1842), 181
Wellington, Duke of (1769–1852), 11, 17, 73, 405, 419–20; and Peninsular War, 203, 397–8; and Waterloo, 204; Prime Minister, 422, 425–7, 436
Wesley, Charles (1807–88), 74–6
Wesley, John (1703–91), 12, 14; early life, 73–5; conversion, 75; preaching and organization, 75–7; and Church of England, 77; his political views, 78, 341
Wesley, Samuel (1662–1735), 33, 73
Westminster, 362, 408
—, Convention of (1756), 291
West Indies, British, trade with, 154–5, 161; transportation to, 234; and Treaty of Paris, 168, 312–13; and Vienna Settlement, 182
—, French, 168, 309, 311, 378
—, Spanish, 260, 312, 378, 387
Weymouth, 12, 46
Whigs, origins of, 59–60; and Treaty of Utrecht, 237; and George I, 60–1, 229–30; and Walpole, 250–1; and Elder Pitt, 300, 309; and George III, 315–18, 320; and parliamentary reform, 62, 427–30; decline of, 434, 440. See also Foxites, Rockinghamites
Whipping, penal, 15–16, 18, 19, 124; naval, 194; military, 200; of women, 13, 15, 18, 19, 143; in schools, 12, 32, 30, 35–7, 233; in families, 17, 122, 148, 390
Whitefield, George (1714–70), 74–5
Whitworth, Joseph (1803–87), 135
Wilberforce, William (1759–1833), 62, 80–1, 82
Wilkes, John (1727–97), 11, 28; and North Briton, 323–5; and Middlesex Election, 331–4, 337–8; as magistrate, 17, 338
Wilkinson, John (1728–1808), 119, 134
William IV (1830–7), 47, 426, 430
Winchester, 12, 32
Wolfe, James (1727–59), 168, 202, 301, 305
Wollstonecroft, Mary (1759–97), 97
Women, education of, 35–6, 122; married life of, 35, 148; in employment, 17, 143–4; punishment of, 13, 15, 17–19, 123; and fashion, 28–31, 148, 388
'Wood's Halfpence', 216, 253
Wordsworth, William (1770–1850), 85, 99–100, 401
Workhouses, 26–7, 438–9
Wren, Sir Christopher (1632–1723), 104
Wyatt, James (1746–1813), 107
Wyvill, Christopher (1740–1822), 349, 363
York, Frederick Augustus, Duke of (1763–1827), 202, 377
Yorktown, 59, 174, 347, 352
Yorkshire, 6, 27, 56, 138, 349, 362
Young, Arthur (1741–1820), 110–11, 113, 117–18, 125, 152
Young, Edward (1683–1765), 95